Multiengine Flying

Multiengine Flying

Second Edition

Paul A. Craig

McGraw-Hill

New York   San Francisco   Washington, D.C.   Auckland   Bogotá
Caracas   Lisbon   London   Madrid   Mexico City   Milan
Montreal   New Delhi   San Juan   Singapore
Sydney   Tokyo   Toronto

Library of Congress Cataloging-in-Publication Data

Craig, Paul A.
   Multiengine flying / Paul A. Craig.—2nd ed.
      p.   cm.
    ISBN 0-07-013452-9 (hardcover).—ISBN 0-07-870624-6 (disk).—
ISBN 0-07-013453-7 (pbk.)
    1. Multiengine flying. I. Title.
TL711.T85C73 1996   96-44272
629.132'5243—dc20   CIP

McGraw-Hill

A Division of The McGraw·Hill Companies

7 8 9 10 DOC/DOC 0 9 8 7 6 5 4 3 2

ISBN 0-07-013453-7 (PBK)
ISBN 0-07-013452-9 (HC)

The sponsoring editor for this book was Shelley Chevalier, the editing
supervisor was Fred Bernardi, and the production supervisor was Pamela
Pelton. It was set in Times by McGraw-Hill's Professional Book Group
composition unit, Hightstown, N.J.

Printed and bound by R. R. Donnelley & Sons Company.

McGraw-Hill books are available at special quantity discounts to use as premiums and sales
promotions, or for use in corporate training programs. For more information, please write to the
Director of Special Sales, McGraw-Hill, Professional Publishing, Two Penn Plaza, New York, NY
10121-2298. Or contact your local bookstore.

This book is printed on recycled, acid-free paper containing a minimum
of 50 percent recycled, de-inked fiber.

Dedication

By the time you read this, you are probably not a beginner in aviation. Multiengine flying is usually not the first step when learning to fly, so it's likely that you, like myself, have invested a certain amount of time and money into the great field of aviation.

If you have been a part of the flying community for any length of time, you might have noticed the disturbing downward trend in the interest in aviation among our youth. My research is unscientific, but I just do not see as many kids hanging on the airport fence anymore. I do not see many who are willing to wash an airplane in exchange for an airplane ride. The number of student pilot and private pilot certificates is down. Are our kids trading the thrill and spirit of aviation for the shopping mall and MTV?

My dedication for this book is simply to future young pilots. I challenge you, as a current aviator who has gotten far enough along to need a book on multiengine flying, to help rekindle the spark in flying among our young people. Have you given any airplane rides lately? Have you shown a group of Girl Scouts or Boy Scouts an airplane? Have you spoken about aviation at your son's or daughter's school? Let's put aviation back on the map. We cannot afford to lose the interest in aviation to the television, the CD player, the telephone, and the Internet.

I hope this book, and others, will be a great help to you as you continue to embark on the adventure of flight. But remember, as you learn, it becomes your duty to pass on your love of aviation to the next group of future pilots. Fly for fun, fly as a career, fly for the challenge, but pass it on!

PC
June 1996
Franklin, Tennessee

Contents

PART III: ADVANCED MULTIENGINE FLIGHT

8 Turboprops   121

9 High-altitude operations   131

10 Cockpit resource management   157

11 "Glass cockpit" systems   165

PART IV: EARNING A MULTIENGINE RATING

12 Multiengine flight training   185

Acknowledgments

Like all others, this book is actually the product of many people in many ways. The greatest appreciation, of course, goes to Dorothy, Ziggy, and the two dogs, Aileron and Fowler Flap.

Thanks also to Eric Stout of Middle Tennessee State University. Eric helped with editing, advising, and preparing this book. Eric is a gifted critical thinker of aeronautical situations. When it comes to multiengine airplanes, nobody can out-troubleshoot him or out-teach him.

Special thanks to John Benton who always had wise advice on this book and so many other things. Thanks, John, for so many great years at LCC!

Eric Kreahemann, a former student, built and wind-tunnel-tested the multiengine engine and airfoil section used in the book for data on accelerated slipstream and windmill drag. Thanks again, Eric. Also thanks to Sheila Johnson who built and tested an airfoil for use in a boundary layer experiment.

Thanks to Charles L. Buchanan, photographer for the Kinston *Free Press* and instrument pilot. His desire to fly is surpassed only by his talent behind the camera.

Captain Ken Futrell of United Airlines deserves many thanks for help and encouragement from the days when we were starving CFIs together until today.

Special thanks to several pros at the FAA's Flight Standards District Office in Nashville, Tennessee: Robert Cope, Wes Jones, Jim Perkins, and Larry Skelly, and to Larry Lambert at the Raleigh FSDO.

Thanks to Joel H. Pritchard of Frasca International for help understanding the difference between a simulator and a ground trainer and all their levels.

Thanks to Grady Jones, my college and Aerospace Technology professor at Middle Tennessee State University, for his help through the smoke.

Thanks to William R. Nelson, Senior Marketing Executive, TRO Aviation Training Services, for help with aviation courseware.

ACKNOWLEDGMENTS

I have several to thank and appreciate at Middle Tennessee State University: Dr. Earl Keese, Ron Ferrara, Don Crowder, Wally Maples, Bill Herrick, Terry Dorris, Billy Cox, Dewey Patton, Mike Schukert, Bob Phillips, Steve Gossett, Matt Taylor, and Gail Zlotky.

To my parents, Floyd and Anne Craig, who bought me my first flight simulator in 1963, I thank you so much. I certainly could not have pulled this one off without you and the Craig Communications Inc. offices in Nashville, Tennessee.

I have been a chief flight instructor for over a dozen years now, and in that position, I am supposed to teach young flight instructors the tricks of their trade. As it turns out, I learn as much from them. I have had the privilege of teaching and learning from some of the best flight instructors anywhere: Steven Wright, Aaron Hedman, Keith Morehead, Lauren Bandy, Bruce Thomas, Kevin Keener, Scott Simmons, Shawn Collins, Servando Gomez, John Pritchard, Lenora Day, John Waddell, Tracy Whitt, and Brandon Lovell. And of course, thanks to my past students and my current group at Middle Tennessee State University. And, after a few years to think about it, it probably would not be all that bad having a class full of Phil Hietmans.

Introduction

I went through most of my life without pondering why the *Spirit of St. Louis* had only one engine. I guess I believed that multiengine airplanes had not been invented yet. But multiengine airplanes had been invented, and they were common. Lindbergh's competitors in the race to Paris were flying multiengine airplanes. Why did Lindbergh insist on an airplane with only a single engine?

Lindbergh had wrestled with a question that many pilots even today do not fully understand. In certain circumstances, a multiengine airplane is not twice as safe as a single-engine airplane; rather, it is twice as dangerous.

One of Lindbergh's financial backers in St. Louis suggested that the *Spirit of St. Louis* be designed with three engines instead of just one. One of Lindbergh's rivals was going to attempt the flight in an airplane with three powerplants. Lindbergh responded, "I'm not sure three engines would really add much to safety. There'd be three times the chance of engine failure, and if one of them stopped over the ocean, you probably could not get back to land on the other two. A multiengine plane is awfully big and heavy. A single-engine plane might even be safer, everything considered."

On another occasion Lindbergh was questioned about his single-engine decision. "Slim," the man asked, "don't you think you ought to have a plane with more than one engine for that kind of flight?" Lindbergh answered, "Suppose one of the engines cuts out halfway across the ocean. I could not get to shore with the other two. Multiengine planes are more complicated; there are more things likely to go wrong with them."

The general public and other pilots perceived that two engines were always better. It would be logical on a flight across the Atlantic that Lindbergh have the best equipment. If you automatically thought "multi" was better, you would have also coached him into a multiengine plane.

What did Lindbergh know that most pilots then, and even today, did not? He knew that the step to multiengine flying is a serious step. Today we are the beneficiaries of more reliable engines, better aerodynamics, and better equipment than Lindbergh ever dreamed of, yet the potential danger of a multiengine airplane remains a constant.

But the multiengine airplane does have distinct advantages over single-engine airplanes in many areas. The most important advantage is redundancy. Provided that the airplane has enough airspeed, two engines can be a lifesaver. Increases in the thrust-to-weight ratio of engines and better aerodynamics have made it possible for a twin-engine airplane to fly to safety on the remaining good engine. The safety of multiengine redundancy goes beyond the obvious fact that there are two engines. There are also two electrical systems, two vacuum systems, and two fuel systems on most twins. Two engines will often (but not always) produce faster flight speeds. Multiengine airplanes can shrink the aeronautical chart.

The disadvantages fall into two groups: economic considerations and safety considerations.

Economic considerations Multiengine airplanes cost more to buy, operate, and maintain. Having two of just about everything means that there are twice as many parts that can fail. Fuel consumption will be at least double on a twin, but groundspeed will not double.

Safety considerations Most of this book will deal with the significant risks that exist when one engine fails and the airspeed gets too slow. There is grave danger involved with multiengine airplanes and the minimum controllable airspeed (V_{MC}).

Attempts have been made to enjoy the benefits of multiengine airplanes (redundancy, speed, and high-speed safety), while eliminating the dangers of V_{MC} (low-speed danger), the most visible of which is the Cessna Skymaster.

The Skymaster beat all the odds. The marketing people inside Cessna did not believe that a twin-engine airplane with one engine in front and one engine in back would be a commercial success, but pilots in the company who knew about the conventional- twin low-speed control problems persevered, and the Skymaster became a bestseller.

Cessna sold more than 1,400 Skymasters with retractable landing gear, designated the Cessna 337. There were military versions and even a pressurized Skymaster. Why was it so popular? The design offered the best of both worlds. At the time, it was faster than a single. It could stay in the air and fly to safety with either the front or the back engine dead. Best of all, no V_{MC}. When one engine fails, the airplane does not have any additional turning tendency, which is so dangerous with conventional wing-mounted multiengine airplanes.

Cessna originally thought that single-engine pilots would fly the Skymaster without any additional pilot rating, but that idea was dashed when *Flight Standards Service Release No. 467* was published. The FAA required Skymaster pilots to earn a new rating, named *airplane multiengine land—center thrust.*

The Skymaster stopped production in the United States in 1980. Although there are still many Skymasters around, your multiengine flying career will most likely be in conventional twins. This means that you will need to have a healthy appreciation of the pros and cons of multiengine flying.

Flying twins offers some real advantages, but also some real risk. Reducing risk requires knowledge, understanding, proficiency, and hard work. I hope this book gets you started toward those goals.

Multiengine Flying

PART I

Multiengine basics

1
Multiengine aerodynamics

THE BASICS OF LIFT OPPOSING WEIGHT, AND THRUST OPPOSING drag still hold true with multiengine airplanes. But multiengine airplanes have more complex thrust vectors, are heavier, and have greater drag than single-engine airplanes. In addition to these basics, the prospective multiengine pilot must learn the difference between performance and controllability.

When flying a single-engine airplane, we typically use V speeds to attain the greatest performance from the airplane. ("V speed" is actually redundant. The "V" stands for velocity, which is basically the same as speed. However, the term is now part of the pilot jargon.) A pilot might need to climb out after takeoff at V_X in order to get over a powerline. The pilot knows that by flying the airplane within a close tolerance of this speed, he or she will be getting all the airplane and its powerplant can offer.

Also, flying a proper V speed instills an unspoken confidence of safety. Pilots figure that if they fly a certain speed, they are just duplicating what test pilots have already done. The speed is proven to be not only for best performance but for safety. The speed is reliable.

This line of thinking starts making us believe that V speeds are only numbers used to provide a certain performance. We assume that a published V speed is also a speed that provides safety and avoids disaster. Single-engine pilots take V speeds for granted.

Multiengine pilots must have a deeper understanding of how speeds affect both performance and control. A multiengine pilot might fly a certain V speed perfectly and still crash. Most pilots memorize a set of V speeds just prior to a checkride. They have a textbook definition of each one ready just in case the examiner asks about speed, but they truly do not comprehend the speed implications.

STALL SPEEDS

Airplanes must move forward to allow airflow over the airfoils. Anytime the airflow is interrupted or stopped, the airfoil stops producing differential air pressure and lift is no longer produced. The moment this interruption takes place, the airfoil stalls. This moment is determined by the angle of attack and not necessarily the speed. So the term "stall speed" is not actually correct. The more correct term is "stall angle." But most pilots correlate the stall to speed because the airspeed indicator is all that we have to go by. Angle of attack indicators are just not commonly found on light general aviation planes.

V-speed	Definition	Airspeed indicator location
V_{s1}	Stall speed with landing gear and flaps up	Slow end of green arc
V_{so}	Stall speed in landing configuration	Slow end of white arc
V_{xse}	Best angle of climb with only a single engine	No airspeed indication
V_{yse}	Best rate of climb with only a single engine	Blue radial line
V_{sse}	Safe single-engine speed for training	No airspeed indication
V_{mc}	Minimum Control Speed	Red radial line

Fig. 1-1. *Summary of V speeds*

V_{S1}

V_{S1} (also called V_S) is the designation for the stall speed, or angle, that produces airfoil stall in a "clean" configuration. This means that both the wing flaps and the landing gear are up. With multiengine airplanes V_{S1} also means zero engine thrust. When the engines are providing thrust, the slipstream off the engines cross the airfoils and produce lift. A true V_{S1} stall would be with the power off to avoid this "engine producing lift."

V_{S1} is marked by the slowest end of the green normal operating range arc of the airspeed indicator. Theoretically, the airplane would stall as the airspeed indicator passed below the green arc while experiencing 1G loading. If a loading of greater than 1G exists, an "accelerated" stall will occur while the indicator still is in the green arc. The airspeed indicator lies to the pilot anytime the airplane has a load factor above 1G.

V_{S1} is a control speed. While flying at or faster than V_{S1}, the airplane should remain under control. A situation could arise, especially on a hot day at high altitude, where the V_{S1} speed is being held, but the airplane is in a descent. In this case the airplane is under control, but there is no performance because the airplane is still going down. Therefore, V_{S1} only guarantees that control surfaces will work to allow the pilot to keep the sky up and the ground down; however, it does not guarantee that the airplane can climb from danger. This V_{S1} idea holds true for both single- and multiengine pilots.

V_{SO}

V_{SO} is the stall speed "dirty." This is also called *stall speed in a landing configuration* because the stall happens with both the flaps and the landing gear down, just like an approach to landing. Since this speed corresponds to a situation with flaps down, it is slower than V_{S1}. With the flaps down, the airfoil camber is increased, and therefore, the airflow speed over the camber is increased. This provides more lift and allows this extra lift to be traded for less airspeed.

V_{SO} is marked on the airspeed indicator at the slow end of the white flap operating range arc. V_{SO} is the flaps-down control speed. Again, performance is not necessarily provided when flying at V_{SO}; only control is provided. The maneuver routinely performed by student pilots, called *minimum controllable airspeed* (MCA), is an experiment in airplane control at slow speeds. The maneuver is not called MPA for minimum performance airspeed.

Many hours of my flight time was spent with a student with flaps full down, nose high, airspeed between V_{S1} and V_{SO}, full power, but with the vertical speed at a minus 200 feet per minute. At that moment, V_{SO} will not allow for a climb (performance).

As a flight instructor, one of my worst nightmares is to have a student pilot on final approach against a stiff wind. The student has full flaps and is low. The student adds ever-increasing amounts of power to remedy the situation, but the trainer airplane does not have enough power to give. The airplane is under control but will land in the approach lights and not on the runway.

MULTIENGINE V SPEEDS

All the speeds discussed so far apply to single-engine airplanes and multiengine airplanes with all engines operating. This section looks at speeds specific to the problem of multiengine flight and how these speeds are affected when one engine quits on a twin-engine conventional airplane.

V_{XSE}

V_{XSE} (best angle of climb with a single engine) is the speed that will give the pilot the greatest gain in altitude over a set distance. If a pilot is ever forced to use this speed, he or she would do so to get out of a very tough situation. Picture a pilot attempting to fly a multiengine airplane off a 1,500-foot airstrip that has 100-foot trees at both ends. Soon after liftoff, one engine quits. In addition to dealing with all the problems associated with losing the engine, the pilot must also clear those trees. The V_{XSE} speed gives you the best chance (although chances are still not good) to make it out in one piece. V_{XSE} allows, under good atmospheric conditions, the ability to control the airplane and also get the best performance out of the remaining engine. The pilot should only hold V_{XSE} until the obstruction is cleared and then lower the nose to increase speed.

V_{YSE}

V_{YSE} (best rate of climb with a single engine) is the speed that allows the airplane to achieve the greatest altitude in the shortest elapsed time with just one engine. This speed is on airspeed indicators of multiengine airplanes certified after 1965 and is designated by a blue line, often referred to as a "blue radial line." If an engine failed during climbout, V_{YSE} is the best speed to hold if no obstructions are present. During an obstruction clearance takeoff after one engine failure, the pilot should go to V_{XSE} until the plane is higher than the obstructions. The pilot should then speed up to V_{YSE} for the remainder of the climb.

Single-engine climb performance of light twins is alarmingly poor. The "best performance" might still be a descent, but at either V_{XSE} or V_{YSE}, the airplane should still be fast enough to provide aircraft control.

V_{SSE}

V_{SSE} (safe single-engine speed) is the slowest speed that the manufacturer recommends for practicing engine-out operations. Manufacturers know that pilots in training must shut down an engine occasionally in order to feel and understand how the airplane will fly with only one engine operating; however, manufacturers give the V_{SSE} speed to pilots as a final warning. V_{SSE} is more legal loophole than V speed.

PERFORMANCE AND CONTROL

Understanding airplane performance dominates flight training. We try to understand density altitude and make sense out of eye-crossing charts. We ask important questions: How fast? How far? How much fuel? How much runway? How much weight? Unfortunately, the questions overlook something vital. All the questions assume that the airplane is under control, and that the pilot is in command of the airplane.

Performance is icing on the cake for the multiengine airplane. The actual "cake" is the pilot's ability to manipulate the ailerons, elevator, and rudder to control the airplane. If the airplane ever gets "out of control," those performance charts and their numbers will be of little interest. We begin understanding multiengine aerodynamics by understanding that airplane performance and airplane control are completely different ideas.

A pilot aligns the multiengine airplane with the runway centerline. The voice over the radio says, "You are cleared for takeoff on Runway 5." The pilot adds full power, checks the engine instruments, and the airplane begins to roll. The airplane accelerates to a speed where the pilot rotates the craft into the air. The airplane lifts off and the runway passes behind.

Then, at this delicate moment, one engine coughs and quits. What should be this pilot's first priority: control or performance? Be careful how you answer. It is easy to say that performance is the most important factor because obviously this pilot needs to climb to a safe altitude, and rate of climb is a performance factor. But wait. A climb assumes that the pilot has control of the airplane. The first priority must be airplane control or an airplane climb will not be possible under any performance-limiting situation. Consider the consequences if the pilot does not recognize the control priority.

Multiengine performance is important and is subsequently detailed, but to set priorities straight, airplane control must be discussed first. Some commonsense ideas must be understood. First, two engines are better than one. Second, if one engine quits, adding power to the operating engine would be a necessity. Does common sense hold true in these examples? The answer is a definite maybe. Whether commonsense ideas work in actual practice depends on airplane speed because speed determines control.

The first question: *Are* two engines better than one? If you were flying high over a mountain range at night in a single-engine airplane and the engine quit, you would be in big trouble. If the airplane had two engines and one failed, you would be better off. But "flying high over the mountains" assumes that the airplane is traveling with enough forward speed to be under control.

If the engine quits while a single-engine airplane is slow, for instance during takeoff and initial climb, the airplane is obviously going to come back down. A multiengine airplane might also come back down, even with one engine running. The single-engine airplane should be controllable on the way down (if not stalled), but the multiengine airplane might go out of control. Both pilots are going to crash in this situation, but the single-engine pilot will land wheels down (assuming fixed-gear), and the multiengine pilot lands wheels up. Which is more survivable?

Two engines are very good sometimes and very bad sometimes. How can a pilot determine when two engines are good and when they are bad? Where is the borderline that must be crossed in order to make multiengine airplanes safer than single-engine airplanes? The borderline is a particular speed value called *minimum control speed* or V_{MC}, which is the most important multiengine speed.

The second question: If one engine quits, adding power to the operating engine would be a necessity. Again, if you were flying high above a mountain range and one engine quits, additional power would be required from the operating engine to maintain level flight. When one engine fails on a multiengine airplane, the total airplane drag shoots up and more power is required to overcome this extra drag. Without additional power, the airplane will gradually sink into the mountains.

What about a slower situation, for instance, takeoff and initial climb? If the pilot of a multiengine airplane has one engine fail, there is a range of slow speeds where power from the good engine is a problem. If the pilot pushes the throttles to full power in this situation, the airplane will depart controlled flight and flip, cartwheel, and crash;

therefore, two engines are very good sometimes and very bad sometimes. How can a pilot determine when they are good and when they are bad? Where is the borderline between safe and fatal?

Again, the threshold between safe and unsafe is the multiengine minimum control speed (V_{MC}). The FAA has established guidelines to determining this critical speed. Most pilots spend time reading the Federal Aviation Regulation Parts 61 and 91 because those two parts have direct influence on pilots and aircraft operation. Part 23 is unknown to most pilots but is crucial because the rules in Part 23 make an airplane safe and legally airworthy to fly. Part 23 defines the conditions of the minimum control speed (V_{MC}) for multiengine airplanes.

FAR Part 23.149: "V_{MC} is the calibrated airspeed, at which, when the critical engine is suddenly made inoperative, it is possible to recover control of the airplane with that engine inoperative and maintain straight flight either with zero yaw or, at the option of the applicant [for an airworthiness certificate], with an angle of bank of not more than five degrees. The method used to simulate critical engine failure must represent the most critical mode of powerplant failure with respect to controllability expected in service."

The last sentence is key. The phrase "with respect to controllability" clearly means that there is a difference between airplane performance and airplane control that is recognized by regulation.

The regulation then defines the exact condition of V_{MC}: "For reciprocating engine powered airplanes, V_{MC} may not exceed 1.2 V_{S1} (where V_{S1} is determined at the maximum takeoff weight) with:

1. Takeoff power or maximum available power on the engines.
2. The most unfavorable center of gravity.
3. The airplane trimmed for takeoff.
4. The maximum sea-level takeoff weight (or some lesser weight necessary to show V_{MC}).
5. Flaps in the takeoff position.
6. Landing gear retracted.
7. Cowl flaps in the normal takeoff position.
8. The propeller of the inoperative engine.
    i. Windmilling.
    ii. In the most probable position for the specific design of the propeller control.
    iii. Feathered, if the airplane has an automatic feathering devise.
9. The airplane airborne and ground effect negligible."

Many unexplained terms in this regulation are essential to understanding the issue. The regulation refers to a "critical engine" and uses the term "windmilling." Phrases such as "most unfavorable center of gravity" and "most critical mode of powerplant failure" appear but are not clearly defined. When it is all boiled down, this regulation is painting a picture of the worst possible multiengine situation that a pilot might get into when it is still possible to recover. If anything gets worse than the situation outlined in this regulation, then there will be no recovery possible and the airplane will depart controlled flight—the plane will crash.

Test ride redline

In order for a multiengine airplane to obtain an airworthiness certificate, a test pilot must take the airplane for a ride. Picture the test pilot up there on a new multiengine airplane's first flight with a full slate of text maneuvers planned. The test crew has loaded the airplane with weights so that the center of gravity is at the aft limit of the CG range and the total airplane weight is at maximum allowable for takeoff.

The pilot climbs to a safe altitude, sets the cowl flaps and wing flaps to the normal takeoff positions (cowl flaps usually open, wing flaps usually up), leaves the landing gear up, and then pulls the throttle of the left engine back to idle. The pilot now banks the airplane 5° to the right—the direction of the good engine—and adds full power to the right engine. Now the pilot allows the airplane's nose to rise and the airspeed to melt away . . . slower . . . slower . . . .

To keep the airplane straight, the pilot is applying more and more right rudder until he can push the rudder no more. The nose of the airplane starts to move to the left, even though the pilot is applying full right rudder. At that very moment, the pilot reaches up with a red grease pencil and marks the position of the airspeed indicator as the airplane rolls over on its back. This is V_{MC}!

Airspeed indicators on multiengine airplanes do have a red "radial" line, although it probably is not actually first marked with a grease pencil (but it is a good joke that Bill Kershner often tells). The red radial line indicates the position of V_{MC} on the indicator, but it is dangerous to assume that you are safe just because the indicator reads faster than the red line because airspeed indicators lie.

The red radial line is placed on the indicator by the "book" value and is based on the FAR Part 23.149 criteria. Pilots can find themselves in situations where the actual V_{MC} is different than the red radial lines indication of V_{MC}. Every multiengine pilot must understand what makes the speed of V_{MC} fluctuate.

Most light twin-engine airplanes have one engine on each wing; yet the airplane's center of gravity is in the fuselage. This causes the problem. Neither engine's thrust is pulling through the center of gravity, so yaw forces are produced by engine power. A yaw force makes the entire airplane pivot as if the airplane were stuck on a pin through the center of gravity and twirled side to side. Under ideal conditions, both engines will produce the same thrust and therefore pull the airplane with equal force. But if one engine pulls harder than the other, the airplane will pivot, and the airplane's nose will swing away from the stronger pulling engine.

It is difficult for many pilots to picture the pivot force and understand why the nose moves the way it does while the forces are uneven. To get a commonsense understanding, think of driving your car down a paved road with a sandy shoulder. The wheels and tires provide equal force while on the pavement. The left and right "drive" wheels are turning the same speed to propel the car down the road. Both wheels have equal traction on the road. Both are producing equal thrust. This equal power allows the car to travel in a straight line.

You swerve to miss a pothole and the right wheels drop off the pavement and into the sand. What will happen now? (Fig. 1-2). When the left drive wheel is on the pavement and the right drive wheel is in the sand, they will not produce the same thrust for the total car. This will cause the car to pivot or yaw. Which way will the front of the car sway? In this example, the car will pivot to the right, away from the greater thrust. The left side of the car is trying to "outrun" the right side of the car. The left side moves ahead while the right side lags back and the result is unwanted yaw.

Multiengine airplanes unfortunately do the same thing. Anytime one engine produces more power than the other, the side with the stronger engine pull will try to outrun the weaker side. This will pivot the airplane's nose away from the stronger force. The problem becomes more and more dangerous as the difference between power outputs of the engines gets greater; therefore, the most dangerous situation would exist when one engine was producing full power while the other engine was producing no power. This full power/no power combination would produce a fast and strong pivot force that might be impossible to stop.

Imagine what would happen to the space shuttle if after liftoff one of the solid-rocket engines were to fail while the other continued to burn (Fig. 1-3). The shuttle is a multiengine craft. Its two solid-rocket boosters are attached on either side for liftoff. These engines do not push through the center of gravity, just like a conventional light multiengine airplane—except for a little more power! If one of those solid-rocket engines were to fail while the other continued to burn, the operating engine would try to continue upward. The failed engine would try to fall downward. The result would be a "yaw cartwheel" which would certainly be unrecoverable.

If this unwanted yaw occurs in cars, airplanes, and spacecraft, how is the yaw force counteracted? If you were the driver of the car with the left set of wheels on the pavement and the right wheels in the sand, which way should you turn the wheel? The front of the car would be pivoting to the right; to keep the car straight you must turn the wheel to the left in hopes of counteracting the yaw.

Your only hope of keeping the car straight would be if the steering wheel's left turning force is at least equal to the car's right turning force. If both forces are equal, they will in effect cancel each other out, and the car will continue straight ahead. But if the forces are not equal, the car will continue to pivot, maybe to a point where control is lost.

What provides the counteracting force in an airplane? Airplanes do not have steering wheels that provide any help to prevent pivot. Airplanes move in three axes: pitch, yaw, and roll. This pivot takes place in the yaw axis (Fig. 1-4), which is controlled by the rudder. Of course the airplane control surfaces require airflow to function properly. All pilots test the control surfaces during a pretakeoff check to ensure that they are moving in the proper direction; but the airplane does not pitch, or roll, or yaw, because the airplane is standing still with minimal airflow. Airspeed makes the control surfaces effective.

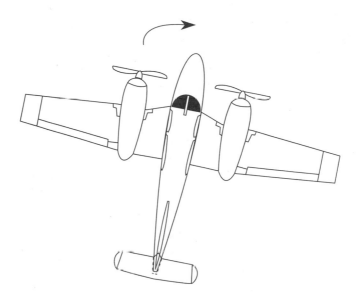

Fig. 1-2. *If the right engine fails, the airplane will yaw to the right just like a car will sway to the right if the right wheels fall off pavement into sand.*

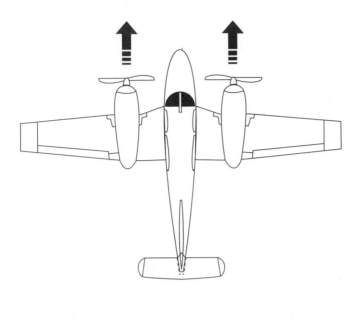

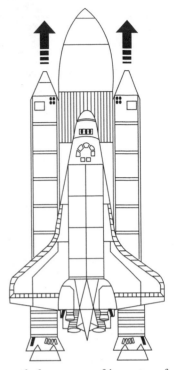

Fig. 1-3. *The twin solid-rocket boosters on the space shuttle do not pull through the spacecraft's center of gravity, much like a conventional twin-engine airplane. If one of the solid-rocket boosters were to fizzle out after liftoff, how much rudder pressure would be required to keep the vehicle on course? What is the space shuttle's V_{MC}?*

My first instructor wanted me to feel how "sluggish" the flight controls were during slow flight and stalls. This sloppy feel of the controls was due to their lack of effectiveness, which in turn was due to the reduced airflow at slower speeds. So the pilot's ability to make the airplane yaw by using the rudder is a function of just how fast the airplane is traveling through the air. If the pilot needs the yaw force of the rudder to counteract an uneven thrust from the engines, the pilot's ability to overcome this force depends on airspeed.

A car driver uses the steering wheel to overcome unwanted yaw. An airplane pilot uses rudder to overcome unwanted yaw, but the rudder does not always give the pilot what is needed.

Many forces are at work when uneven thrust exists. The "pulling ahead" force and the "lagging back" force produce the yaw in one direction. Airflow past and around the rudder can produce yaw in the opposite direction. If all these forces are equal and cancel out, then the airplane can continue straight ahead under control. As airflow gets slower, the rudder counterbalancing yaw gets weaker and soon the engine yaw overpowers the rudder yaw. This overpowering point is the airspeed that is just too slow to

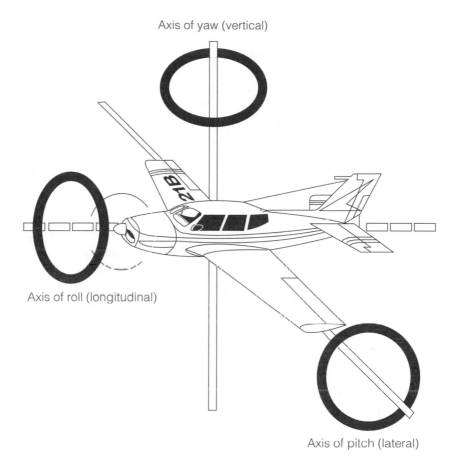

Axis of yaw (vertical)

Axis of roll (longitudinal)

Axis of pitch (lateral)

Fig. 1-4. *The battle for control is fought in the yaw axis.*

make the rudder work strong enough to counteract the uneven engine yaw. This exact speed now depends on the magnitude of all these factors.

FACTORS AFFECTING V_{MC}

The exact speed of V_{MC} fluctuates and is not always as indicated by the red radial line on the airspeed indicator. The exact speed of V_{MC} is actually a battle between opposing forces. Like two armies marching toward each other, the forces eventually clash. If both armies are of equal strength the battle line will become stationary. But if either army emerges as the stronger of the two, the stronger army will push back the weaker opponent. Anything that strengthens or weakens either army will change the position of the battle line. Our battle line is drawn by V_{MC}. On one side of V_{MC} is aircraft control and the opposition side is no aircraft control. The "good" side relies on fast airspeed and the weakness of the enemy's force. The "bad" side relies on slow airspeed and its own yaw strength. Certain forces can strengthen or weaken the "bad" side.

Power produced

The greatest pivot/yaw force would occur when one engine is operating at maximum power and the other engine has zero power. They would only occur on takeoff, outside of a training maneuver. If one engine failed and the other continued to operate at maximum power upon takeoff or during initial climb, the yaw would be the greatest. Couple that strong yaw with the relative slow speed of takeoff and the ability to counteract the yaw would be at its lowest. This is why takeoff in a multiengine airplane can be so dangerous.

More power from the engines usually is a good thing. But if one engine should fail, any "extra" power from the operating engine will produce greater yaw force. This additional yaw force can only be counteracted with additional rudder yaw force, but at slow speeds this "additional" force might not be available or even possible.

So, in an engine out situation, extra power from the good engine is bad. Anything that allows the power produced from the engine to become greater strengthens the "bad" side of V_{MC}. This requires a faster speed to overcome the extra yaw. Anytime more speed is required for control, the "bad" side is winning the battle.

Several factors can cause the engine to produce more power, but the most influential is density altitude. Engines breath air. Reciprocating engines draw air inside, mix it with fuel, squeeze it with a piston in a cylinder, and burn it with a spark plug. Turbocharged engines do the same thing, except they presqueeze the air before sending it to be burned. Turbine engines do the same thing. They draw in air, squeeze it with a rotor, mix it with jet fuel, and burn it in the combustion chambers. Even rocket engines in space breathe air; the spacecraft carries air as liquid oxygen.

The engines draw in air, which is a mixture of many gases. The gas that we are particularly interested in is oxygen because oxygen burns like a fuel. The other gases that get pulled into the engine are used as well. They get hot and expand, which helps push a piston down, but oxygen causes the fuel to give up its energy.

Because the air is a partner to fuel in combustion, it makes sense that when there is more air, there is more combustion and vice versa. Why do hot coals glow red when blown upon? Because more fuel (air) is added. Why does a candle eventually flicker and go out when left burning in a jar? Because the fuel (air) is all used up. In an engine, when the content of air goes down, the combustion goes down and less power is provided from the engine.

Gravity holds the atmosphere tight to the Earth. At sea level, the atmosphere's gas molecules are crushed together under the weight of the atmosphere. Humans have a hard time understanding this "weight" because we simply do not feel it. The pressure of this weight is inside and outside our body. We do not feel the weight because everything cancels out.

Low in the atmosphere, near sea level, the air flows like a river into engines. But high in the atmosphere, above the majority of air molecules, engines gasp for air. To the engine, climbing up into the atmosphere is like slowly turning down the fuel supply. The engine gradually loses power until it can climb no more. Power loss with a gain in altitude restricts aircraft operations.

Many pilots have been forced to go around a mountain range instead of going over it. The limiting factor is the ability of the airplane to get well above a ridge and its turbulence. Density altitude considerations are usually a no-win situation. Anytime density altitude is considered, it usually means aircraft performance is in question. The outcome is a loss in performance. Density altitude is a paradox for multiengine aerodynamics: disadvantageous to performance, advantageous to V_{MC}.

Anytime the power of an engine is reduced, the ability of that engine to produce yaw is also reduced. Less yaw from the engine relaxes the need for the rudder to counteract yaw forces. The airplane requires less airflow across the rudder to keep the nose straight; therefore, V_{MC} gets slower.

A cold day at sea level will allow the engine to produce its maximum power, which is bad for V_{MC}. A hot day in the mountains will deprive the engine of its power, which is good for V_{MC}. But remember, a good situation for V_{MC} might not necessarily be good for performance. Here again, control of the airplane and performance of the airplane are two completely different things.

Power can also be reduced by simply pulling the throttle back. Manually reducing power on the good engine improves airplane control by reducing V_{MC}. The problem is that the airplane might not climb or even stay level with a reduced power setting on the good engine. Here is the crux of the matter. Low to the ground and with an airspeed at or slower than V_{MC}, a pilot does not have any good choices. The pilot must reduce power on the good engine for a slower V_{MC} and stay under control.

This reduced power setting is not strong enough to pull the airplane to a safe altitude. The pilot needs to understand that no matter what he does, the airplane is going to crash. The only choice is to crash right side up or upside down. Instinctively, pilots will push the throttle forward in a futile attempt to climb away. But increasing the power on the good engine produces extra yaw that cannot be overcome by rudder at this slow forward speed. As the power comes up, V_{MC} comes with it and the airplane begins to roll and yaw out of control.

The only hope of a noncrash recovery is altitude. The pilot could reduce the power on the good engine and therefore reduce V_{MC}. Then, using the altitude below the airplane, lower the nose and trade altitude for airspeed. As the airspeed gets faster, the pilot can afford to add more power because the additional speed will allow the rudder to overcome the additional yaw. If enough space is remaining between the ground and the airplane, the pilot can continue walking this speed/control tightrope until the available performance is achieved.

This entire idea is foreign to our original single-engine training. I was told by my first flight instructor to go-around anytime that I was not completely comfortable with a landing approach. Go-around means full power. So we associate "get out of trouble" with "full power." But in certain multiengine circumstances, for instance, low to the ground and slower than V_{MC}, full power is fatal.

Multiengine pilots must do everything possible to avoid that situation. But if such a situation does arise while one engine has failed, the pilot must have the in-depth understanding that will allow a split-second decision to pull back on the power and then accelerate, or if no altitude is available, to accept a forced landing. It is simply against the pilot's nature to sit quietly, holding throttles back, and watch the ground come up. Pilots cannot allow themselves to get painted into this corner.

Uneven drag

Another misunderstanding: When one engine fails, 50 percent of the total aircraft power disappears. Even though the power is being reduced by half, the aircraft performance might be reduced as much as 80 percent. The difference is due to the increased drag that can form on the airplane with one engine out (Fig. 1-5). Recall the concept that the good-engine side causes yaw by attempting to "outrun" the bad-engine side. Now consider that drag will pull the bad-engine side rearward, while the good-engine side pulls forward.

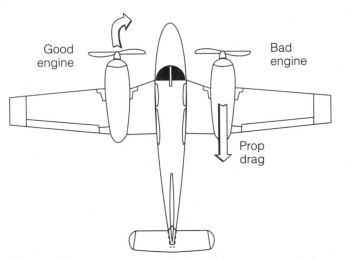

Good engine

Bad engine

Prop drag

Fig. 1-5. *When half the power is lost due to an engine failure, as much as an 80 percent loss in performance can result due to the uneven drag.*

The pilot is in between these two forces, sitting on the pivot point. Left alone, these two forces will "flat spin" the airplane. The pilot must hope that there is enough rudder effectiveness to overcome this twirl. The airplane will require considerable forward speed and corresponding airflow over the rudder to stop this dangerous yaw from taking place. The only way out is to reduce the forward force on the good engine's wing (reduce power) and reduce the rearward force on the bad engine's wing (reduce drag). The propeller that is not producing thrust has become a liability by causing drag.

When one engine quits, the engine instruments do not immediately tell the pilot which engine failed. The airflow will continue to turn the propeller like a pinwheel. This is why you cannot determine the failed engine just by looking. The propellers will look as though they are both running just fine. The propeller of the dead engine is turning, which causes the tachometer to read as it always does. There might be a slight reduction in RPM because relative wind, not combustion, is causing the crankshaft to turn.

The manifold pressure gauge is also no help. The wind that drives the propeller is also driving the pistons to rise and fall in the cylinders; the valves are opening and closing with the proper rhythmic timing. Every intake stroke draws air in past the manifold pressure port that reads the airflow just as any normal situation.

The propellers look normal, and the tachometers and manifold pressure gauges look normal, but the nose is yawing and great amounts of rudder are required to keep the nose straight and the airplane under control.

Propeller drag must be reduced. The propeller can do one of three things:

- Be left alone to fan in the breeze.
- Have blades stopped.
- Have blades turned into the wind.

The condition where the blades turn by the pressure of the relative wind alone is called *windmilling*. The condition where the blades turn edge-on to the relative wind and stop rotating is called *feathering*.

A test airfoil was designed to prove the drag production of the propeller in three conditions (Fig. 1-6). The airfoil section represents the wing section that holds the engine of a conventional light twin airplane. The airfoil/engine combination is shown in Fig. 1-6 in the slow-speed wind tunnel where the tests were completed. The propeller was powered by a small electric motor. In the series of tests conducted for drag, the engine and propeller were installed but the electric motor was turned off. The engine therefore was producing no thrust and the propeller became a drag producer.

In the first test, the limp propeller was allowed to windmill in the tunnel. The tunnel's airflow turned the propeller just as relative wind turns a dead engine's propeller in flight. Figure 1-7 displays the test results of the power-off, propeller-windmilling test.

In the second test, the propeller was stopped and prevented from windmilling in the airflow (Fig. 1-8). Comparing the two graphs tells the story of propeller drag. Examine the coefficient of drag at 8° angle of attack on each graph as one example. When the propeller was windmilling, the C_D was 0.7. With the propeller stopped, the drag was reduced to a C_D of 0.56. That is a 20 percent reduction in drag just because the propeller was prevented from windmilling. A turning propeller is essentially a disk in the wind (the diameter of the disk is the diameter of the propeller arc), not simply two or three blades in the wind.

(This principle applies to single-engine airplanes as well. The pilot can get a much better glide distance—20 percent better in this example—by stopping the propeller of a single-engine airplane. The pilot would have to raise the nose and reduce the airspeed. At a certain speed, the drag from within the engine would be greater than the airflow and the propeller would stop. For the remainder of the glide, the pilot would have more choices. Be careful because raising the nose to reduce the airspeed has its hazards and should be done with plenty of altitude.)

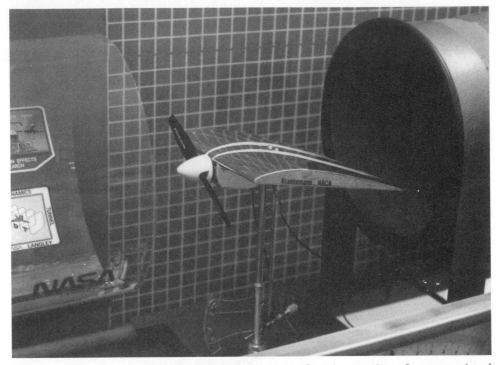

Fig. 1-6. *This airfoil/engine combination represents the wing section of a conventional multiengine airplane where the engine is mounted. The test airfoil/engine was placed in a wind tunnel to test propeller drag in three configurations: windmilling, propeller stopped, and propeller feathered.*

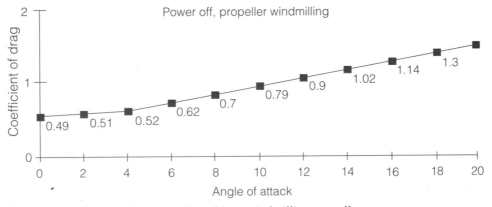

Fig. 1-7. *Coefficients of drag produced by a windmilling propeller.*

For multiengine airplanes with one engine failed, this reduction in drag would cause the airspeed of V_{MC} to get slower. Less drag on the dead engine side would mean less rudder to overcome the drag. So, any drag reduction caused by the propeller will be good for V_{MC}.

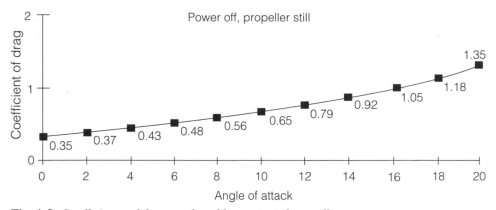

Fig. 1-8. *Coefficients of drag produced by a stopped propeller.*

Propellers on multiengine airplanes have one more drag reducing feature: feathering. When the propeller blades are stopped, the airflow still strikes the blade on the face. The propeller blade is designed to be streamlined when rotating. Without rotation, the relative wind hits the blades head-on. A propeller feathering system allows the propeller blades to twist into a position that is more streamlined. The relative wind then hits the blades edge-on and drag is further reduced.

The last drag test using the sample airfoil was conducted using a feathered propeller (Fig. 1-9). This photo shows the twist on the propeller blades. As before, the tunnel's airflow was allowed to pass by the airfoil in the feathered position. Figure 1-10 shows the feathered test results. Comparing as before the 8° angle of attack setting, the coefficient of drag is 0.43. This is a 38.6 percent reduction in drag compared to the windmilling condition.

These results are from an independent test of a generic airfoil and engine and do not necessarily represent the drag savings of any particular airplane. The results do illustrate the science involved with any multiengine airplane.

If a multiengine pilot experiences a low altitude/slow airspeed failure of one engine, the sooner that the dead engine's propeller is feathered, the safer the situation will be. A feathered propeller produces less drag, which requires less rudder effectiveness and airspeed. A feathered propeller is good because it causes V_{MC} to become slower. A windmilling propeller forces the dead-engine side rearward, which requires a strong rudder to pull the dead-engine side forward. Windmilling increases V_{MC}.

THE LAW OF THE LEVER

To this point, the forces discussed were not amplified. The forces shown in Fig. 1-5 were relatively simple. One force pulls forward; the other pulls rearward. But forces present in a multiengine airplane become more and more complex the closer you look. Not only is the presence of a force important, but the location of the force is important and might have a great impact on the eventual magnitude of the force. This is a very old idea applied to the multiengine airplane.

Fig. 1-9. *Front view of the test airfoil/engine combination with the propeller feathered.*

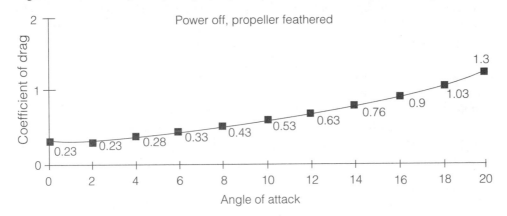

Fig. 1-10. *Coefficients of drag produced by a feathered propeller.*

The idea is so old it goes back to biblical times. Pilots do not own the science of weight and balance; a book on the topic was published as early as 250 B.C. entitled *Centers of Gravity of Planes* by Archimedes. I do not think the term *planes* in the title meant airplanes. Archimedes was a famous Greek scientist and mathematician. He understood something before the birth of Christ that multiengine pilots need to know today. He wrote the law of the lever: "Magnitudes balance at distances from a fulcrum in inverse ratio to their weights."

Loosely translated, this means that two kids on a teeter-totter will only balance if the kids weigh the same. It also means that a lighter weight could balance a heavier weight as long as the lighter weight has a longer arm (distance) from the balance point. Archimedes knew that a small force could be turned into a large force if a lever was used for mechanical advantage. Pilots who struggle with weight and balance problems have Archimedes to blame for the equation

Weight × arm = moment

(Archimedes also became famous for his help in defending his hometown of Syracuse, Sicily, against Roman invaders. The story, which might be more legend than fact, describes the attacking Roman Army entering the Port of Syracuse on a sailing ship. In anticipation of the attack, Archimedes constructed a huge lever with one end underneath the water's surface.

When the Roman ship crossed over the lever, Archimedes and his men jumped on the other side of the lever. This mechanical advantage caused the far end of the lever to rise from the water and flip the ship. Archimedes died in 211 B.C. when the Romans attacked Syracuse on land instead of water, but the law of the lever survived.)

When dealing with uneven forces, such as uneven thrust or drag, the position of the force determines the magnitude of the force. V_{MC} determines the speed required to overcome the force, so V_{MC} and the law of the lever must be understood together.

THE CRITICAL ENGINE

To understand why one engine might be considered more critical than another engine, basic propeller theory must be understood. Recall the terms *P-factor* or *asymmetrical thrust*. Both terms refer to an inevitable turning force that results when a propeller turns in an inclined geometric plane. Most pilots have heard about the force, but few truly understand it. We know that during a full-power climb in a single-engine the airplane tends to turn left and that right rudder cures the problem. But why does the airplane turn? What does turning have to do with V_{MC}? What does all that have to do with Archimedes?

When the airplane is flying straight and level, the thrust from the propeller is centered. The descending propeller blade cuts through the air at a particular angle, and this produces forward thrust. At the same time, the ascending blade makes the same size cut into the air and therefore produces the same amount of forward thrust. When thrust from both sides of the propeller disk is equal, the thrust pulls as if through the spinner.

Things change when the airplane is in a climb with the nose pitched up and the entire airplane tilted back (Fig. 1-11). This tilt increases the descending blades' cut into the air, simultaneously reducing the ascending blades' cut into the air. The descending blade will produce more thrust because the blade is taking a bigger bite of the air; the ascending blade will produce less thrust because it is taking a smaller bite of the air.

The propeller's *thrust pattern* has shifted. Initially, the effective thrust came from the propeller's spinner. Now, with the nose inclined, the focal point of the thrust shifts toward the descending blade. The center of thrust moves from the center of the

21

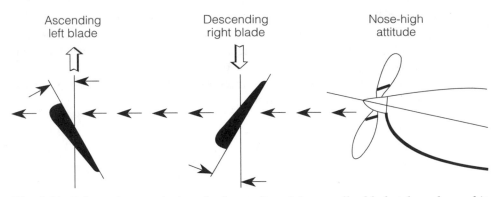

Ascending
left blade

Descending
right blade

Nose-high
attitude

Fig. 1-11. *P-factor is caused when the descending right propeller blade takes a larger bite of the air than the ascending left blade.*

propeller to somewhere closer to the descending blade. A single-engine airplane's propeller turns clockwise as seen from the pilot seat. This means that the descending blade is on the right side. When the center of thrust shifts to the right side, the airplane will turn left because the right side of the blade has more thrust and tends to outrun the left side. This causes the entire airplane to turn left and pilots stop this turn with right rudder.

Apply this to a multiengine airplane climb. Both descending blades will be taking a bigger bite of the air; both thrust patterns will be shifted to the right. Figure 1-12 shows the thrust from both sides of the turning propellers. The left-side thrust arrows are shorter than the right-side thrust arrows, indicating the greater force on the right. The airplane's right side will try to fly faster than the left side. But because both sides are connected by the rest of the airplane, the result is a left-turning tendency. This situation is normal and presents no real problem. All a pilot must do to correct the situation is apply right rudder.

What would happen if one of the two engines quit while this uneven thrust was taking place? The airplane would yaw in the direction of the dead engine. This fact has already been established, but the *critical engine* concept considers the degree of yaw force. In the situation shown in the diagram, a failed left engine would produce a greater degree of yaw force than a failed right engine. The reason the left engine is the "critical" engine takes us back to the lever and Archimedes.

The pivot point of the airplane is the center of gravity. Usually when we think about center of gravity, we are attempting to properly balance the airplane. Using standard weight and balance theory in an elementary sense, we place weights of different magnitudes along the line from nose to tail. Each weight is a force pointing down to the center of the Earth that must be offset in order to balance the fuselage. Considering V_{MC}, we must view the forces from above and look along a line from wingtip to wingtip. The forces as described are thrust vectors of different magnitudes that must be offset not by weight but by rudder force.

The farther a force is from the center of gravity, the more leverage it will have. The force is simply magnified by its position relative to CG. Looking at the diagram one

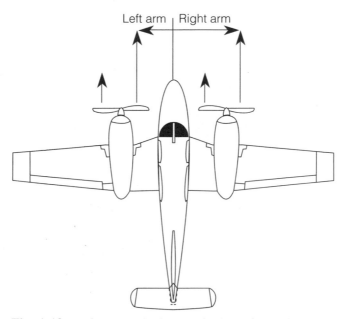

Fig. 1-12. *With a nose-high attitude, both descending propeller blades produce P-factor. This causes the center of thrust to shift to the right. When the right engine's thrust shifts, it gets farther from the airplane's center of gravity. The right lever arm increases while the left lever arm decreases.*

more time, which propeller force is farthest from the CG? The force coming from the right engine's descending propeller blade is farthest. This means that in a situation where a left engine failed, the operating right engine would produce a greater yaw force. This greater yaw force can only be overcome with a greater right rudder force. Greater rudder force can only come from greater airflow past the rudder, and greater airflow only happens with greater (faster) airspeed. So, the reason one engine is more critical than the other is because one engine's failure makes V_{MC} get faster.

In multiengine airplanes where both propellers turn to the right, the left engine is the critical engine. If the right engine quits, you still have a problem on your hands, of course. But the distance from the left engine's center of thrust to the airplane's center of gravity (the arm) is shorter and therefore the yaw force is weaker.

V_{MC} is improved as the P-factor of the left engine starts to shift the center of thrust toward the right. This is because as the thrust shifts to the right on the left engine, it narrows the gap to the airplane's center of gravity. The shorter the lever arm, the less yaw force produced, and the less force required to counteract.

Losing either engine is bad, but losing the critical engine is worse. Recovery from a situation where the critical engine has failed requires a faster airspeed because V_{MC} gets faster.

Picture a situation where a pilot is climbing out with an airspeed just slightly faster than the published V_{MC} (red radial line):

- The right engine fails and the airplane yaws to the right. The current airspeed allows for enough rudder effectiveness to offset this yaw and the pilot maintains control.

- The left engine fails and the airplane yaws to the left. The force of this yaw is greater because the yaw has greater leverage. The V_{MC} quickly gets faster than the published value. The pilot sees the airspeed indicator showing faster than V_{MC}, but the rudder force at this speed cannot overcome the magnified right-engine yaw force, and control is lost.

Attempts have been made to solve the critical engine problem. The best solution is to eliminate the critical engine altogether by making the propellers turn in opposite directions. Many general aviation twins have counterrotating propellers. As seen from the cockpit, the left engine turns clockwise and the right engine turns counterclockwise. This means that both descending blades are on the inside and therefore both are equally close to the airplane's center of gravity. If either counterrotating engine fails, the problem will be bad, but left and right are equally bad. V_{MC} remains the same regardless of which engine fails.

Maintenance on a counterrotating twin can be more expensive because certain parts are unique to a left-turning or a right-turning engine. Many parts cannot be interchanged, but the expense is worth it in a critical situation. You can't "buy" airspeed.

WEIGHT AND BALANCE

The loading of the multiengine airplane also has a large effect on V_{MC}. Pilots say weight and balance, and then refer to the calculation of center of gravity. Weight and balance must be separated and treated as singular topics for an understanding of V_{MC}.

Flying small airplanes, we are very mindful of the airplane's total weight. We are very careful not to flirt with that upper limit of "max gross." We learned that weight was bad and a lighter airplane was a safer airplane. Here again, V_{MC} is a paradox. A heavy airplane is actually better for V_{MC}. A heavy airplane is bad for performance, but remember that V_{MC} is a matter of control, not performance. The pilot must understand this important point: An airplane should not be flown heavier than its maximum allowable weight, but the closer that the weight is to the maximum allowable, the slower V_{MC} will become.

A heavy airplane is a stubborn airplane. The more mass the airplane has, the more inertia it will have. Think about this illustration: Two pilots are at the bowling alley playing on adjacent lanes. One pilot is bowling with a regular bowling ball (heavy weight) and the other pilot is bowling with a volleyball (light weight). They both roll their respective balls at the bowling pins. While the balls are rolling down the lanes, a bowling alley employee opens a side door and a powerful crosswind sweeps across the lanes. The crosswind strikes the bowling ball, but the bowling ball is hardly affected. The same wind strikes the volleyball, and the volleyball's path is deflected into the gutter.

The wind was the same for both balls. We will assume that the balls were rolled with equal force and that both rolled down the center of each lane. Why did one drop in the gutter while the other did not? Weight. It takes a much greater force to move a heavy object.

When I see a pilot report about turbulence, I immediately look to see what type of airplane the report came from. Severe turbulence reported by a Cessna 150 and severe turbulence reported by a Boeing 757 is a misrepresentation of the conditions because the two airplanes do not weigh the same. It takes a large force of air to throw an airliner around, but not very much force to toss a Cessna.

If one engine of a light twin fails, the entire airplane will start to yaw. A heavy airplane will resist any movement. It will take a greater yaw force to move the nose of a heavy airplane than a light airplane. What if a huge cruise ship lost the use of one propeller on one side of the ship? Would the ocean liner quickly begin a yaw turn? No, the turn would be slow and labored. The ship is massive and therefore sluggish. What about a rowboat propelled with the same power as those cruise ship propellers, but only from one side? What will the rowboat do? It will turn immediately. The turn will take effect quickly because the rowboat is light and is pushed around easily.

Any yaw force caused by a failed engine will have less effect on a heavy airplane. When yaw has less effect, there is less force required to balance forces; therefore, less airspeed is required. V_{MC} is slower when heavier. When yaw is produced by a failed engine of a light airplane, however, things can happen faster. More rudder force and greater airspeed will be required. V_{MC} is faster when lighter.

Effect of CG

The location of the weight also affects the speed of V_{MC}. All pilots have calculated a weight and balance problem before. Take the weight of fuel, people, baggage, and the airplane, and determine where the focal point of all this weight rests. That point, the center of gravity, must then be placed in proper proximity to where the wing's lift is being generated in order to have proper aircraft stability. A center of gravity outside the safe range can be fatal, but for multiengine pilots, there is another reason for concern.

The "rudder arm" is shortened when the center of gravity moves to the rear of the airplane (Fig. 1-13). Remember that the pivot point of the airplane is the center of gravity. When the airplane yaws, it turns side to side around this crucial point. When the distance between the rudder and the center of gravity is long, the effective force will be magnified and therefore strong. (Archimedes would be proud.)

But as the gap narrows, the force gets weaker. If the rudder force is weak, it might not be able to overcome engine-out yaw forces at all. The airplane might be under the maximum allowable weight, and the center of gravity might be within the safe range, but V_{MC} gets faster with every increment of aft CG shift.

If an engine fails, the nose will begin to swing. The pilot will step on the rudder to stop the swing and straighten the nose, but with an aft CG, the application of rudder does not yield enough results. The engine yaw might overpower the weak rudder yaw, and aircraft control is quickly lost. The only way the rudder can avoid being overpowered is to have greater effectiveness through greater airspeed. V_{MC} goes up when CG moves back.

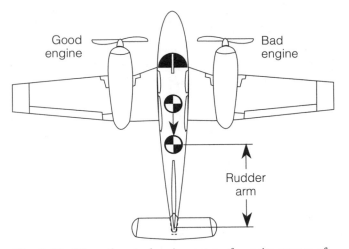

Fig. 1-13. *When the airplane's center of gravity moves aft, the distance (arm) between the pivot point and the rudder is reduced. This weakens the rudder's effectiveness.*

COORDINATION AND SIDESLIP

How the airplane is flown also has an impact on the speed of V_{MC}. Differences in airplanes and opinions have fueled a debate for many years on just how a multiengine airplane should be controlled when an engine has failed. At one time, it was preached that a pilot should never turn the airplane toward a dead engine. If the heading was north and a turn to east was required, the pilot would turn left—the long way to east—if the right engine had failed. Because FAR Part 23.149 specifies that the bank angle for V_{MC} testing be "not more than five degrees," many took the 5° bank as the absolute gospel.

These are the facts: Anytime the airplane's flight path is not parallel with the airplane's nose-to-tail line, drag will increase. Anytime a slip occurs, the rudder effectiveness will suffer. Both factors, drag and rudder effectiveness, have a big impact on the speed of V_{MC}. Anything that tampers with drag or the rudder also changes V_{MC}; therefore, the pilot must understand what is taking place.

If the pilot flies with the wings level and the ball of the inclinometer is in the center while one engine is failed, V_{MC} will get faster. All previous single-engine training has taught that "ball in the center" is a good thing. Your flight instructor spent many hours trying to convince you that staying coordinated during turns and takeoffs, especially during stalls, was vital. But when one engine fails, once again V_{MC} is a paradox. To get best results with V_{MC}, you must go against previous single-engine training. The slowest speed that can be obtained for V_{MC} takes place at *zero sideslip*.

To understand what zero sideslip means, the pilot must first understand what a sideslip is and why it is being produced. A slip takes place when the airplane does not travel in the direction that the nose is pointed. This can happen when flying through a crosswind, but for this discussion wind will not be a factor.

When flying with one engine out and compensating for uneven thrust with rudder, two forces are being canceled out. If the right engine is dead, the operating left engine will yaw the airplane's nose to the right. The pilot must apply left rudder to swing the nose back to center. If the rudder force is strong enough to balance the engine force, control is maintained. These two forces are in balance, but simultaneously there are two other forces present that are not in balance.

The "other" forces that are unbalanced will cause the airplane to slip. The right engine is dead in Fig. 1-14A. The left engine is producing two forces:

- Engine yaw force to the right
- The forward force of thrust

Meanwhile, the rudder is also producing two forces:

- The rudder yaw force making the nose pivot to the left
- A "sideways lift"

The two yaw forces (labeled 1 and 3 in Fig. 1-14A) offset each other and cancel out, but the left propeller's forward thrust force and the rudder's sideways lift force do not offset and therefore do not cancel out.

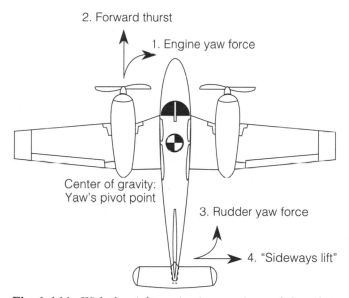

Fig. 1-14A. *With the right engine inoperative and the pilot holding left rudder, four forces go to work on the airplane.*

What is *sideways lift*? The vertical stabilizer and rudder combination acts just like the wing and aileron combination. When an aileron is deflected down, the airflow on the wing's upper camber has a greater distance to travel. This additional distance causes the air molecules to speed up. When the airflow gets faster, the drop in pressure is greater. This drop in pressure creates more lift and the wing rises.

The same thing happens with the rudder. When the rudder is deflected, airflow velocity increases in the area that the travel distance lengthens. The faster that the molecules of air travel, the lower pressure that is produced. When the left rudder pedal is pushed, the rudder's trailing edge moves left. This produces a greater camber on the right side of the vertical stabilizer/rudder combination. A lower pressure then forms on the right side of the stabilizer. The entire tail section then is drawn into the area of low pressure. When the tail moves to the right, the airplane pivots on the center of gravity and the airplane's nose moves left. The sideways lift is a differential of pressure on opposite sides of the vertical stabilizer.

Thrust pulls the airplane forward; rudder force pulls the airplane sideways. The two forces acting on the same body come to a compromise: a slip. The slip is actually the resultant vector of the two forces (Fig. 1-14B). Thrust, as you might have already determined, is much stronger than sideways lift; therefore, the resultant is more forward than to the side. But as sure as the airplane is moving forward, it is also moving sideways, and anytime that the airplane is not completely traveling forward, there will be greater drag. The greater drag is a result of the relative wind striking the airplane from the side rather than from straight on. So, sideways lift causes drag and drag causes V_{MC} to get faster.

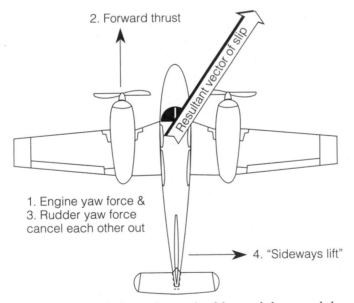

2. Forward thrust

Resultant vector of slip

1. Engine yaw force &
3. Rudder yaw force
cancel each other out

4. "Sideways lift"

Fig. 1-14B. *A sideslip is the result of forward thrust and the rudder's "sideways" lift joining forces.*

Also, the slip damages the rudder's ability to do its job. If the travel path of the airplane is not straight, then the airplane's relative wind is not straight. Figure 1-15 shows the airplane in a sideslip to the right. The right engine is dead. The resultant vector of thrust and sideways lift are producing a travel path that is forward, but also to the right.

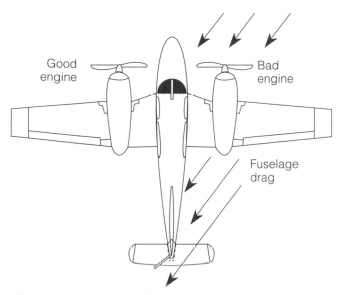

Fig. 1-15. *When the airplane is in a slip, the relative wind produces more drag by striking the fuselage on the side, and rudder effectiveness is lost because the relative wind crosses the rudder with a more parallel angle.*

Look at the way the wind strikes the deflected rudder. The greatest force is produced when the wind hits an object head-on. In this situation, the wind is almost parallel to the plane of the rudder. This makes the rudder force weaker and drives V_{MC} faster.

So, a sideslip is bad for V_{MC} and airplane control. To stop the sideslip, the airplane must be banked into the good engine until the airflow again is parallel with the airplane's nose-to-tail line. How much bank is required? Whatever bank that is necessary to stop the sideslip, which is the same as achieving zero sideslip.

Five degrees is not the magic number. For most twins, the number is closer to 3° bank. V_{MC} is lowered approximately 3 knots for every degree of bank closer to zero sideslip. If the "perfect" angle were 3°, but the pilot elected to fly with wings level, the result would be a 9-knot increase in V_{MC}. If the pilot forgot about zero sideslip and automatically used 5° of bank, the pilot would be penalizing performance by raising V_{MC} an unnecessary 6 knots. These speed differences seem small, but even 1 knot under V_{MC} is fatal on takeoff.

How can the best bank angle be determined? I recommend an old-fashioned way: Use a yaw string. If you are training in a multiengine airplane without a yaw string, your training is lacking. It is easy to do. Take some heavy string and attach one end to the nose of the airplane. Make sure that the string is attached exactly on the airplane centerline. Many airplanes have a seam in the metal that runs along the centerline back to the windshield. Use this seam as the reference line. If there is no convenient seam, mark the centerline with a piece of tape.

While in normal, two-engine flight, the string will flutter in the relative wind, but it will be straight along the centerline (Fig. 1-16). Now, reduce the power on the left engine to simulate zero thrust and initially fly the airplane with wings level. You will see that with the wings level, the yaw string does not lay along the centerline, but the ball is in the center (Fig. 1-17).

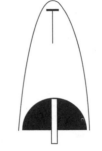

Fig. 1-16. *As seen from the left pilot's seat, the yaw string is standing straight back with both engines operating. The fuselage centerline seam is your reference with the string. The tip of the string will flutter due to the faster, two-engine speed.*

Fig. 1-17. *The left engine is inoperative, and the wings are level. Sideslip is noted by the position of the yaw string, right of the centerline. The ball is held in the center of the inclinometer.*

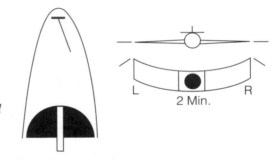

Remember that anytime the yaw string is not on the centerline, the relative wind is coming from the side and drag is increased on the fuselage. Anytime the yaw string does not stretch across the centerline, the rudder is less effective. Both factors tell you that anytime the yaw string is not on the centerline, V_{MC} is faster.

Now, bank into the good engine until the yaw string is on the centerline (Fig. 1-18). When the string centers, the airplane's bank angle has achieved zero sideslip. Now over-bank and watch the string move past the centerline; V_{MC} starts to increase again.

A curious thing happens to the ball during the yaw string exercise. While flying straight and level, the yaw string is not on the centerline, but the ball is centered (Fig. 1-17). When the yaw string is on the centerline, the ball is about halfway out of center in the direction of the good engine (Fig. 1-18). The paradox of V_{MC} is proven again: Straight and level with the ball centered is not as good as a bank with the ball halfway out of center.

FLAPS AND LANDING GEAR AND V_{MC}

Flaps and landing gear affect the speed of V_{MC}. Up until now the factors affecting V_{MC} have involved an asymmetrical situation where something happened on one side of the airplane that did not happen on the other side: engine out. Flaps and landing gear are

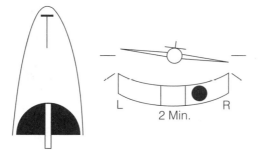

Fig. 1-18. *The airplane has been banked toward the right, the direction of the good engine. The airplane is now flying with zero sideslip, which is noted by the string on the centerline and the ball out of the center, also in the direction of the operating engine.*

supposed to go up or down in unison and no asymmetrical situation occurs. Lowering flaps and landing gear in many twin-engine airplanes can reduce the speed of V_{MC}.

Extended flaps or landing gear act as stabilizers. Jet fighter planes often require drag chutes to stop. Usually a parachute pops out the back and the air resistance of the chute helps stop the fighter. Wing flaps produce drag, so imagine that your airplane has two small drag chutes, one per wing. When simultaneously deployed, the chutes would pull each wing back.

The yawing motion, which is so dangerous to multiengine pilots when one engine quits, will pull the wing with the good engine forward; however, if the flaps are down and additional drag is present, the forward movement of the wing as it pivots on CG will be opposed by flap drag. This dampens the yaw. Less yaw means less rudder force is required; therefore, less speed is required: V_{MC} is lowered.

The landing gear works much the same way. Sailboats have a long keel that sticks down deep underneath the hull of the boat. The keel's job is to grip the water and provide stability to the boat. When the landing gear and tires stick down into the relative wind, they grip the air and will resist yaw.

So, lowering wing flaps and landing gear can slightly improve airplane control, but unfortunately it will devastate performance. The extra drag of flaps and gear will bring the airplane down. Trying to pull flaps and gear through the air with only one engine is a losing battle. For this reason, a pilot should not rely upon the application of flaps and landing gear to solve V_{MC} problems, except under extreme conditions.

Obviously, anything that causes more drag on one side of the airplane while flying on one engine is terribly bad. It would be a disaster to have only one wing flap lowered. If a pilot making an approach to landing got too slow and too close to V_{MC}, then hit the flap control and only a single flap went down, the result would adversely affect V_{MC}. As the split-flap condition developed, especially if the flap went down on the dead-engine side, a great yaw force would develop and V_{MC} would skyrocket past the approach speed.

Before takeoff, run the flaps through their paces. Make sure that they go up and down together. Always keep your hand on the flap control while the flaps are in transition, or at least until you are sure they are lowering evenly.

One other caution: When operating with only one engine and flaps down, be ready for the good engine's wing to rise if you go full power. Airflow from off the propellers streaks back across the wing flaps of conventional twins. This *accelerated slipstream* will produce faster airflow over the camber.

When one engine has quit, the accelerated slipstream will only exist on one side and the spanwise lift pattern will be asymmetrical. In other words, the wing with the operating engine will have more lift and this starts a yaw turn that will raise V_{MC}.

This particular situation might occur when a single-engine go-around is attempted. A single-engine go-around is a very bad idea. The ability of the operating engine to pull you back to a safe altitude, together with the faster V_{MC} during a flap-down application of full power, makes this very dangerous. It might be better to land in the grass beside the runway.

SITUATIONAL AWARENESS

Now that the theory has been explained, it is time for some practical application. You are flying a conventional twin-engine lightplane. Your current airspeed is just faster than the published V_{MC} and one engine has already failed. How will the following situations affect the speed of V_{MC}? Do any of these situations make the pilot "less safe"?

1. Density altitude is 8,000 feet.
2. The dead engine's constant-speed propeller control cable breaks.
3. The airplane is flying with full fuel, all seats filled with passengers, and full baggage compartments. It is at maximum gross weight.
4. A full set of golf clubs is in the aft baggage compartment.
5. A circuit breaker pops leaving both wing flaps stuck down.

The question "Are you safer or less safe?" is too simple for these situations because what is good for V_{MC} is often bad for performance. What is "safer" for V_{MC} might at the same time be "less safe" from a performance standpoint. Because the question calls for a speed just faster than V_{MC}, we will consider "safer" to mean a margin of speed that is faster than V_{MC}.

What about situation number 1? The speed of V_{MC} will definitely be slower. The power output of the operating engine will be severely reduced while the engine gasps for air. Many pilots just do not completely understand the concept of density altitude. Some pilots can even calculate density altitude on a calculator-type flight computer, but they have no idea how to apply the information.

Can you be at 2,000 feet MSL and have an 8,000-foot density altitude? Of course. Can you be at 2,000 feet and have a "negative" density altitude? Of course. Multiengine flying requires pilots to get back to basics. The importance of the basics is amplified when applied to multiengine flying. When the engine produces less power and less yaw, there is less need for airspeed to cross the rudder; however, an 8,000-foot density altitude is "less safe" for performance, especially if you are attempting to climb over a mountain ridge.

The answer for situation number 2 depends upon the airplane's individual systems, which are covered later. But for now, assume that when the cable that operates the propeller's blade angle breaks, you lose the ability to pull the propeller into the feathered position. Being unable to prevent the propeller from windmilling will increase drag and increase the speed of V_{MC}.

In situation number 3, the airplane will have poor performance characteristics such as rate of climb, but V_{MC} will be slower. Never try to justify flying at or heavier than maximum gross weight by using the fact that V_{MC} is improved.

Number 4 is interesting. A full set of golf clubs is very heavy, which can be dangerous if you magnify this weight by placing the clubs in the aft compartment. Even if the CG shift caused by the aft weight is still in the safe CG range, V_{MC} is going to be faster. The distance between CG (pivot point) and center-of-rudder force is reduced and weakened. When one engine quits and you step on the rudder to overcome the yaw, you will run out of rudder before the job is done. Consider putting the clubs in the back seat or renting clubs when you get there.

Number 5 is safer because some small degree of extra stability will slow V_{MC} slightly. Remember that if this happens down low, maintain control and land on something flat. Do not ask the airplane to do something that is impossible and lose airspeed below V_{MC} in the attempt.

You can certainly make up other V_{MC}/performance scenarios. The key is to completely understand what will affect what. This closing table summarizes everything covered in the chapter. Do not simply memorize the table's information; only through understanding the information will you be able to safely fly a multiengine airplane.

What changes the airplane's minimum control speed?

Factor	Higher V_{MC} (bad)	Lower V_{MC} (good)
Prop rotation	Critical engine; Props turn same way	No critical engine; Counter-rotating props
Prop condition	Windmilling	Feathered
Power produced	High; Low altitude; Cold temperature	Low; High altitude; Hot temperature
Total weight	Light	Heavy
Center of gravity	CG aft	CG forward
Coordination	Ball centered; Sideslip	Ball half out; Zero sideslip
Bank	Wings level	Banked to good engine

2
Multiengine takeoff and landing

TAKEOFF IN A MULTIENGINE AIRPLANE IS MORE HAZARDOUS THAN ANY other maneuver. When the airplane has reached a safe altitude and speed, having a second engine is great, but in the transition zone between slow and fast, two engines double the dangers. Multiengine pilots must plan every takeoff with the expectation that one engine will fail. If an engine fails during takeoff, it will be a surprise to the pilot; how the pilot reacts should not be a surprise.

SPEED MILESTONES

As a normal takeoff progresses, the plane and pilot will pass definable points of decision that I call "speed milestones." The proper action taken by the pilot when one engine quits on takeoff changes according to what milestones have been passed. In order to do the right thing, the pilot must understand that different speeds produce different reactions from the airplane (Fig. 2-1).

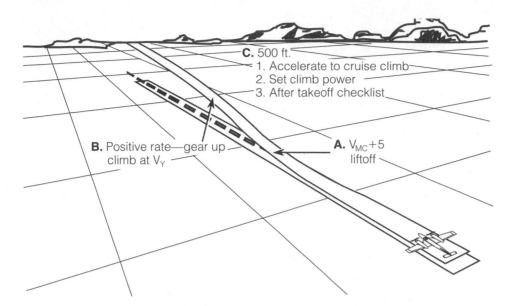

C. 500 ft.
1. Accelerate to cruise climb
2. Set climb power
3. After takeoff checklist

B. Positive rate—gear up
climb at V_Y

A. $V_{MC}+5$
liftoff

Fig. 2-1. *Normal multiengine takeoff.*

Zero

The first speed milestone is zero knots. Before letting the airplane move down the runway, the pilot must be absolutely certain that the airplane is ready. It is a good practice to align the airplane with the runway centerline and then pause for a few seconds. While holding the brakes, run the engines up to takeoff power, and make sure that the engine instruments show green. Verify that the manifold pressure and RPMs are acceptable. Be sensitive to any shudders or shakes that are unusual.

Normal pretakeoff runups are done with less than takeoff power, so this is the first time you can check the airplane at this higher power setting. If there is any indication of a problem, you would rather discover it while standing still; you can turn your full attention to engine observation. When you let go of the brakes, you will be too busy with steering, crosswinds, and other distractions to carefully watch the engine instruments.

Taking the runway, but delaying takeoff for an engine test does have its hazards. The controllers in the tower do not like pilots to make unannounced delays on an active runway. Observe the traffic load by listening to the tower or unicom frequency before you call "Ready for takeoff." This will build your airport situational awareness. If the traffic is heavy, with one airplane after another landing, it will be best to advise the tower that you will need some time on the runway before you begin the roll. Just say, "November . . . is ready for takeoff, and we will need a 15-second delay on the runway."

The controller should know exactly what you are doing and might be able to space traffic accordingly. At uncontrolled airports, an unexpected delay could cause another pilot to go around. Protect yourself by checking that everything is working properly before letting the airplane move, but be courteous as well.

V$_{MC}$

When V$_{MC}$ is reached and surpassed, another speed milestone passes. The minimum control speed must be observed and the airplane held on the ground through this speed. It is a good idea to observe the airspeed indicator for these milestones to pass. At the very beginning of the takeoff roll, the airspeed indicator will not move because most indicators do not go as low as zero. The plane must be into the takeoff roll several seconds until the airspeed indicator starts to move. This is when I say out loud "airspeed's alive" even if I am alone. This verifies that the airspeed indicator really works, which is a nonspecific speed milestone.

V$_R$

The next speed milestone is reached at the liftoff speed or V$_R$. V$_R$ stands for rotation and is the speed when the pilot pulls back on the wheel and rotates the nose up and off the ground. The V$_R$ speed can never be safely slower than V$_{MC}$. If V$_R$ were slower than V$_{MC}$, and at this speed an engine failed, the pilot would be unable to control the airplane. A safe recovery would be unlikely at such a low altitude. Allowing the airplane to become airborne at a speed slower than V$_{MC}$ should never be acceptable to the pilot.

Check the recommended V$_R$ speed in the operating handbook. Ordinarily, V$_R$ is equal to V$_{MC}$ plus 5 knots (V$_R$ = V$_{MC}$ + 5). The zero speed milestone and the V$_R$ milestone form the first takeoff "decision zone." Ask yourself: "If an engine fails now, do I stop or continue to take off?" Between zero and V$_R$, the decision is easy: Stop.

If anything happens in this speed range that makes you suspicious about the condition of the airplane, immediately reduce power on *both engines*. Pilot examiners predictably present engine problems to multiengine checkride applicants during this decision zone. They not only want to see that you will abort the takeoff while between zero and V$_R$, but that you will bring the power back on both engines.

The examiner might say, "You have low oil pressure in the left engine." If the multiengine applicant pulls back the throttle on only the left engine, the checkride will be over. If only one engine is reduced, the other engine at full power will likely pull the airplane off the centerline and into the runway lights. You do not have time during this part of takeoff roll to do much troubleshooting. Just pull everything back, steer with your feet, bring the airplane to a stop, and inform the control tower or make an announcement on the CTAF.

V$_{YSE}$

Decisions become more complicated after liftoff. V$_{YSE}$ is the next milestone speed—the best rate of climb speed using only one engine. V$_{YSE}$ is marked on the airspeed indicator with a blue radial line. It should probably be called the best one-engine performance speed because sometimes the best performance is still a descent. Nevertheless, V$_{YSE}$ is a milestone of significant importance.

If an engine fails after reaching V_{YSE}, the pilot is already at the best speed for that predicament. In this case, the pilot could move attention to identifying the failed engine and reducing drag, rather than changing speeds. V_{YSE} would equal V_R in a perfect world.

If it were possible to safely hold the airplane on the ground until it accelerated to V_{YSE}, then an engine failure would occur at best performance speed. Holding the airplane on the ground is unsafe because wheelbarrowing might occur. If a pilot holds the wheel forward too long in an attempt to increase liftoff speed, the main wheels might lift off when the wings have enough lift and the nose wheel remains on the ground. The airplane would look just like a wheelbarrow being pushed along.

The airplane might start to "buck" as the wings pull the airplane up and the pilot fights to keep it down. It is not a new problem. So many takeoff accidents have been attributed to wheelbarrowing that the FAA published an advisory circular in 1968 (AC 90-34).

The greatest danger is a combination of wheelbarrowing and crosswinds. If the airplane were allowed to ride up on only the nosewheel, a crosswind could easily pivot the airplane into the wind like a weather vane and directional control would be lost.

The airplane should be allowed to become airborne at $V_{MC} + 5 = V_R$ and then accelerate when free of the ground to V_{YSE}. While the airplane is accelerating through the zone of decision between V_R and V_{YSE}, the proper pilot action to take in the event of an engine failure depends on several factors: density altitude, runway length, wind, and obstructions to climb over.

If an engine quits in this zone (between V_R and V_{YSE}), the best option is to pull both throttles back, and land straight ahead on the remaining runway. Never retract the landing gear while there is runway ahead and the airplane is accelerating through this zone. The landing gear does produce drag, but if the best decision is to land anyway, drag is not a big problem. Retract the landing gear only after reaching V_{YSE} or reaching a position where no landing spot is available ahead.

If strong yaw occurs in this zone and plenty of runway is available, retard both throttles. It can happen so fast that there will be no time to think about which engine has failed. Even if you do figure out which one has failed, reducing power on the failed engine does not help. The good engine would still be producing takeoff power, and this would continue the yaw force. If an engine quits, pull both throttles back and correct for yaw and land.

A multiengine pilot must understand the airplane's abilities and limitations in this speed range of critical decisions; otherwise the pilot might inadvertently ask the airplane to do something that it cannot do.

THE CLASSIC MISUNDERSTANDING: MULTI VS. SINGLE

Who is safer when one engine quits just after takeoff? The single-engine pilot or the multiengine pilot? Picture a purely hypothetical situation where two pilots face a takeoff on parallel runways. Takeoff conditions are identical for both airplanes. One airplane has two engines and the other has one engine.

Both pilots add takeoff power and the airplanes begin to roll. Both accelerate at the same speed. Both rotate and break ground at the same place. Each pilot has the same amount of runway ahead with trees at the end. At this moment, each airplane loses an engine.

The single-engine pilot's decisions are already made: Control the airplane until it hits the ground. Without an extra engine to complicate things, the single-engine pilot turns his attention to the only situation left, a forced landing. It never enters the single-engine pilot's mind to attempt to stay in the air.

The multiengine pilot might entertain the idea that a forced landing might be avoided because the airplane has an extra engine. Staying in the air and avoiding a hazardous forced landing is the best option, but just because a pilot thinks that this is possible does not mean that the airplane is capable of staying in the air.

Certain speed and altitude situations will prevent the multiengine airplane from climbing to a safe altitude or even maintaining altitude. Just like the single-engine pilot, the decision might already be made—a forced landing. If the forced landing option is not realized, the multiengine pilot might waste valuable time and airspeed trying to milk the airplane higher; hence, the airspeed falls below V_R speed as the pilot aims the nose to the sky, then the airplane falls below V_{MC} and control is lost.

There are times when the multiengine pilot must accept the fact that a climb is not possible and a forced landing is inevitable, even with one engine operating at takeoff power. The pilot has no good choices, but the best option left is to land ahead, under control.

The other option is a trap. The operating engine might deceive the pilot with the promise of extra safety, but airspeed is lost while chasing the climb and the airplane lands (crashes) out of control. The old saying is true in this speed range: "Below V_{YSE}, if one engine quits, the operating engine simply takes you to the scene of the accident."

Dealing with differences

Remember that every airplane and every takeoff is different. Certain airplanes will pull out of a situation when other airplanes will crash. Density altitude conditions will allow an airplane to climb to safety one day, but other days the exact same airplane cannot climb to safety. I could not write down an exact engine failure procedure that would guarantee safety between the milestones of V_R and V_{YSE}.

The only way to ensure a safe getaway on one engine is to lower the airplane's nose until an adequate speed is obtained and then start a climb at V_{YSE}. The problem with that statement is that it calls for a trade-off of energy: airspeed gained due to altitude lost. It is assumed that the pilot has no altitude to give if the airplane has just left the ground; therefore, the pilot is in a catch-22 situation. The pilot needs airspeed but cannot get any without altitude, and he cannot get altitude without some additional airspeed.

Milestone planning

The best way to avoid all these problems is to plan the takeoff milestones. Decide prior to takeoff just what you will do if an engine fails between V_R and V_{YSE}. Take all factors into consideration, make a plan, and then stick with the plan. This way, if an engine fails, you will not waste time, airspeed, and altitude during a state of indecision. The decisions up until this speed range have been easy.

Speed range	*Pilot action when one engine quits*
Zero to V_{MC}	Retard both throttles and brake (easy decision).
V_{MC} to V_R	Retard both throttles and brake (easy decision).
V_R to V_{YSE}	Optional (tough decision). Option 1: Retard both throttles and land ahead. Option 2: Lower nose to gain V_{YSE}, then climb to safe altitude.

Option 2 might not be possible. If option 2 is not a true option, it is better for the pilot to accept option 1 early. By making an honest evaluation of the airplane's single-engine climb performance, the pilot should commit to either option 1 or option 2 before ever taking the runway for takeoff (Fig. 2-2). The pilot should say, "If I lose an engine before reaching 88 knots (V_{YSE}), then I put it back down in the smoothest place I can find."

Single-engine takeoff

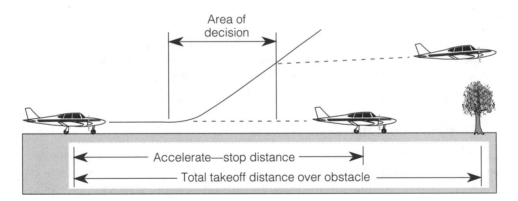

Fig. 2-2. *The area of decision between V_R and V_{YSE}.*

The 88-knot V_{YSE} is only an example, but it reflects what should be going through the pilot's mind when anticipating takeoff. If an engine quits at 79 knots while airborne, the pilot has already made the tough decision to land ahead. No time will be wasted trying to figure out what is better. Multiengine pilots must know the airplane's V speeds and milestones by heart in order to make safe decisions.

Making safe decisions

The pilot should consult several aircraft performance charts during preflight planning. The performance charts provided by the aircraft manufacturer usually are best-case numbers because they were derived by an experienced test pilot flying a new airplane. Pilots should know how to use the performance charts to get the numbers, but understand that actual performance will most always be worse than the chart numbers predict.

Start with the ground-roll graph. These numbers predict the distance, in feet, from initiation of the takeoff roll until liftoff. Figure 2-3 is a typical ground-roll graph. These graphs require a steady hand, and I usually close one eye so the lines do not run together. Use a plastic overlay, and draw lines on the plastic rather than the chart. If you draw the lines on the chart and then erase the next takeoff calculation, the graph will not last very long.

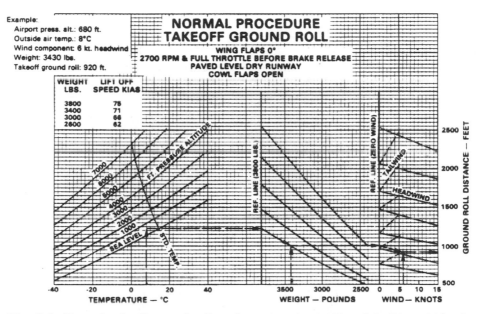

Fig. 2-3. *Normal takeoff ground-roll performance chart. (Copyright Piper Aircraft Corporation. Used with permission. **WARNING:** This performance chart is presented for illustration purposes only and is not intended to predict the performance of any specific airplane. Piper Aircraft Corporation is not involved with publishing this book and does not endorse any statements made herein.)*

To get any information from this maze, you first must determine the following variables:

- Pressure altitude of the airport.
- Temperature in degrees Celsius.
- Weight of the airplane.
- Wind on the runway.

The manufacturer has provided a sample on this graph: pressure altitude is 680 feet, temperature is 8°C, aircraft weight is 3,430 pounds, and a headwind component is 6 knots. Starting at the lower left on the temperature scale, trace up the graph at 8°C until you hit the 680-foot pressure altitude line. Surprise! There is no 680-foot altitude line. This is where the eye squinting comes in. You must estimate where 680 feet should be between the sea-level and 1,000-foot lines.

This rough estimating of position always scares me because a mistake here will change the answer to the problem, and it is upon this answer that safe takeoff decisions will be made. From the estimate of 680, make a 90° right turn and move horizontally to the first reference line. From the reference line, move diagonally with the sloping weight lines. From the base of the graph, find the airplane's weight and start up. When the diagonal sloping line meets the aircraft-weight line, stop and go horizontal again.

Move across until meeting the second reference line. From here, move either up diagonally or down diagonally depending upon whether there is a tailwind or head-wind. In this example, there is a 6-knot headwind, so you slope down the index lines until intersecting the 6-knot position. Now the home stretch. Move horizontally to the right and read the ground roll distance, 920 feet in this example.

Does this mean that it would be safe to take off from a 1,000-foot runway? No. Recall that these numbers are best-case numbers and do not allow for the performance of your airplane and mistakes that were made reading the confusing graph. The 920 feet also assumes that the engines are in perfect working order and are evenly producing takeoff power. What happens when one engine quits? To answer that question, we need yet another graph.

Distance determination

The accelerate-stop distance graph is much more valuable than the ground-roll graph because it presents a better distance value required for safety. The *accelerate-stop distance* is the distance that it takes an airplane to begin the takeoff roll from zero, accelerate to liftoff speed (V_R), have an engine quit at just that speed, and be followed by immediate action by the pilot to retard throttles and safely brake to a stop—ideally on the runway. Broadly defined, the distance required to go from zero to V_R and then back to zero is usually more than twice as long as the calculated ground roll.

Figure 2-4 is a typical accelerate-stop distance graph. The manufacturer provides a sample problem with virtually the same conditions as before: 680 feet pressure altitude, 8°C, 3,430-pound airplane, and a 5-knot headwind component. Perform the graph calculation as before. The accelerate-stop distance answer is 2,050 feet of runway; the ground roll from the previous graph was 920 feet.

Multiengine pilots must look at these numbers realistically. Provided that the graph numbers are correct, a pilot could get into the air with only 1,000 feet of runway, but if anything goes wrong, the pilot will need 2,100 feet to get stopped again. The 2,100-foot number also assumes that the pilot recognized the problem of engine failure at the instant it occurred, and in the next instant the pilot pulled throttles and applied brakes simultaneously.

If the pilot is the least bit surprised, or panic prevents immediate action, that 2,100 feet will grow to 2,500 feet quickly. What if the airplane becomes airborne,

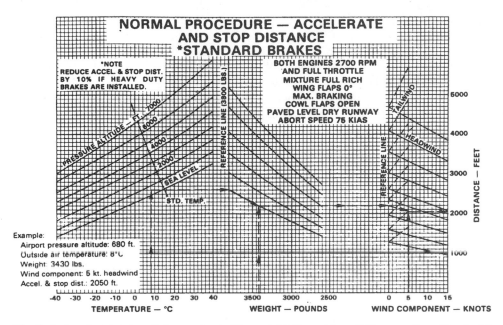

Fig. 2-4. *Accelerate-stop distance chart. (Copyright Piper Aircraft Corporation. Used with permission. **WARNING:** This performance chart is presented for illustration purposes only and is not intended to predict the performance of any specific airplane. Piper Aircraft Corporation is not involved with publishing this book and does not endorse any statements made herein.)*

then an engine quits while the airplane speed is between V_R and V_{YSE}? If the decision is to pull throttles and land, then brake, the distance needed to stop can grow to 4,000 feet or farther. The decision becomes tougher when the runway is only 3,500 feet long.

Imagine yourself in the pilot's seat, no more than 35 feet in the air after takeoff, and one engine has just failed. Airspeed is between liftoff and best single-engine climb speed. It would take 4,000 feet of runway to get stopped, but the total runway length is 3,500 feet. Only 1,500 feet of runway, then a fence, lie ahead of you. What should you do?

Option 1: Attempt to climb to safety.

Option 2: Land and brake.

If you knew for a fact that a climb to a safe altitude was possible, then you should add full power to both throttles (this ensures that the good engine is at full power) and then clean up the airplane by bringing up the landing gear, retracting flaps, and feathering the prop on the failed engine.

If you knew for a fact that a climb was not possible, then you should bring both throttles back, land on the remaining runway surface, and brake hard into the fence. It is always better to hit a fence while decelerating on the ground than to hit trees or terrain while accelerating (downward) in the air.

TOUGHEST QUESTION

How can you know for a fact if the airplane will climb on one engine? This is the toughest question of the book. The ability for a light twin-engine airplane to climb on only one engine is determined by many factors. The biggest misconception comes from believing that when half the engines stop, then half the power is gone. The ability of an airplane to climb is based upon its excess-thrust horsepower.

Excess refers to the airplane's power beyond what is required to maintain level flight. The airplane must have a surplus of thrust to climb. When one engine fails, 50 percent of the power disappears, so it would be easy to assume that the airplane's climb performance would also be reduced by 50 percent. But when asymmetrical thrust and drag are figured in, the actual performance loss is closer to 80 percent.

Can any airplane climb with a sudden 80-percent loss of thrust? Not many light twins can. Compare the two performance charts (Figs. 2-5 and 2-6). The first chart considers the airplane climb capability with both engines operating; the second chart considers the airplane climb capability with only one engine operating. The manufacturer provides the same sample problem as before. Under the conditions of 680 feet pressure altitude, 8°C,

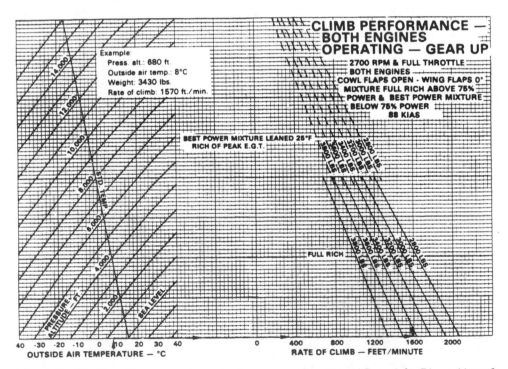

Fig. 2-5. *Climb performance chart: both engines operating. (Copyright Piper Aircraft Corporation. Used with permission. **WARNING:** This performance chart is presented for illustration purposes only and is not intended to predict the performance of any specific airplane. Piper Aircraft Corporation is not involved with publishing this book and does not endorse any statements made herein.)*

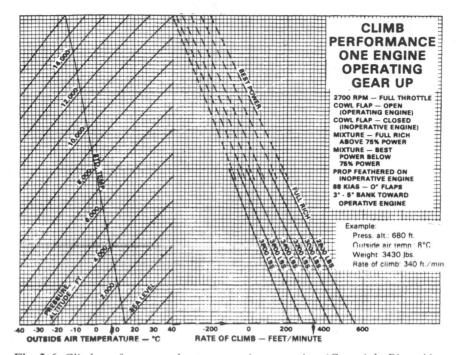

Fig. 2-6. *Climb performance chart: one engine operating. (Copyright Piper Aircraft Corporation. Used with permission. **WARNING:** This performance chart is presented for illustration purposes only and is not intended to predict the performance of any specific airplane. Piper Aircraft Corporation is not involved with publishing this book and does not endorse any statements made herein.)*

and an airplane weight of 3,430 pounds, the graph says that the airplane will climb at 1,570 feet per minute with both engines operating and landing gear up.

Now look at the same conditions with only one engine. This sample yields a climb rate of only 350 feet per minute. The difference between two-engine climb (1,570 fpm) and single-engine climb (350 fpm) is approximately a 78-percent reduction in performance.

Now look at this single-engine climb performance chart a different way. Read it "backwards." Start at the rate-of-climb scale. Go to the zero-climb position and work back through the chart. If the airplane weighed 3,600 pounds and the temperature was 30°C, the airplane could not climb when starting above a pressure altitude of approximately 4,000 feet. At a maximum weight of 3,800 pounds, the airplane cannot climb on one engine above about 3,000 feet. If this does not scare you, it should, because takeoffs are often made at these pressure-altitude values, even when the airport elevation is near sea level.

If an engine failed just after takeoff (a 3,800-pound airplane and 3,000-foot pressure altitude), the pilot could not climb to safety. It is impossible. Any seconds the pilot uses up trying to convince the airplane to climb is time wasted. Physical science says the plane will not fly to safety, and the pilot should spend these seconds preparing for a landing, even a crash landing, rather than on a vain attempt at an impossible climb.

Other circumstances

Even if a climb is possible, flying to safety might not be possible due to the area surrounding the airport. A 350-fpm climb is very weak. Where will the airplane be upon reaching 1,000 feet AGL? The distance across the ground can be calculated. Multiply the climb rate by 60 and divide by the groundspeed to get the feet climbed per nautical mile (nm). Divide the altitude above ground level that you want to climb to by the feet per nautical mile.

If the light multiengine in the example has a groundspeed of 90 knots, the pilot would be 4.28 nautical miles from the airport when reaching 1,000 feet AGL (350 fpm × 60 = 21,000; 21,000 ÷ 90 knots = 233.33 fpm; 1,000 feet ÷ 233.33 fpm = 4.28 nm).

This height of 1,000 feet and a distance of 4.28 nautical miles forms a very shallow climb gradient from takeoff to 1,000 feet AGL. Any obstruction or terrain that intersects this gradient would force the pilot to maneuver an ailing airplane that is already requiring his full concentration to maintain a shallow climb.

Hypothetically, the worst-case scenario would place the airport down inside a bowl-shaped valley. The rim of the valley is 1,000 feet higher than the airport and the bowl's radius is 4.0 nautical miles. The airplane cannot get out of the valley on a straight-line course; turning the ailing airplane to remain clear of the rising terrain would be difficult.

Worse circumstances

What if the conditions were worse than this? Assume the airplane's weight is 3,800 pounds and the temperature is 30°C, but this time the pressure altitude is 5,000 feet. Working the graph with these numbers yields a "best" performance of –100 fpm. The absolute best climb in this case is a descent. If you were the pilot in this situation and did everything correctly (holding V_{YSE}, 3°–5° bank, gear up, etc.), you would still come back down to the ground.

This presents the pilot with two choices:

- Abort the takeoff at the first sign of engine failure by landing and braking.
- Attempt to fly away but the airplane will settle to the ground anyway.

The airplane is going to land or crash-land either way. The second choice will place the accident farther from the airport, which means farther from flat terrain and rescue crews. Flying away will also tempt the pilot to raise the nose in a hopeless effort to gain altitude; hence, the airspeed will bleed away to V_{MC} and the airplane will go out of control.

A pilot must only accept a climb that is steep enough to provide safety. If the pilot elects to continue an engine-out takeoff and subsequent climb, but the airplane is not climbing fast enough to reach a safe altitude, the accident will just take place farther from the airport.

This adds another item to the decision list:

Speed range	Pilot action when one engine quits
V_{YSE} to V_Y	Option 1: Retard throttles, land ahead, start braking.
	Option 2: Accept single-engine climb rate, climb to safety.

The pilot cannot breathe easy and decide that the takeoff has been successful until an altitude is reached where, if an engine quit, he could maintain altitude clear of any obstacle, or he could descend back to the airport. I affectionately call this V_{BE} for "breathe easy" speed. (V_{BE} is not a recognized V speed in aircraft operation manuals or training syllabuses.) The milestones then are:

Milestone	Pilot action when one engine quits
Zero	Tow airplane back to hangar.
V_{MC}	Control but no climb, abort takeoff.
V_R	Liftoff but no climb, abort takeoff.
V_{YSE}	Best single-engine performance, accept or reject climb gradient.
V_{BE}	Safe altitude is available back to airport.

Get into the habit of reading and working the performance charts for your airplane and make the go–no-go decision before takeoff. The decision requires more thought than just the runway length; think about the terrain surrounding the airport. Look for a single-engine escape route that will permit a safe single-engine climb (Fig. 2-7). When a safe altitude is reached, you can afford to return to the airport and land.

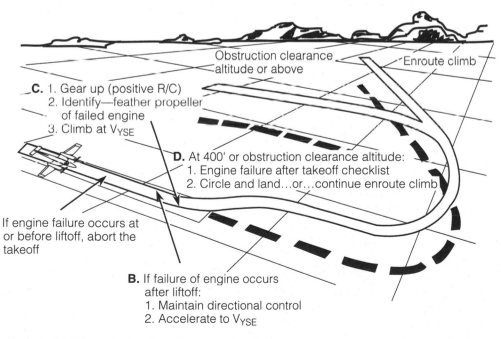

Fig. 2-7. *Flight profile: engine failure on takeoff.*

It is also a good idea to prepare a card that will force you to work the performance problems and help you make an informed takeoff decision. Figure 2-8 is a sample take-off decision card. Fill in the appropriate data for your airplane and make some copies. Fill in the weather information of pressure altitude, temperature, and wind before every takeoff. Work through the performance graphs and determine the ground roll, accelerate-stop distance, and climb performance. Comparing the crucial information on a one-stop reference card will make the go–no-go decision easier.

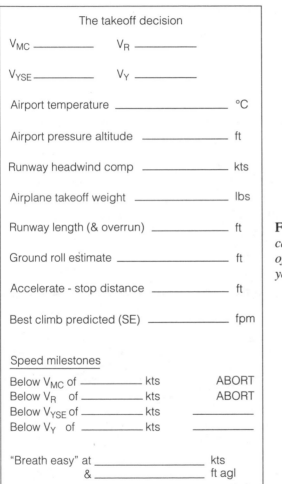

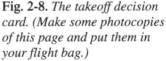

Fig. 2-8. *The takeoff decision card. (Make some photocopies of this page and put them in your flight bag.)*

HIGH TECHNOLOGY ASSISTANCE

With so many speeds, climb rates, engine settings, and decisions, the pilot has a tough job. Considering the number of high-technology products that make a pilot's job easier, you would think there would be something to help with the go–no-go takeoff decision. There is, the *takeoff performance monitoring system* (TOPMS).

The NASA Langley Research Center in Hampton, Virginia, took up the challenge of providing real-time takeoff information to pilots as a result of the Air Florida crash in Washington, D.C. (The Air Florida 737 crashed after takeoff and hit a bridge before sinking into the Potomac River.) Investigators subsequently determined that the accident was probably caused by improper engine instrument readings as a result of ice buildup. The takeoff might have been aborted and the accident might have been avoided if the pilots had had supplemental information. NASA set out to provide just such information.

Every spring for the past several years I have taken my flight dynamics class to NASA Langley to visit the wind tunnels. One year the visit included a session with David B. Middleton, NASA aerospace engineer, to discuss the monitoring system. TOPMS is essentially computer software that acts like a stethoscope on the airplane systems. If anything is ever detected that is below performance standards during takeoff, the computer will determine this much faster than the pilot. The system will then warn the pilot of the problem.

The TOPMS system was tested in NASA's flying laboratory, a Boeing 737. The front of the airplane has a standard cockpit and panel (Fig. 2-9). The cabin has an entirely different rear cockpit (Fig. 2-10). The airplane can be flown by remote control from the rear cockpit. Flying from the rear cockpit allows NASA flight crews the opportunity to evaluate new computer hardware and software for future use.

Fig. 2-9. *The forward cockpit of NASA's Boeing 737 has a standard panel.*

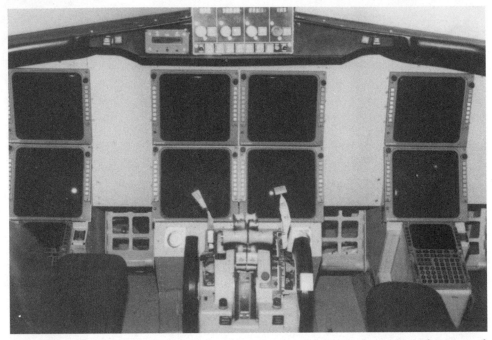

Fig. 2-10. *The rear cockpit of the NASA 737 is a "glass cockpit" where new software, such as TOPMS, is first tested.*

Before takeoff, the TOPMS computer evaluates airplane center of gravity, gross weight, flap settings, ambient temperature, pressure altitude, wind direction, wind velocity, and runway rolling-friction coefficient value. The factors are just like the factors used in the takeoff performance charts. The computer will calculate the expected takeoff performance from these numbers, then determine the distance from the beginning of the takeoff roll to V_R. It also predicts the accelerate-stop distance from zero to V_R and back to zero.

During the takeoff roll, the computer constantly compares the expected performance with the actual performance. The computer evaluates airplane flap setting, left and right throttle positions, left and right engine thrust, calibrated airspeed, airplane acceleration, and groundspeed. The pilot is alerted anytime the predicted numbers and actual numbers do not match.

The alert is either an instrument display on the panel, or a head-up display projection on the inside of the pilot's side window. Figure 2-11 is a photo of the panel and head-up display as seen from the pilot's seat. Figure 2-12 shows the head-up display with greater detail.

Computer-aided decisions

The pilot sees an airplane proceeding down a runway. The triangle that is midway down the runway display is the predicted position of V_R. The white bars on either side

NASA Langley Research Center

Fig. 2-11. *Pilot's TOPMS instrument display.*

NASA Langley Research Center

Fig. 2-12. *TOPMS head-up display.*

of the runway display indicate the power output of each engine. Both engines are shown here with proper takeoff power. If one engine falters, the power bar of the corresponding engine would become shorter, indicating a percentage reduction in power. An engine failure would cause the power bar to turn red on the side of the engine failure. The number 77 on the left of the display indicates the airplane's current calibrated airspeed.

The pilot would see Fig. 2-13 when the computer has detected a problem that will prevent a safe takeoff. An unmistakable stop sign appears and there is an X on the runway. The X displays where the airplane will come to a stop if the pilot initiates immediate abort action now. This display indicates that the airplane could be stopped safely on the remaining runway.

A TOPMS system has yet to be installed in an air carrier. TOPMS is still several years away from affordability for general aviation. At one time, a global positioning satellite receiver in a general aviation airplane was unheard of. Can TOPMS be very far from reality? (I will trade the GPS for a TOPMS whenever possible because a takeoff monitoring system will make my flight safer than having a satellite navigation system.)

Even if high-technology takeoff monitoring does become available to pilots, every takeoff must be evaluated with respect. Don't ask yourself "What will I do if one engine quits?" Make a declaration: "An engine *will* quit and this is what I will do about it!"

Fig. 2-13. *A problem has been detected, and the airplane can be stopped safely.*

TAKEOFF STANDARDS

The following is an edited excerpt from the multiengine practical test standard describing what pilot examiners expect from would-be multiengine pilots on takeoff. The first item on the list refers to the ability to "explain the elements of normal takeoff, including airspeed configurations." This means you will discuss the speed milestones for your particular airplane on the checkride.

Objective. To determine that the applicant:

- Exhibits knowledge by explaining the elements of normal and crosswind takeoffs and climbs including airspeeds, configurations, and emergency procedures.
- Adjusts the mixture control as recommended for the existing conditions.
- Notes any obstructions or other hazards in the takeoff path and reviews takeoff performance. (Elements of takeoff performance are also required discussion topics.)
- Verifies wind condition.
- Aligns the airplane on the runway centerline.
- Applies aileron deflection in the proper direction as necessary.
- Advances the throttles smoothly and positively to maximum allowable power.

- Checks the engine instruments.
- Maintains positive directional control on the runway centerline.
- Adjusts aileron deflection during acceleration, as necessary.
- Rotates at the airspeed to attain liftoff at V_{MC} plus 5 knots or the recommended liftoff airspeed and establishes wind-drift correction as necessary.
- Accelerates to V_X (best angle of climb airspeed) ±5 knots.
- Retracts the wing flaps as recommended at a safe altitude.
- Retracts the landing gear after a positive rate of climb has been established and a safe landing cannot be accomplished on the remaining runway, or as recommended.
- Climbs at V_Y plus or minus 5 knots to a safe maneuvering altitude.
- Maintains takeoff power to a safe maneuvering altitude and sets desired power.
- Uses noise abatement procedures, as required.
- Establishes and maintains a recommended climb airspeed, within plus or minus 5 knots.
- Maintains a straight track over the extended runway centerline until a turn is required.
- Completes the after-takeoff checklist.

If a crosswind condition does not exist, the applicant's knowledge of the task will be evaluated through oral testing. The examiner will:

- Ask the applicant to explain the elements of normal and crosswind takeoffs and climbs, including airspeeds, configurations, and emergency procedures.
- Ask the applicant to perform normal and crosswind takeoffs and climbs, and determine that the applicant's performance meets the objective.

MAXIMUM PERFORMANCE TAKEOFF

Single-engine pilots are required to do short-field and soft-field takeoffs, which fall into a maximum-performance category. Multiengine pilots are also faced with takeoffs requiring the airplane and the pilot to perform their best. The maximum-performance takeoff in a multiengine airplane is not subdivided to short- and soft-field. A soft-field technique can be practiced by holding more elevator in the takeoff roll, which reduces the load on the nosewheel, but the airplane should never be allowed to leave the ground with the airspeed at or below V_{MC}.

The maximum performance takeoff requires the pilot to be in even greater control of airspeed because the airplane must be placed in a climb that is steeper and slower than normal. If the climbout is slower, it is also closer to V_{MC}. After V_R and liftoff, the nose of the airplane is raised to achieve the best angle of climb, V_X. This climb angle places the airplane at the highest possible altitude in the shortest distance across the ground to clear an obstruction at the end of the runway.

Normal takeoff and climb can be divided into three segments:

- Takeoff roll from zero to V_R.
- Climb at V_Y until a safe altitude is reached.
- Adjust power and pitch to achieve a cruise climb and best cooling airflow through the engines.

A maximum-performance takeoff adds one more segment that includes another speed milestone:

- The takeoff roll accelerates from zero through V_{MC} to V_R, which is at least V_{MC} plus 5 knots.
- The airplane leaves the ground and continues to accelerate, but the pilot raises the nose higher than normal and stops the acceleration at V_X. The speed of V_X is held steady by the pilot until all obstructions are clear.
- The pilot allows the nose of the airplane to fall and the airspeed to accelerate to V_Y until a higher, safer altitude is reached.
- A cruise climb is established.

Standards

The following edited version of the FAA's Multiengine Practical Test Standards regards maximum performance takeoffs. The examiner will ask the applicant to explain the elements of a maximum performance takeoff and climb, including the significance of airspeeds and configurations, emergency procedures, and the expected performance. The examiner will also ask the applicant to perform a maximum performance takeoff and climb, and determine that the applicant's performance meets the objective. The examiner's objective is to determine that the applicant:

- Exhibits knowledge by explaining the elements of a maximum performance takeoff and climb, including airspeeds, configurations, and expected performance for specified operating conditions.
- Selects the recommended wing flap setting.
- Adjusts the mixture controls as recommended for the existing conditions.
- Positions the airplane for maximum runway availability and aligns it with the runway centerline.
- Advances throttles smoothly and positively to maximum allowable power.
- Checks engine instruments.
- Adjusts the pitch attitude to attain maximum rate of acceleration.
- Maintains positive directional control on the runway centerline.
- Rotates at the airspeed to attain liftoff at V_{MC} +5 knots, or at the recommended airspeed, whichever is greater. (The applicant explains the extra takeoff segment during a maximum performance takeoff.)

- Climbs at V_X, ±5 knots, or the recommended airspeed, whichever is greater until obstacle is cleared, or to at least 50 feet above the surface, then accelerates to V_Y, +5 knots. (The applicant explains the extra takeoff segment during a maximum performance takeoff.)
- Retracts the wing flaps as recommended at a safe altitude.
- Retracts the landing gear after a positive rate of climb has been established and a safe landing cannot be made on the remaining runway, or as recommended.
- Climbs at V_Y, ±5 knots, to a safe maneuvering altitude.
- Maintains takeoff power to a safe maneuvering altitude and sets desired power.
- Uses noise-abatement procedures as required.
- Establishes and maintains a recommended climb airspeed, ±5 knots.
- Maintains a straight track over the extended runway centerline until a turn is required.
- Completes the after-takeoff checklist.

After the initial climbout has been completed, most airplane manufacturers recommend that the pilot "clean up" the airplane. Most light twins use full power during takeoff, but full power is not required during the entire climb to altitude. It is a good idea to establish a power-reduction routine that is followed after every takeoff. I call for a "500-foot check," which means that I am at least 500 feet above the ground with no obstructions.

The power can be reduced from full takeoff power to a cruise climb power setting. The manifold pressure is usually reduced to 25". Be careful. Most multiengine students mistakenly look at the tachometer; make absolutely certain that you are looking at the manifold pressure gauges. Propellers can be adjusted for an efficient climb after the power is properly set.

The RPMs are usually brought back from full forward to 2,500 RPM. This 25"/2,500 RPM combination is sometimes referred to as "squaring off" and can just be called *25/25*. The nose should also be lowered and airspeed allowed to accelerate from V_Y to a "best cooling" climb speed. Check your airplane's handbook for this speed. The cruise climb can continue with the engine and propellers at 25/25 and good airflow through the engine compartments.

Never let your guard down when it comes to takeoff. Study the existing conditions and predict the airplane's performance. Decide *before* you taxi onto the runway what you will do when an engine quits. Make the takeoff in your mind and simulate engine failures at every speed. By doing this, your actions during an emergency will be swift and undelayed by indecision. You have a better chance of making the correct decision during the calm of taxi when a takeoff is still an option, rather than in the heat of battle on the runway.

MULTIENGINE LANDINGS

The multiengine airplane employs the same aerodynamics for landing as a single-engine airplane. The major difference is that approach speed is faster. Good planning for a short runway is essential so that excessive braking or an unnecessary go-around can be avoided.

The pilot must first get accustomed to slowing the airplane down during traffic pattern entry or at some position during a straight-in approach. Then airspeed control must be maintained throughout the pattern to final approach. Approach speed should be V_{YSE} or the blue line until over the runway and at the beginning of the flare for touchdown. This lengthens the landing, but it will pay off during a go-around.

An engine failure in flight will make you very anxious to find a suitable runway and get on the ground. There is some good news. Landing with one engine failed is no more of a problem than a normal landing. The correct normal landing procedure involves gradual power reductions closer to touchdown, eventually reducing the power to idle when the landing is made.

The yaw tendency is reduced every time power is reduced. Rudder correction diminishes through touchdown, when it will probably be unnecessary. Stay well above V_{MC} until over the runway and concentrate on a normal touchdown.

Normal, crosswind, and single-engine landings, and go-arounds, are discussed in detail in chapter 12, regarding multiengine flight training.

3
Engine-out procedures

Wʜᴇɴ ᴀɴ ᴇɴɢɪɴᴇ ᴅᴏᴇs ғᴀɪʟ, ᴛʜᴇ ᴘɪʟᴏᴛ ᴍᴜsᴛ ʀᴇᴀᴄᴛ ᴄᴏʀʀᴇᴄᴛʟʏ ᴀɴᴅ without hesitation. Having two engines is an advantage, but the pilot must place the airplane in a position to utilize the advantage. The first reaction from the pilot depends on the airplane's speed when the engine fails. If the airplane's speed is slower than V_{MC}, the pilot must reduce the power on both engines. If the speed is faster than V_{MC}, the pilot must increase power on both engines. Making the wrong choice here is fatal.

If one engine fails, the pilot will feel the sway-yaw of the airplane. It can happen fast, and in that first second before you realize what is happening, it can surprise even the most veteran multiengine pilot. In that second, it might be unclear which engine has failed because the airplane is reacting to the failure faster than the pilot can recognize it.

Because the exact engine's failure has not yet been positively determined, the action taken by the pilot should include both throttles. By moving both throttles in unison, the pilot is sure to affect the operating engine, even if the pilot does not know which one is operating during this moment of confusion. It is better to move both throttles even though one is dead than to waste time figuring out which one works and which one does not work.

PROPER THROTTLE ADJUSTMENT

Now we understand that both throttles should move together, but which way should they move? If the airplane is slower than V_{MC}, both throttles should be pulled back. If the pilot pushes the throttles to a higher power setting, directional control will be lost. If both throttles are brought forward, the dead engine will continue to produce no power, but the operating engine at full power will produce the yaw that the rudder cannot overcome while slower than V_{MC}.

This idea of "pull back when in trouble" goes against our earlier training. In single-engine airplanes, the remedy for a stall was to push forward on the wheel to break the stall and push forward on the throttle. We associate recovery with full power. Some of us have become "Pavlov's pilots" because we hear a horn and add power without thinking.

Below V_{MC}, power must be reduced on both throttles; the power output from each engine will be the same: zero. Having zero power is not good, but at least it is equal power and no yaw will result. With the power pulled back on both engines, lower the nose and gain airspeed.

When the airplane is traveling faster than V_{MC}, the pilot can afford to add power on the good engine while opposing yaw with rudder. This requires the airplane to have sufficient altitude to gain the speed. If there is no altitude, the pilot should land straight ahead on the flattest, softest thing available.

If the airplane's speed is faster than V_{MC} when an engine failure is felt by the pilot, both throttles should go forward. The greatest power will set up the best possible climb performance for the situation. Unfortunately, the pilot cannot throw both throttles forward if the propeller controls are back. If the engine failure occurs during cruise flight, the props will be back.

Asking the propeller in a high-pitch/low-RPM setting to take on full engine power is like putting the force of a cannon through the barrel of a rifle. It is not matched and can damage the propeller and engine. This is why it is the proper procedure to place the prop controls full forward for takeoff and for landing.

In this position, if full power is required, the props are already prepared to handle the extra load. Most manufacturers also recommend that the engine mixtures be at full rich because a faulty mixture might cause an engine to fail. Consult your own airplane's manual, but usually the proper response to a faster-than-V_{MC} engine failure is:

1. Both mixtures forward (rich).
2. Both propeller controls forward (high RPM).
3. Both throttles forward (high power).

These steps should be taken when the pilot feels the yaw of an engine failure. At the same time, the pilot must "fly the airplane." If the airplane's speed is faster than V_{MC} at the time of the failure, the pilot cannot allow depletion of the airspeed to V_{MC} while working in the cockpit to understand and fix the problem.

MAINTAIN AIRSPEED

When the yaw of engine failure is first felt, add rudder to keep the airplane straight, adjust the airplane's pitch as necessary to maintain a speed above V_{MC}, then go to work on the problem. Many pilots have panicked here, and while they were moving levers and throwing switches, the airplanes sank below control speed and crashed.

The safe multiengine pilot must have a little savvy. The safe multiengine pilot takes calculated time to fly the airplane and then go to work on the airplane. The mental checklist would read:

1. Apply rudder as the unknown yaw sets in.
2. Control airspeed above V_{MC}.
3. Both mixtures to full rich.
4. Control airspeed above V_{MC}.
5. Both prop controls to high RPM.
6. Control airspeed above V_{MC}.
7. Both throttles to full power.
8. Control airspeed above V_{MC}.
9. Use additional rudder as the power comes up on the good engine.
10. Maintain airspeed above V_{MC}.

This all needs to happen fast, but not in a mindless blur. Multiengine pilots must be alert because the thought process can be challenged at any moment. When the initial shock and reaction has passed, and the airplane is under control, it will be time to think about performance.

Recall from chapter 2 that single-engine climb performance is bad at best. In order to give the airplane the best chance of staying in the air, the pilot must now reduce drag so the remaining good engine can do its job.

The wing flaps are also drag producers, and they should be retracted to achieve the best possible climb unless the manufacturer has prescribed a "best-climb flap setting." If the airplane is "stabilized" in level flight or in a climb, the pilot should also bring the landing gear up.

It is vital that the decision to continue flight, as opposed to landing on the remaining runway (if any), is made before gear retraction. The thinking here is that if you are going down anyway, you should have the landing gear out to help absorb the shock of impact. But if a climb is possible, the landing gear sticking out into the wind is a tremendous drawback to performance and the pilot is better off with gear up.

The thought progression to take care of the power is: mixture, props, and throttles. Also verify that the fuel pumps are on, then reduce drag: flaps up and landing gear up.

A pilot must set priorities to manage this engine-out crisis. Each move the pilot makes is calculated to yield the best airplane result at the best time:

1. Understand that an engine has failed.
2. Counteract yaw with rudder.
3. Control airspeed.
4. Mixtures rich.
5. Props high RPM.
6. Throttles to full power.
7. Wing flaps retracted or to recommended setting.
8. Landing gear up when level or climbing.

The first three items assure airplane control. The next five items work toward giving the airplane the best performance. Now it is time to find out what has happened to the airplane.

AIRBORNE DETECTIVE

The failed engine must be identified before any further corrective action can be taken. Remember that no instrument on the panel clearly spells out which engine has failed. The failed engine will still be turning because it is being driven by the wind; therefore, the tachometer will show nearly the same RPM on both engines, even though one is not producing power.

When the propeller turns, the pistons are still moving up and down in the cylinders and still drawing in air. For this reason the manifold pressure gauge is also reading near normal. The windmilling propeller on the dead engine is still turning fast enough so the blades are blurred to invisible. This means that the pilot cannot tell which engine is the problem by just looking at it, unless smoke or oil is evident.

The dead engine is identified by "feeling" the yaw produced by the good engine. If the dead engine is on the right side, the airplane will yaw to the right. This will require the pilot to push the left rudder pedal. With left rudder applied, the nose (speeds above V_{MC}) can be returned to a straight position.

Now the pilot must hold the left rudder continuously in opposition to the good engine's yaw. At this time, there is no need for any right rudder, so the pilot's right foot is not required. This leads to the saying "Idle foot/idle engine," meaning that the side where no rudder is needed is also the side of the failed engine. Determining which engine is inoperative is accomplished with the feet.

When the failed engine is identified, the pilot should verify that the correct decision has been made. This is done by pulling back the throttle on the engine that is believed to have failed. If the pilot has made the correct decision, nothing will happen because the engine has quit anyway, and the throttle position does not matter.

If the wrong decision is made and the good engine's throttle is pulled back, the pilot will instantly feel the difference. The good-engine yaw will go away, and the cockpit will be much quieter. If you do pull back on the wrong engine throttle, reapply full power.

This is where the engine-out checklist has evolved so far:

1. Understand that an engine has failed.
2. Counteract yaw with rudder.
3. Control airspeed.
4. Mixtures rich.
5. Props high RPM.
6. Throttles to full power.
7. Wing flaps retract or to recommended setting.
8. Landing gear up when level or climbing.
9. Identify failed engine (idle foot/idle engine).
10. Verify failed engine (reduce failed engine's throttle).

Perform the checklist as soon as a faster-than-V_{MC} engine failure is recognized. Items 1–3 ensure airplane control. Items 4–8 give the airplane the best possible performance. Items 9–10 determine which engine has the problem. But after item 10, the pilot reaches a crossroad.

FIX OR FEATHER?

Fix means the pilot attempts to get the engine restarted; feather means that the pilot either aborts an engine restart or has no time to consider a restart. The determining factors in the decision to fix or feather are airplane speed, airplane altitude, time available, and the reason the engine failed.

If the airplane is high and fast at the time an engine fails, the pilot might pause after item 10 on the mental checklist and attempt to discover the problem. Height and speed give the pilot the luxury of time. The reason the engine has quit could be *relatively* minor. Perhaps improper fuel management has caused a tank to run dry, and subsequently an engine quits; the pilot could switch the fuel valve to a tank that still contained fuel and restart the engine.

But at low altitudes and slow airspeeds, the pilot is robbed of time to fix the problem. Even if the engine failure were fixable, the pilot could not spend time attempting a fix during a takeoff or initial climbout. In those critical situations, the best thing to do is reduce drag by feathering the prop.

If the pilot determines that it is safe to attempt a restart, the following troubleshooting checklist might be helpful. Always consult the airplane's operating handbook for specific instructions.

TROUBLESHOOTING

1. Complete procedures for engine failure (items 1 through 10).
2. Decide to fix or feather. If the decision is to fix, do not feather and initiate troubleshooting.
3. Troubleshoot.

a. Fuel selectors ON.

b. Primers LOCKED.

c. Carburetor heat ON.

d. Mixture ADJUST.

e. Fuel quantity CHECK.

f. Fuel pressure CHECK.

g. Oil pressure and temperature CHECK.

h. Magnetos CHECK.

i. Fuel pumps ON.

An improperly set fuel selector, carburetor ice, improper mixture, or low fuel pressure can cause an engine to quit. This troubleshooting checklist covers all the *minor* problems that could arise and be corrected to get the engine up and running again; perhaps your knee inadvertently hit the magneto switch. You cannot be a mechanic in the air, but if time and altitude permit, you should check what is possible. If, after these troubleshooting items are complete, you realize that the engine cannot be restarted, then feather the prop and secure the engine (described in the next subsection).

If the engine failure occurs on takeoff or during the initial takeoff climb, there will be no time for the troubleshooting checklist. After the failed engine has been properly identified and verified, feather the propeller using the manufacturer's guidelines. Usually this means pulling the prop control all the way back into the feather position.

Most multiengine prop controls have a detent in the travel of the lever. The detent is a place where the lever rubs in its track. If a pilot pulled back on the prop control inadvertently, she would feel this resistance on the lever before going as far as the feather position. Theoretically, a propeller can only be feathered on purpose.

Always go through the identify-and-verify process before feathering the propeller. Just about the worst thing you can do (besides landing gear up) is to feather the good engine. When the decision is made to feather, follow the feather procedure provided in the airplane's manual.

Secure the engine

After the propeller has been feathered, the job is still not done. If the airplane is up high, the pilot should secure the engine. If the airplane is down low, and the pilot is struggling to maintain control and climb, then the last thing on the pilot's mind will be another checklist. Use good judgment here. Problems might worsen without securing the engine. Follow the manufacturer's recommendations to secure an engine. This checklist is an example:

1. Mixture IDLE CUT OFF.

2. Fuel selector OFF.

3. Fuel pump OFF.

4. Magnetos OFF.

5. Alternator OFF.

6. Cowl flap CLOSED.

7. Reduce electrical load as required.

8. Maintain at or above V_{YSE}.

Without such a list, fuel would continue to be pumped to a hot, disabled engine, which might cause a fire. You have enough problems without also starting a fire. After the engine is secure, the pilot can turn attention to safely getting back on the ground. Reduce power on the operating engine, if that is possible, to protect that engine from overheating and wear due to extended use at a power setting that is higher than normal.

ENGINE FAILURE SUMMARY

When an engine quits, the pilot's mind cannot. The engine failure events look like this:

1. Engine quits.

2. Pilot recognizes that an engine has quit.

3. Pilot controls airplane.

4. Pilot gets best performance from airplane.

5. Pilot decides to fix or feather.

6A. Pilot feathers prop using proper procedure. (Go to step 7.)

6B1. Pilot troubleshoots the problem, and the engine restarts. (Pilot continues flying, but monitors the situation closely and considers a precautionary landing to determine what happened.)

6B2. Pilot troubleshoots the problem, and the engine fails to restart. (Go to step 6A.)

7. Pilot secures engine.

8. Pilot lands safely.

Each step requires the pilot to fly skillfully and make decisions correctly. All these events can happen quickly. Items 1 through 7 might take place in less than a minute with no warning. Multiengine pilots must be able to handle emergencies with swift, accurate, and knowledgeable action. Multiengine pilots are only safe if they are competent disaster managers.

PART II

Multiengine airplane systems

4
Multiengine propeller systems

THE PROPELLERS AND PROPELLER SYSTEMS OF A MULTIENGINE AIRPLANE must be capable of doing more than a single-engine propeller. The biggest difference is that a propeller must be stoppable on a multiengine airplane. The value of a featherable propeller was proven in chapter 1 on multiengine aerodynamics. The speed of V_{MC} skyrockets when a prop is windmilling, versus when a prop is feathered. Multiengine airplanes must come with a propeller system that will allow for this drag reduction, and V_{MC} reduction, to occur.

To become a commercial pilot, an applicant must have a minimum of 10 hours training in an airplane that has retractable landing gear, retractable flaps, and a constant-speed propeller system. If you train for the commercial pilot certificate in a single-engine airplane, you will become familiar with a propeller system that changes blade angles, but does not feather. For building-block purposes, it is usually best to progress from a fixed-pitch propeller airplane to a constant-speed propeller, to a constant-speed, full-feathering propeller.

ANGLED FOR EFFICIENCY

It is important to understand why propeller blade angles need to change. Fixed-pitch propellers are manufactured to maintain only one angle, but no single angle will provide the best efficiency all the time. A fixed-pitch propeller is like having only first gear in a car. If the only gear you have is first gear, then everything is great when pulling away from a stop sign, but when you get to about 15 miles per hour, first gear becomes very inefficient. First gear at speeds above 15 mph will strain the engine and burn extra gas.

Fixed-pitch props are usually set with blade angles efficient for either climb or cruise. Flying a single-engine airplane equipped with a fixed-pitch climb propeller is like being stuck in first gear. You get off the runway just fine, but when you level off for cruise, the prop will hold the airplane back, just as first gear prevents the car from going faster.

Most flight schools own single-engine airplanes with the props in a fixed-pitch climb angle because student pilots need the best takeoff and climb performance to remain safe while learning.

Changing blade angles allows pilots to shift gears as if in a car. At a car speed faster than 15 mph, the driver should shift into second gear, which makes the engine and drivetrain operate more efficiently. A controllable propeller allows the pilot to shift gears. Several systems were designed to accomplish this task. The most common is the constant-speed propeller.

PROPELLER DYNAMICS

What causes propeller efficiency? The propeller blade is simply an airfoil that swings around to create relative wind. Each blade is twisted. Each blade's angle of attack is greatest near the spinner; the angle of attack is gradually reduced moving toward the tip. The blade tip is moving faster than the inner parts of the blade, so the tip requires less angle of attack to produce thrust.

If the propeller blades did not twist, but had a constant angle of attack throughout the length of the blade, then the tips, because of their greater speed, would produce the greatest thrust (Fig. 4-1). But that would cause a problem because the tips are thin and weak. The thrust, if allowed to be greatest at the tips, would bend the tips forward, and this could damage or destroy the propeller.

Fixed-pitch propellers actually have many blade pitches when you consider the different locations along the blade (Fig. 4-2). Now consider just one location on any propeller. Let's look in detail at what is happening at a position 6 inches from the tip, toward the spinner. This position has a particular blade angle, and this angle will always be the same on a fixed-pitch propeller.

Relative windmill

As the blade moves, the air that passes around the blade is the blade's relative wind. Just like the relative wind on the airplane's wing, this relative wind is always

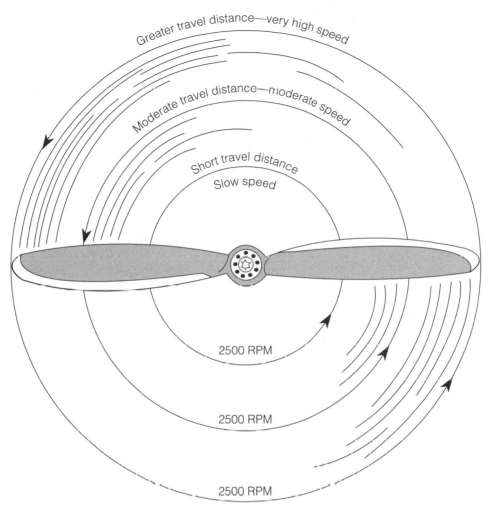

Fig. 4-1. *Every airfoil section along the propeller blade is traveling at a different speed. This requires the blade to "twist" in order to produce an even thrust pattern.*

moving in the opposite direction to the blade's travel path. When the prop blade is moving down (the right side of the propeller arc as seen from the pilot's seat), the relative wind at that position is up. When the prop is moving up (left side of propeller arc), the relative wind is moving down. This means that a fixed-pitch propeller is most efficient when the airplane is not in motion! Think about it.

The greatest thrust is produced when the angle of attack is greatest per given RPM. When the airplane's engine is running, but the airplane is not in forward motion, the angle of attack will be the greatest. Here is why: Angle of attack is determined by the angle between the airfoil's chord line and the relative wind. As the prop blade goes down, the relative wind comes up, and this forms the angle. When the airplane is not

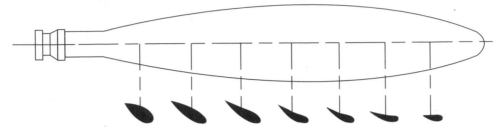

Fig. 4-2. *Each airfoil cross section is called an element. Each element has a different angle of attack. Near the hub, where the blade element moves slowly, a high angle of attack is set. At the blade tip, where the speed is greatest, the angle of attack is small. The result is an even pattern of thrust.*

in forward motion, the relative wind comes straight up. But when the airplane starts to move, the relative wind also starts to move forward because when the airplane is in forward motion, the prop blade is moving down and also forward.

The result is that the blade is moving in a corkscrew path. As the blade moves down and forward, the path of the blade is actually a slant forward (Fig. 4-3). Because relative wind is always opposite the travel path, a slanted travel path will produce a slanted relative wind. This means that the relative wind no longer comes straight up into the blade, but now from more in front of the blade. Because the actual prop blade angle has not changed, this cuts down the angle of attack and this cuts down the prop's ability to produce thrust. In other words, the prop efficiency has been reduced. The faster the airplane goes, the more inefficient the propeller becomes.

But what if the prop blade moved forward when the relative wind moved forward on the prop blades? This would preserve the angle of attack. When the relative wind moves forward, the blade angle also moves forward, and the result is the angle of attack stays the same and the ability of the blades to produce thrust remains the same. This would maintain propeller efficiency. This is exactly what a controllable propeller does. The entire blade twists in its socket to chase the shifting relative wind. In effect, the prop blade shifts gears to remain efficient.

Taking off

For takeoff, the blade angle should be set to a low angle of attack. Because the airplane will have a slow forward speed during takeoff, the propeller blade's angle of attack will be efficient. But a low angle of attack on the blades also reduces drag and allows the engine to turn as fast as possible. Just like any airfoil, the production of lift produces induced drag.

When the drag on the prop is high (large angle of attack), the engine will labor under this additional strain and the RPMs will be reduced. When the drag on the prop is low (small angle of attack), the engine has less to hold it back and the RPMs increase. A low-pitch/high-RPM setting is best for takeoff because this allows more total thrust.

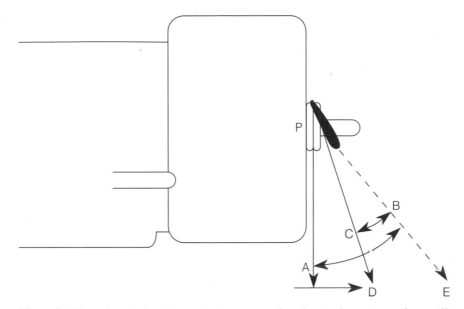

Fig. 4-3. *When the airplane's engine is running, but the airplane is standing still, the propeller blade moves from position P to A. Relative wind is always opposite the direction of travel, so relative wind is from position A to P. The chord line of the blade's airfoil is the extended line P to E. The relative wind and chord line make up the angle of attack, which is angle A to B. When the airplane begins to move forward, the blade moves both down and forward in the direction from P to D. This changes the relative wind to the direction D to P. If the propeller blade does not change its chord line position, the angle of attack is cut down to angle C to B. This lowers efficiency because the "bite" of the air is actually less. The only remedy is to move the blade's chord line out, which is what a constant-speed propeller does.*

Each time the prop rotates, the blades will take a smaller bite of the air, but because this setting produces less drag, the prop can turn faster and take more bites than would be the case with a higher pitch setting.

This idea of blade angles and RPMs is hard to visualize because you cannot actually see the blade angle while the blades are in motion. To help understand why low pitch equals high RPM and high pitch equals low RPM, substitute low angle with low drag and high pitch with high drag.

Use the example of a lawn mower. Will the engine run faster in high grass or low grass? The answer is low grass because the engine has less to impede its blade motion. Low grass produces low drag and high RPM. A thick, high lawn produces more drag, and the engine is burdened and runs slower.

I often ask students this question: "Why don't we take off with a low-RPM and high-pitch blade setting? That way each swing of the prop would take a bigger bite of

73

the air and we could get in the air faster." I hope they respond to this question by saying something about how the higher blade angle will produce more prop drag and that means less prop swings per minute. The smaller number of prop swings, the smaller the total thrust. Even though the bite of air is smaller with a low blade angle, you get more bites.

HARDWARE

This is the physical science reason why a movable propeller blade system is needed, but how does it actually work on the airplane? The constant-speed propeller systems typically move the prop blades to various angles in unison. The most efficient blade angle can be maintained at all flight conditions and without much input from the pilot. The pilot uses a propeller control in the cockpit to set the proper speed, and then the system maintains that speed and efficiency.

The prop control is to the pilot what a stick shift is to the car driver. The car driver might only have five forward speeds, but the pilot's prop control has an infinite number of "gears" to choose from. After the pilot selects the proper RPM for the flight condition, the prop system will maintain that RPM setting by automatically changing the blade angles.

When the RPMs get faster than the prop setting, the prop system will raise the prop drag by increasing the blade angle, and the RPMs will slow down to the prop setting. When the RPMs get slower than the prop setting, the system will reduce the blade angle and RPMs will speed up to the prop setting.

The system is based on a unique balancing act. Systems differ only slightly from manufacturer to manufacturer. Most systems start off with the ability of the blades to turn. Constant-speed propeller blades that turn to various angles are cylinder-shaped where the blade enters the spinner (Fig. 4-4). Fixed-pitch blades usually still have an airfoil shape at the spinner (Fig. 4-5).

The spinner of a fixed-pitch propeller is just for window dressing and drag reduction. The spinner of a constant-speed system is usually fatter because the spinner contains either a large spring, an air pressure chamber, or both. The spring is called the *hub spring* (Fig. 4-6), and left alone, it will push the prop mechanism. The *prop mechanism* is a piston that moves either forward or aft inside the spinner. The piston is connected to the prop blades so that when the piston moves, the blades turn to a different angle of attack.

In many systems, the hub spring will push the piston aft, which will cause the prop blades to go to a high-pitch/low-RPM position. In order for the blades to return to a low-pitch/high-RPM position, the piston must move forward again in opposition to the force of the hub spring. This opposition force is supplied by engine oil.

Engine oil from the oil pan is allowed to pass into a *prop governor pump* that raises the oil pressure high enough to push the hub spring forward. High-pressure oil is lead to the aft side of the spinner's piston. If the oil pressure is stronger than the hub spring pressure, then the piston will move forward, causing the prop blades to move to a low-pitch/high-RPM position. The balancing act is between oil on the back side and a spring on the front side of the piston.

Fig. 4-4. *This airplane has a constant-speed propeller, which can be easily identified by the shape of the propeller as it enters the spinner. This blade shank has a cylindrical shape that allows the blade to turn in its socket.*

Fig. 4-5. *This airplane has a fixed-pitch propeller. The blade's airfoil shape is intact as the blade enters the spinner. This blade cannot twist in the socket.*

Fig. 4-6. *This is the large hub spring of a constant-speed propeller. The photo of the spring is taken through the round opening where the propeller blade would be attached. The spinner would cover this entire assembly.*

Certain systems balance oil against air pressure, and other systems route oil to the front side of the piston so that oil pressure is on both sides. No matter how it is done, the blade angles are determined by oil pressure going to the spinner.

How does the system know when to send oil in and out of the hub? The brain of the system is the *propeller governor* (Fig. 4-7), a combined unit that contains the previously discussed governor pump and a speed-sensing oil valve. The governor regulates the amount of oil that goes to the hub and therefore regulates the propeller RPM setting.

Whenever the water level in a lake behind a dam gets too high, the dam operator can open up the flood gates, allowing water to flow through the dam and downstream. The prop governor is the flood gate operator. When the system requires more oil, the governor opens the gate. When the system requires less oil, the gate is closed by the governor.

How is the prop governor so smart? How does it know when to open the oil gates and when to close them? The prop governor relies on a delicate balancing act to operate. The opposing forces are the force of a small spring and centrifugal force. The pro-

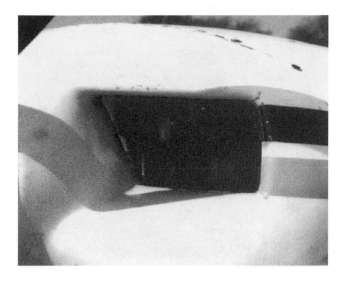

Fig. 4-7. *The propeller governor is often hidden inside the engine nacelle.*

peller governor has a smaller spring inside called the *speeder spring*. Never confuse the larger hub spring, which is inside the spinner, with the smaller speeder spring, which is inside the governor.

When the pilot moves the prop control inside the cockpit, the speeder spring (Fig. 4-8A) is either tightened or loosened; the pilot sets the force of the spring. The spring rides atop a spinning shaft that is connected by gears to the engine. The spinning shaft will speed up or slow down with the engine's RPMs. Two flyweights are attached to the spinning shaft. When the shaft spins fast, the flyweights fling out; when the engine slows down, the centrifugal force on the weights becomes less, and the speeder spring pulls the flyweights back in (Figs. 4-8A and 4-8B).

The flyweights are connected to a high-pressure oil valve: the flood gate. In this example, when the engine slows down, the spinning shaft also slows down, which reduces centrifugal force on the flyweights and the weights come together under the pressure of the speeder spring. When the flyweights come together, they move a pilot valve (flood gate), then oil floods into the prop hub and pushes against the hub spring. The prop blades move to a lower pitch and this reduces prop drag. With less prop drag, the engine speeds back up to the setting that the pilot placed on the prop control.

All this happens instantly. Usually the pilot does not know it happened. Study and understand the prop governor system on the airplane that you fly because system configurations might vary from model to model. (Get to know the whole airplane.)

Governing a chandelle

The governor is in constant operation and continuously adjusting to even minor changes in RPM. Take a look at the propeller blade angles and prop governor actions during a common flight maneuver, the chandelle. A *chandelle* is a maximum-performance

Fig. 4-8A. *The speeder spring is small in comparison with the hub spring. In this photo, the flyweights (held in position by the thumb and forefinger) are closed as they would be in a slow-speed condition.*

Fig. 4-8B. *The same speeder spring and flyweights now placed in the proper location inside the governor. The flyweights are also shown retracted, as if at slow speed.*

climbing turn where airspeed is sacrificed for altitude. The maneuver starts by setting the propeller to the proper RPM, usually a climb or takeoff position. This setting will be 2,500 RPM on most airplanes with constant-speed props. The prop governor's job will be to maintain 2,500 RPM throughout the maneuver.

The maneuver starts at design maneuvering speed (V_A) with an easily seen object near the horizon on one wingtip for reference. Some airplanes require a slight descent to achieve V_A. During this descent, the engine will tend to increase speed. When the airplane goes "downhill," gravity assists this motion and not as much energy is required from the engine. With the engine less burdened at the same power setting, the engine RPM increases to perhaps 2,600 RPM.

This rise in RPM is instantly sensed by the prop governor because the spinning shaft inside the governor and the crankshaft are geared together; most systems use the camshaft. The increase in RPM produces an increase in the governor's shaft speed, which increases the centrifugal force on the flyweights. The flyweights will tend to move out (Figs. 4-9A and 4-9B), and this pulls the pilot valve up, releasing oil pressure from the back side of the piston.

Fig. 4-9A. *The governor's flyweights in the extended position, as they would be at a fast RPM.*

Fig. 4-9B. *The spring and flyweights in the governor, this time with the flyweights thrown out, as would be the case at high speeds due to centrifugal force.*

With no oil pressure in opposition, the large hub spring then squeezes out the oil by moving the piston aft, and simultaneously altering the prop blade angle to a higher pitch. The higher pitch produces higher drag on the prop, which labors the engine just enough to slow it back down to 2,500 RPM.

Later in the chandelle, the nose is raised above the horizon, and the airplane struggles against gravity to reach a maximum climb. The engine must work against gravity during the climb to pull the airplane higher. This extra burden causes the RPMs to be reduced, perhaps to 2,400 RPM. The prop governor instantly swings into action.

The governor's shaft slows down so that the flyweights have less centrifugal force and fall back in. This moves the pilot valve into a position where the high-pressure governor-pump oil is allowed to pass to the aft side of the hub's piston. The oil overpowers the hub spring and the piston moves forward. This twists the propeller blade to a lower angle of attack. The lower angle reduces drag, and the RPMs move back to 2,500.

What a chain reaction this is! It sounds like the song, "the ankle bone is connected to the leg bone, the leg bone is connected to the knee bone, the knee bone . . . ." The progression is crankshaft, camshaft, prop governor, flyweights, pilot valve, oil pressure, hub-piston movement, blade-angle change, drag change, RPM change. Again, please check your airplane's governor operation. Some do not work exactly as described here, but all work to constantly maximize propeller efficiency.

FEATHERING

In addition to maximizing propeller efficiency, the multiengine system must also have a mechanism that feathers and unfeathers the propeller (Fig. 4-10). This mechanism does not rely entirely upon governor pump pressure, but rather a combination of oil pressure and centrifugal force. It is not a good idea to use oil pressure alone to feather the prop blades because if the governor oil pump failed, the propeller could not feather.

Recall from chapter 3 regarding engine-out procedures that when a prop needs to be feathered, it *really* needs to be feathered; therefore, a truly dependable system must be used. Nothing is more dependable than the basic forces of physics, such as centrifugal force. Propeller blades that feather have counterweights attached to the shank of the blade. The counterweights are often hidden by the spinner.

Fig. 4-10. *This propeller is in the feathered position. It is easy to see that a propeller in this edge-on position will greatly reduce drag.*

During normal operation, the turning prop blade acts as an airfoil. We know that variations of pressure act on the surface of the blade. Taken together, these pressures tend to turn the blade angle to a lower pitch, called *aerodynamic twisting force*. Centrifugal force opposes the aerodynamic twisting force. That opposition tends to throw through the blades to a high pitch.

Usually these two forces cancel each other out, and the combination of oil pressure and a hub spring moves the blades. When the prop blade angle is low, the counterweights are tucked in and have little effect. When the blade angle gets higher, the counterweights rotate with the blade into a new position. This new position places the counterweight's center of gravity farther out from the spinner.

This essentially gives the counterweights an arm, and the centrifugal force is magnified through this arm. The magnified centrifugal force becomes stronger than the aerodynamic twisting force, and the blades move into an even greater pitch angle. The greater the pitch angle, the closer to the feather position.

Many systems also have air charges, or even an additional spring, to help push the blades all the way to the feathered position. These systems will cause the prop blades to feather within only a few seconds of placing the prop control into the full-feather position.

Featherable propellers also have locking pins to prevent feathering below a certain RPM. Consult the operating manual for the proper RPM setting during engine shutdown. Using the pins properly will prevent the blades from feathering during start-up and shutdown.

Autofeathering

Some systems employ an autofeather feature, usually only on high-performance turboprop airplanes. When an autofeather system is in use, the propeller will automatically move to the feathered position when an engine fails, without the pilot moving any controls. When the system is turned on, an electrical sensor compares engine power output to the position of the power levers (throttles). If the power output does not match what should be produced at a given power-lever setting, the system activates, and the prop feathers.

This system cuts down the time between engine failure and feathered prop because it effectively cuts out the time a pilot would take to decide to feather, and then manually move the prop control to feather. The system puts the airplane in the best low-drag configuration as quickly as possible, which frees the pilot to control the airplane. If an engine does fail while in flight, and the prop is feathered, the best thing to do is land as soon as practical.

Restart

Instructors routinely feather props at altitude during a training flight to teach students how to fly with only one engine. The engine has to be restarted, which requires a system that will bring the propeller away from feather and into normal blade angles. When feathered, the blade angle is never precisely 90°. Instead, the blade's farthest travel is approximately 85°–87°. This position lets the airflow help the engine starter during an in-flight restart from feather.

To air-start a feathered engine, place the propeller control into the normal operating range. Crank the engine. As the engine begins to turn, and the blades eventually windmill, the blades will move out of feather within a few seconds. An *accumulator* on certain airplanes helps the governor move the blades out of feather. The mechanism accumulates oil pressure to be deployed at the moment of unfeather. Accumulators (Fig. 4-11) use the pent-up oil pressure to bring the blades from feather to windmill by simply placing the prop control full forward.

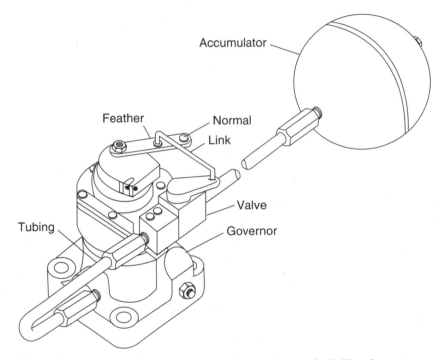

Fig. 4-11. *An accumulator stores up a charge of air and oil. The charge is released to help the governor bring the propeller out of feather.*

REVERSE-THRUST PROPELLERS

Some propellers can throw a thrust force in the "wrong" direction. The blade's direction of rotation does not change, and the angle of attack moves to a negative position. This system is found on turboprops. The reverse-thrust position of the propeller is mainly used to shorten a landing roll or to stop without using brakes on a slick runway. Reverse thrust can be used during taxi to get into or out of a tight spot, or even to back into a parking space. Reverse thrust could also be used in-flight for an emergency descent.

RANGE OF OPERATION

We have discussed three ranges of propeller angles: positive, feathered, and reverse. The feathered position is edge-on and occurs near 90°. The 0° blade-angle position would provide minimal drag and high RPM, but minimal thrust, as well. Normal operations take place from 0°–90°. Takeoff might be 8° and cruise near 12°. The positive-angle range from 0°–90° is the *alpha range*. Reverse thrust is developed when the propeller's blade angle moves to a negative angle. Negative angles from 0° to approximately –20° are in the *beta range* (Fig. 4-12).

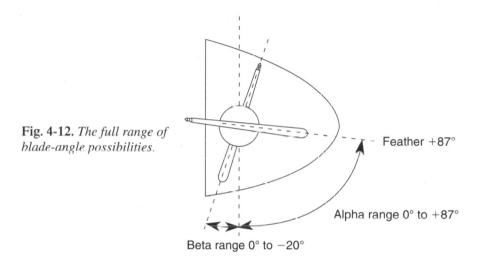

Fig. 4-12. *The full range of blade-angle possibilities.*

Feather +87°

Alpha range 0° to +87°

Beta range 0° to −20°

CHECKING AND SYNCHRONIZING THE PROPS

Always check the prop governor and feathering mechanism during the pretakeoff checklist. Place both prop controls full forward. Advance the throttles and match the RPMs. This test can be done during the engine run-up, so use the run-up RPM setting. Slowly pull back one prop control until the RPMs drop by 100, then bring back the other prop control until the RPMs drop by 100. This proves that the governors are operating.

Look at the position of the left and right prop control levers. Chances are good that they are not exactly lined up; they are *split*. The cables that connect the prop control lever to the prop governor are never exactly the same for each engine. This means that if you place the two prop controls exactly together, the RPMs from both engines will not be in synchronization.

The props are synchronized in flight by adjusting the controls to the proper split. It is best to know what the proper split is before leaving the ground so that you know what to expect while in flight. By performing this test on the ground, you determine the prop control split for synchronization. Check the airplane's operating handbook for the exact procedure.

Oscillations from unsynchronized propellers will be unnerving. To put the props in sync, set the desired RPM on the left engine first. Set the right-engine RPMs to match the left-engine RPMs. Tachometers are not always perfect, so after matching the RPM numbers, use your ears. You will be able to sync the props by sound with a little practice.

Automatic synchronization

A multiengine airplane might have a device that will synchronize the propellers automatically (Fig. 4-13). The system uses a much more accurate RPM reading than just a tachometer, determined by magnetic pick-ups on the engine. The pick-ups turn at the speed of the engine and make contact once per revolution. The revolutions are accurately counted by the number of times the contact is made.

Upon contact, an electrical pulse is sent to a control box. The control box receives

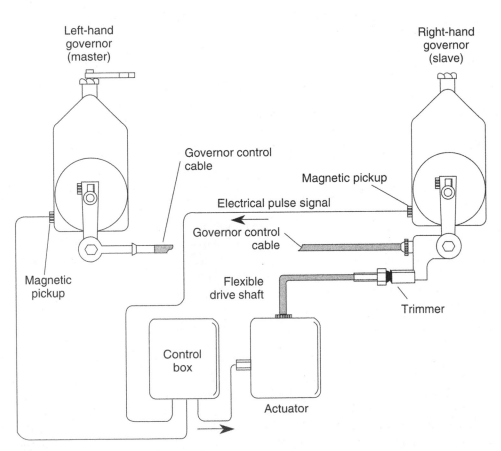

Fig. 4-13. *Propeller synchronization system.*

pulses from both engines and compares them. The left engine is usually considered the master engine; the right engine is the slave. The left engine's RPM is used as the starting point, and the right engine is matched to the left.

A signal is sent to an actuator if the control box determines that the right engine is not turning at the same speed as the left. The actuator changes the RPM of the right engine, using the prop governor, until the two engine's speeds are equivalent. Each time the control box sends a signal, the actuator changes the right engine's speed a predetermined amount—a *step*. It might take several steps to completely synchronize the propellers.

The right engine follows the left engine only through a narrow speed range. If the left engine's speed changes drastically, the right engine will not follow. This is a good idea. What if the pilot feathered the left prop, and the prop sync system feathered the right prop so they would be the same? The pilot can turn the prop sync system off for takeoffs and engine-out operations.

PROPELLER ICE CONTROL SYSTEMS

An airplane with two engines cannot automatically fly safely into any weather. Most light-twin airplanes have absolutely no anti-ice or deice equipment; however, larger airplanes will likely have an ice control system. According to federal regulations, airplanes without ice protection should never be flown into a known-icing condition. Don't let an ice protection system give you a false sense of security. You must become completely familiar with the limitations of an ice protection system.

Ice can form on propeller blades and cause real problems. First, the airfoil shape can become distorted by the ice accumulation, which reduces the blade's ability to produce thrust. Second, the ice might form on the blade unevenly, which unbalances the blades; a destructive vibration can start. Eventually, large ice chunks will be thrown off the blades, which could damage other parts of the airplane.

Two systems have been designed to prevent the ice from accumulating on a propeller: fluid and electrical. The fluid system employs anti-icing liquid, commonly isopropyl alcohol, that is pumped from a tank to the propeller hub (Fig. 4-14). At the hub, the fluid is passed from the stationary line to the spinning propeller through a *slinger ring*. Centrifugal force pulls the fluid from the slinger ring onto the blades.

In some systems, the fluid will travel inside the blade through a narrow strip of rubber, called a *feed shoe*, and be dispersed on the outside of the blade.

The electrical system uses a *hot blade* to keep ice clear. These propeller blades have a heating element that is either inside the blade or mounted externally. The airplane's electrical system power is transferred from stationary wires to the spinning prop by using contact brushes that ride on a rotating ring. When the electrical current makes the leap to the prop, the heating elements are activated just like the heated wires that melt frost off a car's rear window. The prop ice must melt uniformly to prevent vibration; therefore, the intensity of the heat is controlled.

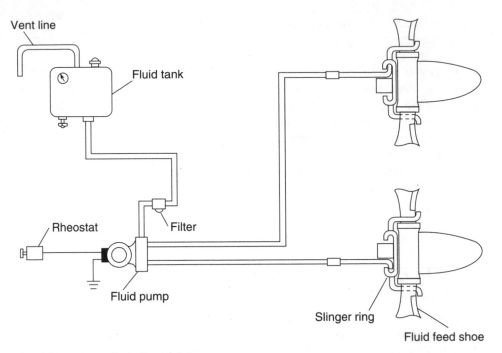

Fig. 4-14. *A propeller's liquid deice system.*

5
Multiengine fuel systems

BASIC COMPONENTS OF A SINGLE-ENGINE AIRPLANE FUEL SYSTEM ARE THE same on a multiengine airplane, except that there might be more fuel tanks and the ability to crossfeed fuel between tanks. Many multiengine airplanes have more than one fuel tank in each wing because fuel consumption is higher: two engines, each with more horsepower, versus one engine with lower horsepower. Additional fuel will also extend the range of the airplane. Extra tanks might also be a space requirement or meet a structural need.

The tank with the greatest capacity is usually the main tank, and all others are auxiliary tanks. Auxiliary tanks can be in the wing, wing tips, or fuselage. The main and auxiliary tanks are filled separately, are vented separately, and might feed the engine separately.

Some systems require fuel to be transferred from a wingtip tank to an inboard main tank. The quantity of fuel in the main tank must be low enough for the fuel transfer to occur. Also, adequate time must be allowed for the fuel transfer to take place. Obviously, the pilot must fully understand the system to accomplish proper fuel management.

Fuel normally stays on one side of the airplane; the fuel from all left-wing tanks is used in the left engine, and all right-wing fuel is used in the right engine. This works fine until one engine fails in flight. If the failure occurs while flying in heavy IFR weather, you might need all the range you can get. You might determine that the fuel supply for the operating engine will run out before you can land. In this situation, the fuel from the dead engine side can be transferred across the airplane to the good engine.

CROSSFEEDING

Study the airplane's operating handbook to determine the exact valve settings to crossfeed and how to maintain the crossfeed system. Because the crossfeed line will not be used as often as the normal lines, the crossfeed line is very susceptible to water and debris accumulation. Many airplanes will have a separate place to draw a crossfeed-fuel sample. Find the crossfeed drain sump and take a fuel sample before each flight.

Test the crossfeed operations on the ground. While taxiing out for takeoff, switch the valves so that crossfeed fuel goes to the engines, and allow enough time for the fuel to arrive at its destination engine; however, before takeoff, switch the valves back to the normal position and allow time for that flow to take place. This ensures that the crossfeed will work when airborne, and a single operating engine will continue to run in the critical situation.

The valve system on light twins is usually very simple. The settings are ON, OFF, and CROSSFEED (Figs. 5-1 and 5-2). Normally, both valves are on, meaning that fuel is moving from the left tank(s) to the left engine, and fuel is moving from the right tank(s) to the right engine. When an engine fails and the need for crossfeed arises, you must know exactly how to position the valves.

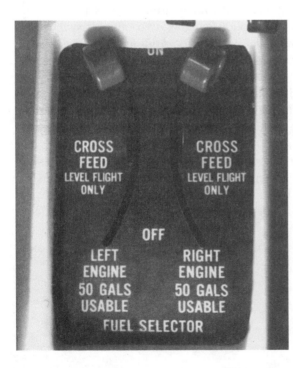

Fig. 5-1. *Fuel selector valves for a multiengine airplane with one fuel tank in each wing.*

Fig. 5-2. *Fuel selector panel for a multiengine airplane with main and auxiliary fuel tanks.*

If the left engine fails and cannot be restarted while the fuel selector valve is in the ON position, it will be important to turn the fuel valve to OFF. The airplane's operating handbook will have a securing-engine checklist, which is used as damage control. You do not want to send fuel to the problem-engine. Follow the manufacturer's recommendations to turn off fuel pumps, and stop the flow of fuel. If the flow is not stopped, a fire could start, turning the engine-out emergency into a catastrophe.

After the fuel flow is stopped to the dead engine, fuel consumption to the good engine will increase because the higher power setting is required to maintain level flight. The pilot should fly to the nearest suitable airport and land. It might become necessary to use fuel on the dead-engine in the good engine. Turn the good engine's fuel selector from ON to CROSSFEED, and turn the dead engine's selector to OFF (or as prescribed in the operating handbook). You cannot normally mix fuel from both left and right; fuel comes exclusively from one side or the other.

Crossfeeding fuel will also help balance the airplane. If one side's tank burns down to near empty, while the other side is near full, aircraft control will become awkward. This condition could even be dangerous if a crosswind landing must be made.

FUEL PUMPS

Multiengine pilots must also become familiar with fuel pump operations. Many of us learned to fly in high-wing airplanes that did not have an electric fuel pump to worry about. Gravity did the work and we never thought much about it. Pilots of low-wing airplanes are accustomed to fuel-pump switches. Most light-twin airplanes are low-wing; therefore, understanding the pumps are part of understanding the airplane.

Fuel pumps are either engine-driven or electric. Engine-driven pumps are geared to the engine and turn anytime the engine is turning. These pumps move the fuel under pressure through the line and to the engine. The pumps very rarely fail, but if they fail, the engine could stop due to fuel starvation. Electric fuel pumps are provided as a backup system.

The electric pump operates only when it is switched on; power comes from the airplane's electrical system. The electric pump is first used for engine start-up because the engine-driven pump cannot supply fuel pressure. This is the only time when the electric pump is working and the engine-driven pump is not working. All other times, when the engine is running, the electric pump is used as a supplement to the engine-driven pump.

Pumps should be tested prior to takeoff. If the electric pump is used to start the engine, turn off the pump after the engine begins to run. Whenever you turn off a fuel pump, immediately look at the fuel-flow or fuel-pressure gauge (Fig. 5-3). Depending on the airplane, a noticeable change in pressure might be seen. If the fuel pressure falls below the green arc of the gauge, and stays there, an engine-driven fuel pump has failed. You must look at the fuel-pressure gauge; if you do not catch the pressure problem early, the engine will stop.

Theoretically, when both electric and engine-driven pumps are functioning, there will be a higher pressure than when the engine-driven pump alone is working. But two-pump

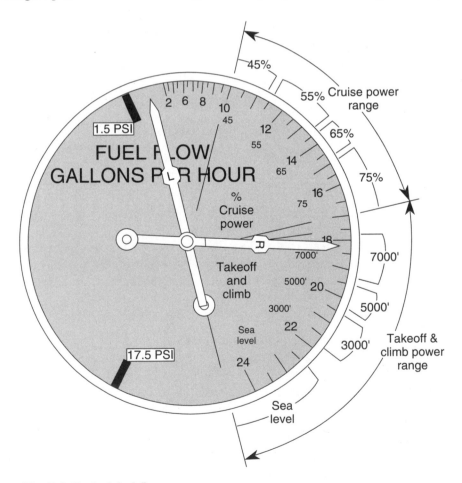

Fig. 5-3. *Typical fuel flow meter.*

and one-pump pressure should be within the green arc of the fuel-pressure gauge. When the electric pump is switched on, a rise in pressure should be seen, and this will verify the operation of the electric pump.

There are crucial times when an engine failure would be particularly dangerous, for instance, takeoff. All fuel pumps should be operating during crucial phases of flight; if one pump fails, the other continues to push the fuel to the engine. After a crucial phase of flight has passed (arriving at cruise altitude), the electric pumps may be turned off.

Never turn both pumps off at the same time. Turn one engine's pump off, and watch the fuel-pressure gauge to ensure that the engine-driven pump is still maintaining pressure in the green arc. When that engine's fuel flow is stable, turn off the second engine's pump, and watch the pressure on that side.

Improve your fuel-management safety margin by locating the nearest airport before turning off any pumps or switching any tanks. Switching tanks over an airport is an ideal procedure en route. One decision is already made if you must seek safe haven due to a fuel system malfunction.

FUEL WEIGHTS

Fuel management usually addresses weight and balance and range concerns, but in many multiengine airplanes it is also a structural topic. A certain amount of fuel might be required in the airplane for the airplane to be strong enough for flight. The fuel in the tanks can actually make a wing stronger. Which soft drink can is easier to crush? The full, unopened can, or the empty can? The empty can, of course. Which fuel tank is easier to bend? The empty one. Nobody would deliberately allow a fuel tank to run dry, but there might be danger in even letting it run low. There are two important terms to know about: *minimum fuel for flight* and *zero fuel weight*.

The minimum fuel for flight is a fuel reserve, but not for the normal reasons. Most pilots can tell you about the VFR day, VFR night, and IFR fuel reserve regulations, but the writer of these regulations did not have the structure of the airplane in mind. These regulations are written to allow lost pilots to find an airport before the fuel runs out. Minimum fuel for flight is different.

Some airplanes must have a particular weight of fuel, or greater, to remain structurally sound. The fuel usually rides in the wings. The design of the wings allows for the weight of fuel. When the fuel runs low, the wing becomes too light, and the wing will rise higher. The lack of fuel allows the wing to flex too far for safety.

The junction where the wing meets the fuselage is like your shoulder joint when your arm is extended. When the wing has the proper weight, it's as if your arm were held straight out from the shoulder, parallel to the ground. When the wing is light, lift pulls the wing up, like raising your outstretched arm. The joint only has so much play, and structural damage (wing bending), or failure (wing breaking off), might occur if the joint is pushed passed the limit of play. When flying an airplane that lists a specific minimum fuel for flight, running out of gas is the least of your problems. It is more dangerous to run low than to run out.

Zero fuel weight is also related to structure. If an airplane has a zero fuel weight, or zero fuel condition, the amount of payload other than fuel is limited. Zero fuel weight is the maximum an airplane can weigh without considering the weight of usable fuel. Figure 5-4 is a sample weight and balance form from a typical light-twin airplane.

The zero fuel condition of this airplane is 3,500 pounds. This means that the total weight of the airplane, pilot, passengers, and luggage cannot exceed 3,500 pounds. The airplane's maximum takeoff weight is 3,900 pounds. In other words, it is possible to overload the cabin and fuselage without exceeding the maximum gross takeoff weight. Multiengine pilots must pay close attention to this fact so they do not fly too long and go below the zero fuel weight.

WEIGHT AND BALANCE LOADING FORM

Model _____ *Duchess 76* _____   Date _____

Serial No. _____   Reg. No. _____

Item	Weight	Mom/100

1. Basic empty condition
2. Front seat occupants
3. 3rd & 4th seat occupants
    or bench seat occupants
4.
5. Aft baggage
6. **Sub total** zero fuel
    condition (3500 lbs max.)
7. Fuel loading (gal.)
8. **Sub total**
    ramp condition
9. *Less fuel for start,
    taxi, and takeoff
10. **Sub total**
    takeoff condition
11. Less fuel to
    destination
12. **Landing condition**		

*Fuel for start, taxi, and takeoff is normally 16 lbs at an average
mom/100 of 19.

Fig. 5-4. *Sample weight and balance loading form. Item number six on the form refers to a "zero fuel condition" of 3,500 pounds maximum.*

Figures 5-5, 5-6, and 5-7 illustrate the complexities of multiengine fuel systems. If you are more accustomed to airplanes without fuel pumps and only an on/off fuel valve, familiarize yourself with all aspects of a complex airplane's fuel system, and develop routine operating habits that foster safety.

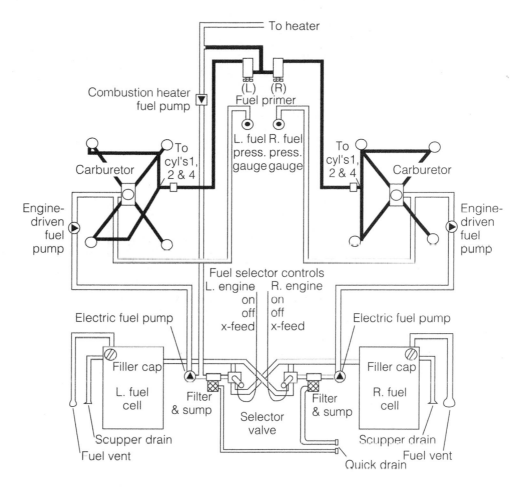

Fig. 5-5. *Piper Seminole fuel system. Note the crossfeed, the cylinders that are primed, and where fuel for the cabin heater comes from.* Piper Aircraft Corporation

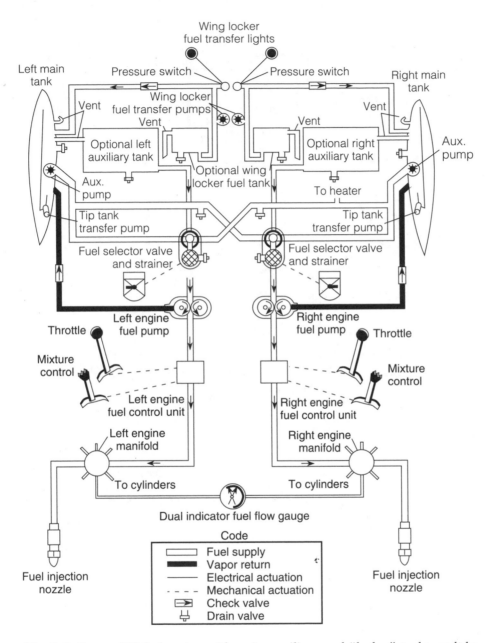

Fig. 5-6. *Cessna 310 fuel system with main, auxiliary, and "locker" tanks, and the wingtip fuel transfer pumps.* Cessna Aircraft Company

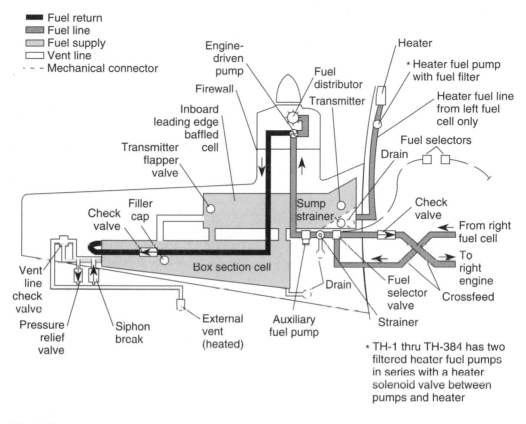

Fig. 5-7. *Beechcraft 55 fuel system. Note the position of the engine-driven and electric auxiliary fuel pumps and the crossfeed.* Beech Aircraft Company

6
Multiengine electrical systems

MANY PILOTS HAVE A LIMITED UNDERSTANDING OF THE AIRPLANE'S electrical system because they have a poor foundation of knowledge about electricity. Pilots back off after taking one look at all those circuit breakers, wires, and electrical schematic diagrams. All pilots need a working knowledge of the airplane's electrical system in order to diagnose in-flight electrical problems and troubleshoot the system.

CURRENT KNOWLEDGE

The first step in understanding electricity is to have some concept about what it actually is. The good news is that electricity is not mysterious, and it is really easy to grasp. Recall from physical science classes what you learned about atoms and the parts of the atom. My favorite part was always the electron because it flew around the stationary center part called the nucleus.

An atom becomes more complex when more electrons start orbiting the nucleus. The electrons orbit in layers. Each layer is farther from the center. The electrons that travel in that farthest layer can escape the grasp of that atom and travel freely to other atoms.

When free electrons move in a pattern from one atom to the next, an *electric current* is produced. Some atoms will give away electrons easier than others. Atoms from elements that give up electrons freely are called *conductors*. Atoms that tend to hold their electrons are called *insulators*. An electric wire will be made of material that conducts, or passes, the electron flow. The covering that is wrapped around the wire is an insulator that keeps the flow on the proper course.

How does electricity move so fast? When you hit a light switch, the light instantly comes on. How did the electron move from the switch to the light so quickly? The fact is that a single electron did not move that fast. In reality, the electron at the switch started a chain reaction of electron flow down the wire to the light.

Imagine a length of pipe with ping-pong balls stacked up one after another inside the length of the pipe. If you were to push a new ping-pong ball into one end of the pipe, a ping-pong ball at the far end of the pipe would be pushed out. The inserted ball does not have to roll all the way down the pipe in order for a ball to fall out. The inserted ball pushed all the balls that were already in the pipe; therefore, the end ping-pong ball fell out of the pipe at the exact instant that the new ping-pong ball was pushed in.

In this analogy, the ping-pong balls are free flowing electrons. The pipe is a wire's insulation. When an electric switch is turned on, one electron pushes electrons that were already in the wire until the electron at the far end of the wire is pushed into the light bulb. All electrical devices work the same way, whether the device is an electric razor, or an airplane landing light, or a transponder.

Forcing the issue

For the current flow to take place, a force must move the first electron in the chain. The ping-pong ball was pushed into the pipe. The push is called *electromotive force*, which can be thought of as electrical pressure. This pressure is measured in *volts*. If the ping-pong ball is gently placed into the pipe, a low voltage would exist; if the ball were thrown into the pipe, a high voltage would result.

The number of electrons (ping-pong balls) that pass by a certain position along the wire in a given amount of time is the *electron flow rate*. This rate is measured in *amperes*. When a large number of electrons flow, there will be a greater number of amps.

The electrons will also encounter some resistance as they move. *Electric friction* will slow the electron's flow. This resistance is measured by a unit called an *ohm*.

Grounded

The flow of electricity must move in a loop. If electrons flow into a light bulb, there must be a path for the electrons to return from the light to the power source. In airplanes, wire (and weight) is often saved by using the frame of the airplane as the return-wire from most electrical equipment. This means the electrons flow from a power source to an electrical device through a wire. When leaving the device, the electrons are led to a *ground* wire that is attached to the airplane. The electrons flow through the airplane, back to the power source, and the loop is completed.

The battery or an *auxiliary power unit* (APU) provides power before an engine starts. When an engine has started, a generator or alternator will be turned by a gear off the engine. As the generator or alternator "comes on-line," the electrical system takes over from the battery. The battery is out of the loop, and its charge is no longer utilized.

Flowing

A generator need only be turned to generate an electric current flow. This seems simple enough, but the generator's current flow is affected by engine RPM. This can be annoying while taxiing at low RPM or during final approach with the engine power pulled back. Delicate electric circuits can be damaged by wavering tides of electrical current coming from a generator.

An alternator, on the other hand, delivers a predictable and equal flow, regardless of RPM. The alternator uses a *magnetic field* to produce the required current. (The magnetic field is triggered by a small electric current.) Alternators are preferred more than a generator for the equal current flow.

Each engine of a multiengine airplane has an independent electrical system. In most cases, one engine's alternator electrical system is capable of supplying sufficient electric power for the entire airplane's. It is a great feeling to know that if one alternator fails when flying IFR, the other alternator should take up the slack and you fly home safely.

SYSTEM SAVVY

When both engines and alternators are running properly, the electricity drawn from the alternators is shared equally from each side. Figure 6-1 illustrates a simple generic multiengine electrical system. Even though there are two engines, two starter motors, and two alternators, there is only one battery.

The battery is grounded to the frame of the airplane to accept returning electron flow from devices located all over the airplane. The electron flow from the battery will have a series of switches, contacts, or solenoids to pass through to reach the starter motors and the bus bar. When the engines are started, electrons are allowed to flow from the battery by closing the battery switch, known as the *master switch*.

The current reaches the starter motor when the starter switch for that particular engine is closed. The starter switch can be activated by the pilot using a toggle, a button, a key, or a rocker switch. The current enters the starter motor, then passes out to the ground, and goes back to the battery. When a loop of current is connected, the engine turns over. The engine that is closer to the battery should be started first. When the electrons have a shorter distance to travel, there will be less resistance and less drain on the battery.

When the engines have started running, the alternators will be turning because they are geared to the engine. Recall that solely turning the alternator will not produce a current flow. A small amount of current must first enter the alternator to activate the magnetic field circuit.

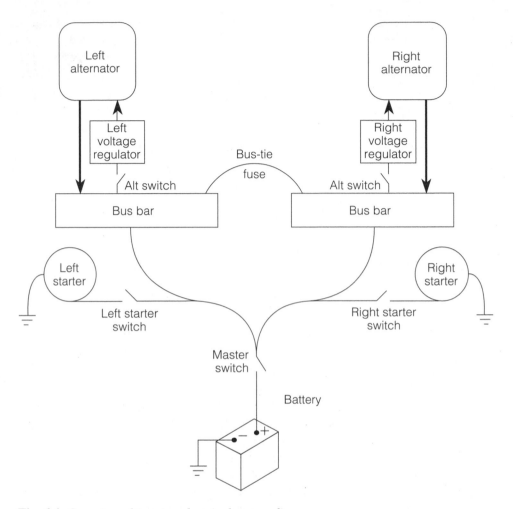

Fig. 6-1. *Generic multiengine electrical system diagram.*

The bus to alternator lines in Fig. 6-1 indicate a small wire with a small current flow. This small current is taken off the bus bar and fed into the alternator. The small current excites the field circuit, which couples with alternator rotation to produce a larger current. The alternator to bus lines represent larger wires that carry the larger current back to the bus bar.

BUS STOP

The *bus bar* is the junction for all other electrical devices in the airplane. A main power line will branch off to supply electricity to individual homes in a neighborhood. The bus bar is a power line, of sorts, that branches off to the lights, flaps, radios, turn coordinator, and all other airplane electrical devices.

The bar is lined with circuit breakers. Each breaker is like a traffic cop. The cop lets in only the proper amount of current to the device. If the current flows too fast or too strong, the cop will stop the electronic traffic flow to the device, which protects the device. The circuit is broken when the breaker opens and interrupts the flow of electrons.

Certain multiengine airplanes utilize a common bus bar. Figure 6-1 illustrates a system with two bus bars. One alternator feeds one bus bar. If an alternator fails, the remaining alternator can provide current to both bus bars through a *bus-tie fuse*.

CONTROL

A certain amount of current from the alternator is recycled to continually supply the alternator's field circuit current. This can lead to a problem. If the field circuit current gets too large, the output of the entire alternator could become too large. This would send more power around the loop back to the field circuit, which would increase the alternator current to even higher levels; hence, the system starts to "feed itself."

Alternator current levels might get so high that circuit breakers will start popping. The electrical devices will shut down, and the alternator will run away. A *voltage regulator* is placed in the system to prevent this from occurring. The regulator acts like a funnel in the field circuit line. It only allows a certain amount of current through. Even if a larger current enters the funnel, only the proper amount exits to the field circuit. The entire alternator's output is under control when the field circuit is under control.

The voltage regulator (funnel) can also widen its opening when the system needs more current flow. Demand is the greatest at night when all the interior and exterior lights are turned on in addition to radios and all other electronic devices. The voltage regulator is able to sense the increased demand and increases the flow to the field circuit, which causes an increase in total alternator output and the electrical demand then is met.

INSTRUMENTATION

The pilot can observe the electrical system through the electrical monitoring instruments. Some airplanes have load meters that display the amps or percentage of capacity. Other systems use ammeters to indicate whether the alternators are supplying sufficient power, or if the battery is tapped for power.

All systems will have a system-failure light or gauge. If the current to the alternator field circuit gets too low or too high at any time, the voltage regulator will cut off the current to protect the system. This dumps the entire electrical load on the battery or the other engine's alternator.

You need to consult the operating handbook to determine the proper course of action to bring the alternator back on-line. If one alternator fails, you need to ensure that the other alternator is indeed providing the proper amount of current, and that the current is being delivered to the proper locations.

Multiengine airplanes provide redundancy, which provides some peace of mind. Two independent alternator systems failing on the same flight would be a very rare occurrence. The multiengine pilot must recognize any evolving electrical problems early, then quickly take constructive action to solve or diminish the problem based upon knowledge about that airplane's electrical system.

7
Minimum equipment list and AFMs

A S PILOTS, WE ARE VERY FAMILIAR WITH PREFLIGHT INSPECTIONS
to determine airworthiness. We are also aware of the regulation that puts us completely to blame if we fly an airplane in an unairworthy condition. But what is "legal airworthiness"? When you move up to multiengine airplanes, there are many more items you need to check, and therefore, many more items that could render the airplane not airworthy. While conducting an unscientific survey of pilots, I found that surprisingly few were sure about how to handle inoperative equipment or understood the term "legal airworthiness."

For instance, say that while performing a routine preflight inspection of an airplane, you discover the suction gauge that monitors the vacuum system is broken. Can you legally take off with the gauge inoperative? Is the airplane legally airworthy? The commonsense answer is yes. After all, the suction gauge has nothing to do with the operation of the engines, nor with the wings' ability to create lift.

Because it does not involve the structural integrity of the airplane, it should not affect airworthiness, right? Wrong! Actually, it does factor into legal airworthiness, but not in a way that most pilots would consider. As pilots, we are primarily concerned that the airplane will fly, the engines will run, and the airplane will stay in one piece. But legal airworthiness goes much further than all that.

Recently the FAA made a ruling that allows a pilot to fly a plane even if certain items on the airplane are inoperative. The ruling says that inoperative equipment may be flown "as long as the equipment is not essential to the safe operation of the aircraft." So who determines what is essential and what is not? Ordinarily, the answer to an airworthiness question lies within the judgment of the pilot, but in this case, several regulations must guide the pilot's judgment. There are presently two paths to follow: 1) developing a minimum equipment list and 2) FAR part 91.213.

OPERATIONS WITH A MINIMUM EQUIPMENT LIST

Minimum equipment lists (MEL) have been around since 1964 for air carriers, and since 1978 for Part 135 operators with multiengine airplanes. In December 1988 the FAA established the program for Part 91 operators to use MELs.

An MEL is simply a list of the equipment on a specific airplane and a statement as to whether the aircraft can be flown if a certain piece of equipment is inoperative. When an item is discovered to be inoperative, the pilot goes to the MEL, finds the entry for that item, and checks if the plane must be grounded until maintenance is performed. Once an MEL is in place, it is quick and easy to use. But getting it into place is the problem.

The MEL under Part 91 is approved for one individual airplane at a time. The process begins when the airplane is first manufactured. During the airplane's type certification process, the manufacturer submits what is known as a *proposed master minimum equipment list* (PMMEL) to a branch of the FAA called the *Flight Operations Evaluation Board* (FOEB). The FOEB is composed of FAA personnel who are avionics, airworthiness, operations, and aircraft certification specialists. The PMMEL is a working document that is used by the people at the FOEB.

Eventually, the FOEB determines the minimum operative instruments and equipment required for safe flight, and they transform the list into a master minimum equipment list (MMEL). The FOEB specialists make recommendations to the FAA's *Aircraft Evaluation Group* (AEG), who are responsible for the publication of the MMEL.

The approved MMEL is then passed on to the various *flight standards district offices* (FSDO) across the United States. The FSDOs have the capability to download MMELs of many different airplanes. In fact, the FAA has developed MMELs for most of the FAA type certificated aircraft in use today. Single-engine airplanes can get a generic MMEL. Multiengine airplanes require a specific MMEL, such as for a BE-76.

In order to have your own MEL for your own airplane, you must first obtain a copy of your airplane's master minimum equipment list, and the MMEL's preamble from the nearest FAA flight standards district office. An FAA inspector and the operator must meet with you to discuss operations using an MEL. After the inspector is convinced that you fully understand MEL operations, a *letter of authorization* (LOA) is issued (Fig. 7-1).

Now you must do some work. Using the MMEL, airplane flight manuals, and maintenance manuals, you need to revise the list to meet the individual needs of your airplane. Not all airplanes have carburetor air temp gauges, but for those that do, there must be instructions for how to proceed if this gauge is inoperative. To customize your list, you will use what are called "M and O procedures."

Flight Standards District Office
Portland-Hillsboro Airport
3355 N.E. Cornell Road
Hillsboro, OR 97124

July 25, 1991

Mr. John Dough, President
John Dough Enterprises
Hangar 9, Suite 203
Portland-Hillsboro Airport
Hillsboro, OR 97124

Dear Mr. Dough:

This letter is issued under the provisions of FAR § 91.213(a)(2) of the Federal Aviation Regulations (FAR) and authorizes John Dough Enterprises only to operate Cessna Citation 500, N81149, Serial No. 12345, under the Master Minimum Equipment List (MMEL), using it as a Minimum Equipment List (MEL).

This letter of authorization and the MMEL constitute a Supplemental Type Certificate for the aircraft and must be carried aboard the aircraft as prescribed by FAR § 91.213(a)(2).

Operations must be conducted in accordance with MMEL. Operations and maintenance (O and M) procedures for the accomplishment of rendering items of equipment inoperative must be developed by the operator. Those procedures should be developed from guidance provided in the manufacturer's aircraft flight and/or maintenance manuals, manufacturer's recommendations, engineering specifications, and other appropriate sources. Such operations or maintenance procedures must be accomplished in accordance with the provisions and requirements of FAR Part 91, Part 145, or Part 43.

A means of recording discrepancies and corrective actions must be in the aircraft at all times and available to the pilot in command. Failure to perform O and M procedures in accordance with Part 91, Part 145 or Part 43 as appropriate, or to comply with the provisions of the MMEL, preamble, O and M procedures and other related documents, is contrary to FAR and invalidates this letter. All MMEL items that contain the statement "as required by FAR" must either state the FAR by part and section (e.g., 91.205) with the appropriate FAR carried aboard the aircraft, or the operational requirements/limitations required for dispatch must be clearly stated. When the MMEL is revised by the Flight Operations Evaluation Board (FOEB), John Dough Enterprises will be notified by post card of the revision. John Dough Enterprises must then obtain a copy of the revision from this Flight Standards District Office (FSDO), or the FSDO having jurisdiction, and incorporate any changes as soon as practicable including O and M procedures as required.

John Dough Enterprises must develop O and M procedures that correspond with those listed in the MMEL. John Dough Enterprises must also list the "as required by FAR" by specific FAR part and section, or state the operational requirements/limitations for aircraft dispatch. These items must be contained in a procedures document that is placed in the office of the

Fig. 7-1. *Sample letter of authorization.*

In the MEL, items are listed in columns. Beside each item is the letter "M" for maintenance or the letter "O" for operations. "M" indicates that a specific maintenance procedure must be accomplished before takeoff. This usually means a qualified maintenance person must do the work. "O" indicates that the procedure required can be accomplished by the pilot or flightcrew. The letter of authorization together with the MMEL, preamble to the MMEL, and the M and O procedures becomes your airplane's MEL. The process flow chart is shown in Fig. 7-2.

After all the MEL parts are together, the MEL is also considered a *supplemental type certificate* (STC) for that one specific airplane. The STC allows that airplane to be operated by the MEL conditions and not the Federal Aviation Regulations. In a sense, the STC becomes the federal regulations for that one airplane. The STC cannot be transferred. If you sell the airplane, the STC is void, and the new owner must start the process over again.

As you can see, getting an MEL has many steps and each can be time-consuming. However, once the MEL is in place, it can make life easier. For instance, say a pilot is at an airport far away from the home base and company maintenance shop. Before takeoff for a flight home, the pilot sees that the right fuel gauge is not working. According to FAR 91.213, the airplane would be grounded because 91.213 requires that each tank have an operating fuel quantity indicator. The pilot would have to get the gauge repaired before takeoff, delaying the flight and requiring out-of-town maintenance work, which could be expensive.

However, if the airplane has an MEL, the pilot might be able to bypass the FARs. I have an approved MEL for a multiengine airplane that allows the airplane to legally fly with one fuel gauge broken. In the MEL there is an O procedure listed by the fuel gauge entry, directing the pilot to top off the fuel tank in question and then fly less than two hours. The pilot in that situation could simply fill the tank and take off for home. If home was more than two hours away, a fuel stop would be needed. Either way, the airplane will get fixed at the home base and the flight is not delayed.

You can see that it would not take too many of these situations before the MEL will pay for itself.

MELs are revised by the pilot or operator, so they can be very practical and pilot-friendly once developed. Contact your local FSDO to get your airplane's MMELs and help throughout the process.

OPERATIONS WITHOUT AN MEL

Option two, the use of FAR 91.213, is available to any aircraft that does not have an MEL and falls into one of these categories:

1. Small rotorcraft
2. Non-turbine powered airplanes
3. Glider
4. Lighter-than-air aircraft

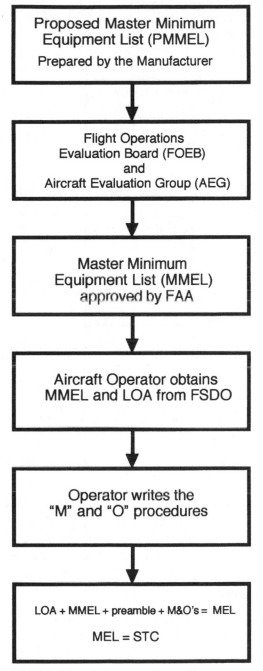

Fig. 7-2. *The minimum equipment list process.*

Light twins with reciprocating engines, therefore, are not required to have a minimum equipment list. If an approved MEL is not used, the pilot then determines airworthiness by using what I call the "four-step test," shown in Fig. 7-3. If the inoperative or

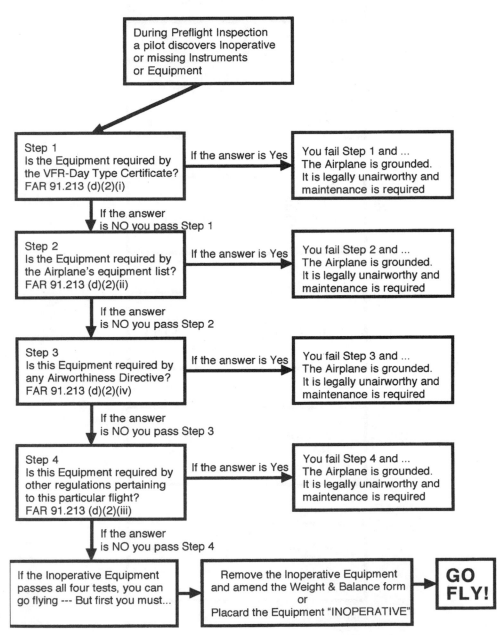

Fig. 7-3. *FAR 91.213. The four-step test.*

missing instruments or equipment passes all four steps, you can fly the airplane if the equipment is taken out or placarded.

Let's look at each step of the process individually.

Step 1

Step 1, adopted from FAR 91.213(d)(2)(i), asks, "Is the inoperative equipment in question required by the VFR-day type certificate?" The VFR-day type certificate is the set of rules that were followed when the airplane's design was originally certificated to fly by the FAA. The problem is that most of today's general aviation airplanes were certified under some very old regulations. The airplane might be younger than the regulations, yet the airplane might still be "certificated" under the old regulations. In fact, these regulations are so old they are not Federal Aviation Regulations, but rather Civil Aviation Regulations (CARs).

The old CAR Part 3 still has jurisdiction over airplanes today when not specifically superseded by a newer FAR. When the FARs replaced the CARs, the CAR Part 3 became FAR Part 23. But Part 23 even today refers back to its regulation ancestor. So CAR Part 3 is still used to determine the VFR-day type certificate requirements.

Although you probably have never even seen CAR Part 3, I'll bet you know some of its rules. For instance, most pilots know that fuel quantity indicators are required for each fuel tank and that the only time that gauge must read accurately is *when the tank is empty*. This calibrated-to-empty rule is well known, but you won't be able to find it in the FAR. It is in CAR 3—CAR 3.672 to be exact. Do you know what regulation requires an airplane to have a compass correction card? It's CAR Part 3.758. Are airplanes required to have a master switch? Yes, according to CAR 3.688.

There are several others like this that we have taken for granted. So where can these old rules be found? In a library, perhaps, or an FSDO office, or maybe no place. So here they are, the dusty, but still applicable, Civil Aviation Regulations:

CAR 3.655—Required Basic Equipment
The following table shows the basic equipment items required for *type and airworthiness certification of an airplane:*

(a) Flight and navigational instruments
  (1) Airspeed indicator
  (2) Altimeter
  (3) Magnetic direction indicator
(b) Powerplant instruments
  (1) For each engine or tank
      (i) Fuel quantity indicator
     (ii) Oil pressure indicator
    (iii) Oil temperature indicator
     (iv) Tachometer

(2) For each engine or tank (required in reference section)

    (i) Cylinder head temperature indicator

    (ii) Fuel pressure indicator (if pump fed engines used)

    (iii) Manifold pressure indicator (if altitude engines used)

    (iv) Oil quantity indicator

(c) Electrical equipment (required in reference section)

    (1) Master switch arrangement

    (2) Adequate source(s) of electrical energy

    (3) Electrical protective devices

(d) Miscellaneous equipment

    (1) Approved safety belts for all occupants

    (2) Airplane flight manual if required by 3.777

Now compare this list to today's FAR 91.205, the regulation that lists the instruments and equipment required to fly a United States registered airplane during the daytime in VFR conditions:

FAR 91.205 (b)

1. Airspeed indicator

2. Altimeter

3. Magnetic direction indicator

4. Tachometer for each engine

5. Oil pressure gauge (each engine)

6a. Temperature gauge (each liquid-cooled engine)

6b. Oil temperature gauge (each air-cooled engine)

7. Manifold pressure gauge (each altitude engine)

8. Fuel quantity gauge for each tank

9. Landing gear position indicator (retractable gear airplanes)

10. Floatation gear and flare gun (flights over water beyond glide-to-shore distance if operated for hire)

11. Safety belts

12. Front seat shoulder harness

13. Emergency locator transmitter

You can see that 91.205 (b) is the offspring of CAR 3.655. Although the lists are very similar, they are not identical. Using FAR 91.205 (b) in Step 1 of the four-step test can still leave the pilot vulnerable. The best way to determine exactly what your airplane requires is to obtain what is called a *type certificate data sheet* (TCDS) for your specific airplane. The TCDS is a document issued by the FAA that describes the aircraft's airworthiness requirements relating to a specific type, make, and model of aircraft. Although the TCDS can be obtained from the FSDO, ask your mechanics first; they probably already have one.

What books and manuals are required to be carried in the airplane? There is always a debate over operating limitations and where these limitations can be found. Different manufacturers publish pilot operating handbooks (POH), and others offer information manuals. Are any of these publications required for airworthiness? Once again, the old CAR 3.655 (d) helps answer the question.

CAR 3.655(d) Miscellaneous equipment
(2) Airplane Flight Manual if required by 3.777.

In regard to an Airplane Flight Manual, CAR 3.655 refers us to CAR 3.777. The old CAR 3.777 states:

(a) An Airplane Flight Manual shall be furnished with each airplane, having a maximum certified weight of more than 6,000 pounds.

(b) For airplanes having a maximum certified weight of 6,000 pounds or less, an Airplane Flight Manual is not required. Instead, the information prescribed in this part for inclusion in an Airplane Flight Manual shall be made available to the operator by the manufacturer in the form of clearly stated placards, markings, or manuals.

So while the old CARs were the only regulations to go by, an airplane weighing 6,000 pounds or less did not require an airplane flight manual. But in 1979 the newer FARs were in force, and the regulations changed to include airplanes that were less than 6,000 pounds. FAR Part 21 concerns the certification procedures for aircraft products and parts. It states:

(a) With each airplane that was not type certificated with an Airplane Flight Manual and that has had no flight time prior to March 1, 1979, the holder of a type certificate shall make available to the owner at the time of delivery of the aircraft a current approved Airplane Flight Manual.

This means that airplanes heavier than 6,000 pounds always required an airplane flight manual (AFM), but after March 1, 1979, all airplanes, regardless of weight must have an approved AFM.

What then constitutes an "approved" airplane flight manual? FAR 23.1581 also spells out the AFM requirements. FAR 23.1581 says that the AFM must be kept in a binder so that pages can be inserted (no bound books) and that the AFM must be kept in a "suitable fixed container" that is readily accessible to the pilot. FAR 23.1581 goes on to say that the AFM must contain a table of contents and must include all that is required in FAR 23.1583, 23.1585, and 23.1589. As you might imagine, these regulations seem to go on forever, so here are the highlights:

The AFM must include information on the airplane's maximum weight, maximum landing weight, and maximum takeoff weights for each altitude, ambient air temperature, and required takeoff distances. There must be center of gravity limits, speeds, flight maneuvers, and kinds of flight operations (IFR, VFR day, VFR night). The AFM must have the airplane's serial number, not just tail number, on the title page, and the entire book must be "updatable."

The owner subscribes to a service whereby the manufacturer will send revision pages to the owner as revisions are made. When the owner receives a revision page, he or she removes the old page and replaces it with the new page. This is why the book must not be bound, but rather loose-leaf in a binder.

This requirement illustrates the difference between an airplane's POH and an approved AFM. The POH is a reprint of the AFM at the time of publication, but the POH is not updated. Any revision that comes out will not be replaced in a POH, and the POH will therefore become obsolete. The POH in most cases is still adequate as a reference book for study purposes and is definitely cheaper than an approved AFM.

So if you are flying an airplane that had no flight time before March 1, 1979, you must fly with an approved airplane flight manual on board or the airplane is to be grounded. I personally double-laminated all my airplane's AFM title pages so that the required serial number page could not accidentally tear out with wear and render the airplane unairworthy.

If any inoperative equipment is one of the items on the type certificate data sheet list or if the AFM is missing, then the airplane cannot legally leave the ground. If the inoperative equipment is not on this list and you have an approved AFM, then, congratulations, you passed the first test and can graduate to the second test.

Step 2

The second step comes from FAR 91.213 (d)(2)(ii) and asks, "Is the inoperative equipment specifically required by the manufacturer in the aircraft's equipment list?" To find this answer, you must go to the aircraft's operating handbook (Fig. 7-4) or other documents that contain the equipment list. After finding the list, you must understand the manufacturer's code.

ITEM NO	EQUIPMENT LIST DESCRIPTION
D67-A	Recorder, Engine Hour Meter
D82-S	Outside Air Temperature Gauge
D85-R	Tachometer Instillation, Engine
D88-S	Indicator, Turn Coordinator
D88-O	Indicator, Turn & Bank
D91-S	Rate of Climb Indicator

Fig. 7-4. *Sample equipment list. (Not specific to a particular airplane.)*

Some manufactures append a letter to a part number that signifies that a particular piece of equipment is required for flight on their airplane. For example, in part number R-001, the *R* stands for "required," and therefore, this equipment must be in good working order before flight.

Other letters are also used as codes. *S* can mean "standard." Equipment listed as standard means that the equipment comes with the airplane when it is built, but it can be broken and still legally fly. *A* can mean "additional." Just like options for a car, additional equipment must be ordered separately from the basic airplane. Additional equipment is usually not required for airworthiness, and therefore, an inoperative piece of additional equipment can be flown unless the additional equipment substitutes for a required piece of equipment. These codes can be found in the equipment list of the airplane's handbook.

Other manufacturers code differently. In Fig. 7-5 the pressure gauge for instrument air has a minus (-) sign under the columns marked VFR day and VFR night. This means that the manufacturer does not require this gauge to be operating for VFR flight. However, note the "1" that appears under the IFR day and IFR night columns. This means that one operating instrument air gauge is required by the manufacturer before the airplane can be flown into IFR conditions.

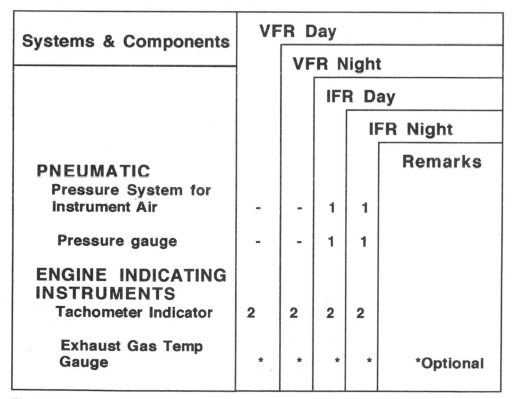

Systems & Components	VFR Day	VFR Night	IFR Day	IFR Night	Remarks
PNEUMATIC **Pressure System for Instrument Air**	-	-	1	1	
Pressure gauge	-	-	1	1	
ENGINE INDICATING INSTRUMENTS **Tachometer Indicator**	2	2	2	2	
Exhaust Gas Temp Gauge	*	*	*	*	*Optional

Fig. 7-5. *Sample equipment list. (Not specific to a particular airplane.)*

In the same figure, note the heading "Engine indicating instruments." Here, two engine tachometers are required for any flight. Although listed under the manufacturer's requirements, tachometers for every engine are also a requirement of 91.205. (This is obviously a twin-engine airplane, since two tachometers are required.) There is no regulation or manufacturer requirement, however, for the next entry, "Exhaust gas temperature" indicator. This instrument has an asterisk (*) under every column to indicate that this piece of equipment is optional and can therefore be flown when broken.

Every pilot should become very familiar with the manufacturer-provided equipment list of the airplanes that they fly. The second inoperative equipment test can only be passed with assistance from the POH or FAA-approved AFM.

Step 3

The third step comes from FAR 91.213(d)(2)(iv) and asks the question, "Is the inoperative equipment specifically required by any airworthiness directives?" An *airworthiness directive* (AD) is a recall. When parts of aircraft are found to be defective, they must be fixed or replaced. But how do aircraft owners find out about the problem?

Here is the process: A problem with an aircraft part is often determined by the National Transportation Safety Board (NTSB) through similar accident reports, by the FAA, or by the aircraft manufacturer themselves. When a part needs repair or replacement, the FAA is notified and a mailing is sent out to owners of that particular aircraft. The FAA knows who owns the airplanes because of the aircraft registration.

Once the owner gets the word of the AD, he or she must comply with the provisions of the AD. The AD might specify that the aircraft cannot be flown until a repair is made, or it might allow the repair to be made at the next scheduled inspection. The AD might even be reoccurring, requiring the owner to have a particular item inspected periodically for the life of the aircraft.

If any airworthiness directive states that a particular part or instrument must be operating in a particular airplane for flight, and if that part is in fact found to be inoperative, then the aircraft does not pass Step 3 and must be grounded.

If you are a renter pilot, you might not have ready access to information concerning ADs. The actual AD notice goes to the owner, but you, the pilot, are held responsible for flying only legally airworthy airplanes. If you get ramp-checked by an official of the FAA, how can you prove that the airplane you have flown is completely airworthy? You cannot pass the buck by saying, "I just rented this plane." The pilot is held accountable for the complete airworthiness.

Since a pilot could easily get hung by this situation, it is always best to rent from a dependable FBO that has a good maintenance track record. Spend some time with the chief mechanic and have the mechanic show you the existing ADs of the airplane you intend to rent. Ask about their AD tracking and research system. Educate yourself so that you will know what items and inspections might be required on a particular airplane. After doing some research if you discover that an inoperative piece of equipment is not specifically required by an airworthiness directive, then the equipment passes the third step.

Step 4

The fourth and final step depends on the particular conditions of the flight: "Will the weather conditions, the time of day, or the airspace to be flown in require specific equipment?" If the flight will be at night, the airplane will need instruments and equipment all operational that are listed in 91.205(c) for VFR night flight. If the flight will penetrate IFR flight conditions, even more instruments and equipment are required under 91.205(d) for IFR flight. Certain airspace types, namely airspace A, B, and C, require a Mode C transponder, so when you are flying into one of these airspace types, an altitude reporting transponder becomes required equipment.

Flights above certain altitudes and for specific duration require the availability of supplemental oxygen. For instance, if the flight was planned to fly above 15,000 feet in a nonpressurized airplane, supplemental oxygen for each person would also be required equipment.

The fourth test, listed under FAR 91.213(d)(2)(iii), says that "any other rule" applies. That means regulations 91.205, 91.207, 91.211, 91.215, and others must also be consulted before inoperative equipment can pass the final test.

Let's assume that all four tests are passed. Can the pilot now legally fly the airplane? No, not yet! FAR 91.213(d)(3) says that we are not finished. Before flight the inoperative equipment must:

1. Be removed from the aircraft, or deactivated under 91.213(d)(3)(i) or,

2. Be placarded with a sign that says "Inoperative" under 91.213(d)(ii) and,

3. The discrepancy is recorded in the maintenance records of the airplane under FAR 43.9.

Removing inoperative equipment from aircraft is usually not very practical. In addition, if you take equipment out of the airplane, the weight and balance form for the aircraft will become inaccurate, grounding the airplane anyway. The easiest method is to deactivate the equipment and place a sticker that says "Inoperative" or simply "Inop" over the equipment. Deactivation of electrical equipment can be accomplished by pulling the equipment's circuit breaker and placing a plastic collar around the breaker. This will prevent the breaker from inadvertently being pushed in.

To be completely legal, you might have to fly with a panel of "Inop" placards, which will not instill much confidence in your passengers. And, of course, you would expect the FAA to stipulate the type of sign, and they have not let us down. Advisory Circular 91-67 says the placard must be a label or decal with letters at least ⅛ inch high.

How long can you fly with an "Inop" placard on a piece of equipment? Not forever. FAR 91.405 (c), titled Maintenance Required, says that "the owner or operator of an aircraft shall have any inoperative instrument or item of equipment permitted to be inoperative by 91.213(d)(2) to be repaired, replaced, removed, or inspected at the next required inspection." The next required inspection is usually a 100-hour inspection or an annual inspection. This means items that pass the four-step test and then are properly placarded still have a deadline to be fixed or removed.

APPLYING THE FOUR-STEP TEST

The question posed at the beginning of the chapter asked whether you can legally take off with an inoperative suction gauge that monitors the vacuum system. Let's look at how we can apply the four-step test to answer this question.

Step 1 Is a suction gauge (or instrument air gauge) required for VFR flight during the day under part 91.205 and/or a TCDS? After looking down a sample TCDS list, we see that a suction gauge is not on the list of required items, so this gauge passes the first test.

Step 2 Is a suction gauge required by the manufacturer? Look back at Fig. 7-5. This gauge is not required for day or night VFR. If the proposed flight will remain in VFR conditions, the second test is passed.

Step 3 Is the suction gauge required due to an airworthiness directive? You'll need to do some research to say for sure. If a visit to the maintenance technician's office did not reveal such an AD, the gauge passes the third test.

Step 4 Is this suction gauge required for the specific conditions of this flight? No regulation requires a suction gauge just because you fly to a certain type airspace or to a specific altitude. As long as this flight remains VFR, the gauge passes the fourth test.

The suction gauge made it all the way through without grounding the airplane. Now the suction gauge must be labeled as inoperative and the discrepancy must be recorded. Now you can take off with the assurance that flight even with this equipment broken is legal.

RAMP CHECKS

The issue of flight with inoperative equipment is a complicated one. With all the paperwork required of an MEL and all the regulations involved with operating without an MEL, the pilot can get confused. But when you taxi in someday and are greeted by a person saying, "Good morning, I'm from the FAA and this is a ramp check," it will be a bad time to be confused. Study your airplane's AFM, the regulations, and apply the four-step test.

A last word on FAA ramp checks. The FAA performs these inspections on three occasions:

1. For normal surveillance
2. When an FAA inspector observes an unsafe operation
3. After an accident or incident

The inspector will ask the pilot for:

1. The pilot's, and any other required crew member's, Pilot Certificate and Medical Certificate.
2. The airplane's Airworthiness Certificate. The airplane's tail number and Airworthiness Certificate numbers must match, and the certificate must be original—no photocopies.

3. The airplane's Registration Certificate with matching numbers. If the airplane's ownership has changed within the past 120 days, there should be a pink temporary registration certificate. If 120 days have passed since the temporary certificate was signed, then the airplane is grounded until the permanent certificate arrives. If this certificate is late, call your local FSDO for assistance.

4. The radio station license.

5. POH, or an FAA-approved AFM, whichever is required.

6. The current and up-to-date weight and balance data sheet.

The FAA inspector who performs the ramp check must also have identification. He or she should present to the pilot an Aviation Safety Inspector's Credential, FAA Form 110A. This credential allows the holder access to aircraft, airports, and accident sites. In addition, the inspector might need an FAA form 8000-39 to gain access to secured areas of airports without escort. Both these credentials will have the inspector's photo on it.

The inspector will not board the aircraft without permission, but if permission is denied, you can bet that the inspector will write down the airplane's tail number and will then take action to ground that airplane and that pilot so that an inspection can be made at some point. The FAA's policy is not to do blanket ramp checks at air shows, fly-ins, wings weekend seminars, and so forth. The FAA inspector is also not supposed to cause a delay to a flight while doing the ramp check inspection.

It is also possible to get an evaluation from the FAA as to the complete airworthiness of your airplane without threat of enforcement by attending a PACE program. PACE is the Pilot and Aircraft Courtesy Evaluation where the FAA inspectors wear the white hat. During the PACE inspection, an FAA inspector will perform a courtesy ramp check and report to you any problems. This gives the pilot/operator the opportunity to become aware of any items that could have gotten them into trouble. After you complete the PACE program, the inspector gives you a T-shirt that says "I survived PACE"!

PART III

Advanced multiengine flight

8
Turboprops

THE STEP UP FROM A RECIPROCATING (PISTON) ENGINE TO A TURBO-prop (turbine) engine is a significant one. Turboprops are not necessarily more complicated, but progressing to this type of engine usually means that someone has shown some confidence in you. Although most pilots do not start out on turbopropeller-driven airplanes, they are an inevitable rung on the career ladder. Some pilots do not believe that they have "arrived" until they start burning kerosene.

The turboprop is a gas turbine engine and propeller combination. To the layperson, it's a jet with a prop, and for this reason, it's also called a "propjet."

This combination offers the best of two worlds. Propellers are great at slow speeds, like initial takeoff roll. The prop bites into the air and pulls the airplane forward. A pure jet engine relies on accelerating intake air, so it is slow to accelerate during initial takeoff roll when there is low forward speed. But at fast speed the propeller looses efficiency. The prop simply gets in the way and holds the airplane back. A pure jet engine that has no propeller does not have this problem.

An engine that is both jet and prop is a great compromise. It can get into and out of short runways that pure jets could not. The fast speed inefficiencies of piston/propeller combinations are partially overcome by turboprops by increasing the prop blade angles (chapter 4). The turboprop can afford to reach for higher blade angles because of its increased turbine engine power. Turboprops provide greater fuel economy for their speed range and offer reverse thrust.

TURBOPROPS

Because of these advantages, most charter, corporate, and commuter airlines use turboprops. For this reason, you should understand the basic principles of a turboprop.

Like all other systems, there will be variation from one airplane to another. You will spend hours learning the intricacies of the particular turboprop that you fly, but all have basic principles in common. They all take air in, compress that air, mix fuel with the air then burn it, and eventually turn the resulting expansion of gases into propulsive energy.

TURBOPROP PRINCIPLES

You might not know it yet, but the basic principles of the turboprop are already familiar to you. To get the big picture let's construct a turboprop step by step. Figure 8-1 shows a propeller in profile. The blades are rotating on the shaft, and as a result, air is being pushed behind (in this illustration, to the right).

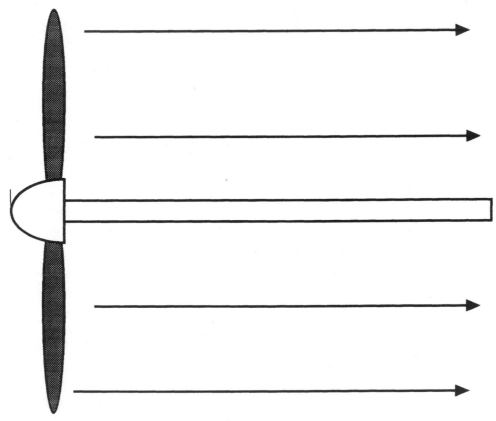

Fig. 8-1. *Airflow behind a rotating propeller.*

This is a normal situation. Every time you fly in a propeller-driven airplane, you take advantage of this "prop-wash." The greater the rush of air backward, the greater the move forward. The air comes spinning off the propeller and is blasted behind without a second thought. But moving air is a form of energy, and it really is a shame to just waste that energy. The essence of the turbine engine is to harness this energy.

If moving air produced by a rotating blade transforms energy that we can use, why not have several additional blades to move even more air? Figure 8-2 illustrates a rotating shaft with multiple blades whipping the air. One blade passes air back to the next blade, and in doing so, increases the movement of air. The idea here is that more is better. More blades push more air, and this increases the airflow.

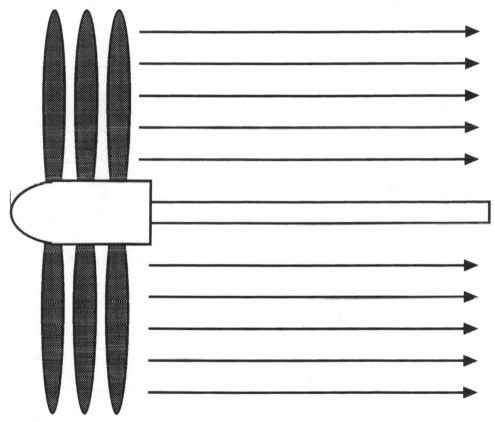

Fig. 8-2. *Airflow behind a compressor.*

When this airflow is led into a confined area, the air molecules start to get jammed up and the air's pressure increases. This compression of the air molecules acts somewhat like a supercharger, and therefore, this engine could climb much higher above sea level without a power loss. But Figs. 8-1 and 8-2 cannot be real because there is nothing to turn the propellers on the shaft in the first place. How will the rotation of the propellers be accomplished?

Figure 8-3 has the answer. A wheel placed in the airflow will turn the shaft, which will turn the blades. Just like a windmill, this rear wheel spins when air flows through

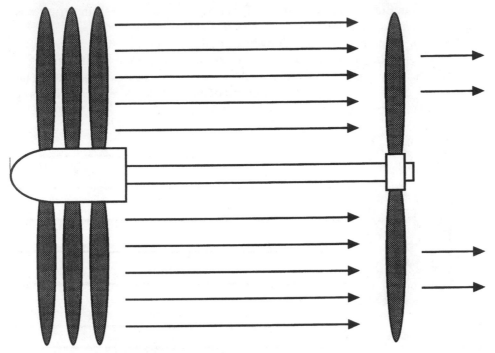

Fig. 8-3. *Compressor and propeller combination.*

it. (The wheel is called a *turbine*, hence the engine's name.) The forward blades make up the *compressor*, and they feed the turbine and make it spin.

As you can see, there is still a major problem. The compressor blades cannot spin without the turbine driving the shaft, and the turbine cannot spin without the airflow from the compressor. They need each other. But the compressor/turbine combination alone cannot sustain itself. There must be one more ingredient.

Figure 8-4A adds the combustion chambers to the diagram. Air coming from the compressor blades goes in two directions. Approximately 75 percent of the air is used to keep the combustion chambers cool, or at least within tolerable temperatures. The other 25 percent is led into the combustion chambers, where fuel is injected and mixed with the air. The mixture is designed to provide a combustible ratio that will burn when exposed to an ignition source. The ignition source (fire) is provided in the combustion chamber, and the mixture starts to burn.

When the mixture burns, it gets hot and expands. The expanding gases are led out of the chamber and directly into—you guessed it—the turbine wheel. The turbine wheel must be designed to withstand high temperatures, since the gases come rapidly from the combustion chamber. As the expanding gases strike the turbine wheel, it will begin to turn. This turns the shaft, which, in turn, turns the compressor blades. The compressor blades continue to supply airflow to the combustion chamber, and the cycle continues as long as there is fuel to burn.

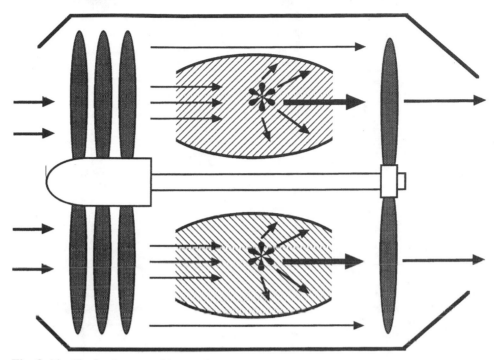

Fig. 8-4A. *The basic gas turbine engine.*

The energy used to turn the turbine/shaft/compressor combination is approximately 60 to 80 percent of the engine's total energy. This means that as little as 20 percent of the total energy produced ultimately ends up as "jet blast" out the exhaust.

Figure 8-4B compares the turbine engine to the reciprocating engine. The four-stroke reciprocating piston engine moves from the intake stroke to the compression stroke, followed by the power stroke and, finally, the exhaust stroke. The strokes follow one after the other in repetition.

Notice that the turbine engine has the same functions. The turbine engine has an intake, along with air compression, power/ignition, and finally, exhaust. The difference is that all four functions are performed simultaneously and without interruption. The piston engine functions must take turns with each stroke because all four functions take place at the same location: the cylinder. But the turbine engine has a separate location for each function, and therefore, all can be performed at once.

Because in the turbine engine, intake, compression, combustion, and exhaust occur continuously, fire must continuously burn within the combustion chamber. There is no need for ignition "timing"; you light the fire once and it simply stays lit until the fuel is turned off. Nor is there a need for intake and exhaust valves, push rods, rocker arms, or camshafts. There is also no need for all the parts that produce intermittent ignition, such as magnetos, distributors, and spaghetti spark plug wires. In principle, the turbine engine is much less complicated than the reciprocating engine.

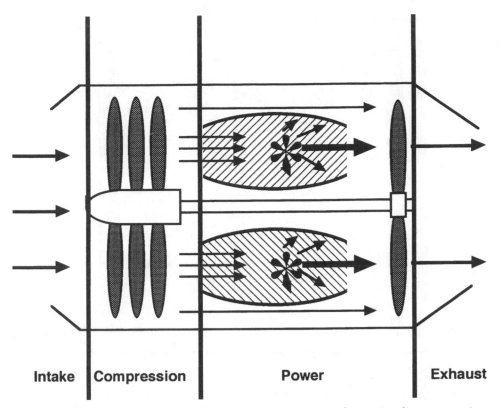

Intake | **Compression** | **Power** | **Exhaust**

Fig. 8-4B. *The gas turbine engine, like a reciprocating engine, has an intake, compression, power, and exhaust stroke. The difference is that all these functions take place continuously and simultaneously inside the turbine engine.*

Figure 8-4A is a pure jet, not a turboprop. The gas turbine engine is the core of the turboprop, but Fig. 8-4A only shows the inside. To make this engine a turboprop, a propeller must be attached. But it is not that simple.

Propellers are attached directly to reciprocating engines. In other words, the propeller and engine crankshaft are turning at the same speed. But the reciprocating engine turns at between 2,500 and 3,000 RPM maximum. The turbine engine may turn at 33,000 RPM.

If a propeller were attached directly to a shaft turning at 33,000 RPM, trouble would ensue. The propeller blade tips, which travel faster than any other part of the blade, would go through the speed of sound. Shock waves would form on the blades, increasing the drag to levels that would destroy the blade. The other forces that act on a turning propeller blade, such as centrifugal, torque bending, thrust bending, and twisting forces, would be so great the propeller would surely fail and fly apart.

To avoid this problem the propeller is attached to the turbine engine only by way of a reduction gear system. The reduction is approximately 15 to 1. Therefore, the turbine engine shaft may be turning 33,000 RPM, while the propeller is turning a mere 2,200.

Think of the power advantage of those numbers. When you have 2,200 RPM backed up by 33,000 RPM, you can increase the propeller blade angle (chapter 4) to degrees higher than with a reciprocating engine without laboring the engine. This allows the turboprop to take a bigger bite of the air, which increases cruising speed and delays the onset of propeller inefficiency. The increased efficiency saves fuel and is the principle reason the turboprop is used so widely today.

Figure 8-5 illustrates a sample turboprop. The propeller blades turn and provide thrust in the same manner as propeller blades of piston engines. At the same time, air comes rushing off the propeller and into the engine itself. The air is then compressed, combusted, and expelled.

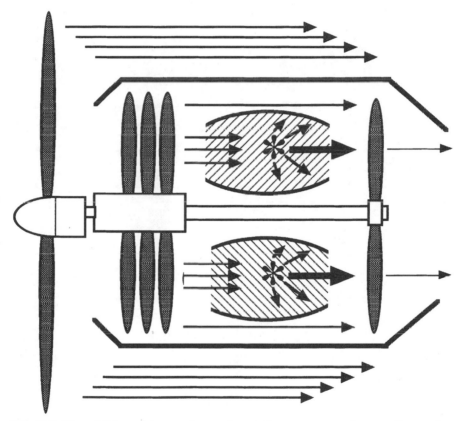

Fig. 8-5. *The addition of the gearbox and propeller creates a turbopropeller engine from the basic gas turbine engine.*

The turbine drives the compressor, the reduction gear assembly, and the propeller, so up to 85 percent of the total energy is absorbed by the turbine. This leaves only 15 percent for the exhaust blast; however, this blast is not a factor, since the propeller is providing the thrust.

TURBOPROP VARIATIONS

The basic turboprop powerplant can have many variations. Figure 8-6 shows a common design. This version ducts the air to the rear of the engine first and channels the flow forward. The sharp turn that the air must make is a safety precaution. Debris that might be in the air travels in a straight line because of its inertia and cannot make the turn. This arrangement, called an *inertial separator,* prevents debris from entering and damaging the engine's internal parts.

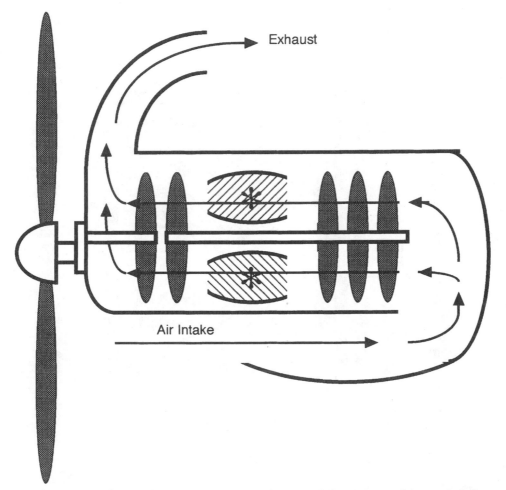

Fig. 8-6. *A turboprop variation with intake at the rear of the engine and forward airflow through the engine.*

The airflow then moves forward through the engine; first through the compressor section, then into the combustion chamber. After ignition, the hot, expanding gases are directed into two turbines. The first is the compressor turbine whose shaft runs rearward, back to turn the compressor. The second is the power turbine whose shaft runs forward into the reduction gear assembly and propeller.

Notice that this is a split shaft. There is no interconnection between the compressor and power shaft. This should give you a sense of the power of the expanding gases. The reduction gears and propeller run off airflow alone like a pinwheel in the wind, yet they provide more than enough power to operate the system. After passing through and driving both turbines, the air is led out and some thrust is actually obtained due to "blast" from the exhaust.

Figure 8-7 illustrates yet another example. This variation has a common shaft between the compressor blades in the front and the turbine blades in the rear. Air enters the engine and is compressed by the blades, then ducted around to the back of the engine. The air enters the rear combustion chamber, where fuel is added and ignited. The resulting hot, expanding gases then move forward in the engine across the turbine blades. The turbine wheel turns, and the gases are led out the exhaust.

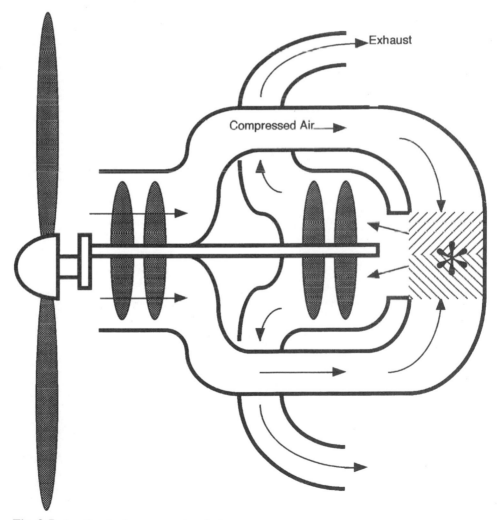

Fig. 8-7. *Another turboprop engine design.*

TURBOPROPS

Other arrangements, for use in helicopters, turn the shaft 90° through the reduction gear assembly and a rotor is attached. This variation is called a *turboshaft engine*.

Of course, the illustrations are simplified—just concepts, really. When you actually fly airplanes with these types of engines, you should become completely familiar with that particular system's fuel, lubrication, ignition, cooling, accessories, pressurization, and all subsystems. Review chapter 4 of this book for information on the types of propellers used on turboprop airplanes and their operation.

9
High-altitude operations

IN 1982 THE NATIONAL TRANSPORTATION SAFETY BOARD (NTSB) MADE a recommendation to include high-altitude training as a "transition" course for pilots learning to fly airplanes in high-altitude situations. The recommendations were made as a result of a string of fatal accidents. Each accident in the study listed "lack of flightcrew knowledge and proficiency at high altitudes" as a contributing factor. Nine years later, in 1991, the FAA added regulations pertaining to pressurized airplanes that fly above 25,000 feet in response to the NTSB recommendations. FAR 61.31(f) states:

> No person may act as pilot in command of a pressurized airplane that has a service ceiling or maximum operating altitude, whichever is lower, above 25,000 feet MSL, unless that person has completed the ground and flight training specified in this section and has received a logbook or training record endorsement from an authorized instructor certifying satisfactory completion of the training.

The regulation has several parts. First, it says that no person can act as pilot in command of a pressurized airplane capable of flying higher than 25,000 feet MSL. This training is not required if you fly a nonpressurized airplane that has the capability of flying that high. Of course, in that case, you would have other supplemental oxygen requirements to meet (FAR 91.211). The regulation does not say that this high-altitude training is required only when flying above 25,000 feet, rather it says that the training is required anytime you fly an airplane that is capable of 25,000 feet even if you choose to fly at a lower altitude.

As an example, is this high-altitude endorsement required when flying such an airplane on a short trip and only to 10,000 feet? Yes. Even though you do not choose to climb to 25,000 feet, if the airplane is capable of climbing to that altitude, the PIC would need the required high-altitude training and endorsement.

No training is required if you acted as pilot in command of an airplane capable of flying higher than 25,000 feet prior to this law coming into effect on April 15, 1991. If you did not act as PIC in this type of airplane prior to that date, then FAR 61.31(f)(1)(i) outlines the ground training that is required for you. Specifically:

- High-altitude aerodynamics
- High-altitude meteorology
- Respiration
- Effects, symptoms, and causes of hypoxia
- High-altitude sicknesses other than hypoxia
- Duration of consciousness without supplemental oxygen
- Causes and effects of gas expansion and gas bubble formations
- Preventive measures for eliminating gas expansion and bubble formation
- Physical phenomena and incidents of decompression
- Any other physiological aspects of high-altitude flight

This chapter discusses all the topics, and more, that are required for the ground portion of the high-altitude operations endorsement. Use this chapter as your textbook to higher altitudes.

HIGH-ALTITUDE AERODYNAMICS

The aerodynamic factors of high-altitude flight center around the fact that the air to fly through is so thin. When calculating lift, drag, and thrust, you must consider the density altitude. At high altitude where the density altitude or weight of the air is low, the airplane simply cannot perform as it does near sea level. The engines gasp for air to breath in and compress for combustion, and the wings yearn for more molecules to accelerate in order to produce lift.

Also, the airspeed indicator loses efficiency. A certain amount of air pressure must be present to indicate a particular airspeed, which is true at any altitude; however, at high altitude where there are less molecules to begin with, it takes a greater forward speed (true airspeed) to produce that certain air pressure in the pitot tube. Because of this, an airplane's true airspeed increases, while its indicated airspeed remains constant.

This increased error in the airspeed indicator with altitude can be very confusing. If a pilot held a nose pitch angle of 6° near sea level, that attitude, together with a power setting, would yield a particular indicated airspeed (IAS) and true airspeed (TAS). That same 6° angle of attack and power setting at high altitude will produce the same IAS but a greater TAS.

If a pilot chooses a high angle of attack, the wing might near the critical angle and begin to stall. But at the same time, the airplane has a very fast TAS and might near the mach buffet. The *mach buffet* occurs when a combination of subsonic and supersonic airflow crosses the airplane's surfaces. The airplane is not going faster than sound, but since wings and other airplane surfaces accelerate airflow, the air around the airplane might be faster than sound. This produces shock waves and buffeting (the sound barrier). The location where high-speed mach buffet, IAS, and critical angle of attack all merge is called the *Q corner*, or "coffin corner."

The Q corner is the airplane's aerodynamic ceiling. The airplane can neither go faster nor slower. A faster speed would exceed the limits of the airplane's speed envelope. A slower speed/higher angle of attack would cause airflow to separate from the wing, and the wing would stall. The pilot is maintaining airplane stability and control on the point of a pin. At this point, any maneuver such as a turn or roll from turbulence will result in a decrease in control effectiveness and loss of stability. The only escape is to descend back down into thicker air.

HIGH-ALTITUDE METEOROLOGY

The weather at high altitudes is also a challenge. Although some problems associated with low-altitude weather flying are reduced when up high, there are new problems. The biggest difference between down low and up high is the wind and its associated turbulence. As low-altitude pilots, we view the winds and temperatures aloft information from the bottom up. When a FSS briefer begins reciting the winds from 18,000 and 24,000 feet, we usually tune them out and attempt to catch up on our notes about what was previously said. The one thing we do know is that, ordinarily, the wind gets faster as altitude gets higher. This fact has everything to do with the tropopause.

The near-Earth layer of our atmosphere is called the *troposphere*, or the "weather" sphere. The troposphere is where we live and where most of us fly. It is also where most of the moisture and, therefore, clouds and precipitation occur. The air is warmed in the troposphere mostly by the compression of the air, not by direct energy from the sun. At sea level the air is warmer because there is a greater amount of air molecules above pushing down. This pushing or compression causes friction between molecules, and friction produces the heat. As altitude increases through the troposphere, the temperature is reduced because compression is reduced. This is why it is usually cooler in the mountains than at the beach.

HIGH-ALTITUDE OPERATIONS

If you go high enough, however, the temperature will stop getting colder and actually start to get warmer again. When the temperature switches its trend, you enter the stratosphere. The outside temperature in the stratosphere is still very cold by human standards, but the air does increase its temperature because of sunlight and ozone reaction and other phenomena. The thin boundary between air with troposphere and stratosphere characteristics is called the *tropopause*.

Near the Earth's poles the air is cold and thick, so it crunches down near the surface. The tropopause in this area is low, about 20,000 to 30,000 feet. Over the equator the air is warmer. The molecules spread out and rise. This pushes the tropopause very high, like a fountain, to around 50,000 to 65,000 feet.

The United States is situated between the low polar tropopause and the high tropical tropopause. The problem is that these two do not blend well. There is not a smooth tropopause slope from 20,000 to 65,000 over our heads. Instead, the tropopause starts high in the south and in a very short distance drops off to low. This drop-off or break is the area where hot and cold, sparse and dense, polar and tropical air collide. When this happens, something has got to give. The result of these different pressures coming together is the jet stream. The jet stream is the ricochet of the colliding forces.

Pilots can find the jet stream at the altitude of the tropopause. In the summer months the warm air is stronger and pushes the cold polar air back, and its lower tropopause moves far to the north. Therefore, in the summer the jet stream is far to the north generally in the northern United States and Canada. But in the winter the cold air is stronger and wins the north-south battle by breaking out and pushing back the warm air to the south. The boundary and, therefore, the jet stream patterns move south for the winter.

The airflow of the high-altitude winds and jet stream is usually west to east, but just like the rising and falling of the tides, the polar and tropical fronts move back and forth, so the jet stream can wander a curved course where the winds can travel north and later south. The speed of the jet stream is also faster in the winter. This is true because of the greater differences in temperature that exist in the winter from north to south.

Whenever a horizontal shaft of fast-moving air cuts through otherwise still air, a ripping will occur in the boundary between the two air masses. Since the jet stream is very fast (50 knots or greater to be classified a jet) and the larger air mass is relatively motionless, any pilot flying across this area would move from still air to fast air quickly. This transition causes *clear air turbulence* (CAT). CAT occurs where there are no clouds and, therefore, with little warning. The best indication of oncoming CAT is a rapid change in the outside air temperature, which is indicative of the crossing horizontally of the sloping tropopause. The CAT is stronger on the polar side of the jet.

The clouds at high altitude are virtually all frozen ice crystals in the form of thin cirrus. Icing at high altitudes is not as common as at low altitudes because the clouds are already frozen and the particles simply bounce off the airplane. The remaining cloud problem at high altitude are the tops of thunderstorm clouds. A towering cumulonimbus cloud can reach beyond 60,000 feet and can build vertically faster than most airplanes can climb. Pilots should make every effort to circumnavigate these clouds. The tops of these clouds, like the remainder of the thunderstorm, are filled with heavy turbulence, wind shear, and supercooled water that rises through the cloud and will freeze on contact with an airplane.

Flight planning at high altitudes is greatly affected by the weather at high altitudes. Generally, flights to the west should avoid the tropopause and the jet stream. Flights to the east could take advantage of the jet if turbulence precautions are taken.

No matter which way you fly, monitor the airplane's groundspeed. The effect of strong headwinds can change your fuel planning, fuel tank switching, and even your destination. Flying against a headwind could eat away at fuel reserves to the point where a fuel stop short of the intended airport is necessary. Strong high-altitude head-winds often bring on the need for a fuel service/credit card directory so the pilot can figure out where to land and get more fuel.

RESPIRATION

Every cell in the human body needs oxygen to survive. Without oxygen, we die; it is that simple. The body, in order to live, must feed oxygen to the cells. It must deliver oxygen from the environment outside the body to the environment of tissues inside the body. The delivery system sustains life and is made up of three phases (Fig. 9-1).

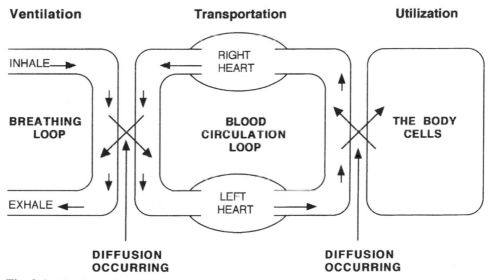

Fig. 9-1. *The three phases of respiration.*

The outside air is brought into the body when we inhale. All gases of the atmosphere get inside, but it is only the oxygen that is important for this process. The air passes through the mouth or nose, down the trachea (windpipe), and into the bronchial tubes, where the air is divided up between the two lungs.

The lungs are great mazes with seemingly endless passages. Each passage is smaller than the last until reaching the end at the *alveoli*. The alveoli are tiny air sacks and are the link between the outside world and the bloodstream. Adults have between 250 and 350 million of these air sacks.

The blood arrives through microscopic capillaries, and when capillary meets alveoli, you have a capillary junction. It is at this junction where the air and the blood get together to make an exchange of gases.

Figure 9-2 shows the air giving the blood its oxygen while the blood deposits its carbon dioxide in the air. The oxygen travels on in the blood, and the carbon dioxide is swept out in the next exhale. The transfer of these gases is called *diffusion*. This diffusion must occur efficiently or the gas transfer does not take place properly. In that event, oxygen cannot get in and carbon dioxide cannot get out. This situation will rapidly cause problems for the person involved.

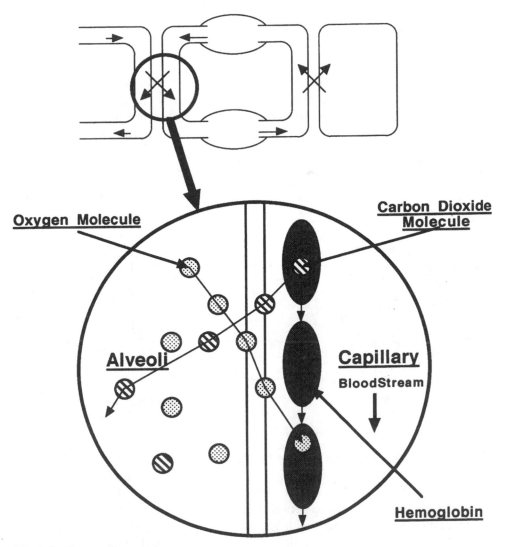

Fig. 9-2. *The capillary junction.*

The blood drops off its carbon dioxide in the lungs and loads up with oxygen bound for the cells. In order for the blood to move to the cells for the delivery, it gets pushed along by the left side of the heart muscle. When the oxygen-filled blood arrives at the cells, another diffusion takes place. The cells get the oxygen they need and discard into the blood the carbon dioxide waste they have used up. The blood delivers the good stuff and carries away the bad stuff. This is called *metabolism*. The blood gets a second push from the right side of the heart into the lungs, where the process starts all over again.

This works great in theory, but other factors are involved that can reduce this system's ability to do its job. Some of these factors are common to pilots who routinely leave the safe confines of the atmosphere near sea level and travel to places that the body is not used to. Going up makes the efficiency of the respiratory system go down.

HYPOXIA

Hypoxia is a lack of oxygen that is being metabolized by the body's cells. The problem comes from some breakdown in the links of the respiration system. To really understand hypoxia we must get microscopic. We must look at the capillary junction where the actual transfer of oxygen occurs.

The blood itself has many components, but not all of these carry the oxygen. The oxygen carrier is called the *hemoglobin*. It is the hemoglobin that actually catches the oxygen and makes the delivery to the cells. The oxygen arrives in the alveoli, and the blood with its hemoglobin arrives in the capillaries on opposite sides of a very thin wall. The actual transfer requires a force to push the oxygen through the wall and into the blood where the hemoglobin can soak it up. The force required is the pressure of the air itself.

Air pressure is sometimes hard to understand and accept. We always set our altimeters for barometric pressure before each flight; however, since we truly cannot feel the air pressure, we take it for granted. Though we have heard that on a standard day at sea level there is a pressure of 14.7 psi from the air's weight above pushing down, we do not actually notice it. The reason we do not feel the pressure from above is because it is also from all around and even inside our bodies pushing out. There is equal pressure inside and outside of our bodies, so we feel no net effect.

But we would feel a difference if the air were water. You can feel the weight of water on the body when swimming. Refer to Fig. 9-3. If you dive to the bottom of the deep end of the pool, you notice the force of the water against the body. The shallow end does not provide as much pressure because there is simply less water above you to bear down on you. Picture the Earth's atmosphere as a swimming pool. The surface of the water is the edge of space where there is no longer a usable atmosphere. The bottom of the pool is the surface of the Earth. The bottom of the deep end of the pool is like sea level. The shallow end is Mount McKinley. When at the "deep end" of the atmosphere (sea level), there is greater pressure from the air above because there just is a greater amount of air above. When higher in the atmosphere, there is less pressure because there is less air above.

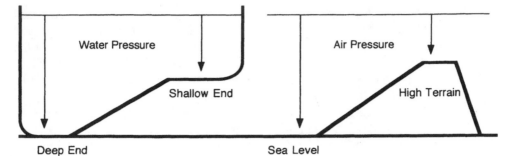

Fig. 9-3. *Air pressure at sea level is like being at the bottom of the deep end of a swimming pool.*

This air pressure from above is what pushes the oxygen through the alveoli wall and into the bloodstream. When we fly to high altitudes where the pressure is less, there is less force to push the oxygen across, and consequently, less oxygen gets to the cells. This is hypoxia.

The air is only approximately 21 percent oxygen. The other 79 percent is made up of all the other gases found in the atmosphere of the Earth. Since oxygen is only part of the air, it is also just one part of the pressure that makes up the air. If the total air pressure were 14.7 psi, then the portion of that pressure that is from oxygen would be only about 3.0 psi or 21 percent of 14.7 psi.

This means that on a standard day at sea level, there is approximately a 3-psi force that pushes the oxygen through the wall and into the blood. At 10,000 feet above sea level the standard pressure is about 10 psi, which would mean that the oxygen push would only be 2.1 psi. At 18,000 feet the total pressure is 7.34, and therefore, the part of the pressure that is oxygen would be down to 1.5 psi.

You can see that as we go up, the partial pressure of the life-giving oxygen goes way down. There must be a pressure gradient that is forceful enough to do the job of pushing the oxygen into the bloodstream. If you ever fly so high that the force pushing the oxygen is not as strong as the alveoli wall, then the oxygen simply will not get through.

We humans have made several attempts to artificially replace the pressure so that the cells will again receive the oxygen. We can breath 100 percent oxygen from a canister rather than 21 percent from the atmosphere. The pressure from the canister does not need to be as great as the atmosphere because, being 100 percent, there is no partial pressure; it's all oxygen. So even 3 psi would be like the normal atmosphere at sea level.

We have tried "pressure breathing," using a device that blows the air into the lungs and increasing the pressure to acceptable levels. But the most common device (and most comfortable) to artificially provide breathing pressure is the pressurized airplane cabin. The only reason we need to pump up the inside of an airplane is to allow enough partial pressure to push the oxygen over the edge and into the hemoglobin.

This reduction of oxygen partial pressure is often called *altitude hypoxia*, but there are other forms. To understand the different forms, let's use an analogy. Let's say that the air sacks (alveoli) where air collects is like a subway station. The capillaries are the tubes that the subway train runs through, and the hemoglobin cells are the subway train cars. The people who want to ride the train will represent the air molecules.

Under normal circumstances, when the train pulls up to the station, the doors open and people rush off the platform and into the subway cars. This represents the situation at sea level; there is plenty of oxygen (people) and plenty of pressure for the people to get on board.

What would happen if when the train pulled up to the station, the doors opened, but the people were too slow and did not get on the train in time. The doors would close and the train would move on, but with fewer people (oxygen molecules) on board. This would be the effect of breathing at a high altitude, and the result would be altitude hypoxia.

What would happen if, when the train stopped at the station and the doors opened, some "bad" people pushed onto the train first and kept the "good" people (oxygen) from even getting on the train. In this case the train would pull away from the station without the needed oxygen, but with pollutants instead. The "bad" molecules in this example could be carbon monoxide, alcohol, cigarette smoke, or over-the-counter drugs such as cold remedies and antihistamines. These molecules can take the place of the oxygen in the bloodstream. The hemoglobin can become filled will unwanted, unhealthy, and even dangerous molecules.

The hemoglobin will actually soak up the toxic molecules faster than it will oxygen molecules, so when oxygen attempts to get on board the train car, the train car could be already full of the bad stuff. The toxic molecules are poison to the cells. When the cells get a delivery of poison rather than oxygen, they begin to malfunction. This form of hypoxia is called *histotoxic hypoxia*, and it is much more common than you might think.

Histotoxic hypoxia is what causes intoxication. Being drunk is simply the restriction of oxygen to the brain. When a pilot drinks alcohol, it brings on histotoxic hypoxia, and brain functions slow down. When this is combined with a flight in an airplane, altitude hypoxia is added to compound the problem. This is why two drinks will have the effect of six drinks if you are at high altitude. Histotoxic and altitude hypoxia together are killers.

Then there is the case when the subway train enters the station, but the train does not have the usual amount of cars. There is plenty of oxygen and plenty of pressure, but not sufficient room to carry all the oxygen that is needed. This is called *hypemic hypoxia*, or *anemia*. When a person is anemic, they do not have enough healthy hemoglobin cells to deliver the oxygen to the tissues. People who suffer from anemia will often feel tired, run down, and without energy. They simply do not get the proper amount of oxygen, and the body's cells operate in slow motion.

What if the train pulled into the station, the doors opened, the people rushed on board, but the train did not move on. If the blood flow stops, the hemoglobin also stops, and the oxygen is no longer transported. This is *stagnate hypoxia*. This form is a problem when pilots pull heavy G loads. The force of the G factor can be stronger than the heart's ability to pump the blood upward to the brain. When the blood cannot be pumped to the brain against a G force, a blackout will result. And, of course, the most serious source of stagnate hypoxia is when the heart stops pumping altogether. This will cause the oxygen to be stranded at the station, while the cells throughout the body begin to die.

Finally, what if the train pulled up to the station platform, the doors opened, but there were absolutely no people to get on board. Eventually, the doors close and the train moves on, but with no oxygen at all. This lack of oxygen is called *anoxia*, which leads to suffocation.

Effects of hypoxia and TUC

No matter which type of hypoxia a pilot might be exposed to, reversing the trend immediately is vitally important. The problem is that hypoxia can sneak up on a pilot. The symptoms might be so subtle that the pilot is unaware of the danger until it is too late. It is possible for a pilot to lose consciousness and therefore be unable to take life-saving action. The time span from first exposure to hypoxic conditions until unconsciousness is called the *time of useful conscience* (TUC). The TUC varies from person to person and from altitude to altitude, but the following table shows the averages:

Altitude above MSL	TUC w/o activity	TUC w/ activity
22,000	10 minutes	5 minutes
25,000	5 minutes	3 minutes
30,000	1 minute	45 seconds
35,000	45 seconds	30 seconds
40,000	25 seconds	18 seconds

These times are shockingly fast. If a pilot is exposed to an altitude of 30,000 feet while sitting quietly in the airplane, on a good day he or she has only 45 seconds to figure out what to do. Solving this problem will require some quick action and thought, but response time and clear thinking are among the first faculties to be robbed by hypoxia. A pilot really only has about 15 seconds to effect some sort of corrective action before he or she will no longer be able to think straight.

Hypoxia is hard to self-diagnose. The symptoms that tell the pilot of the onset of their own hypoxia vary from person to person. Some common symptoms are the following:

- Tingling in fingers and toes
- Reduced peripheral vision
- Exhaustion and fatigue
- Warm or cold sensations
- Dizziness
- Perspiration

- Weak muscles and sluggish movements
- Loss of muscle coordination
- Slurred speech
- Change of attitudes: overaggressive, overconfident, or timid
- Euphoria

Each person will experience different symptoms and in a different order. I placed "tingling in fingers and toes" first on the list because that happens to be my first hypoxia symptom, but it might not be your first symptom. It is very important to know what symptom your body will display first, second, and third so that when these symptoms do occur, you can start getting on oxygen.

The only way to learn what your hypoxic symptoms are and the order the symptoms present themselves is to experience hypoxia. The safest place to do this is during a joint FAA-Military-NASA sponsored physiological training program. The programs are available to any person who is at least 18 years old and holds a current airman medical certificate. The course consists of classroom lectures on physiological topics such as hypoxia, vision, disorientation, and survival. The focus of the training is a "flight" to high altitude in an altitude chamber. The following is a list of facilities that offer the course:

- FAA Aeronautical Center, Oklahoma City
- Andrews AFB, Maryland
- Barbers Point NAS, Hawaii

- Beale AFB, Texas
- Brooks AFB, Texas
- Brunswick NAS, Maine
- Cherry Point MCAS, North Carolina
- Columbus AFB, Mississippi
- Edwards AFB, California
- Ellsworth AFB, California
- El Toro AFB, California
- Fairchild AFB, Washington
- Jacksonville NAS, Florida

- Laughlin AFB, Texas
- Lemoore NAS, California
- Little Rock AFB, Arkansas

- MacDill AFB, California
- Mather AFB, California
- NASA Johnson Space Center, Texas
- Norfolk NAS, Virginia
- Patuxent River NAS, Maryland
- Pease AFB, New Hampshire
- Peterson AFB, Colorado

- Point Mugu NMC, California
- Reese AFB, Texas
- San Diego NAS, California
- Sheppard AFB, Texas
- Vance AFB, Oklahoma
- Whidbey Island NAS, Washington
- Williams AFB, Arizona
- Wright AFB, Arizona
- Wright-Patterson AFB, Ohio

Figure 9-4 is a copy of my own physiological training card from Cherry Point NAS, near the coast of North Carolina. To schedule a course you must first contact your nearest Flight Standards District Office of the FAA and receive an application for the training. The pilot then sends the application to the Mike Monroney Aeronautical Center in Oklahoma City for processing.

PHYSIOLOGICAL TRAINING

This is to certify that the following person has met the requirements for the Physiological Training Program as prescribed by the Federal Aviation Administration.

NAME

AIRMAN CERTIFICATE NUMBER

DATE OF TRAINING

PHYSIOLOGICAL TRAINING UNIT

SIGNATURE OF PHYSIOLOGICAL TRAINING OFFICER

FAA Form 3150–1   (3–67)

Fig. 9-4. *Certificate for completion of the physiological training course.*

The course costs $20.00. The courses are taught to about 20 people at a time, so the individual sites where the course is offered collect the applications until they have enough for a course to be scheduled. Applicants are notified of a course date within 30 to 60 days after applying.

I have taken student groups for this physiological training for many years and have learned some very valuable tips. You should plan to go with a group. Consider taking a CAP chapter, flight school members, or the entire charter department. By scheduling an entire group, you will not have to wait long for a class date. If you put just one or two names in, you will have to wait until 18 others have also signed up. That might take some time and planning might be difficult.

Second, do not even think about going into the altitude chamber unless you are feeling good, have eaten well for a few days, had plenty of sleep the night before, and do not have a head cold! Last, plan to stay overnight after the class in the city where the class is given. Do not attempt to drive several hours home after a bout with full-blown hypoxia. The chamber will make a believer out of any skeptic that hypoxia is serious. Hypoxia leaves you spent and worn out. Afterwards, you will want to do nothing but eat, sleep, and feel normal again.

The chamber is a long, narrow, mobile home-sized box with thick windows. The students and instructors climb in and sit down at various stations inside. Each station has an oxygen mask. Great care is taken by the instructors inside and to observers outside to ensure safety. When everything is ready, the air is slowly sucked out of the chamber to simulate high altitude. While everyone is on oxygen, the instructors give several demonstrations of altitude effects.

The chamber eventually arrives at the target high altitude. This is where the fun begins. Half the students in the room are instructed to take off their masks and perform simple duties such as writing on a tablet, stacking blocks, playing patty-cake, or inserting pegs through a hole.

The hypoxia effects are almost immediate. I have seen students continue writing without the pencil ever touching the paper. I have also seen students, who only moments before had normal coordination, slap each other instead of each other's hand in a game of patty-cake. Smokers drop like flies. I even saw one pilot attempt to punch an instructor. Later, the pilot said that he thought the instructor was coming to take his mask away, when in reality, he was coming to replace the mask. Hypoxia had completely stolen his ability to see what was actually taking place.

Each station is numbered, and an outside observer is assigned to watch the person through the windows at that station. When the observer thinks the student has had enough, he or she radios, for instance, "Get number 7!" to the inside instructor.

Later, the second half of the room gets their shot at hypoxia. When it's all over, air is slowly added to the room to simulate a descent back down to real-world pressure.

Once outside the chamber, you can review the symptoms and the order of the symptoms that overcame you at altitude. It seems that everyone has a different first symptom, but we are all in agreement that we would hate to be in that condition and still be required to fly an airplane. The instructors and doctors keep you around for about an hour after leaving the chamber just to make sure there are no additional effects of the altitude change.

OTHER HIGH-ALTITUDE SICKNESSES

The effects of low atmospheric pressure can be harmful and even painful on other parts of the body. Whenever you climb to higher altitudes, the atmosphere that is inside the body will want to come out. If this expanding gas ever gets trapped and cannot get out, the pilot will experience discomfort and pain. This air is all through the body and can cause several problems.

Air exists inside the middle ear behind the eardrum. A small tube called the *eustachian* connects the middle ear with the nasal cavity. When we climb, the air inside the ear starts experiencing more pressure than the air outside. Eventually, the air comes out and equalizes. We say that our ears have "popped." When we descend, the air pressure outside will start increasing, and the air will want to go back into the ear through the tube to equalize.

A problem arises when the eustachian tube becomes blocked. This can happen when you get a head cold and the air pressure cannot equalize naturally. Even with a head cold, the ear usually pops on the way up because the small pocket of air works its way out from inside. But the air has a harder time going back through the swollen tube. Therefore, coming down can be painful and hearing can be affected. The medical term for this is *barotitis*.

The same type of problems exist with *barosinusitis*, which is a blockage of the sinuses due to nasal congestion, and *barodontalgia*, which is tooth pain. Gum or root abscess and air trapped behind a tooth filling can cause great pain. If you experience any unusual tooth pain when flying, see a dentist and tell him or her you are a pilot. Last, pain and cramps can be caused by expanding gases anywhere in the digestive system.

CAUSES AND EFFECTS OF GAS EXPANSION AND BUBBLE FORMATIONS

One of the most dangerous potential effects of high altitudes is decompression sickness. As indicated earlier in this chapter, the atmosphere is made up of more than just oxygen. The largest portion of the air is nitrogen. Usually the nitrogen that we breath into our bodies gets pushed right back out when we exhale. But some of the nitrogen is absorbed into our tissues. Normally the nitrogen is dissolved into a liquid and held by the cells. This does not cause any problems unless the nitrogen rapidly changes back to a gas in the form of bubbles.

The bubbles form according to Henry's Law, which says that "the amount of gas dissolved in a solution is directly proportional to the partial pressure of the gas over the solution." This law can be observed when you open a soft-drink bottle. When the cap is on the bottle, there are no bubbles in the drink. When you take the cap off, however, the bubbles appear from the drink, and the drink might overflow. When capped, the pressure was contained over the soft drink, and this held the gas in the liquid state. But when the pressure was released, there was no force to hold the gas in the liquid state, so it quickly bubbled up.

When this bubbling-up occurs in the tissues throughout the body, it can cause decompression sickness, or "the bends." This extremely painful, potentially fatal disorder is associated with scuba diving as well as flying. When a diver comes up to the surface, the pressure changes on the body from heavy pressure under water to reduced pressure above water. Pilots likewise travel from high pressure at sea level to reduced pressure at altitude.

These gas bubbles will first become evident in the joints. Bending the joints seems to give temporary pain relief, hence the name. In severe cases the victim will experience pain in the chest and begin to cough. There will be the feeling of "air hunger." The gas bubbles in the skin might cause tingling, itching, and rashes. Finally, the bubbles can affect the central nervous system, causing sight problems, loss of muscle control, seizures, and paralysis.

The treatment for decompression sickness is recompression. For the pilot, this means quickly getting to a lower altitude. Usually symptoms will subside when the pressure is increased. If they continue, however, an airman medical examiner should be contacted. The examiner might recommend that the victim be treated in a repressurization chamber.

The altitude chamber, discussed earlier as the means to induce hypoxia, draws air out of a chamber. A repressurization chamber is just the opposite; it blows air in and holds it like a balloon that cannot expand. This additional pressure around the body will force the gas bubbles back into the liquid state.

As if you did not need another reason to lose weight, fatty tissue contains more nitrogen than all other tissue. So being overweight makes decompression sickness a greater threat. In addition, mixing flight after scuba diving is a very bad idea. You or anyone you fly with should wait an adequate length of time between diving and flying.

VISION

Finally, vision is affected at high altitude. The higher you climb, the farther from moisture and the associated haze you get. Without haze acting as a filter, the sky seems to be darker and the sun's rays are more intense. Because the sky is darkened, shadow areas in the cockpit are even harder to see, while sunlit areas are more glaring. When you are flying in bright sunlight, shaded instrument panels with overhanging dashboards might make instruments unreadable.

All this makes wearing the proper sunglasses important. Do not wear the type of glasses that change with illumination. The glasses won't know what to change to when you are looking at both dark and brightly lit areas. Dark, single-color, graded-density sunglasses will cut down on the glare yet not black out the shaded areas.

The anatomy of the eye is also affected by high altitude. The eye requires large doses of oxygen to work properly, especially at night. The eye is able to see because it uses a film called the *retina* to transfer light to nerve impulses that the brain can interpret. The retina actually has two types of film: daytime and nighttime. The daytime films are called *cones*, and humans, because they have adapted to daylight, have more of these than other creatures. The nighttime films are the *rods*. Rods produce a light-sensitive substance called *rhodopsin*, or visual purple, that aids in night vision.

The production of rhodopsin requires oxygen. Since we do not rely on rhodopsin in the day, oxygen is less critical in the daylight. But at night our vision is greatly diminished when we have a reduced oxygen supply, as would be the case at higher altitudes. Pilots flying at night need supplemental oxygen at lower altitudes than during the day, or they can plan to fly lower at night (obstruction clearance provided, of course).

FLIGHT TRAINING

The flight portion of the high-altitude operations training required for the endorsement must be conducted in an airplane that has a service ceiling or maximum operating altitude (whichever is lower) above 25,000 feet, or in a simulator that meets the requirements of FAR 121.407. The simulator referred to here is not a basic desktop or motionless ground trainer. Its exact qualities are quite lengthy; however, essentially they are simulators of specific airplane types and versions of types (Boeing 737-400, for instance). We'll discuss simulators at greater length in chapter 13.

FAR 61.31(f)(1)(ii) requires the following to be a part of the flight lessons:

- Normal cruise flight operations above 25,000 feet MSL
- Proper emergency procedures for simulated rapid decompression without actually depressurizing the airplane
- Emergency descent procedures

Like any other lesson, a high-altitude flight lesson should follow a plan. The instructor should begin with a review of the ground school topics and an overview of the upcoming flight. The preflight briefing should allow time for questions from the students. Plenty of time, possibly divided over several sessions, should be allocated to cover the actual airplane systems in general and those specific systems designed for high-altitude operations.

Before flight the high-altitude weather should be discussed, including the wind, position of the jet stream if applicable, and pilot reports about clear air turbulence. A vertical flight profile should be covered that would include the climb to altitude; the use of supplemental oxygen; the pressurization controls and instruments; regulations pertaining to Mode C transponder use, distance measuring equipment, and altimeter settings; fuel management; and the planned descent. The lesson should cover all that would be involved in a normal flight from one airport to another via a high altitude.

During the flight the airplane procedures for climb to altitude should be followed. When climbing above 12,500 feet in nonpressurized airplanes, supplemental oxygen requirements should be met. When climbing through 18,000 feet, the altimeter should be set on 29.92" Hg and left at that setting until descent back through 18,000 feet. Passing above 18,000 feet, you will be entering the Positive Control Area, so unless you have some authorization otherwise, you must be on an IFR flight plan. Above 18,000 feet, the term "flight level" is used, and altitude designations change from 21,000 feet to Flight Level 210. Above Flight Level 240, the airplane is required to have DME. Above Flight Level 250, a pilot in command is required who has the high-altitude endorsement in his or her logbook.

Simulated emergencies should be conducted as well. In order to achieve the high-altitude endorsement you must complete at least one simulated rapid decompression and emergency descent. This simulation does not have to begin above FL 250; it can be performed at any safe altitude. The cabin does not have to be depressurized in the simulation. Real decompression is simply too dangerous for simulated training purposes, but everything else should be done. Pilots should use the quick-donning oxygen masks, activate the supplemental oxygen, reconfigure the airplane as guided by the manufacturer for the emergency descent, and get down fast. Pilots should consider aircraft speed and engine cooling limitations on the way down.

Finally after the flight, the student and instructor should review the flight step by step. The accomplishment of a high-altitude endorsement might take more than one flight. This decision is made by the flight instructor. The high-altitude endorsement that is recommended, Advisory Circular 61-65, says:

> I have given Mr./Mrs. _____, holder of pilot certificate number
> _____, the ground and flight instruction on high-altitude operations required by FAR 61.31 (f).

The endorsing instructor must then date and sign the endorsement, together with their flight instructor certificate number and expiration date.

Any flight instructor with a high-altitude endorsement can give the ground and flight instruction required by FAR 61.31(f)(1) and make high-altitude endorsements like the one above in students' logbooks.

PRESSURIZATION SYSTEMS

If going up so high takes humans out of their natural habitat with the result being hypoxia, decompression sickness, and worse, why do we go? Aside from the possible increased groundspeed from high tailwinds, the answer is fuel economy and best engine operation. Turbine engines are most efficient when they turn near their highest continuous speed and upper limit of their temperature range. This highest engine RPM and temperature would ordinarily thrust the airplane faster than is safe.

So where can the engine be run at maximum speed yet provide thrust that will be within speed limitations? Only where thrust is reduced because of reduced air density. And where is the air density reduced? High altitude, of course. So up high is great for the turbine engine, but potentially deadly to the airplane's occupants.

The solution is to simply reproduce a high-pressure atmosphere artificially inside the airplane. This is done by blowing air into the cabin continuously. When you blow up a balloon, the air pressure inside the balloon rises, but the air is also trapped. If we "blew up" the cabin of an airplane this way, we would increase pressure, but soon there would be problems. The system must provide circulation and continuous fresh air for the breathers (occupants) inside.

Imagine a balloon that is continuously being blown up from one end while a pinhole releases air out the back side. The pressure inside the balloon would be both increased and circulating. This is the basic idea behind an airplane pressurization system.

More air is blown into the cabin than is released. The air comes from either an engine-driven turbocharger or from a turbine engine's compressor section. The inflow is constant. The outflow is regulated by a valve. When the valve is open wide, as shown in Fig. 9-5, more air will be released through the opening, and the cabin pressure will be reduced. When the valve narrows, the air cannot get out as quickly, and the pressure goes up. The mechanism that operates the valve varies from system to system. Some systems use differential pressure, some are electric, but all do the same thing: they let less air out than gets in.

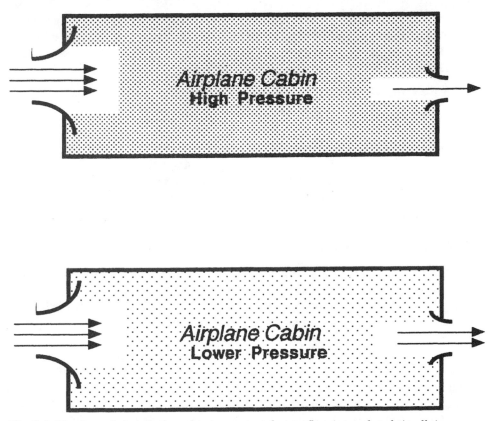

Fig. 9-5. *The flow of air into the cabin is constant, but outflow is regulated. At all times more air is going in than is coming out.*

Pressurized airplanes usually fly very high where outside air temperatures are extremely cold. This being said, why do these airplanes have air-conditioners instead of heaters? Heaters really are not necessary because compressed air becomes very warm. When air molecules are sealed in a container, they fly around. What keeps a balloon inflated are the constant inner-wall impacts of the contained air molecules. The air pressure inside is just a measure of the force of internal air-molecule wall impacts. The molecules not only bounce off the interior walls of the container, they ricochet off each other. When they collide with each other, friction is produced, generating heat. This is why, as discussed earlier, it is warmer at low elevations and cooler at higher elevations.

Now think about the increased collisions and, therefore, increased friction produced when air molecules are jammed together in a container against their will. They get hot. In fact, the air from the blowers would be so hot, humans would no longer be able to function. To cool down the compressed air to more comfortable levels, the air is first passed through an intercooler. The intercooler is an air-flow radiator. Cool outside air circulates around the lines carrying the pressurized air. In addition airplanes use Freon-type air conditioners to further cool the inflowing air.

Today's pressurization systems can maintain safe cabin pressures even when the engines are operating at low RPM. Instrumentation allows the pilot to compare the outside cruise pressure with the inside cabin pressure. Additional controls can vary the rate at which the pressure changes so that transition is smooth and comfortable. Consult an instructor who knows the specific pressurization system of the airplane to be flown. Study and follow all the manufacturer's recommendations as outlined in the airplane's approved flight manual.

SUPERCHARGERS AND TURBOCHARGERS

The purpose of both supercharging and turbocharging is to allow an engine to produce its maximum power even when operating at high altitudes. Just like the human body needs air under pressure to operate properly, so does the engine. As we climb to heights where the air is thin, the engine cannot produce the power it could at sea level.

Figure 9-6 illustrates two identical pistons and cylinders. Cylinder A has a dense population of air molecules because it is at sea level. Cylinder B has the same inside volume, but because it is represented at high altitude, the population of air molecules is sparse. During the cylinder's power stroke, the expanding air moves the piston, which then moves the propeller. When the air is sparse, the power is sparse.

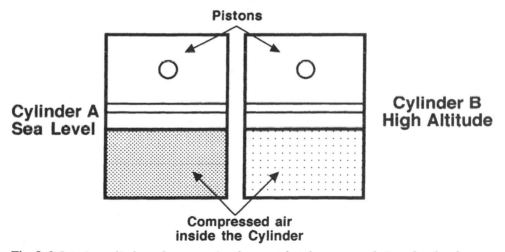

Fig. 9-6. *Interior cylinder volume remains the same, but the amount of air molecules that fill the space decreases with altitude.*

Many systems have been invented to cheat nature and add air pressure to the engine when the outside air pressure is reduced by high altitude. In every system some form of air blower or air pump attempts to "inflate" the engine's cylinders in order to increase or at least maintain sea-level power.

Superchargers and turbochargers do the same thing: increase air pressure to the engine cylinders. The difference between the two is in how this increase in pressure is produced. Superchargers use energy directly from the engine's crankshaft to turn a device that pumps air—an *impeller*. A turbocharger also uses an impeller, but the energy to turn the impeller comes from exhaust gases, not directly from the crankshaft.

Superchargers

Figure 9-7 is a generic supercharger system. This diagram is by no means a technical drawing, but rather a concept drawing of how a supercharger system works. The airplane's propeller is turned by the crankshaft. The crankshaft turns when it is pushed by the piston/connecting rod combination. The piston is pushed down by the burning and, therefore, expanding gases of the air/fuel mixture.

The problem is that when the air portion of the air/fuel mixture begins to diminish, the power begins to diminish. The supercharger attempts to solve this problem by attaching an impeller to the back of the crankshaft. The air/fuel mixture coming through the carburetor is led into the impeller. The impeller is spinning, and when the air/fuel mixture comes in contact with the impeller, the air/fuel molecules are slung out in all directions.

The impeller spins in a housing that catches the air/fuel as it speeds up and travels away from the impeller. The air is collected and channeled toward the cylinders. The air/fuel mixture enters the impeller housing at about atmospheric or ambient air pressure but leaves the impeller at a pressure that is much higher than ambient. The engine cylinders are now being fed air at a pressure that simulates a lower altitude. This enables the engine to retain its power and fly to higher altitudes.

The supercharger impeller does put an additional strain on the engine. Anytime you attach an accessory to be driven off the engine, it adds to the friction horsepower of the engine. Friction horsepower reduces the engine's ultimate horsepower that could be used to produce thrust. Magnetos, oil pumps, fuel pumps, alternators, tachometers, and vacuum pumps are all common examples of accessories that are run from the engine. We must pay a power penalty for each one. But is the benefit of the item greater than the penalty? Turning the supercharger impeller has its price, but the benefit of the compressed air to the cylinders far outweighs the penalty. An impeller gives back more than it takes.

Between the crankshaft and the impeller is a gear train. To provide the advantage of compressed air, the impeller must turn faster than the engine, so the gear ratio is high. There have been some impellers that turn at the same speed as the engine, but no compressed air was provided. Called a *distribution impeller*, this system simply mixes the air/fuel better.

To produce above-ambient air pressures, the impeller must turn faster than the crankshaft. Many system variations have been developed to do this job. Some systems have more than one impeller speed. In other words, they have a first and second gear. First gear is used for the initial climb when only a 3:1 ratio is required to produce full power. At high altitude, however, second gear is used, and its 5:1 ratio continues to allow for full power. These ratios given here are examples only; every system is somewhat different.

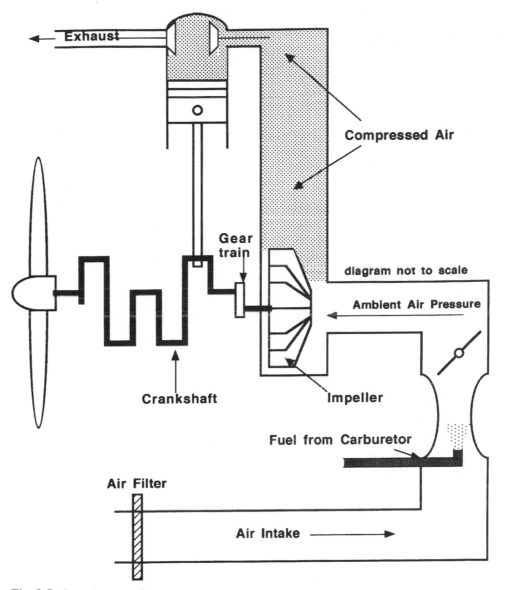

Fig. 9-7. *Generic supercharger system.*

When air pressure is increased by an impeller, this is called a *stage*. Some systems have more than one stage and, therefore, more than one impeller. A multistage system would compress air several times, making every effort to reach maximum pressure.

As the impeller turns faster, its friction with the incoming air/fuel molecules causes heat. This heat is carried on by the air/fuel mix. Also, when air is compressed, heat is produced because molecules collide with each other more often. The two heat sources, friction with the impeller and friction with tightly packed air molecules, can

151

affect the combustibility of the air/fuel mixture. If the mix gets too hot too early, this will adversely affect the power stroke.

To solve this problem some systems will run the hot, compressed mixture through an intercooler. The intercooler, like those described in the previous section on pressurization, is simply an air radiator. The hot, compressed air is passed through tubes. The outside of the tubes have cool air, usually just ram air, circulating around them. This transfers some heat out of the compressed air and away with the ram air. The air/fuel mixture then is prepared for use in the cylinders. The pressure is higher than ambient and the temperature is under control.

Turbochargers

Although the actual term is *turbosupercharger*, the shorter form, *turbocharger*, is used throughout the industry. By either name, this system provides compressed air to the engine cylinders but does not attach to the crankshaft. Instead, the energy of the hot exhaust gases is used. Normally, exhaust gases are just thrown overboard. But these gases contain heat, and heat is energy, so why not design a system that will use that heat energy? The turbocharger does just that: it recycles energy.

Figure 9-8 looks rather complicated at first glance, but it can be broken down into parts that are easily understood. (Again, this is a concept diagram, not a technical drawing.) Shown are the flow of air, the flow of fuel, and the flow of oil. The airflow enters the diagram at lower right, is compressed by an impeller, eventually is combined with fuel and burned in the engine cylinder (top middle of diagram), and then the exhaust is tossed out. Before the exhaust is tossed out, however, it passes over and turns a turbine (lower left of the diagram). The turbine wheel is connected by a shaft to the impeller. The impeller turns to compress the air and the cycle starts over again.

The system sounds great; it's almost like getting something for nothing. Unfortunately, there are problems. If the compressed air produces more power, we also would get more exhaust. More exhaust would turn the turbine wheel faster. Because they are connected, a faster turbine wheel would make the compressor impeller go even faster. A faster impeller means even more air pressure. More pressure means more power and even more exhaust, which would result in still faster turbine wheel speeds, which would . . .

You can see the possibility that the system would "run away." The pressure would become greater and greater until eventually the pressure would be more than the engine could handle. Something would have to give.

For the turbocharger to work safely, the speed of the turbine wheel must be controllable. This is accomplished by using a *waste gate*. The waste gate is located between the cylinder's exhaust valve and the turbine wheel. When the speed of the turbine needs to be reduced, the waste gate opens and the exhaust gases are dumped out early. When the gate is open, the majority of the gases bypass the turbine wheel and the wheel slows down. When the gate is closed, most of the gases will reach the wheel and it will increase its speed. Figure 9-8 shows the waste gate partially open so that some gases get out and some get to the wheel. The gate never completely closes for fear that it might get stuck closed.

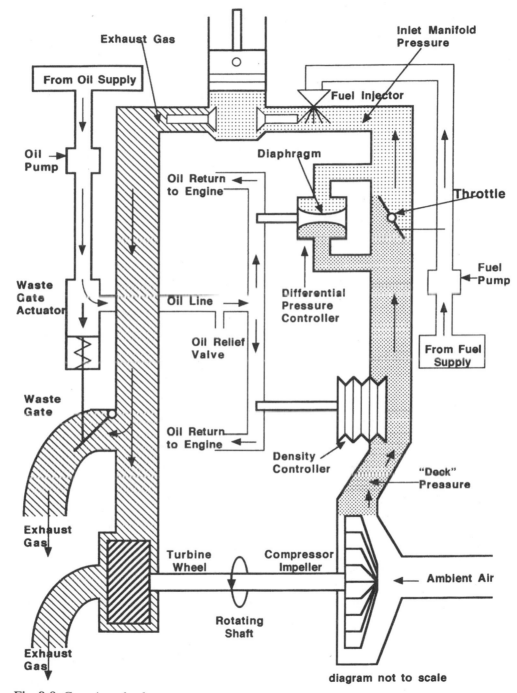

Fig. 9-8. *Generic turbocharger system.*

So the waste gate, by its opening and closing, controls the speed of the turbine wheel and prevents runaway. How does the waste gate know when to open, when to close, and when to remain partially open? The pilot does not control the waste gate manually; the position of the waste gate is dictated by two devices that monitor the air's pressure. The brains of the system are the density controller and the differential pressure controller.

As its name implies, the *density controller* monitors the density of the air as it leaves the compressor and before the air reaches the throttle valve. The pressure of the air as it comes out from the compressor impeller is called *deck pressure*. The density controller measures both the temperature and air pressure of the deck. It is actually a bellows that can expand or contract. The bellows is exposed to the deck pressure that will enter the engine. When temperature increases, the bellows, usually filled with dry nitrogen, expand. When pressure increases, the bellows contract. The expansion or contraction of the bellows is connected to an oil valve.

The flow of oil in the system is not used for lubrication, but rather for movement of the waste gate. Oil comes from the engine and is pumped to the waste gate actuator. Inside the actuator the oil is pressed up against a wall with a spring behind it. If the oil pressure is stronger than the spring, the wall will be pushed back and a rod will close the waste gate (see Fig. 9-8). If the oil pressure is weaker than the spring, the wall will move with the spring and the rod will pull open the waste gate. Coming out of the actuator, the oil passes through a line. The line branches off and one path takes the oil to the density controller.

If the deck pressure gets too low for the engine to produce full power, the bellows expand. This expansion causes the mechanism of the density controller to block the flow of oil. When the oil flow is blocked, or restricted, the oil pressure begins to back up in the oil lines. Oil is a liquid and, therefore, cannot be compressed, so when pressure is increased on the oil, something has to give. The spring in the waste gate actuator is what gives first. The spring is pushed back by the pent-up oil pressure, and the waste gate is closed.

With the waste gate closed, more exhaust gases are directed to the turbine. The turbine wheel and compressor impeller both speed up, and the deck pressure to the engine is increased. The low pressure problem is solved, and now deck pressure is high enough to produce full power.

If the deck pressure ever got too high, the opposite reaction would take place. High pressure would contract the bellows. The mechanism would release oil pressure back to the engine. The release of oil would relieve pressure back at the actuator, and the spring would expand. This would open the waste gate and vent exhaust gases away from the turbine wheel. The wheel and compressor impeller would both slow down and the deck pressure would reduce to an acceptable level.

This all works great, but there is another problem. The density controller opens or closes the waste gate with relation to full power. What about the times when the pilot brings the throttle back and wants to fly with partial power, as for a cruise power setting? When partial power is desired, the density controller blocks the oil flow because the bellows is not sensing full power. To get around this situation, the *differential pressure controller* takes over.

When the throttle valve is wide open, the pressure before and after the throttle valve is the same. During this situation, the density controller regulates turbine wheel speed. But when the throttle valve is partially closed across the airflow passage, this will block some air pressure (see Fig. 9-8). In this case the air pressure before and after the throttle is different. The "before" pressure is the deck pressure, and the "after" pressure is the *inlet manifold pressure*.

The differential pressure controller has two vents, one to the deck (before throttle) pressure and one to the inlet (after throttle) pressure. The vents lead to a chamber that is divided with a flexible diaphragm. If the deck pressure becomes higher than the inlet pressure, the diaphragm will bulge in the direction of the inlet pressure. This bulge will open an oil valve and release oil pressure back to the engine. The release of oil pressure will reduce the tension back on the actuator spring, opening the waste gate. When the waste gate opens, more exhaust gases will bypass the turbine wheel and it will reduce speed. This also reduces the speed of the compressor impeller, which will reduce the deck pressure back to a desired level.

Remember that if the deck pressure gets too high, the dangerous cycle of overpressurization could start, so the differential pressure controller acts to open the waste gate and prevent the problem. If the deck pressure ever gets too low, the lack of diaphragm movement will block the oil flow, which will increase oil pressure, compress the spring, and close the waste gate. A closed waste gate increases turbine and impeller speed, which will increase deck pressure and solve the problem.

The system also has an oil relief valve that will open and protect the system if everything should ever get blocked (see Fig. 9-8). The spring in the waste gate actuator should give way and move before the relief valve is pushed open. But the relief valve is provided to save the system if for some reason the waste gate actuator or spring ever gets stuck.

As you can see, oil is a very important part of this system's operation. The same oil that is used for internal engine lubrication is also circulated through the turbocharger system. For this reason, the proper oil level and adequate engine oil warm-up time is essential.

The fuel flow portion of the system is on the right side of Fig. 9-8. The fuel comes from the fuel tanks and is pushed through the lines by an engine-driven fuel pump. Some airplane might also have an electric fuel pump that is used as a backup and during critical phases of flight such as takeoff and landing. The flow of fuel after the pump is dictated by the airflow past the throttle. The fuel is injected into the high-pressure air in the proper proportion at or near the cylinder's intake valve. The flow of fuel is continuous even though the intake valve is not open all the time.

Shown in Fig. 9-8 is an extremely simplified view of the fuel metering device. As the throttle opens and more air passes through, more fuel is also allowed to pass through. When the throttle is closed and, therefore, airflow is restricted, the fuel flow is also restricted. This raising and lowering of flows should ensure that the proper ratio of air and fuel get together at the intake valve.

HIGH-ALTITUDE OPERATIONS

You should notice that the supercharger increased the pressure of both the air and the fuel together, while the turbocharger increases the air alone. The use of compressor impeller and fuel injection together offers many advantages. The delivery of fuel in the proper proportion to the compressed air is more accurate with fuel injection, and there is faster response from the throttle during an emergency go-around situation.

Of course, there is a limit to how high you can fly even with superchargers and turbochargers. Every engine has a critical altitude. Above this critical altitude the engine's power will gradually diminish. For engines that do not have either supercharging or turbocharging, the critical altitude is the airport's elevation, because the engine's performance begins to fade right away. For supercharged engines the critical altitude is reached when the compressor impeller is turning as fast as it can go, yet only sea-level pressure can be produced. A climb any higher than this will yield less than sea-level pressures in the engine even at maximum impeller speed.

For turbocharged engines the critical altitude is reached when the waste gate is closed as far as it can go. This dumps almost all the exhaust gases into the turbine and will produce the fastest turbine speed. A climb higher than this will leave the turbine behind. The engine will ask for more pressure, but with the waste gate already closed, the turbine is doing all it can do. The deck pressure will gradually decrease with the climb even though the turbine and compressor are going as fast as they can go. Eventually all three engine examples (normally aspirated, supercharged, and turbocharged) will reach an altitude where no more excess horsepower can be produced.

Excess horsepower is the extra power needed to climb. When there is zero excess horsepower, the airplane cannot climb any higher. This is called the *absolute ceiling* of the airplane.

High altitude is yet another of the great challenges of flight—especially multi-engine flight. Like most all areas of flying, it is not dangerous as long as you are prepared to meet the new challenge. Seek the instruction of a qualified instructor who will take the time to cover all required areas and resolve all your questions.

10
Cockpit resource management

COCKPIT RESOURCE MANAGEMENT (CRM) HAS INCORRECTLY BEEN considered a "big airplane" concern. A distinction should be made between crew resource management and cockpit resource management. Traditionally, CRM was a topic involving several people working together on a flight deck. For those of us who fly single-pilot airplanes, CRM did not seem necessary; you have no need for crew coordination if there is no crew. CRM to the single pilot once was nothing more than folding your charts correctly before takeoff and having the next radio frequency stored. That notion of single-pilot CRM is simply not up to date.

The idea of CRM is to effectively combine all resources available to the pilot so that the greatest safety and efficiency can be maintained. What is a resource? A resource is any person, reference manual, chart, or aircraft system that provides information or assistance to pilots in doing their job. Of course, the pilot's job is to operate the airplane with safety, which comes from complete situational awareness.

The pilot in command is an orchestra conductor. The string section, woodwinds, and percussion instruments are all the conductor's resources that must be blended together in the correct proportions to make the music. In the final analysis, it is the conductor that uses all the different parts, together with his or her own experience and judgment, to make the work excellent.

The goal of CRM is to reach a synergy. Synergy is a system where the output of all of its parts is greater than the sum of its parts. In other words, if two people working together can produce more in cooperation than they could working individually, a synergy is achieved.

Our aviation heritage is very anti-synergy. The image of the single-pilot hero-warrior became part of the romance of flight. When you are flying an airplane all alone with no outside contact, you have only yourself to rely on. This self-reliance became a way of life and formed the personality of many pilots. If you were Charles Lindbergh flying across the ocean with no copilot, no radio, and no human contact, it was necessary to develop a me-against-the-world attitude. But today that attitude is out of place and dangerous.

Unfortunately, old habits die hard. Many pilots find it difficult to move from a pilot-only system to a pilot-resource system. This is not to say that the responsibility of pilot in command has changed. Whether flying single-pilot or as a captain of a three-person crew, the PIC is the final decision maker. The hope, however, is that those decisions will be informed and will consider all factors involved.

WORKING TOGETHER AS A FLIGHTCREW

Anytime people work together, there are bound to be some conflicts. Most airline interviews contain several questions that are aimed at evaluating the prospective pilot-employees ability to work with a crew. "What would you do if your captain flew below the decision height without having the runway in sight?" "What would you do if you smelled alcohol on your captain's breath?" "What would you do if your captain missed an ATC instruction?" These and many other questions like them attempt to place the applicant in a difficult position—one that might be encountered on the job.

So, how *do* you correct other members of your crew without being combative? How do you change the actions of your captain without undermining the authority of the captain? I suggest you use the phrase: "Captain, I'm not comfortable with. . .". This statement will alert the other pilot to a concern you have without coming across as judgmental. It might be that the other pilot, who has more experience and savvy than you, will now give you a lesson on why the procedure is in fact correct. Or maybe the other pilot will use your statement to change the course of action. The statement gave the other pilot an "out" without accusing the pilot of being wrong.

But what about the single-pilot operation? The important fact to remember is that in today's system, the pilot is never alone. There might only be one pilot in the airplane, but he or she can interact with hundreds of others. Yes, it is important for the pilot to arrange the cockpit efficiently with charts, flashlight, pencil, and clipboard within reach, but CRM is more. It is the effective use of all resources, the largest segment of which is outside the airplane.

IN-FLIGHT COCKPIT MANAGEMENT

Most pilots get weather information by telephone or DUAT, plan their flights, then get in the airplane and never access the weather information system again. They isolate themselves from the wealth of information available on their radio if they only knew how to get it. Pilots even will call in flight plans but be unable to activate the plan once airborne because they do not know how to get into the system.

Many VFR pilots use their radios when departing an airport, but then the radio goes essentially unused for the remainder of the trip. Pilots then fly across the land, listening to downwind reports at distant airports and idle chatter on the unicom frequency when vital information passes them by on the FSS frequencies.

Before takeoff, you should write down the FSS frequencies that you can receive along your route of flight. Then while in flight, monitor the frequency that will do you the most good. In this way, vital decision-making information will come to you. You won't have to scramble for it.

If the weather broadcast in the AIRMETs, SIGMETs, and CWAs (air route traffic control Center Weather Advisories) are so important, why are they only broadcast at certain intervals, allowing for the possibility that a pilot misses an alert? This question is being addressed by a new system that brings all these alerts under one umbrella: the Hazardous Inflight Weather Advisory Service (HIWAS).

HIWAS is a continuous broadcast that summarizes information from all existing AIRMETs, SIGMETs, CWAs, and PIREPs. When a HIWAS alert is issued, the announcement can be heard on all ARTCC, FSS, and airport terminal frequencies. The announcement instructs airborne pilots to contact the continuous HIWAS frequency in their area. The pilot can then switch frequencies (or use the "both" feature of the audio panel) and hear the recorded message.

HIWAS is not yet a nationwide service. In areas where HIWAS has been installed, the local FSS and ARTCCs will stop broadcasting alert messages at time intervals around the clock and rely on the HIWAS system. In your preflight briefing, you should ask if the area along your route of flight has HIWAS service.

If you are monitoring a frequency and an alert is broadcast, your next step is to talk with someone. With the exception of an FSS phone call, all the services discussed thus far involve a pilot listening to a recording or a computer-generated voice. But to get the best information, you need to ask questions unique to your situation.

If hazardous weather is in your area or along your route of flight, you'll be faced with the classic decision: whether to continue the flight as planned, stop at an interim airport, or turn around and go back to where you came from. FAR Part 91.5 speaks to the required pilot action in the event that something causes you to consider changing plans: "For an IFR flight, or for a flight not in the vicinity of an airport. . . [the pilot must familiarize himself with] alternatives available if the planned flight cannot be completed." If while in flight you hear a weather alert or actually see bad weather ahead, you need information immediately to help you make your decision.

The best thing to do is to talk to someone who has access to real-time information. If the situation concerns precipitation and/or thunderstorms, you want to talk to someone who is watching a radar screen. Your first attempt at communicating should be to a flight service station.

The easiest way to contact a flight service station is on a discrete frequency. A *discrete frequency* means that you dial in the correct numbers and broadcast, then in return, the person at the FSS talks back to you on that same frequency. A control tower is another example of a discrete frequency.

These frequencies can be found on the top of a thick-lined FSS information block on a sectional chart (Fig. 10-1). If an FSS and a VOR are co-located, then the entire VOR information block is outlined with a thick line. The frequencies of the FSS are located outside the block on the top thick line. The discrete frequencies are those without the letter *R* beside them.

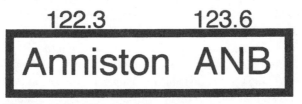

Fig. 10-1. *The FSS "thick line" box.*

Every flight service station has 122.2 and 121.5 as standard frequencies. So even if you could not find the information block, you could try to contact an FSS on 122.2. The emergency frequency is 121.5, and all FSSs listen in on that channel as well.

When you speak to the FSS with the discrete frequency tuned in, you can address them with the term "radio," followed by the name of the FSS. The briefer will reply back to you on the same frequency. Now you can get the valuable information on which to base your decision.

What if, due to the line-of-sight limitations of the VHF radio, you are unable to contact the briefer on the discrete frequency? The answer is certainly not to give up trying to get a personal briefing. You must now fall back to plan B. The FSS system anticipated situations where you would be out of range and designed ways in which the long arm of the FSS could be extended. The range of the FSS and therefore your ability to receive information in flight is extended at certain VOR stations. When a VOR is capable of providing a communications link from your position to the FSS, the VOR information block on the sectional chart will indicate a parent station. Under the VOR block is a bracket. Inside the bracket is the name of the flight service station that monitors that VOR.

Figure 10-2 shows the top of the box, and a frequency is shown with the letter *R* beside it. The *R* stands for "receive." In other words, the FSS can receive your transmission if you talk on the frequency indicated. For this example, the frequency of 122.1 would be placed in the "communications" side of the radio and 115.5 in the "navigation" side of the radio. When you do this, your transmission does not have to travel a long distance to the location of the FSS but only to the nearby VOR.

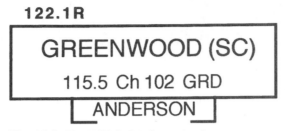

Fig. 10-2. *The VOR link information box.*

Your voice is then relayed by a land line to the FSS. The *land line* is just a dedicated telephone line that is not subjected to line-of-sight limitations, and the message gets through. When the briefer responds to your request, he or she will talk back to you on the navigational frequency of the VOR. Again, the briefer's voice travels over mountains and through valleys on the land line to the VOR, and then through the air to your airplane.

You must remember two things when using this link: (1) Mention to the briefer on which VOR you would like him or her to respond to you and (2) turn up the volume on the navigation side of your radio. Now you can talk on one frequency, and the briefer talks back on the VOR. The valuable communication has now been established over a longer distance.

What if the VOR is out of service or there is no VOR in range that provides the link? You must fall back to plan C. In addition to monitoring VORs, many flight service stations will monitor remote communications outlets (RCOs). The RCO is another radio/land line combination, but it is a discrete frequency and has no navigational function. The RCO is illustrated on sectional charts by a thick blue box with location of the RCO antenna and the letters *RCO*. Figure 10-3 shows an RCO box. The RCO frequency is on the top and the parent station is in the bracket below.

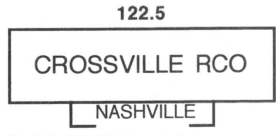

Fig. 10-3. *The RCO information box.*

When you call an RCO frequency, your voice is transmitted through the air to the RCO antenna. Then your voice travels across the land line for the rest of the way to the FSS. The briefer returns the favor, using the land line for the first part of the trip back to the RCO site and then back through the air to your radio. The actual through-the-air part of the transmission can be up to 50 nautical miles, depending on the line of sight.

As the flight service stations consolidate, there will be even more reliance on VOR and RCO communication links.

Air route traffic control centers use RCOs as well. The center's controller might be controlling traffic in an area that is hundreds of miles from the actual location of the center. Just like the FSS, the controller cannot communicate using line-of-sight transmissions across those miles to the place where his or her radar screen has coverage, so the controller uses an RCO that is located somewhere under the radar coverage.

With the direct communication possibilities to a flight service station, together with VOR and RCO relays, the network of coverage is almost nationwide. If you are approximately 3,000 feet AGL or higher, you should be able to use some method to reach weather information. Someday all these communications will be delivered via satellite, and all the present communication links will no longer be necessary. Rather than using land lines to carry voices over mountains and around the curvature of the Earth, we will be able to transmit and receive through an orbiting relay station.

FLIGHT WATCH

If for some reason plans A, B, and C fail to reach a flight service station, you should call the Enroute Flight Advisory Service (EFAS). EFAS goes by another name as well, "Flight Watch." The Flight Watch briefer is an expert in enroute weather; therefore, you should not try to open or close a flight plan on this frequency. The Flight Watch information is no longer shown on sectional charts because now the service is standard nationwide.

Anytime you are flying over the United States at 5,000 feet AGL or higher, you can reach Flight Watch (Fig. 10-4). For flights below 18,000 feet MSL, Flight Watch has a universal frequency: 122.0. If you are not sure which Flight Watch station you are closest to, just call on 122.0 and say "Flight Watch" with your aircraft number.

Basically, the area in which a Flight Watch station has jurisdiction is the same as the ARTCC areas. The Flight Watch specialist is located at an FSS but can communicate by way of RCO over a wide area of responsibility. Flight Watch is usually operated from 6 A.M. until 10 P.M. every day. Complete diagrams of Flight Watch stations and their coverage areas are shown in the Airport/Facility Directory.

The Flight Watch specialist is the "teller" at the bank of pilot reports (PIREPs). The Flight Watch specialist can relay PIREPs, which contain firsthand pilot report information. More often than not, that specialist is the person who recorded the pilot report in the first place. The Flight Watch specialist will often solicit a PIREP from you when you call for information.

When you talk to Flight Watch, you are talking to someone who is looking at all the weather information possible. If you see bad weather ahead on your route of flight, you should call Flight Watch because the person at the other end is already looking at that bad weather on radar. The Flight Watch specialist is in the best position and has the best information to give you decision-making data. How wide is the bad-weather pattern? Which way is it moving? Can I go around the weather safely? If I can go around, which direction is best? When you get the answers to these questions, you'll be able to make important weather-related decisions with confidence.

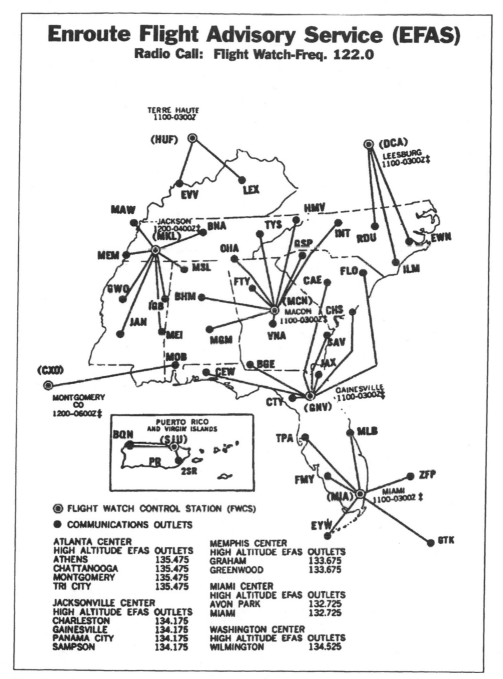

Enroute Flight Advisory Service (EFAS)
Radio Call: Flight Watch-Freq. 122.0

TERRE HAUTE
1100-0300Z

(HUF)

(DCA)
LEESBURG
1100-0300Z‡

EVV   LEX

MAW   HMV

JACKSON   BNA   TYS   INT   RDU
1200-0400Z   EWN
(MKL)

MEM   GSP

GWO   OHA   ILM

FTY   CAE   FLO

fGB   BHM   (MCN)   CHS

JAN   MACON   SAV
1100-0300Z

MEI   MGM   VNA   JAX

MOB   BGE

(CXO)   CEW

CTY   (GNV)   GAINESVILLE
MONTGOMERY   1100-0300Z‡
CO
1200-0600Z‡

PUERTO RICO   MLB
AND VIRGIN ISLANDS   TPA

BQN   (SJU)   FMY   ZFP

PR   (MIA)   MIAMI
2SR   1100-0300Z ‡

EYW   6TK

⊚ FLIGHT WATCH CONTROL STATION (FWCS)
● COMMUNICATIONS OUTLETS

ATLANTA CENTER HIGH ALTITUDE EFAS OUTLETS		MEMPHIS CENTER HIGH ALTITUDE EFAS OUTLETS	
ATHENS	135.475	GRAHAM	133.675
CHATTANOOGA	135.475	GREENWOOD	133.675
MONTGOMERY	135.475		
TRI CITY	135.475	MIAMI CENTER HIGH ALTITUDE EFAS OUTLETS	
		AVON PARK	132.725
JACKSONVILLE CENTER HIGH ALTITUDE EFAS OUTLETS		MIAMI	132.725
CHARLESTON	134.175		
GAINESVILLE	134.175	WASHINGTON CENTER HIGH ALTITUDE EFAS OUTLETS	
PANAMA CITY	134.175		
SAMPSON	134.175	WILMINGTON	134.525

Fig. 10-4. *The "Flight Watch" network.*

Do not forget the radar controllers at the nation's air route traffic control centers, as well as the approach and departure controllers. These people can help find the nearest airport in an emergency, call out precipitation echoes, give you a frequency, tell you

163

a minimum vectoring altitude, or give you any number of other valuable bits of information. Remember, you are pilot in command, and controllers are additional people who work in your crew.

With all these ways to access information, there should never be a time when the pilot is isolated. With all these controllers, briefers, and specialists in your crew, your crew is larger than the flightcrew in the nose of a DC-10. Remember, you are not alone even when you fly alone.

Also, do not forget your maintenance crew members. I recently entered an uncontrolled airport's traffic pattern with a CFI applicant. When he placed the landing gear handle in the DOWN position, the landing gear did not come down. We exited the traffic pattern and ran through the emergency gear extension checklist. The gear was successfully pumped down, and we got a green light on the indicator. We made a normal and uneventful landing, but not before I talked to an A&P mechanic on the unicom frequency. I put that mechanic on my crew even though he was in his office.

Get people involved when there are problems and you have time to talk. The more ideas, the better. You must build situational awareness in order to make the best decisions. People working together have the best opportunity to create situational awareness. This is not piloting by committee. The pilot in command is still in command; we simply want the commander to be well informed.

11
"Glass cockpit" systems

COMPUTERS HAVE INFLUENCED ALL AREAS OF OUR LIVES, AND AIR navigation is no exception. Today in larger airplanes and tomorrow in light airplanes, mechanical flight instruments are being replaced by computer screens. The screens are smaller versions of the monitors of today's personal computers. The screens are small television pictures made of glass, thus the expression, "glass cockpit."

Early in the 1990s this idea of a glass cockpit was reserved for "big" airplanes, but as technology improves and costs come down, the glass cockpit will fill smaller, general aviation airplanes. Already, global positioning systems and "moving maps" have brought a version of the glass cockpit to smaller airplanes; however, much more is on the horizon. Many in the aviation industry hope this technology shift will contribute to a revitalization of the general aviation market.

The general aviation market thrived in the late 1950s through the late 1970s, but has declined steadily ever since. Many factors caused the decline, but the biggest impact was due to product liability. Companies simply chose not to produce many products, from entire airplanes to magnetos, for fear of being sued. These liability concerns drove many manufacturers out of the market or out of business. Since 1978, more than half of the manufacturing jobs in general aviation have been lost. The production of new airplanes dropped year by year, until in 1993, only 800 new general aviation airplanes were built. The picture was very grim.

"GLASS COCKPIT" SYSTEMS

The National Aeronautics and Space Administration (NASA) began an initiative to reverse the trend. NASA, together with the Federal Aviation Administration, universities, and industry representatives, has formed the Advanced General Aviation Transport Experiments (AGATE) consortium. The combined efforts of government, academia, and industry are working on several projects to bring technology and growth back to general aviation.

One of the AGATE projects is the "cockpit concepts" group. Figure 11-1 is an example of the glass cockpit used in general aviation. This concept blends many existing technologies. The pilot would still have some traditional flight instruments, but elements of collision and terrain avoidance systems, weather radar, GPS, NOTAMs, heads-up displays, and engine monitoring would all be combined.

When traveling cross-country, the pilot would have a GPS-provided "moving map" to display position and progress. If hazardous weather was in the area, the boundaries of the weather would be shown on the map display. Circumnavigating the weather or finding an airport to make a precautionary landing would be easy. When other airplanes approached, they would also be displayed on the map, substantially enhancing collision avoidance. The heads-up display will project on the inside of the windshield a series of windows to be flown through on instrument approach. No more relying on needles and dials to conjure up an image of position in the mind. The airplane's horizontal and vertical position will all be seen, not just imagined.

If control towers open or close while the airplane is enroute, this information is passed on to the computer and becomes available to the pilot. The same is true about restricted areas, military training routes, and all types of controlled airspace. The computer will monitor the engines and other airplane systems. If any temperature, pressure, speed, or electrical output should ever exceed a safe range, the computer will display the problem to the pilot, together with a checklist of corrective actions to try.

The system might even have touch-screen and voice interaction between the pilot and the computer. This AGATE concept even has a supplemental restraint system, or air bags. (See the upper right side of the instrument panel shown in Fig. 11-1).

These systems, and the takeoff performance monitoring system (TOPMS) discussed in chapter 2, will become available to general aviation airplanes, and the cost will work its way down. Because of the industry's decline and the gap in general aviation manufacturing, airplanes used to train tomorrow's pilots are still locked in the 1970s. Imagine what a difference bringing 1990s technology to airplanes will do. Think how different your home and office would look today if home/office technology had gotten stuck in the 1970s, as airplane technology did. You would not have fax machines, personal computers, microwave ovens, cellular phones, VCRs, or cable TV with remote controls. Today, I train pilots in airplanes that are older than the students. Imagine how much catching up we have to do and how much pilots will have to learn, beginning now.

If professional flying is your goal, you might transition from airplanes with no new technology to airplanes with completely new technology. This transition can be overwhelming. Flight instructors with whom I have worked have been moving from

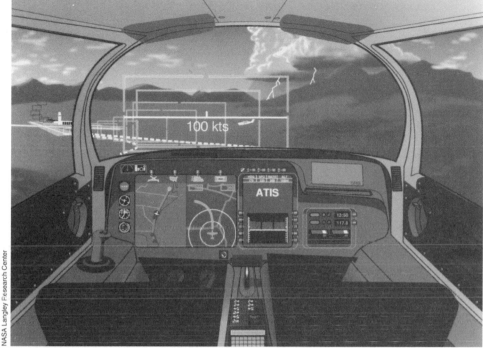

Fig. 11-1. *NASA AGATE general aviation cockpit of the not-so-distant future.*

1981 multiengine airplanes to 1996 glass cockpit airliners overnight. They must play catch-up immediately. On their first day on the job, they are months behind.

The following is a "ground school" on the new technology systems that you will encounter as you climb the aviation career ladder. If you are making this transition in the 1990s, this chapter will help you catch up. If you are flight-training in the future, this technology will be as routine as the magnetic compass is today.

Navigation in the glass cockpit requires a basic understanding of the airplane systems that are providing the pilot with the data. It is also important to understand that navigation in the glass cockpit is not only horizontal or lateral, but vertical as well. The primary purpose of the glass cockpit is to reduce the pilot workload and increase fuel efficiency by integrating a variety of airplane systems. These systems include the flight management computer (FMC), the control display unit (CDU), the autothrottle (A/T), the autopilot flight director system (AFDS), and the inertial reference system (IRS). Integration of these systems is what is known as the flight management system (FMS) (Fig. 11-2).

FLIGHT MANAGEMENT COMPUTER

The flight management computer is a database that contains information relating to the performance and navigation of the airplane. The FMC is accessed by the pilot through the control display unit. By using the CDU, the pilot is able to communicate with the FMC in a compatible language to find the information stored in the databases, and then use the information in a manner that can accomplish the task at hand. The FMC and CDU combined provide the pilot with a flight management tool that performs navigational and performance computations. This is accomplished by accessing the two databases stored in the FMC: the performance database and the navigational database (Fig. 11-3).

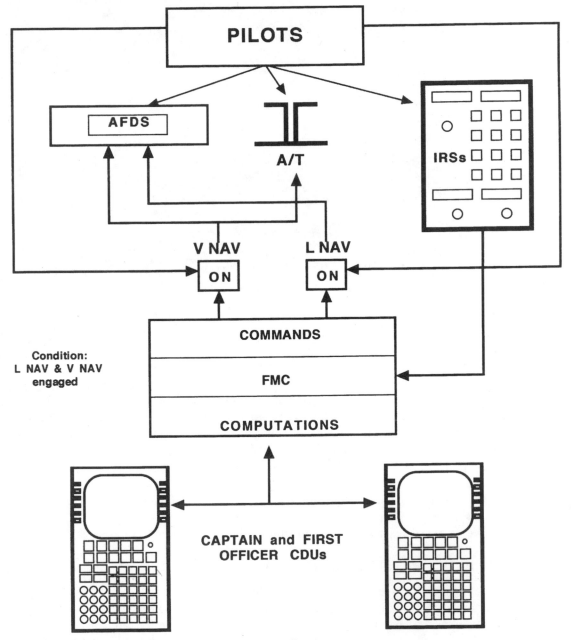

Fig. 11-2. *The flight management system integrates all units.*

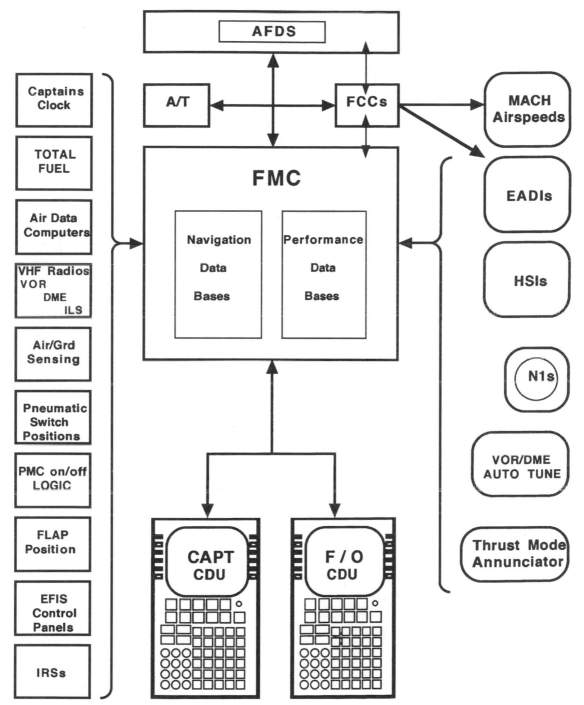

Fig. 11-3. *FMC and CDU interaction.*

"GLASS COCKPIT" SYSTEMS

The purpose of the performance database is to reduce the need for the pilot to refer to the airplane performance manuals. This database also provides thrust-command information to the autothrottles as selected by the FMC or by the pilot. In addition, the performance database is used by the FMC to provide predictions along the entire route of flight, for example, when to step-climb to a higher altitude for increased fuel efficiency.

The performance database contains information relating to the specific airplane and its operating characteristics, along with the average model of the airplane and its engines. Compiled from the design process and flight certification tests, this data has been shown to be accurate in the actual operation of the airplane.

The average database contains information pertaining to climb and cruise performance, maximum and optimum altitudes, certain drag characteristics, and maximum, minimum, and economy airspeeds for different operating conditions. Also in the database is a buffet limit envelope, certificated operating limitations, and altitude and speed of single-engine capability. Information from the performance database is used by the pilot to make decisions about the operation of the airplane.

The performance database, as well as the navigational database, is accessed through an input/output process, allowing the pilot to make entries and receive information based on that particular input. Once the gross weight of the airplane is known by the FMC, an economical climb speed is computed, and an economical altitude is presented, along with an appropriate cruise speed. A descent airspeed is calculated based on weight at the top of descent and the winds aloft. The vertical outputs from the FMC are normally referenced to the best economy profile for climb, cruise, descent, and holding patterns.

Computations of optimum airspeeds for the economy profile are based on a cost index, which is the ratio of operating costs compared to the cost of fuel. Changes in the cost index change the computed optimum airspeeds by the FMC. However, at any time, the pilot can manually select any speed profile other than economy.

The navigation database in the FMC is stored in two parts. One part is active data that is effective until a specific date of expiration. The other part is data to be used for the next period of effectivity. The navigational database is kept up to date by maintenance personnel on a revision cycle that normally coincides with the date of flight manual and chart revisions. Through this method, the data in the FMC is current with the pilot's charts and maps.

The FMC navigational database contains information for all VOR and DME stations in the United States, as well as selected ILS facilities, airports, and runways. Additional information is also stored in the database, such as routes, airways, standard instrument departures (SIDs), standard terminal arrival routes (STARs), and instrument approach procedures.

Depending on the software installed, the database can be applicable to any location in the world. The database is tailored to the specific customer and the areas of operation. The data presented includes most of the information normally obtained from navigational charts, which can be displayed on the CDU or the electronic horizontal situation indicator (EHSI), thereby eliminating the majority of chart reading done in conventional navigation airplanes. (This is not to say charts are to be abandoned in the glass cockpit. However, they are used in a verification process instead of initial course selection.)

The navigation database contains a wealth of information for the pilot. When a pilot enters an airport, the latitude and longitude, station elevation, and magnetic variation of the field are displayed. Upon entering a runway, the latitude and longitude, runway elevation, runway length, and ILS frequency are displayed. When entering a VOR, the frequency, latitude and longitude, elevation, class of VOR, and magnetic variation are all presented to the pilot.

The same information is available for nondirectional beacons. When SIDs and STARs are used, courses, airspeeds and crossing altitudes, and all of the fixes of the transition are presented. For an instrument approach, the inbound course, fixes, and altitudes are made readily available to the pilot.

The FMC and CDU provide the pilot with a tool that performs navigation and performance computations. These computations are both vertical and horizontal. Computations that relate to horizontal or lateral navigation include estimated time of arrival, distance to go, and courses to be flown in accordance with the route or airway. Route segments include published airways, constant headings, or great circle tracks between selected waypoints. Vertical navigation computations include fuel burn data for each phase of flight, when to step-climb to a higher altitude, and airspeeds and altitudes to be flown. All of these items are determined by the FMC and displayed on the CDU.

CONTROL DISPLAY UNIT

The control display unit (Fig. 11-4) is the tool that lets the pilot interact with the FMC. Through the CDU the pilot is able to input required actions to the FMC. The FMC can then perform the task requested by the pilot or inform the pilot via a message why the task cannot be completed. If the request is accepted by the FMC, the task is accomplished and no further communication is required.

The CDU data is displayed to the pilot in the form of pages, which relate to the applicable phase of flight. The pilot can select these pages simply by pushing the button that corresponds to the phase of flight with which the pilot is concerned. The phase of flight selected need not be the one that is currently being flown. For example, during the climb, the pilot can select the cruise page and enter and execute a different cruise airspeed that will become active when the airplane reaches the cruise altitude.

The CDU is used throughout the flight from preflight to parking. During the preflight, the CDU is used to inform the FMC of the route to be flown, altitude selected, requested airspeed if desired by the pilot, gross weight, forecast winds, and latitude and longitude from the inertial reference system (IRS). These entries are the starting point for the FMC and the IRS. After takeoff, the FMC continuously updates the progress of the flight, with all data available through the CDU. Any modification to the progress of the flight can be entered through the CDU.

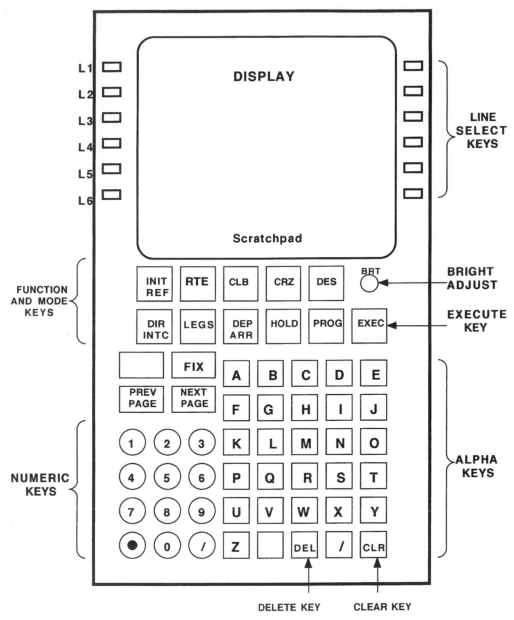

Fig. 11-4. *Control display unit (CDU).*

INERTIAL REFERENCE SYSTEM

The FMC is certified to be accurate within 2 nautical miles per hour when it is in range of accurate VOR/DME facilities. The FMC uses a combination of sources to determine the most accurate position. The position is established by using radio inputs and inputs from the inertial reference system. The FMC automatically cross-checks radio position and updates the facilities every two minutes with a stronger signal.

The FMC position can be derived from information from the IRS only. However, when in range of accurate radio inputs, the position is continually refined. The radio inputs can be from VOR/DME, ILS/LOC, or DME/DME. The IRS position is then checked against the radio position to determine the best position. Using this data, the FMC determines the best position every five seconds.

The IRS provides the FMC with many sources of information essential to navigation. This system provides present position in terms of latitude and longitude, attitude, true and magnetic heading, groundspeed, track, and wind data to all systems that require inertial data. To provide this information, the IRS uses a system of laser gyros that use laser beam frequency shifts to measure movement of a particular axis, and accelerometers that detect acceleration.

Inertial navigation can be defined as being able to determine the present location without any assistance from outside references. In fact, inertial navigation uses no radios at all. Because the airplane can move in a three-dimensional plane, each IRS contains three gyros and accelerometers. Each gyro operates in conjunction with one particular axis. These gyros are referred to as *ring laser gyros*.

The ring laser gyro operates using two laser beams that travel in opposite directions (Fig. 11-5). These laser beams travel in a contained area in opposite directions toward the same point where a measurement is taken. Anytime there is rotation of the axis, one of the beams of light will shorten and the other will lengthen. The difference in the two beams' paths is measured by a detector from a designated measurement point and sent to a microprocessor (computer). The difference in frequency between the two beams is a measure of rotational rate about the axis. The microprocessor then takes the inputs received and applies the Earth's rotational acceleration, the Earth's spherical shape, and the effects of gravity to determine the system outputs.

The IRS uses three other inputs that assist in providing all of the outputs that are used by various airplane systems: initial position, barometric altitude, and true airspeed. The initial position is used by the IRS during the alignment process to become the navigation starting point. Although the IRS stores its last position in memory prior to shutdown, the position entered by the pilot serves as a verification and reference point for the alignment process. Barometric altitude stabilizes vertical navigation, which stabilizes vertical outputs to the system. The TAS allows the system to be able to determine wind direction and speed. The IRUs have been designed to operate with ac power while using dc power as a backup.

AUTOPILOT AND FLIGHT DIRECTOR SYSTEM

The autopilot and flight director system are integrated into the overall system. When the autopilot is engaged, it follows commands from the FMC. These commands include navigation and performance commands. The pilot selects a navigational command and enters it through the CDU to the FMC. The autopilot will follow those commands as long as the lateral (horizontal) navigation function of the autopilot is engaged. If the pilot

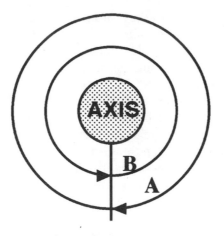

**A & B are light beams that travel
in different directions**

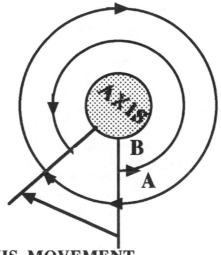

AXIS MOVEMENT

**When the axis moves, the beams of light become
different lengths. The Photocell Detector measures
the difference. This difference is sent to the
microprocessor that determines the axis movement.**

Fig. 11-5. *Laser principle of operation.*

changes a performance command, the autopilot will accomplish the required command as long as the vertical navigation function of the autopilot is engaged.

The flight director is presented to the pilot on the electronic attitude direction indicator (EADI). The flight director presents pitch and roll commands in the form of bars on the EADI. These commands are from the FMC for either the autopilot or the pilot to follow. The flight director follows both lateral navigation and vertical navigation commands as computed by the FMC and selected by the pilot.

AUTOTHROTTLES

The autothrottles, or thrust management system, play an important part of the vertical navigation function. When engaged, the autothrottles receive commands from the FMC. The autothrottles are available from takeoff through landing and provide the proper thrust based on the FMC commands. These commands can be changed at any time by the pilot through the CDU. The commands include proper takeoff thrust, climb thrust, cruise thrust, and thrust necessary to make crossing restrictions during descent.

ELECTRONIC FLIGHT INSTRUMENT SYSTEM

The electronic flight instrument system (EFIS) is actually what is known as "glass" in the cockpit. The term *glass* refers to the cathode ray tubes (CRTs) that are now used in the latest generation of airplanes. The EFIS consists of CRTs that encompass the electronic attitude direction indicator (EADI) and the electronic horizontal situation indicator (EHSI). It may also include all of the engine instruments on a separate CRT. The EADI and EHSI receive attitude, heading, and track information from the IRS, and flight and map information from the flight management system.

The EADI (Fig. 11-6) is displayed much in the same way as conventional ADIs. However, with the CRT screen, much more information can be provided to the pilot. The ADI is able to present conventional information such as attitude deviations, flight director commands, and localizer and glideslope deviations; some even present an airspeed display.

Other information such as TAS and groundspeed, radio altitude, decision height, a pitch limit symbol to alert the pilot of maximum pitch, and windshear information can also be provided to the pilot. A wealth of information can be presented over and above that of a conventional ADI.

The EHSI (Fig. 11-7) is a major departure from conventional HSIs. Although the EHSI has selectable modes for the pilot, the one most commonly used is known as the *map mode*. The map mode presents information against a moving background as the airplane is moving. The map background moves relative to the fixed airplane symbol. Information presented includes current route, magnetic heading, trend vectors, range to altitude, wind speed and direction, distance to next waypoint and estimated of arrival, and selected navigational facilities and airports. The map range can be changed from 10 miles up to 320 miles, with selections in between.

Weather radar is also displayed on the map. The radar depicts weather in relation to the map range selected and shows weather in the proper location in conjunction with

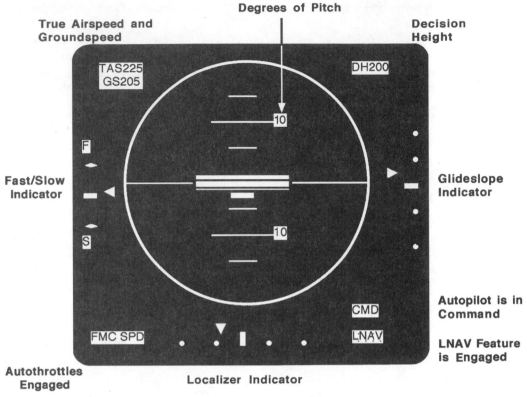

Fig. 11-6. *Attitude direction indicator.*

the moving map. The pilot has the option of selecting conventional VOR or ILS modes for presentation instead of the moving map display.

The symbol generators are the instruments that provide the displays for the CRTs on the EADI and EHSI. These generators receive inputs from the various avionics systems and process the information into displays for the appropriate CRT. Invalid or unreliable data results in an appropriate failure flag or removal of the affected display from the CRT.

NAVIGATION

Navigation in a glass cockpit airplane is quite simple when all the resources available are used. The pilot enters the route to be flown, desired altitude, and desired airspeed if economy is not chosen, and the FMC computes the vertical and lateral computations. The route appears as a line on the EHSI, whether a direct routing or an airway. The line is then followed by the autopilot, or by the flight director if the pilot is manually flying, as long as the LNAV feature is engaged.

Vertical navigation is accomplished by using the autothrottles and pitch control and by engaging the vertical navigation (VNAV) function. The autopilot or flight director will command pitch to maintain the proper climb and descent airspeeds, along

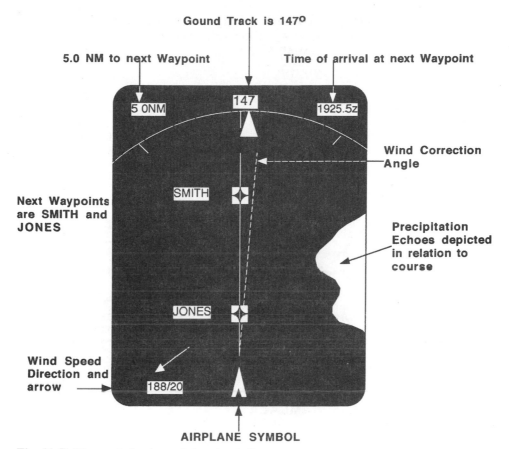

Fig. 11-7. *Electronic horizontal situation indicator.*

with proper thrust provided by the autothrottles. The cruise portion of the flight is also encompassed in the vertical navigation computation.

The pilot enters the route through the CDU to the FMC. The FMC produces a line that corresponds with the entered route and displays the line on the EHSI through the symbol generator. The airplane navigates with reference to the line on the EHSI. Airplane airspeed is controlled by the autothrottles through FMC commands. When a fix requires a crossing altitude and airspeed, the throttles reduce to idle, and the airplane pitches down and crosses the fix at the programmed altitude and airspeed.

The pilot has become an operation overseer. The pilot simply has to make sure the FMC is programmed correctly and verify the airplane will accomplish what the FMC commands.

An example of how the FMS is now being integrated into the airspace system is a FMS transition (Fig. 11-8). These transitions are airport- and runway-specific. The track of the transition is the same track over the ground that the controller would use when vectoring airplanes for the final approach course. When an air traffic controller assigns a FMS transition, the pilot selects the runway and the specific transition

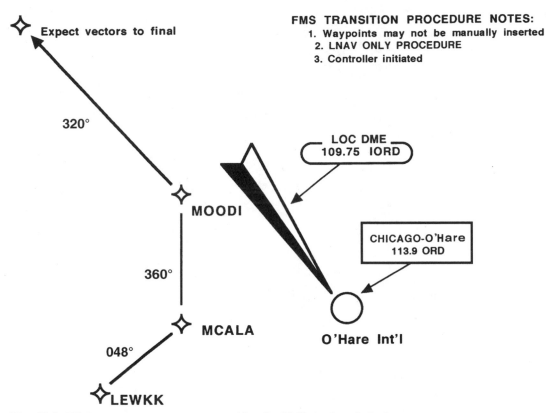

NWRK FMS TRANSITION Rwy 14L (NWRK 1)
(FMS EQUIPPED AIRCRAFT ONLY)
(RADAR REQUIRED)

Expect vectors to final

FMS TRANSITION PROCEDURE NOTES:
1. Waypoints may not be manually inserted
2. LNAV ONLY PROCEDURE
3. Controller initiated

320°

LOC DME
109.75 IORD

MOODI

CHICAGO-O'Hare
113.9 ORD

360°

MCALA

O'Hare Int'l

048°

LEWKK

Fig. 11-8. *Flight management system transition for FMS-equipped airplanes.*

through the CDU. The controller then gives the pilot a clearance direct to the initial fix or a vector to it. With the LNAV feature engaged, the airplane will follow the course.

The advantage of this type of procedure is that the pilot knows exactly the relationship of the airplane to the final approach course. Another advantage is the reduction of talk on the radio—particularly important since radio congestion is becoming a major problem at busy airports.

The conventional method of flying airplanes is always available to the pilot in the glass cockpit. To regain complete manual control of the thrust, the pilot must turn the autothrottles off. By placing the EHSI in the VOR mode and manually selecting VORs and courses to be flown, the airplane can be flown by conventional methods. The features of the glass cockpit just make the overall navigation simpler.

GLOBAL POSITIONING SYSTEM

Global Positioning System (GPS) was originally a military system, and the military still operates the system today. The system uses a "constellation" of 24 satellites that remain in Earth's orbit; at least five of these should be in view anywhere on the Earth (Fig. 11-9).

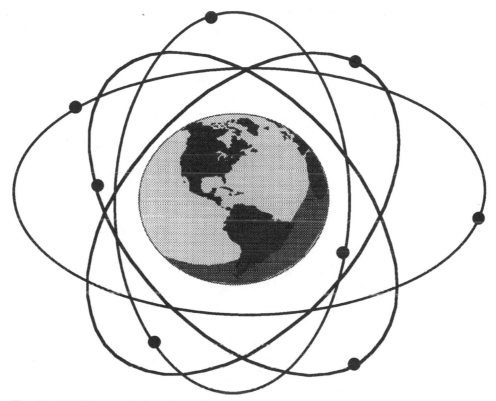

Fig. 11-9. *GPS constellation of satellites.*

The concept depends on cross-checking range and triangulation between receiving satellites to determine aircraft position. When three satellites are received and a fourth is used for timing corrections, GPS can determine location in three dimensions: latitude, longitude, and altitude. Since it comes from above, the navigation information from these satellites has no obstructions. The system is unaffected by weather and can provide service to an unlimited number of users.

There are actually two levels of GPS service. The Standard Positioning Service (SPS) provides horizontal accuracy within 100 meters 95 percent of the time, and within 300 meters 99.9 percent of the time. The Precise Positioning Service (PPS) is even more accurate than the SPS; however, the exact parameters are not published because this portion of the system is still retained for military and other government uses.

GPS has a self-checking feature called *receiver autonomous integrity monitoring* or RAIM. The RAIM feature of GPS can determine if one or more satellites are providing corrupted information. RAIM requires one more satellite than the standard four to be in view, for a total of five satellites; however, if you also have "baro-aiding," only four satellites are needed. *Baro-aiding* uses the conventional pressure altitude corrected for the local altimeter setting to provide the altitude portion of the GPS information. If RAIM does in fact find a corrupted signal, it will need six satellites (or five with baro-aiding) to discover which satellite has the problem and eliminate that satellite's message.

Multiengine airplanes are almost all IFR-equipped, but in the very near future, the phrase "IFR-equipped" will also mean IFR GPS-equipped. Today, not all GPS units can be approved for IFR flight. I have a GPS unit on one of the airplanes that I operate at the university flight school where I teach, but it is an older unit and cannot be converted for IFR use. If you have a GPS unit and want to find out whether it can be approved for IFR, you can read its manual or consult with an avionics technician. To be approved for IFR, GPS units must meet the requirements of TSO C-129, and the installation must be made in accordance with Notice 8110.47 or 8110.48. GPS units that fall under TSO C-115a cannot be approved for IFR.

In addition, you and your equipment must comply with the following six rules for IFR approval:

1. Airplanes that will be approved for GPS IFR must also have an approved and operational backup navigation system such as a VOR. While in flight, the flightcrew does not need to constantly watch the alternate navigation system as long as the RAIM function of the GPS is working. If the RAIM goes out, however, the flightcrew must get the backup system up and running.

2. You must come up with procedures in the event the RAIM does go out. As with emergency procedures for other equipment, such as engine failure, you need a plan for the backup equipment.

3. The GPS must be used in accordance with the airplane's FAA-approved flight manual or manual supplement.

4. Aircraft navigating by GPS are considered RNAV aircraft. When filing a flight plan, you should use the letter *G* as the aircraft's equipment suffix for approved oceanic, enroute, terminal, and approach under IFR.

5. Prior to any GPS IFR flight, you must review NOTAMs. You might need to specifically ask the FSS briefer about GPS NOTAMs.

6. All air carriers and commercial operators must also conduct IFR GPS operations in accordance with their own approved operations specifications.

The GPS implementation has come in three phases. Phase I was the military-only phase, which ended in February of 1994. Phase II began on February 17, 1994, when the FAA declared the system suitable for civilian operators. Phase III began on April 28, 1994, when the first "overlay" approaches were published. An *overlay approach* allows pilots to fly existing VOR, VOR/DME, NDB, NDB/DME, TACAN, or RNAV approaches using the GPS system. ILS, LDA, and SDF approaches are not used as an overlay. The GPS overlay approaches add the phrase "or GPS" to the heading of the approach chart, such as "VOR or GPS RWY 7." The first standalone, as opposed to overlay, GPS approaches were published on July 21, 1994.

In order to fly a GPS approach, the GPS equipment you use must have a database with the specific approach procedure installed, and the information must be retrievable while in flight. The GPS units approved by TSO C-129 will have such a database.

Finally, GPS equipment for use in instrument approaches is further broken down into classes. Class A simply has a GPS sensor and navigation capability. Class A1 has the RAIM function and can be used for nonprecision approaches. Class B has the GPS sensor, but also links the GPS information into a flight management system. Class C has the sensor and integrates the GPS into an FMS, but also hooks up with an autopilot or flight director system.

As these new systems are developed, they will work their way down from multi-million dollar airliners and business jets to the multiengine airplanes that most up-and-coming professional pilots train and build time on. Changes will come faster for today's generation of pilots than for any previous group. Staying ahead of the changes by reading up on the new technology as it evolves will be to your benefit.

PART IV

Earning a multiengine rating

12
Multiengine
flight training

MANY FLIGHT SCHOOLS OFFER FLIGHT AND GROUND INSTRUCTION THAT leads to the multiengine airplane rating. Check out each school as if you were shopping for any other pilot certificate or rating. Do not shop on the basis of cost alone. Look at the airplanes that will be used for the training. Check out the experience level of the multiengine instructor. Ask questions about the ground instruction and the support facilities.

Ask about insurance requirements for renting multiengine airplanes. Contact an aviation insurance company for details about proper insurance to fully protect yourself. The instruction necessary to get a multiengine rating is usually less than 10 hours, but a minimum 25 hours is common for insurability. This means that you might pass the checkride, but still not be able to rent the airplane for a solo flight.

A multiengine course is a course in disaster management. The initial flight is the only flight where the trainee pilot can get accustomed to the airplane. After the first flight, the lessons are filled with presumed malfunctions, equipment failures, and other assorted in-flight disasters that must be dealt with. Multiengine training is all work and no play. (Adding on a seaplane rating has always been considered more fun. Even though a seaplane rating is serious business, training can be intermingled with fishing trips.)

Any good multiengine course must spend a lot of time on the ground. There is no multiengine rating written test. Ground school might be your only opportunity (besides this book) to understand multiengine concepts. The ratio of flight-to-ground instruction should be at least 1-to-1. If the instructor wants to jump right into the airplane with little or no preliminary ground school about the airplane's systems, aerodynamics, and procedures, look for another school.

The transition to multiengine work will be much easier if you have had some previous experience in a complex single-engine aircraft. If you have never worried about landing gear and prop control settings before, and you try to grasp those while also dealing with two engines, you will be way behind the airplane and the learning curve. Log perhaps 5–10 hours in a complex single-engine airplane first.

What is complex time? To be eligible for a commercial pilot certificate, an applicant must have logged 10 hours of complex airplane time, according to FAR 61.129. The term *complex* is unusual because it is not defined in FAR part 1. The only reference to the word complex comes from the FAA's practical test standards for the commercial and flight instructor certificates. The publications describe an airplane that must be used for the flight test.

The airplane must have a constant-speed propeller, retractable landing gear, and retractable flaps. This means that a Learjet is not a complex airplane because it does not have a propeller. Engine horsepower is not mentioned.

Complex should not be confused with the term *high-performance*. A high-performance airplane, defined in FAR 61.31, has 200-horsepower, or the triple combination of constant-speed prop, retractable gear, and retractable flaps. I train commercial pilot and flight instructor candidates in an airplane that has a constant-speed prop, retractable gear, and retractable flaps, but it only has 180 horsepower; therefore, I am teaching in a high-performance airplane because the regulation has that all-important "or" in the sentence. The airplane is also complex.

A flight instructor must make an endorsement in your logbook stating that you have been adequately trained to fly a high-performance airplane before you can log pilot-in-command time in such an airplane. Many students have an endorsement that says "complex" rather than "high-performance" in their logbook. Check your own book. If it says complex, go back and have your instructor change it to high-performance or you will legally be unable to log or act as PIC in that airplane.

Multiengine airplanes used for training are both complex and high performance. For this reason, some students have combined a multiengine rating with a commercial pilot certificate checkride. They receive training and become proficient on commercial maneuvers in a single-engine noncomplex airplane before moving to the multiengine airplane to log at least 10 hours of complex-airplane flight time.

They have two applications for the checkride: commercial certificate and multiengine rating. This is fine except for two possible problems. First, this combination might require the student to move faster than he is capable of. Moving from a Skipper to a Duchess is a big step. The student might be able to fly the airplane after some practice, but his systems experience is very limited. Second, the student will have little or no single-engine complex time, which will be a problem if she goes for a flight instructor certificate.

People pursuing a career as a professional pilot should consider starting multi-engine training after obtaining the commercial pilot certificate and instrument rating. This makes things less complicated, promoting building-block training from one step to the next. Seemingly countless variations of training are certainly possible; the emphasis is don't train beyond your capabilities and sacrifice safety for time.

The multiengine rating comes in two types: VFR or IFR. At one time, a person with an instrument rating who later earned the multiengine rating could then fly IFR in the multiengine airplane. A series of accidents led the FAA to change the law. The FAA determined that IFR in a multiengine airplane was more demanding on the pilot than IFR in a single; yet no additional instrument/multitraining was required.

I received this letter from the FAA in 1984 regarding the matter (edited):

"On July 2, 1981, a Beech 65-A80-8800 crashed near Madisonville, Texas. The NTSB investigation indicated that the accident might have been caused by excessive air loads generated by nose-up control input by the pilot at high speed, which resulted in in-flight breakup of the aircraft.

"A review of the pilot's records indicated that he had acquired an instrument rating in a single-engine aircraft; however, he had limited experience in the operation of multiengine aircraft in instrument meteorological conditions and had not received instrument training in a multiengine aircraft.

"Consequently, the NTSB recommended that the FAA require all holders of an instrument rating and a multiengine class rating to demonstrate their ability to operate a multiengine aircraft under normal and emergency conditions by reference to flight instruments only as a prerequisite to exercising the privileges of an instrument rating in multiengine aircraft.

"The FAA agrees in principle with the NTSB recommendation as it applies to airplanes; therefore, appropriate flight-test guidance material will be amended to reflect that all new applicants for a multiengine airplane class rating who hold an instrument rating for airplanes will be required to demonstrate pilot competency to operate a multiengine airplane solely by reference to instruments.

"Persons who currently hold an instrument rating for airplanes plus the multiengine airplane class rating will not be affected; however, if the applicant elects not to demonstrate competency in instrument flight, the applicant's multiengine airplane privileges will be limited to visual flight only.

"Multiengine ratings restricted to VFR will . . . (state) . . . AIRPLANE MULTIENGINE VFR ONLY. To remove this restriction, the pilot will be required to demonstrate competency to operate a multiengine airplane . . . solely by reference to instruments."

The NTSB investigation of multiengine and related instrument flying accidents led to a recommendation to the FAA that multiengine testing be changed. The FAA took this advice and added three items to the multiengine flight test for IFR privileges:

- Instrument approach with both engines operating.
- Instrument approach with only one engine operating.

- Engine failures during straight and level flight and in turns while flying solely by flight instruments.

This became known as the "first handshake" rule. Multiengine applicants have to declare at the time they first shake the hand of the FAA designated pilot examiner that they are arriving to take either a VFR or IFR multiengine test. The method came about because applicants would say they wanted an IFR multiengine rating. If they failed an IFR item, they would say, "Forget the IFR part, I really only wanted a VFR rating." The rule means that the multiengine flight test is all or nothing.

Decide whether to train for IFR or VFR and tell your instructor. This reemphasizes the importance of obtaining the instrument rating before the multiengine rating.

When investigating flight schools and multiengine instructors, ask to see the flight syllabus to be used. Some schools might not have a published syllabus, but the instructor should have a clear plan of instruction that will take you from proficient single-engine pilot to competent multiengine pilot. The regulations do not require a minimum amount of multiengine dual instruction. For this reason, most multiengine training programs are short, ranging from 6–12 hours of instruction. With a minimum amount of time in the airplane, it is very important that every minute count. If the instructor does not have an efficient plan of action, then look elsewhere.

The following is a sample multiengine course syllabus and a discussion of each item taught. The syllabus that you use might not be exactly like this one, but the topics and maneuvers should be the same. I have used this IFR multiengine rating syllabus a hundred times with great success.

The lessons are not automatically one hour, or even one flight. The student only advances to the next lesson when the completion standards of the previous lesson are achieved. Flight time required depends on the student's ability to grasp the topics, previous experience in complex airplanes, and IFR proficiency.

LESSON 1

Objective: The student will become familiar with the multiengine airplane's systems, controls, and cockpit layout. The student will be introduced to flight at critically slow airspeeds, become familiar with the flight characteristics of slow and stalled flight, and become familiar with the airplane's normal flight characteristics.

Introduce:
Preflight and ground maneuvers
Aircraft systems and airworthiness inspection
Cockpit resource management
Safe engine starting procedures
Taxiing: normal, crosswind, and with differential power
Pretakeoff checklist and systems check
Flight operations
Traffic pattern operations

Four fundamentals:
    Slow flight
    Approach to landing stall
    Takeoff stall
    Steep turns
Heater operation
Autopilot operation
Manual gear extension
Simulated engine failure enroute (instructor demo)
Drag demonstration

Completion standards: The student will be able to perform all the listed ground procedures with instructor assistance. During takeoff and landing, the student will demonstrate good directional control and maintain liftoff, climb, approach, and touchdown airspeed within 10 knots of the correct airspeed. Straight-and-level flight, climbs, and descents will be performed while maintaining assigned airspeeds within 10 knots, rollouts from turns within 10° of assigned headings, and specified altitudes within 100 feet. The student will be able to demonstrate the correct flight procedures for maneuvering during slow flight, steep power turns, and the correct entry and recovery procedures for stalls. All maneuvers at critically slow airspeed must be completed no lower than 3,000 feet AGL.

It is very important during this lesson to become familiar with the airplane. Even though it is tough to become comfortable in any airplane in just one lesson, make your strategy to know the airplane systems and layout during this lesson. The lesson should begin with understanding the airplane's systems, especially propeller, electrical, landing gear, and engine instrument systems. Try to arrive at least 30 minutes early and get permission to look around the airplane, outside and inside, without the instructor. No-cost training such as this will eventually pay high safety dividends.

The panel of even the smallest twin-engine airplane will look much more complicated than a single-engine panel. As you look more closely, you will see the duplication of controls and instruments used to adjust and monitor the separate engines. There will be two of everything pertaining to the powerplants: two manifold-pressure needles, two tachometer needles, two throttles, two oil-pressure needles, and the like.

By grouping the paired instruments and indicator needles in your mind, the panel becomes more comfortable and understandable. The "fistful of throttles" simply becomes like one throttle. Make sure you know where the panel and cockpit components are located: engine instruments, electric switches, power instruments, emergency landing gear extension apparatus, and the like. You never want to hunt for something in flight.

Sit in the pilot's seat and close your eyes. Without peeking, point to the right-engine tachometer indication, for instance. Then open your eyes and see if you are indeed pointing correctly. Repeat the session until you can draw the panel in your mind's eye.

During the formal lesson, the instructor should explain that airplane's systems: prop governors, battery-drain vents, battery airflow vents, airplane heater vents, fuel tank vents, stall warning horns, anti-ice or deice equipment, auxiliary power receptacle, and airplane antennas. Ask questions because you need to know about everything attached to or hanging from the airplane.

Settle into the cockpit and start the engines according to the airplane's checklist. Everything will have a specific order, so be careful not to inadvertently skip any items. The left engine is generally considered the number one engine, but there might be some particular reason why you should start the right engine first. It is a good idea to start the engine that is closer to the battery so that the current flow would have least resistance. If the start order is not specified by the manufacturer, some operators suggest that you alternate the engine started first from one flight to the next. This would keep the time on the engines even.

When the engines are started, check all systems for green, and it will be time to learn to taxi. The combined steerable nosewheel and main gear brakes are not new, but multiengine airplanes are bigger and heavier, and are therefore harder to handle in tight places.

Holding brakes and riding brakes while taxiing is never a good idea, so multiengine pilots must become accustomed to using *differential power* for turns. In a tight right turn, the right-engine power can be brought back to idle while the left-engine power is brought forward. The left engine pulls the airplane around (Fig. 12-1).

You must become completely comfortable with taxiing the airplane. One pilot took a multiengine checkride and failed because he could not park the airplane at the end of the ride. He successfully passed the oral exam and the flight portion. The parking space that was available to the applicant required a tight turn. The examiner allowed five tries to get the airplane into position, but eventually the examiner's patience ran out.

The airplane had always been parked in that same tight spot. The flight instructor did not want the student to damage the airplane; therefore, the instructor had always parked the plane at the end of each lesson. The student had never been allowed to park; he never had the opportunity to learn.

On the retest of the multiengine applicant, the examiner had the applicant pull out of the space, taxi around the ramp like an obstacle course, and park the airplane in the original spot. The student passed. The moral of the story: Learn to taxi the airplane, do not park in extremely tight spaces and, when necessary, shut down the airplane and get a tow bar.

The pretakeoff checks and runup should be done slowly and carefully. Follow the checklist exactly. Ask questions when they come to mind. Try to perform the runup in a location that does not block other pilots. Do not feel pressured to finish the checklist in a hurry and, for goodness' sake, do not become a Hobbs-meter watcher here.

Do not feel slighted if the instructor says, "If anything happens on this first takeoff, I have it." The first takeoff should be normal, so if anything abnormal happens, the instructor will handle it. You will have plenty of chances to deal with emergencies on the runway later. Follow instructions and enjoy that first feel of acceleration pushing you back in your seat.

In the air, you will be pleasantly surprised at how easy the airplane is to handle. It will feel heavy at first, but your touch will develop quickly. It will take some time to synchro-

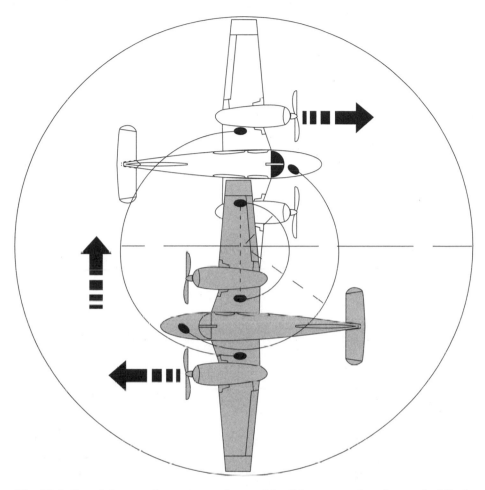

Fig. 12-1. *In a tight spot, the engine on the outside of the turn can be advanced while the inside engine's power remains at idle. This allows the turning radius to become tighter.*

nize the props for the first time. Set one engine and work the prop control to match the RPMs. This takes a little ear training, but it comes with practice. Multiengine training is all business, but initially the instructor should let you fly the airplane to get a very good feel for it without any specific maneuvers. Enjoy the familiarity segment, then get to work.

Steep power-turns

Steep power-turns display airmanship and knowledge of the airplane's characteristics. It is essentially the same maneuver that you have performed in a single-engine airplane (Fig. 12-2):

1. Set the power so that the speed of the airplane is less than V_A.
2. Clear the area with either one 180° turn, or two 90° turns in opposite directions. Make sure that you really look for traffic in the turns.

3. Perform a clean-configuration GUMPS check.
   a. Gas from both engines ON.
   b. Undercarriage UP for this maneuver.
   c. Mixtures rich (or appropriate lean setting).
   d. Props at cruise setting for this maneuver.
   e. Switches or systems (fuel pumps) ON.
4. Begin a roll, either left or right, to a 50°–55° angle of bank.
5. Anticipate the need for elevator back pressure, and raise the nose as necessary while the bank steepens.
6. Stay in the turn through 720° (two circles). While in the turn, observe the outside horizon and keep the horizon in a constant position relative to the dashboard as your pitch reference. Hold pitch and bank constant after establishing the turn; do not chase the pitch and bank.
7. Start the rollout to wings level approximately 20° prior to the entry heading.
8. Complete the rollout on the original heading, and maintain altitude and airspeed.
9. Return to cruise configuration.

Fig. 12-2. *The flight instruments during a steep left turn. The bank angle is 50°–55°, the vertical speed indicator is showing a level turn, the ball is in the center, and there is sufficient airspeed above accelerated stall.*

Slow flight

One excellent way to get the feel of an airplane is airspeed transition maneuvers. Maintaining straight-and-level flight during airspeed changes will make you adjust the pitch and power to new positions. This forces you to feel how slight changes affect the airplane. This fine-tunes your touch to the airplane. The following is the procedure I use to establish the slow-flight maneuver. Double-check your airplane manufacturer's recommendations:

1. Maintain a safe altitude (at least 3,000 feet AGL) and an assigned heading.
2. Reduce power on both engines to 15" manifold pressure.
3. While slowing down execute a clearing turn, either one 180° turn or two 90° turns in opposite directions.
4. As the speed continues to slow from cruise, perform the GUMPS check for a landing configuration:
   a. Gas is turned ON for both engines.
   b. Undercarriage DOWN when the speed of the airplane is slower than V_{LE} (maximum landing gear extended speed).
   c. Mixtures to full rich (or properly leaned for the conditions).
   d. Props forward to high RPM.
   e. Switches. Turn fuel pump switches on.
5. Slow the airplane to 70 knots by lowering flaps, one notch at a time, until fully lowered. Hold altitude by adding power as necessary.
6. Hold 70 knots with a constant heading and altitude.
7. Right and left turns can be made while holding 70 knots and a constant altitude.
8. Return to cruise flight speed:
   a. Both throttles to full power.
   b. Flaps up.
   c. Landing gear up when a positive rate of climb is established.
   d. Accelerate to cruise airspeed.

The slow-flight maneuver helps you understand the pitch and power relationships that are required to change speed and maintain altitude. Also, the slow-flight condition is a good platform for other maneuvers.

Approach to landing stall

Aerodynamics of a stalled wing are the same for either single-engine or multiengine airplanes; however, because the engines are on the wings, stall characteristics are altered because the prop wash from the engines alters airflow over wings. Lift is produced as the airflow accelerates over the upper contour of the airfoil. Faster airflow acceleration creates more lift, which means that lift will be greatest where the prop wash is blown across the wings; therefore, power setting and stall condition are closely related.

Air accelerates off the propellers and back across the airfoil and engine nacelle. This accelerated slipstream produces lift that otherwise would not be present. This is one reason why you should never chop power on a multiengine airplane because you are chopping the wing's lift.

The stall recovery in a multiengine airplane is somewhat different than in a single. The stall recovery usually requires a pronounced lowering of the nose to lower the wing's angle of attack from the critical angle. With a multiengine airplane, the nose-down pitch can be shallower if power is added in the recovery. The addition of power, probably full power, will cause high-energy airflow to be sent over the wings. This brute force of prop wash forces the airflow to follow the wing's camber, which produces lift.

A test airfoil in a wind tunnel proved this point about accelerated slipstream and its effect on lift at slow airspeeds. Test data clearly showed that multiengine stall recovery is greatly enhanced with power. Graphs from the wind tunnel test (Figs. 12-3 and 12-4) show that at a 10° angle of attack, with the prop windmilling, the wing produced a coefficient of lift of 1.93. At the same angle, the wing produced a coefficient of 2.88 when the power was on and the airflow accelerated by the propeller. That is a 67 percent increase in lift without changing the pitch angle.

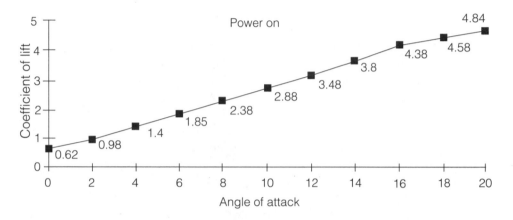

Fig. 12-3. *Wind tunnel test data of lift produced while power is on. The accelerated slipstream from the propeller produces lift as it flows over the engine nacelle and affected wing section.*

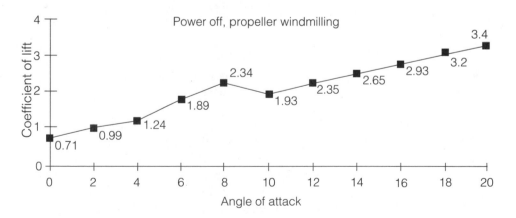

Fig. 12-4. *Wind tunnel test data of lift produced while power is off and the propeller is windmilling. Comparing the chart with Fig. 12-3, the lift advantage provided when the engine has power on is quite clear.*

The effects are even greater when closer to the critical angle of attack. When the test airfoil was placed in the tunnel with a 20° angle of attack, the wing was buffeting wildly and producing a coefficient of 3.4; the engine was turned on and the slipstream created a coefficient of 4.84. This represents a 70 percent increase in lift at the time you need it the most.

This showed that the fastest way to regain lift is engine power in the stall recovery, coupled with a small pitch change. When a single-engine pilot stalls a multiengine airplane for the first time, this fact is sometimes lost, and she will push the nose over too far in recovery. This unnecessarily adds to the altitude loss.

The entire maneuver from start to finish should be accomplished within ±100 feet. Clear the area, and watch for traffic throughout the maneuver. To perform the approach to landing stall maneuver, use the following procedure (Figs. 12-5 and 12-6):

1. Set up the slow-flight platform no lower than 3,000 feet AGL.
   a. 15" manifold pressure.
   b. Clearing turns while reducing speed from cruise.
   c. GUMPS check for landing configuration.
   d. Arrive at 70 knots with full flaps and holding altitude.
2. Reduce power to approximately 13" manifold pressure.
3. Uniformly add pitch to slow the airplane.
4. Hold heading and altitude. The ball of the turn coordinator is in the center.
5. Allow the nose to pitch into a stall attitude. Wait to feel the stall buffet, then go to step 6.

Fig. 12-5. *This photo was taken just prior to a stall. The nose is high, and the vertical speed shows a climb. Note the instrument panel's placard about stalls with only one engine operating.*

Fig. 12-6. *This photo was taken during the stall recovery. The nose is placed on the horizon, the vertical speed shows a descent, and the airspeed is increasing.*

6. Initiate the recovery by simultaneously lowering the nose to the horizon, but not lower than the horizon, and advancing the throttles to full power. Raise the flaps. Retract the landing gear when a positive rate of climb is established.
7. Ease back on the power, and return to normal cruise configuration.

Takeoff and departure stall

Understanding stall characteristics at full power is very important because the deck angle at the time of the stall will be very high due to the accelerated slipstream over the wings. It might not stall until reaching 45° nose-up pitch. This can be a little scary and single-engine pilots are always a little reluctant to pitch that high. You must be careful with any stall; you must be especially careful with a multiengine, power-on stall:

1. 15" manifold pressure. Set up the slow-flight platform no lower than 3,000 AGL.
2. Make clearing turns as the airplane reduces speed.
3. Perform a GUMPS check for a clean configuration.
   a. Gas from both engines ON.
   b. Check that the landing gear is UP and leave it there.
   c. Mixtures rich.
   d. Prop full forward.
   e. Fuel pump switches on.

4. Reduce speed while maintaining altitude until it is time to apply power.
5. Advance power to the desired power setting (21" manifold pressure, climb power, or full power).
6. Raise the nose until the stall occurs. Wait to feel the buffet, then go to step 7.
7. Initiate recovery. Simultaneously place the nose on the horizon and, if power was less than full, add full power.
8. Return to normal cruise configuration of speed, power settings, and prop settings.

Stall tips

Always stall with plenty of recovery altitude. If a cloud deck is at or lower than 3,500 feet AGL, fulfill the ground school portion, and reschedule the flying portion of that lesson. There is a high potential for a spin entry during multiengine stall practice. Regardless of the number of engines, a spin can be entered whenever an uncoordinated stall occurs. An uncoordinated stall occurs when there is yaw present during the stall.

Multiengine airplanes are extremely yaw-prone because the engines do not pull through the center of the airplane. The pilot can never be completely sure that both engines are turning at exactly the same RPM producing exactly the same thrust. When thrust is uneven, the airplane will be uncoordinated. As the pilot raises the nose to reach a stall angle, the engines are turning, but probably not exactly in unison. For this reason, multiengine airplanes are prone to spin.

The recovery from a spin entry in a multiengine airplane will require at least 2,000 feet to initially recognize the spin and pull out. The exact altitude loss is unknown because the FAA does not require multiengine airplanes to be spun for airworthiness certification. This means that if you enter a spin in a multiengine airplane, you become your own test pilot.

Never stall a multiengine airplane while one engine is feathered or while power is reduced on one engine. Stall only when the power settings are as close to symmetrical as possible. Stalls can be performed from straight and level flight or in a turn.

Finally, never look back at the tail, especially a T-tail, when stalling. It is safe, of course, but the tail usually vibrates and sways. This alone can scare you away from stalls.

Simulated engine failure enroute

The first lesson is a good time for the instructor to demonstrate enroute flying with an engine out. Perhaps the instructor will have you follow through, while she is in complete control of the airplane. While the airplane still has an altitude of at least 3,000 feet AGL, the instructor will reduce the power on one engine, and you can feel the rudder pressure that will be necessary to hold the airplane on a particular heading.

With one engine simulating zero thrust, this is a good time to get a feel for the airplane in various drag configurations. Recall from ground school that small twins simply do not climb well on a single engine. Also recall that the performance charts are based upon ideal conditions; the chart numbers are the absolute best you can hope for.

You will see and feel the 80 percent loss of performance. Clear the area and watch for traffic throughout the drag configuration maneuver:

1. From cruise speed in a clean configuration, reduce power on one engine to idle, and advance power on the other engine to full.
2. Add some power to the idle engine to simulate zero thrust (the effect on the airplane if the propeller were feathered). About 11"–12" manifold pressure will do it.
3. Maintain a speed of V_{YSE} (blue line).
4. Reduce power on the operating engine as necessary to maintain level flight.
5. Lower the landing gear, but attempt to maintain altitude and V_{YSE}.
6. Lower the flaps, one notch at a time, until full flaps are down.
7. Add power on the operating engine as necessary in an attempt to maintain altitude. (Chances are that you will be unable to maintain altitude with one engine, even at full power, with the gear and flaps down. It is a helpless feeling to be holding one throttle at full power; yet the airplane is still sinking. Doing this with plenty of altitude is safe. It will surely make you understand that it is impossible to attempt a climb on one engine when the airplane is heavy and dirty.)
8. Initiate recovery from the drag demonstration.
    a. Add power to the idle engine slowly. (The extra rudder pressure will seemingly melt away as the power becomes symmetrical again.)
    b. Simultaneously add power to both engines until reaching full power.
9. Climb back to the desired altitude and resume cruise configuration.

Normal landings

A multiengine airplane will land the same as a single-engine airplane, but the pattern and approach speeds are faster, and you have to control more inertia. A single-engine airplane does not have to slow down very much to enter a traffic pattern. A multiengine airplane must slow down a noticeable amount to safely enter the traffic pattern. The slow-flight maneuver you performed at altitude becomes very important.

Slow down and get set up in the traffic pattern (Fig. 12-7). Compensate for the speed with a pattern that is somewhat wider than a pattern for a single, but not a great deal wider. Review the airplane's handbook for recommended approach speeds. I like to stay 10 knots faster than the blue line for most of the approach, slowing to blue line on final. I stay at blue line speed until the flare. This means that the flare and float will use up some runway at this speed, but I would rather stay at blue line as long as possible just in case a go-around is needed.

Do not chop the power at any time during the approach. Recall that chopping power chops lift; all available lift is crucial when low and slow. You probably will be required to perform power-on approaches where the power is brought all the way to idle only after touchdown.

You might make several full-stop landings and taxi back for takeoffs. Recall that you have more options and improved safety with runway ahead during a multiengine takeoff. A touch-and-go consumes too much of the safety margin.

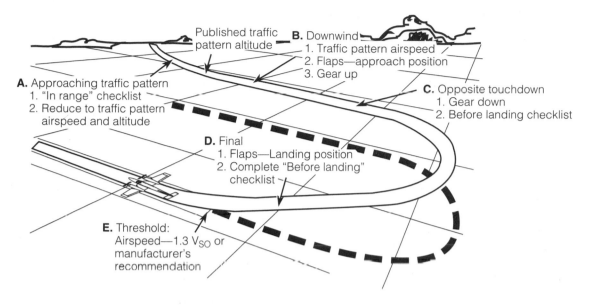

Fig. 12-7. *Normal landing profile.*

After landing

Use the after-landing checklist which is usually an expanded version of "Up, open, and off," which means wing flaps up, cowl flaps open, and fuel pumps off. Prior to engine shutdown, use the checklist to make sure that everything is in order. Stop the engines with the mixture cut-off, not by placing the prop control into feather.

After the engines have stopped and all checklist items are complete, review the flight thoroughly. Resolve any questions that might have come up during the flight. Review the procedures for each maneuver. Plan for the next flight, which should be as soon as possible to facilitate better recall of what you learned this time.

LESSON 2

Objective: The student will practice each of the assigned review maneuvers and procedures to increase proficiency and experience. The student will be introduced to crosswind and maximum-performance takeoff and climb, crosswind and maximum-performance approach and landing, and go-around from a rejected (balked) landing.

Review maneuvers:
Approach to landing stall
Takeoff stall
Steep turns

Introduce:
Maneuvering with one engine at idle

V_{MC} demonstration
Instructor-vectored instrument approach (both engines operating)
Crosswind takeoff and landing
Maximum performance takeoff and landing
Go-around from rejected landing
Normal pattern
One-engine pattern (engine idle on downwind)

Completion standards: The student will perform all the procedures and maneuvers listed for review at a proficiency level that meets or exceeds the criteria set forth in the multiengine-land sections of the appropriate FAA test standards. The new maneuvers and procedures will be evaluated on the adherence to proper procedures, operating techniques, coordination, smoothness, and understanding.

The first lesson always has an introductory atmosphere; the second lesson places more burden for performance on the student. At the beginning of the second lesson, the instructor should pass most of the preflight inspection duties over to you. The instructor should still be present for the preflight, asking the student some questions to ensure comprehension from the first lesson.

Steep turns, slow flight, and the stall series of maneuvers are often grouped together and called "VFR maneuvers." These maneuvers should be practiced at the beginning of the second lesson. The student should now have a good feel for the airplane and be able to perform the VFR maneuvers with precision.

The completion standard for this lesson states that "the procedures and maneuvers listed for review (the VFR maneuvers) (performed) at a proficiency level that meets or exceeds the criteria set forth" in the multiengine practical test standards. This means that steep turns, slow flight, and stalls must be checkride-ready at the conclusion of this lesson.

Maneuvering with one engine

After the VFR maneuvers have been practiced at altitude, it's time to work on single-engine operations again. For this lesson, the engine failure will be simulated by reducing a throttle to the zero thrust power setting. When an engine's power has been reduced to zero thrust, make some turns in both directions. It's OK to turn in the direction of the dead engine; just control your speed.

Many multiengine airplanes have a yaw string attached to the nose. If your airplane does have a yaw string, experiment with the position of the string versus the amount of rudder pressure applied. Use the ball in the inclinometer if no yaw string is used. (Review the yaw string discussion in chapter 1.)

Determine how much rudder pressure will bring the airplane to the zero sideslip position. You will also notice that holding rudder against the engine yaw can be exhausting. You cannot extend your leg and lock your knee; you have to hold muscle pressure continuously while maneuvering. If you can ignore the discomfort in your good-engine leg, the airplane should handle normally.

Demonstration of V$_{MC}$

Before attempting a V$_{MC}$ demonstration in flight, make sure that you understand what is about to happen and why. Review the V$_{MC}$ discussion on aerodynamics in chapter 1. Ask your instructor plenty of questions. You must know the procedures required by your airplane to get into and out of a V$_{MC}$ demonstration. Do your homework. V$_{MC}$ demonstrations are serious business, and it is no place for an unprepared student.

The demonstration is an experiment to prove that there is a speed where airflow over the rudder is simply not strong enough to overcome the yaw from one wing-mounted engine. This speed changes with altitude. The higher you fly, the less dense the air becomes. When the air is less dense, the operating engine will produce less power. Less power from one side of the airplane means less force from the rudder is required to counteract the engine power from the other side. When less rudder force is needed, less airflow (airspeed) is needed and V$_{MC}$ is reduced.

The horizontal axis of the graph in Fig. 12-8 displays the indicated airspeed of the airplane. The vertical axis is density altitude. Air becomes thinner the farther up the graph you go. The line for V$_{MC}$ is slanted. In this example, V$_{MC}$ is 75 knots at sea level where the air is thick and the good engine is strong. But the line bends backward, showing that V$_{MC}$ is only 40 knots at 7,500 feet.

This information makes it appear that the airplane is much safer at high altitude because you could reduce speed a large amount and still be faster than V$_{MC}$. It looks safer, but there is a catch; there always is. The indicated stall speed remains the same

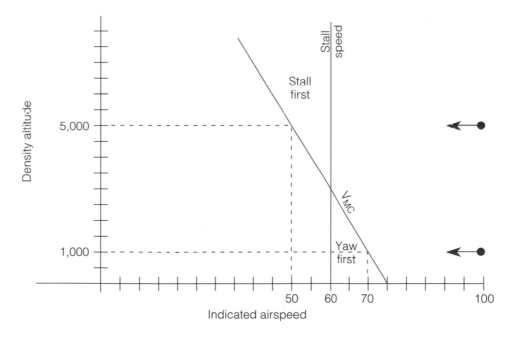

Fig. 12-8. *Density altitude's effect on the indicated airspeed of both stall and V$_{MC}$.*

regardless of density altitude. The graph shows the stall speed to be a straight vertical line at 60 knots. At approximately 3,000 feet density altitude, the stall line and the V_{MC} line cross. This is a very important position to understand.

Now look at the dot and left arrow at 100 knots and 1,000 feet density altitude. If you and I were preparing to do a V_{MC} demonstration in this airplane, we would first reduce power on the left engine and begin to reduce the airplane's speed. The arrow points in the direction of the speed reduction. We would cross the V_{MC} line at 70 knots, and at this density altitude, the airplane would require a full rudder deflection to keep the airplane straight and under control.

With a 1-knot reduction of airspeed, the rudder force produced would not be strong enough to overcome engine yaw. We would lose control of the airplane if we did not initiate a recovery immediately. We entered the yaw-first region of the graph, and the airplane experienced yaw that we were unable to counteract.

Now we try the same maneuver, but this time at a 5,000-foot density altitude. As we reduce speed from 100 knots with the left engine at idle, we add full power on the right engine and raise the nose. When we arrive at 70 knots, the rudder is still effective, and uncontrollable yaw is not present. This is true because the operating engine is weaker in the thin air at this altitude.

We reduce speed to 60 knots. According to the graph, we still have a 10-knot cushion of airspeed above V_{MC}, but 60 is the stall speed. With the 1-knot reduction in airspeed, the airplane stalls and we never get to V_{MC}. We entered the stall-first region.

When students and instructors go out intending to do V_{MC} demonstrations, they very rarely actually do them. True V_{MC} demonstrations can only happen during conditions with density altitudes that are low, but that would probably place the airplane too close to the terrain to safely do the demonstration. You need altitude to be safe, but a high altitude means that the airplane will stall before reaching true V_{MC}. Unfortunately, the first time a multiengine pilot might ever experience true V_{MC} conditions is low to the ground when an engine quits on takeoff.

During the V_{MC} demonstration, the airplane will yaw or stall, perhaps do both. For this reason, the pilot must initiate a V_{MC}/stall recovery at the first indication of uncontrolled yaw or a stall buffet. To play it safe, a recovery should also be initiated when rudder travel on the good-engine side runs out.

Because asymmetrical power is causing the problem of uncontrolled yaw at any speed slower than V_{MC}, the solution to the problem is to equalize the power again. In demonstration, you can do one of two things. You can advance the power on the simulated bad engine to meet the power setting of the good engine, or reduce power on the good engine to equal the bad engine's power setting. In reality, you must reduce power on the good engine because that is the only option available if you have an actual engine failure.

By reducing the good engine's power to idle, the power output from both sides is now equal. The good news is that you no longer have yaw present, and the airplane is under control. The nose should be down, and the airplane should be gaining airspeed.

The bad news is that you now have no power on either engine and you are dropping like a brick. This is why these demonstrations should never be attempted below 3,000 feet AGL. With enough altitude, the airplane can be accelerated by gravity to a safe speed. Good engine power can be added to stop the descent and maintain level flight.

The left engine should be failed for this demonstration. This leaves you with the right engine, which simulates the most adverse situation where the critical engine is operating. (*See* chapter 1, regarding aerodynamics, for details.)

Never attempt a V_{MC} demonstration or a stall with one engine feathered. Although this might be close to realism, it simply does not allow you a safe way out. Practice the V_{MC} demonstration only with an experienced instructor.

Here is the procedure that I teach. Please consult an airplane's operating handbook for its exact V_{MC} demonstration procedure before attempting the maneuver with an instructor onboard:

1. Reduce power on both engines to 15" manifold pressure above 3,000 feet AGL.
2. Make clearing turns.
3. Perform a clean-configuration GUMPS check.
   a. Gas: Fuel selectors ON.
   b. Undercarriage: Verify gear UP for this maneuver.
   c. Mixtures: Rich.
   d. Props: Full forward/high RPM.
   e. Switches: Fuel pumps ON.
4A. Both throttles to full power, then left engine decrease to idle. (Step 4A is more like what would actually happen during an engine failure on takeoff because both engines would be at full power.)
4B. Left engine to idle, then right engine to full power. (Step 4B is more tame and might be preferred for the first demonstration. Either step will yield the desired yaw or stall results.)
5. Establish a 3°–5° bank in the direction of the good engine. Place the ball one-half width out from the center toward the good engine.
6. While the left engine is at idle and the right engine at full power, begin to raise the airplane's nose. Lose approximately 3 knots per second.
7. Use ever-increasing amounts of rudder pressure to maintain directional control.
8. Continue to allow the speed to decrease and the forward travel of the rudder to increase until:
   a. An uncontrollable yaw begins.
   b. A stall occurs.
   c. The rudder pedal touches the floor.
9. At the first indication of yaw, stall, or full rudder travel, initiate recovery:
   a. Reduce the right throttle to a setting where directional control can again be maintained.

b. Lower the airplane's nose and begin to gain airspeed faster than V_{MC} and/or stall.

c. As airspeed increases and directional control is completely regained, add power on the right engine sufficient to stop the descent and achieve straight and level flight at a safe speed of V_{YSE}.

10. Complete the demonstration by smoothly reapplying power to the left engine. Change altitude as necessary. Resume cruise configuration.

Figure 12-9 was taken during the setup to a V_{MC} demonstration. The left throttle is being retarded and the manifold pressure is shown at 18 inches and diminishing. The right throttle is advanced at 25 inches. The vertical speed indicator is seen with a 1,000 fpm climb. This altitude gain will be lost during the recovery. One goal of the maneuver is to recover and stop the resulting descent prior to falling below the altitude used to begin the maneuver. This simulates a climb from the ground, an engine failure, a recovery, and a return to level flight before hitting the ground.

Fig. 12-9. *This photo was taken during the approach to V_{MC}. The left engine power has been reduced. The manifold pressure gauge is visible in the photo. Right engine is set at takeoff power of 25" and the left engine is falling through 18".*

Crosswind takeoff and landing

Crosswind technique is one of the easiest skills to lose. Teaching the crosswind takeoff and landing to student pilots is hard because so many things are happening at once. Many private and commercial pilots are not proficient because crosswind practice might have been rare and abbreviated. Instructor and student must take advantage of any crosswinds that occur during any lesson, which would ensure proficiency.

A crosswind takeoff in a multiengine airplane uses essentially the same technique as a single-engine takeoff. Consult the manufacturer's recommendations for crosswind takeoff and landings. A crosswind component chart is usually included with the airplane's literature. Also check what flap settings are allowed during crosswind operations.

As the takeoff roll begins, the aileron should be turned into the wind. This means that the upwind aileron is deflected up. The upward deflection will hold the upwind wing on the runway. Pilots of multiengine airplanes can use differential power at the beginning of the ground run. By applying more power on the upwind engine, the airplane will resist weathervaning.

The tail is sticking up into the wind. A crosswind strikes the tail on only one side, which tends to pivot the airplane so that the nose aims more into the wind, like a weathervane. If the power is greater on the upwind engine, the differential power will counteract the weathervane force, and the airplane will track straight down the runway centerline.

The rudder will eventually become effective. When the rudder is able to overcome the weathervane force, the pilot should add full power to both engines, and continue the takeoff run as normal. The airplane should be allowed to accelerate through V_{MC} + 5 knots, to a slightly faster than normal rotation speed. This will allow the airplane to pop off the ground. By doing this, the pilot can immediately bank the airplane and establish a crab angle without fear of hitting the upwind main gear or wingtip on the ground. From here, the normal procedures and speed milestones for multiengine takeoff can be followed.

Landing a multiengine airplane in a crosswind is again similar to landing a single-engine airplane in the same conditions. There are two schools of thought.

One method is to hold a crab angle while on final approach and then during the flare to touchdown, apply downwind rudder to take out the crab angle, and align the airplane with the centerline. This requires the pilot to simultaneously apply elevator back pressure and rudder. The elevator and rudder actions require some pilot finesse, but this finesse is hard to come by when both actions happen at the same time.

The second crosswind landing method is to establish a slip on final approach. Aileron holds the upwind-wing down. Opposite rudder prevents the airplane from turning. If the proper amounts of aileron and rudder can be found, the airplane can be held in alignment with the runway. The pilot begins the flare with the upwind-wing low, landing on the upwind main gear first.

The second method does not require the rudder pressure to change during the flare. The pilot should understand what flap settings are allowed while slipping. Avoid the wing-low method when the flaps are deployed beyond the airplane's limit.

No matter which method is used to get on the runway, the aileron should be used during the rollout to hold down the upwind wing. Always use ailerons on the ground for winds. Pull elevator back pressure while taxiing over bumps and while braking. Never stop flying the airplane until it is tied down.

Maximum performance takeoff and landing

The maximum performance takeoff is a short-field takeoff. The goal is to get off the runway early and climb over obstructions quickly. A single-engine soft-field technique is not used because a multiengine airplane is limited by V_{MC} as to when it should be allowed into the air. The single-engine technique allows the airplane into the air at the slowest possible speed while utilizing aerodynamic ground effect. The dangers of multiengine flight close to the ground at or slower than V_{MC} outweigh the dangers of a longer ground roll. For this reason, the airplane should still be rotated and flown off the runway at $V_{MC} + 5$ knots:

1. Hold brakes and add full power to both engines. Verify that full power is being developed, and all engine instruments are indicating in the green arcs.
2. Release brakes and begin ground run. (It might be hard or even impossible to hold the airplane still with brakes against full power in many multiengine airplanes.)
3. Airspeed indicator becomes alive.
4. V_{MC} is passed.
5. $V_{MC} + 5$ knots. Anticipate rotation.
6. Leave the ground and accelerate to V_X.
7. Retract the landing gear as soon as there is no more runway ahead.
8. Hold the pitch attitude that produces V_X speed until obstructions are clear. (Use 50 feet for practice.)
9. When obstructions are clear, lower the nose, and accelerate to V_Y.
10. Hold the pitch attitude that produces V_Y until 500 feet AGL.
11. Perform the 500-foot check: power back, props back.
12. Above 1,000 feet AGL, establish the best cruise climb speed or best speed for engine cooling.

Normal takeoffs have three segments: ground roll, V_Y climb out, and best cruise climb out. The maximum-performance takeoff has four segments: ground roll, V_X climb, V_Y climb, and best cruise climb. The pilot's skill level must be high enough to maneuver the airplane safely within a close tolerance of airspeed while just above the ground. The maximum-performance takeoff will either display the pilot's airspeed skills or expose the pilot's lack of airspeed skills.

The maximum-performance multiengine landing is a short-field approach and landing. The goal is the same for single-engine and multiengine airplanes: Approach over an obstruction to land on a short runway. The multiengine technique requires a near-constant power setting all the way to flare and touchdown. Do not pass the obstruction and then chop power. Plan the approach to be deliberately high, then reduce power gradually, and add full flaps.

The path over the obstruction and onto the runway should be a slanted straight line. Pilots who are not completely familiar with the maneuver or their airplane routinely lower the flaps to the lowest position too early, or while they are too low. This forces them to add power to make the runway. They arrive at the runway too low and too slow, then chop the power, and flop down.

The better technique is to place the airplane high on final approach and deploy full flaps when the airplane is in a position that requires full flaps. The pilot can then gradually reduce power, controlling the airspeed while gliding to touchdown.

Instrument approach: both engines operating

After completing a practice session of the VFR maneuvers, I want to go back to the airport to work on the landings. Returning to the airport is a great opportunity to execute an instrument approach. The student needs to fly at least one IFR approach when no emergencies are taking place. This will convince the pilot that IFR procedures are the same no matter how many engines you have; only the speeds are different.

Perhaps it would be wise to take some dual instrument instruction in a single-engine airplane to assure proficiency before transitioning instrument skills to a multiengine airplane. The IFR workload of the pilot in a multiengine airplane can be overwhelming.

Operate the throttles as if they were only one throttle. Fly the approach like you did when in a single, except make allowances for the faster multiengine speed. You will be required to fly the approach with precision, communicate with ATC effectively, manage the multiengine cockpit, and display excellent situational awareness.

Lower the landing gear and complete the GUMPS check immediately before the final approach fix on nonprecision approaches. Do it no later than glide slope interception on precision approaches. Adjust power as necessary; control speed at approximately 100 knots for most light twins.

If a missed approach is required, smoothly add full power to both engines and climb away faster than V_{YSE}. The prop controls should already be full forward after the GUMPS check, ready to handle the application of full power. When the climb is established, raise the flaps and landing gear according to the manufacturer's recommendations.

Approach and landing: single-engine

Depending on how long it has taken to reach this point in the second lesson, and the stamina of the student, I usually finish with an engine-out approach and landing. This demonstration should be accomplished with the power of one engine reduced to zero thrust. Never take a multiengine airplane below 3,000 feet with an engine completely shut down. All simulated engine-out situations on the runway, during climbout, or in the traffic pattern should be with fuel selectors on, mixtures rich, and one throttle at idle. (If I ever deliberately shut down an engine above 3,000 feet AGL, and then I am unable to restart it, I treat the situation as an emergency.)

For this demonstration, I retard one throttle to zero thrust while on the downwind leg. The student must be careful not to let the pattern get so wide that an excessive power setting from the good engine is necessary to make the field. Also, the student must play the wind properly with correction angles and allowances for a headwind on either base or final.

The student should be able to gradually reduce power from downwind to touchdown. With every increment of power reduction, the rudder pressure that is needed to overcome yaw becomes less. Eventually, the good engine will be at zero thrust, or nearly so, and no yaw will be present. The touchdown is normal. This maneuver presents no dangerous challenges unless a single-engine go-around is forced. Hopefully, this lesson's single-engine approach and landing can be made with no interruptions.

After the second lesson, I expect the student to be very familiar with the airplane. Airspeed control must be excellent. Their understanding of how the airplane acts with only one engine operating should be established. This lesson should be seen as an early milestone in training because the student will be doing most of the flying starting with Lesson 3.

LESSON 3

Objective: The student will practice the review maneuvers and procedures to maintain or gain proficiency. The student will be introduced to engine-out procedures, learn to identify the inoperative engine and initiate appropriate corrective procedures, and maneuver the airplane with one engine inoperative. The student will demonstrate loss of directional control and the recovery technique with an engine out.

Review maneuvers:
Slow flight
Approach to landing stall
Takeoff and departure stall
V_{MC} demonstration
Engine failures enroute
Maneuvering on one engine

Introduce:
Engine failure on takeoff before V_{MC}
Engine failure during climbout after gear is up
Identifying an inoperative engine (student should be able to complete all steps unassisted)
In-flight engine shutdown
Air start
Simulated vectors to approach (single-engine approach)
Approach to landing with one engine
Go-around with two engines and one engine

Completion standards: The student will be able to identify the inoperative engine and use the correct control inputs to maintain straight flight. The student will have a complete and accurate knowledge of the cause, effect, and significance of engine-out minimum control speed, and recognize the imminent loss of control. All engine-inoperative and loss of directional control demonstrations must be completed no lower than 3,000 feet AGL.

Lesson 3 begins true emergency management training. The concepts learned previously must now be applied correctly and aggressively. The flight instructor was your advocate the first two lessons; now the instructor seemingly becomes your nemesis.

Engine failure

Training and checkride prediction: You will be presented with an engine out on the takeoff roll before reaching V_{MC}. The instructor will present a situation that will require you to think fast and react. Somewhere between "airspeed alive" and V_{MC}, the instructor will say something like, "you have a fire in the right engine," or "you have no oil pressure in the left engine," or another problem that indicates an engine failure is imminent.

The instructor should say which engine, left or right, but it really does not matter. Anytime you are slower than V_{MC}, you cannot fly. That decision is made. The situation is actually presented to see if you will pull the power back on both engines and brake to a stop. During the takeoff run, there is absolutely no time for you to do mechanic work. You cannot, in that split second, try to analyze what is wrong and in which engine.

If you only pull back the "ailing" engine's power, leaving the other engine at full power, the airplane might leave the runway. Do not think about left and right. Any problem during the takeoff run requires immediate power reduction on both engines.

When both engines are at idle, brake as necessary to bring the airplane to a stop without leaving the runway centerline. The instructor might allow you to continue a takeoff run after you have made the correct response to the crisis—if the runway is long enough.

An engine failure after takeoff will be presented. This is sometimes referred to as an "engine cut," but be careful with terminology. An engine-out simulation that is below 3,000 feet should be done using reduced throttle, not by cutting engine power with mixture or a fuel selector valve.

After the airplane is in the air and has passed a position where a landing can be made with the existing runway ahead, the instructor will bring the throttle back to absolute idle. The student must act calmly and correctly without hesitation or confusion. Your primary goal is to maintain control of the airplane by keeping the airspeed faster than V_{MC}. Your second goal is to prevent the airplane from descending into the ground; reduce drag, and fly with maximum available performance.

As soon as the power is reduced on one engine, you will see and feel the airplane sway with the engine yaw. Stop the yaw with rudder. If the nose is moving right, use left rudder. If the nose is yawing left, use right rudder. Use as much rudder as necessary to keep the nose straight.

Now that directional control is maintained, observe the airspeed. Adjust the elevator pitch as necessary to maintain V_{YSE}. Your best hope, maybe your only hope, is to hold that blue line.

Airplane control and speed must be brought under control within the first few seconds of engine failure, then establish best performance:

1. Mixtures full rich.
2. Prop controls full forward.
3. Both throttles full forward. Note: Even though one throttle is dead, you should bring both to full power. The emergency has only been taking place a few seconds. Events are taking place faster than you can see, analyze, and reason. In the first second, you cannot positively identify which engine has failed. The good news is that you do not need to know, just push everything forward. You will be pushing something that is right, even if you do not know which it is yet.
4. Flaps UP.
5. Landing gear UP whenever you see that you are level or in a stabilized climb. Do not bring the landing gear up if you are in a descent and there is still the danger of hitting the ground.
6. Identify which engine has failed. Use the idle foot/idle engine method.
7. Verify which engine has failed by pulling back the throttle of the engine you think has failed. If you are correct, there should be no change in the rudder pressure required to hold the airplane straight.
8. Feather the engine. You will not actually feather the engine in training. When a student calls for the engine to be feathered, I advance the dead engine's throttle from absolute idle to a zero-thrust setting. This will reduce yaw just like feathering the prop would reduce yaw.
9. Continue holding the blue-line speed. Climb if possible.

At this point in this lesson, I would give the dead engine back to the student. After full power is regained on both engines, a normal climbout is made. There are some drawbacks to simulating an engine failure by bringing back the throttle, as opposed to using mixture or fuel selectors. The main drawback is that the student can clearly see which engine has been reduced by looking at which throttle has been retarded; the student cannot push both throttles forward. This drawback is not strong enough to overrule the below-3,000-foot-AGL rule. Save the realism for a higher altitude.

The flight instructor will surprise you with a real engine failure at a higher, safer altitude. Even though you know it is coming sometime, it is always a shock. One minute, you are having a friendly conversation; the next minute, the instructor's hand has slipped down toward the fuel selector valve to turn off the fuel to one engine.

The instructor knows that it will take about 30 seconds from the time the valve is moved until the engine actually quits. That is plenty of time for the instructor to continue the pleasant conversation, subsequently making a production out of having her hands nowhere near the mixtures or throttles when the engine actually dies. If the instructor has done the job, your first thought will be that this is a real unexpected failure. Your second thought will be how naive you were to get caught so far off guard.

The position of the fuel selector valve can really help or hinder the stealthy instructor. If the valves are forward under the throttles, the instructor might need to resort to covering the valve panel with the checklist so that you know that something is about to happen but you cannot tell which engine it will be. If the valve is back between the seats, watch out.

I like to turn the valve off and use the 30 seconds before failure to have the student initiate a steep turn. The engine will quit during the turn. While at altitude, I want the student to go through the entire engine-out process. After the initial shock is gone and the student realizes that she is fully responsible to handle the situation, there should be no hesitation:

1. Mixtures rich.
2. Props full forward.
3. Throttles full forward.
4. Flaps up.
5. Gear up.
6. Identify.
7. Verify.
8. Fix or feather. Note: Just above the runway, there is no time to fix the problem, so move quickly to feather the propeller. It is assumed that at altitude, there is time for limited troubleshooting.
9. Decide that altitude allows time to troubleshoot.
   a. Fuel selectors ON. (This must be simulated if the fuel selector valve was deliberately placed in the OFF position for this exercise.)
   b. Primers in and locked.
   c. Carburetor heat ON.
   d. Mixture adjust as necessary.
   e. Fuel quantity check.
   f. Fuel pressure check.
   g. Oil pressure and temperature check.
   h. Magnetos check.
   i. Fuel pumps ON.
   j. Attempt to restart the engine.
10. If the troubleshooting checklist fails to regain engine power, feather and secure the failed engine.
   a. Feather the dead engine's propeller.
   b. Mixture of dead engine to idle cut off.
   c. Dead engine's fuel selector OFF.
   d. Dead engine's fuel pump OFF.
   e. Dead engine's magnetos OFF.
   f. Dead engine's alternator OFF.
   g. Dead engine's cowl flaps closed.
   h. Reduce electrical load as practical.
11. Save the good engine by reducing power as practical and always maintain a speed greater than V_{YSE}.

This is the first time you will be in flight with the engine stopped and the propeller feathered (Figs. 12-10 and 12-11). It is very unusual. The instructor will not let you spend much time flying around while the prop is feathered. For one thing it is not a good idea to leave the hot engine in the icy-cold breeze. It is also not a good idea to overburden the operating engine needlessly. Lastly, the instructor will also be anxious to get the engine going again.

Fig. 12-10. *Maneuvering with one engine inoperative.*

Fig. 12-11. *Feathered right-engine propeller. (This demonstration was conducted on the ramp to safely photograph the feathered propeller up close.)*

For purposes of training the airplane manufacturer probably will include an air-start procedure. The air start might require that the airplane be flown at a particular speed so that the relative wind will help make the propeller windmill. Follow the procedure, and fly the air-start speed. Also, the manufacturer might have specific instructions about the prop control operation and positions.

This procedure does not match every airplane, but it provides some idea about what an air-start checklist requires:

1. Establish air-start airspeed.
2. Fuel selector to the dead engine ON.
3. Dead engine's throttle cracked open about ¼ inch.
4. Dead engine's fuel pump ON.
5. Dead engine's magnetos ON.
6. Dead engine's mixture RICH.
7. Dead engine's prop control full forward.
8. Engage starter to the dead engine. Note: The engine should start to turn, slowly at first, but then faster as the prop comes out of feather. If you have a starter that is temperamental and does not always engage when you start it on the ramp, get that fixed before shutting down that engine in flight. An accumulator that brings the prop out of feather without using the starter is best.
9. After the engine starts, pull prop control back to midrange, approximately 2,000 RPM.
10. Advance the throttle to partial power of about 15 inches. Note: Do not hurry to get all the power back. Allow the engine to run slow until it is warmed up. Keep the cowl flaps closed to retain some engine heat and speed up the warm-up process.
11. Alternator ON.
12. After sufficient warm-up, power can be brought forward to match power on both engines. Perform the cruise checklist.

If the engine cannot be restarted by normal means, the airplane's handbook might have some suggestions about how to get the prop windmilling by alternate means. Of course, flying around with one engine feathered is not a good time to break out the handbook for a little light reading. Look over all the airplane's emergency procedures prior to this flight. If the engine will not restart, and all attempts have failed, proceed below 3,000 feet AGL with extreme caution. Inform the control tower or area traffic of your problem, and this should give you an uninterrupted path to the runway. Be very reluctant to give up the altitude until you absolutely have to.

If an approach must be made with one engine feathered, you must get it right the first time. Single-engine go-arounds will be practiced in your multiengine training, but will be made with one engine at idle not shut down. Actual engine-feathered single-engine go-arounds should be avoided if at all possible; however, the procedure is the same whether the single-engine approach is simulated or for real.

As you approach the runway, be stingy with your altitude. Every single-engine approach has a point of no return (Fig. 12-12). This point is an altitude that might vary with conditions. I usually use 500 feet AGL as my decision altitude. Above 500 feet AGL, if I must make a single-engine go-around, I can (under certain conditions) as long as I immediately go full power with the good engine, reduce drag, and can maintain V_{YSE}.

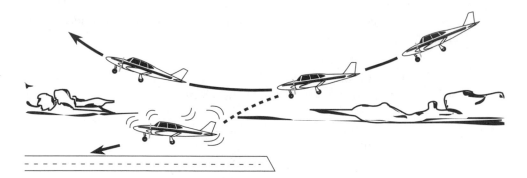

Fig. 12-12. *The decision to go-around on one engine must be made early. There comes a point in each single-engine approach beyond which a landing must be made because a go-around becomes extremely hazardous.*

Below 500 AGL, it is probably safer to continue to the ground, even if that means landing in the grass to avoid someone who has pulled out on the runway. Past the point of no return the pilot must not consider going around; the decision to land is made, no matter what else might happen.

During a single-engine approach, leave the landing gear up until the runway is absolutely made. Anticipate the drag and increased rate of descent caused by the landing gear. Use wing flaps sparingly or not at all.

Single-engine instrument approaches

Recall that the greatest hindrance to an IFR multiengine rating is not the multiengine skills; it is the common lack of instrument skills. Many students show up for multiengine training without instrument proficiency and never give it a thought. When I am working with a student toward an IFR/multi, I expect the IFR procedures, skills, and techniques to already be excellent.

If the student is not instrument proficient, the multiengine training will stall and become very expensive. The elapsed time between instrument rating and multiengine rating might have been several years for some pilots. Do yourself and your budget a big favor. Before getting in a multiengine airplane, regain your IFR proficiency in a less expensive single-engine airplane.

The previous lesson had at least one all-engine instrument approach. I try the first single-engine approach during this lesson, if the student is instrument proficient. A simulated engine failure can occur anytime during an approach. The worst time for an engine failure is between the final approach fix and the missed approach point. Under normal circumstances, the airplane is centered on the inbound course, adjusted for wind, and the proper rate of descent has been established. The inbound course and descent can easily be ruined when an engine fails at this position.

Initial yaw caused by engine failure can take you off the course, especially a localizer. The sudden increase in drag will increase the rate of descent, which might cause you to lose the glide slope. Things can go to heck very fast. The pilot must act quickly and aggressively to accurately control two situations at the same time. First, the pilot must meet the engine-failure emergency. Second, the pilot must continue the instrument approach as if everything else is normal.

The most common error is losing track of the approach while reacting to the loss of an engine. Losing track means flying off course, having an excessively steep descent, forgetting the approach timing, or accidentally descending through an MDA or DH. The pilot's workload will skyrocket, so it pays to have prepared early for the approach, which is another aspect of instrument proficiency.

As soon as the pilot gets things under control during a single-engine approach, landing gear and wing flaps must be dealt with. I prefer to perform the complete GUMPS check before beginning the approach so that all those items are taken care of and my attention can be placed on the instrument approach. This means that if an engine fails during the approach, the landing gear and approach flaps are already down.

Bring the gear up? Initially, I would say no, but it does depend on how the approach is expected to terminate. If I am descending on the approach to a straight-in landing, then I will leave the gear down. The landing gear produces drag, which is OK because I want to come down anyway; however, if I expect to fly level at anytime during the approach, I will retract the landing gear. I would try to make the instrument approach terminate with a straight-in landing for this reason of convenience and safety.

LESSON 4

Objective: The student will review the listed maneuvers required for basic instrument flight: maneuvers and procedures, VOR and/or NDB holding procedures, and a VOR approach.

Review maneuvers:
Maneuvering on one engine
Selected VFR airwork maneuvers
Procedures for shut-down and feathering
Engine restart
Emergency operations
Systems and equipment malfunctions
VOR approach
NDB approach (The approach will be full or vectored or engine-out depending on the student's performance.)
Holding patterns
Missed approach
Single-engine circle-to-land

Completion standards: The student will demonstrate attitude instrument flight while maintaining altitude within 100 feet and headings within 10°. Climbs and descents will be performed within 10 knots of the desired airspeed and level-offs will be completed within 100 feet of the assigned altitude. During engine-out operation the student will be able to readily identify the inoperative engine, shut down, and feather while maintaining altitude within 100 feet and headings with 15°. The approaches will be completed while maintaining the correct approach speed within 15 knots. Holding patterns will be entered correctly and within 10 knots of the proper holding airspeed.

This lesson begins with standard multiengine airwork that should be completely understood. The maneuvers improve proficiency and develop self-confidence. More instrument procedures are practiced after the airwork. I want to get into a holding pattern somewhere and while in the hold I can go through slow flight, and even stalls. Then on to instrument approaches.

The student must handle all the radio communications, fly the airplane with precision, and make all the decisions. In addition to shooting a variety of instrument approaches, I also want to end an approach with a circle-to-land maneuver with only one engine operating.

The previous lesson discussed the decision to keep the landing gear down after engine failure during an approach. Leave the gear down if the landing will be straight in and the path from engine failure to touchdown is a continuous descent. The decision is different if you must fly an extended course while holding a constant altitude during the approach: a circle-to-land maneuver.

The circle-to-land requires the pilot to reach the published approach MDA, fly level around to the other side of the airport, and land. The circling altitude is a mandatory altitude. This is a tricky maneuver under any circumstances, especially with an engine failed.

You cannot legally descend below the circle-to-land minimums until in a position that is within 30° either side of the landing runway's centerline. You cannot climb, or you risk getting back into the clouds, which calls for a missed approach. You cannot go down. You cannot go up. You must maintain straight and level flight with one engine.

Recall the drag demonstrations that showed that a dirty airplane with one engine inoperative might not be capable of flying level. This is a good reason to retract the landing gear in the circle, then reextend the gear when starting final descent to land.

It is also very important to teardrop the approach after a circle-to-land maneuver. Do not try and make a perfect VFR traffic pattern of downwind, base, and final. Play the wind and make the approach one smooth turn to final rolling out on the runway centerline.

Remember that a single-engine go-around from low altitude would be hazardous. Plan the approach properly, and do not overshoot the final approach. If the approach path is faulty, initiate a go-around early. Do not try to salvage a faulty approach with steep-bank turns to realign with the centerline. To do so invites low altitude, unrecoverable stalls.

Plan a point-of-no-return altitude, below which a single-engine go-around is unacceptable. It is possible that your circle-to-land altitude is already at or below your point-of-no-return altitude. This means that when you are committed to a circle-to-land maneuver, you are very close to a full commitment to land.

If you had a choice, you should fly this at an airport with an operating control tower. Inform the tower of the procedure you plan to execute. ATC should be able to keep other airplanes out of the way. At uncontrolled fields, other airplanes might cause an unwanted, and dangerous, single-engine go-around.

A crosswind, partial-panel NDB approach, with an engine failure, concluding with a circle-to-land procedure on the opposite-direction runway, is the supreme test of the pilot's multiengine skills, instrument flying skills, knowledge of the airplane, and good judgment.

LESSON 5

Review and practice:
Fuel flow metering
VOR and/or NDB holding
ILS approach
NDB simulated vector
ILS approach on one engine
VOR and/or approach on one engine (Instructor should try to include a single-engine landing from the approach: straight-in and circle-to-land.)

Completion standards: The student will demonstrate basic attitude instrument flight at a proficiency level that meets or exceeds the criteria specified in the multiengine sections of the applicable FAA test standards. Additionally, the student will demonstrate the ability to perform an approach while maintaining airspeed within 10 knots and altitude within 100 feet on the final approach segment. The student will execute missed approach procedures. If circling approaches are conducted, the student will maneuver the airplane at the MDA in a turn with a radius that does not exceed the visibility minimum for the approach.

Lessons 5, 6, and 7 should all be for proficiency enhancement without much introductory material. The completion standard for Lesson 5 specifically uses the IFR/multi and instrument-rating practical test standards as its benchmark. This means that the student's instrument flying must be checkride-ready from here on. This lesson might take several flights to meet this standard if instrument proficiency was weak to begin with.

The multiengine student should be gaining confidence with each maneuver, approach, and procedure. Pilots at this level are not spectators, but are innovators, and take the lead with decisions. Good judgment should be evident in all actions.

LESSON 6

Objective: The student will practice each maneuver to gain proficiency. The student will learn the procedures required for an engine-out ILS, VOR, and NDB approach.

Review and practice:
All VFR maneuvers
ILS approach on one engine
Nonprecision approach as necessary
V_{MC} demonstration (instrument reference only)
One-engine patterns

Completion standards: The student will demonstrate the ability to perform each maneuver and procedure at a proficiency level that meets or exceeds criteria outlined in the multiengine sections of applicable FAA test standards. After completion of Lesson 6 standards, the student should be ready for the checkride. The last lesson is a mock checkride that is meant to completely prepare the student for the real thing.

LESSON 7

Objective: A chief flight instructor or designated assistant will determine that the instrument-rated student has acquired the proficiency and the performance of the required IFR operations and procedures in the multiengine airplane for successful completion of the FAA flight test.

Review and practice:
All VFR maneuvers
Instrument approach as necessary
Engine failure procedures
One-engine patterns
V_{MC} demonstration
Engine-out taxi

Completion standards: The student will be able to demonstrate each of the listed areas of operations at a proficiency level that meets or exceeds those criteria outlined in the multiengine sections of the applicable FAA test standards. The instrument-rated applicant who desires instrument privileges in the multiengine airplane will be able to demonstrate each of the listed areas of operations at a proficiency level that meets or exceeds those criteria outlined in the instrument-rating test standards.

I have conducted hundreds of these mock checkrides. If I do my job correctly, the lesson will be much tougher than the actual FAA practical test. Lesson 7 should be all encompassing. This means that even if I see something happen that would cause a checkride to be failed, I continue the flight. I want to solve as many potential problems as I can.

On the actual practical test, if the examiner sees something that causes the student to fail, she is supposed to announce it at the time of the failure. The student has an option; stop the test or continue to perform maneuvers after that failure. Either way, the examiner will give credit for the elements of test standards that are passed so that a retest within 60 days applies only to the failed element or elements.

Most applicants are in no mood to continue. The only advantage is to get as much passing credit as possible to shorten the next test session. More often, the test performance after failure goes from bad to worse.

I never say pass or fail during the mock checkride. I continue to test the student even if there are several substandard items. The more problems I can find, the better critique that I can give, and the more help I can give the student in preparing for the actual checkride. That makes this the most demanding lesson of all.

13
Computerized training

IF YOU HAVE TAKEN AN FAA WRITTEN EXAMINATION LATELY, YOU know that they are no longer "written." The FAA began moving away from pencil-and-paper exams and entered the computer age in the early 1990s. Today nobody waits three weeks for test results. The exam is computer-scored and results are given instantly. Previously, students would have to plan well in advance to take the exams so that their results would be mailed in time before the checkride. Now procrastinators can wait until the last minute to take the exam (although I would strongly advise against it).

Computers have invaded aviation as they have all other areas of society. Our tests are taken on computer, our cockpits are enhanced by computers, and even entire airplanes fly by computers. Now computers are being used to help us train to be better pilots.

Schools, corporations, and airlines have learned that much work can be done to prepare pilots for their work environment using computer-based training (CBT). Pilots work one-on-one with computers to receive the training that once was done in large classrooms. In the large group setting, a student's question would be competing with those of all the other class members. The question might not get full attention from the instructor, or it might simply go unasked. When the computer is the instructor, everything is individualized. The computer can lead the student along a customized path of learning.

COMPUTERIZED TRAINING

In today's airline training centers, large classrooms have been replaced by CBT labs filled with individual computer workstations. Customarily, these labs are open 24 hours a day, and pilot/students can work at their own pace through the course.

Just as aviation has its own language, the computer world has its own as well, and today's pilots must learn both. The machines are called hardware. The machines form platforms in which delivery systems can operate. A platform may be combinations of computers (PCs), the monitor, the operating system, CD-ROM, scanners, laser disc players, digital cameras, and speakers.

The operating system allows the computer to run the courseware. Examples of operating systems include System 7 (Mac), OS/2, and DOS. (Windows programs, such as Windows 95, are more accurately called *operating environments,* because they are still DOS-based.)

Many companies and airlines have produced software or courseware to run on these platforms. Courseware available today teaches maintenance courses, safety and survival, air traffic control, inflight services, as well as flight "ab initio" (from the ground up) training.

The system is interactive; a decision made by the student takes the session in a new direction so that each session is potentially different. Also, flight training can use the line-oriented flight training (LOFT) approach. Instead of simply asking the student questions, the computer presents a real-world scenario that requires the student to make decisions based on system knowledge and common sense. In this way, the student learns the information not by rote, but by using correlations with actual situations he or she will face.

The courseware is often more than just a flight simulator program. In addition, it offers detailed moving system diagrams, instrumentation views, and airplane reactions to decisions. The diagrams use high-resolution graphics and digital sound. The courseware does not yet use virtual reality, but it probably will in the near future.

AICC STANDARDS

If you have bought a computer recently, you know that it is practically obsolete by the time you get it home and out of the box. Early on, the need became apparent to standardize the courseware and platforms that would be used to train pilots. In 1995, a group was formed to look at industry needs and to recommend hardware and platforms that could be standardized for aviation CBT programs. The result is the Aviation Industry Computer-Based Training Committee (AICC) standards.

Now if airlines, schools, and corporations follow the AICC guidelines, and courseware producers design programs that will operate within the guidelines, there will be industry-wide agreement. Pilots at a university will be trained on the same or similar platforms as are used in the industry. Pilots who move from a commuter to a major airline will already have exposure to CBT training, and the transition will be smoother. Any airline new hire will have a faster, more cost-effective initial training period.

The AICC has also recommended guidelines for hardware. The objective is to provide a training course delivery system with the ability to operate the largest number of currently available aviation CBT courseware. The recommendations take into consideration four other factors as well: flexibility, expandability, changing technologies, and certification testing.

Flexibility Flexibility is important so that individual users can customize their courses. In addition, airlines or schools might need to network many computers, and nobody wants to buy a computer today that will not run tomorrow's software. Flexibility was strongly considered in the AICC hardware recommendations.

Expandability The AICC understood how fast the computer industry is moving and wanted to recommend platforms that could expand when the need arises. Systems must be upgradable, and any upgrade must be within economic reach.

Changing technologies The AICC proposed to continually update their recommendations when new technologies come out. Virtual reality (VR) might very well be a part of every pilot's training, and there will certainly be ongoing developments that will challenge us to upgrade again.

An independent test lab has been used by the AICC to ensure that all courseware does in fact run on delivery systems that meet the AICC platform guidelines. As of April 1996, AICC began recommending that courseware be developed as a Windows application running under Windows 95. The AICC does list as alternative platforms the Macintosh, PowerMac, PowerPC, and DEC Alpha.

The basic guidelines include:

- A minimum 75 MHz central processing unit (CPU).
- A power supply capable of 110/120 or 220/240 volts, and either 50 or 60 Hz.
- A minimum of 16 MB of random access memory (RAM) with the capability to add more.
- A standard QWERTY keyboard (the letters *QWERTY* are the first six letters on the top letter row of standard keyboards).
- A MPCII 16-bit sound card.
- If a CD-ROM is used, it should be an MPCII-compliant.

This discussion of CBT training should not be limited to "big" airplanes and airlines alone. Courseware is available for light and medium-sized multiengine airplanes. TRO Aviation Training Services of Edina, Minnesota, for instance, offers a CBT course for the Beechcraft Baron and Piper Cheyenne. These courses involve 22 hours of computer work. TRO even has a single-engine CBT for the Piper Arrow.

FLIGHT TRAINING DEVICES

Computers have also helped in the development of what we often call flight simulators. The advantages of flight simulation on the ground are enormous. The time and cost savings of flight simulation over actual flight usually pays for ground training devices quickly.

Flight simulation can add safety to the training as well. Many emergency situations that cannot be safely reenacted in flight can be simulated on the ground. Also, 52 percent of mid-air collisions involve training flights, probably because students and instructors working on scenarios in the airplane do not look outside like they should. Ground simulation removes this danger completely.

Over the years some terminology problems have developed in the world of ground simulation. I often catch myself using the term "simulator" when in fact I mean "ground trainer." Essentially, an airplane simulator must be a full-sized, exact replica of a specific type or make, model, and series airplane cockpit. It must have computer software programs that are necessary to represent the airplane in ground and flight operations. It must have a visual system providing an out-of-cockpit view and a "force (motion) cueing" system that at least provides cues around the three axes of airplane control.

An airplane flight training device (FTD) is also a full-sized replica of an airplane that uses computer software to present ground and flight situations, but it does not move. The FTD's layout can be inside an enclosed cockpit or arranged as an open flight deck. This device can be a generic trainer. In other words, it does not have to duplicate any specific airplane, and visuals are not required.

FTDs have gone by many names in the past, leading to some confusion. Cockpit procedures trainers (CPT), cockpit systems simulators (CSS), ground trainers (GT), and fixed-base simulators (FBS) all now fit under the category of flight training devices. To make it easy: in general, if it moves, it is a simulator. If not, it is an FTD. (Refer to chapter 17 for more detail on the specifications of simulators and FTDs.)

Before any machine is classified and can be used in the training of pilots, it must be approved by the FAA. A principal operations inspector (POI) from the local FAA office must inspect the machine. A simulator or FTD is not a simulator or FTD until the FAA says it is.

Capabilities of both simulators and FTDs vary widely. Some are multimillion-dollar full-motion, holographic, airplane-specific enclosed flight decks; others are not much more than home computers. The FAA has had a hard time keeping up with the explosion in computer technology. Their attempt to categorize these machines has led to a two-tiered, multilevel classification system.

Flight simulators are grouped together and have four levels of complexity: A, B, C, and D. FTDs have seven levels: 1 through 7. In the FTD group, level 1 is currently "reserved" while the FAA tries to figure out what to do with all the home computer flight simulator software programs that are currently on the market. As of this writing, home computers, even with joysticks, are not considered FTDs and cannot be used for pilot training toward certification and currency.

FTD levels 2 and 3 have generic cockpits and do not represent any one specific airplane. I use a Frasca 141, which is a level 3 FTD, primarily to train instrument students who fly in a Cessna 172. The Frasca is not an exact replica of the Cessna; the Frasca could just as easily be used in conjunction with a Piper Cherokee. At this level, the

FTD is not specific. Instead, it represents a group of airplanes that have instrument flight training in common.

FTD levels 4 through 7, on the other hand, do represent a specific airplane. The device is matched to a particular make, model, and series of airplane, for instance, Boeing 737-300.

For the particulars on each level from both groups, you should obtain FAA Advisory Circular 120-45A. You can pick up this AC at your local FAA office or order it from the FAA. The following is the outline of the AC and associated FTD level requirements. Although this list is not complete, you can determine what is required at each level.

I. Functions and maneuvers
    A. Preparation for flight (cockpit only)   Levels 2-7
    B. Surface operations
        1. Engine start   Levels 2-7
        2. Push back   Levels 3-7
        3. Brake operation   Levels 2,3,5,6,7
    C. Normal takeoff
        1. Powerplant check (run-up)   Levels 2-7
        2. Acceleration, nose wheel steering crosswind, landing gear, flap operations   Levels 2,3,5,6,7
        3. Rejected/aborted takeoff   Levels 3,6,7
        4. Continued takeoff with engine failure at most critical point   Level 7
        5. Flight control system failure   Levels 2-7
    D. Inflight operations
        1. Climb. Normal and one engine inoperative (multiengine FTD)   Levels 2-7
        2. Cruise. High-altitude handling, high-speed handling, normal and steep turns, approach to stalls   Levels 2,3,5,6,7
            Engine shutdown and restart, maneuvering with one engine   Levels 2-7
            Specific flight characteristics   Levels 6,7
        3. Descent. Normal and maximum   Levels 2,3,5,6,7
    E. Approaches
        1. Nonprecision—all engines   Levels 2,3,5,6,7
            Nonprecision—one or more engines inoperative   Levels 3,6,7
            Missed approach   Levels 2,3,5,6,7

2. Precision. PAR normal	Levels 3,6,7
ILS normal	Levels 2,3,5,6,7
With engine(s) inoperative	Levels 2,3,5,6,7
Missed approach	Levels 2,3,5,6,7
F. Surface operations	
1. Landing roll	Levels 2,3,5,6,7
Reverse thrust operations	Levels 3,6,7
G. Any flight phase	
1. Aircraft and powerplant systems	Levels 2-7
2. Flight management and guidance	Levels 2-7
3. Airborne procedures	Levels 2-7
4. Engine shutdown and parking	Levels 2-7

The application of computers to flight training is a significant advance. As long as you follow the rules (see chapter 17), computers can save time and money for pilots in training. No matter what type of machine, from the most sophisticated to the least, computers should be used to simulate real-world situations and scenarios. Although the airlines use this method in LOFT (line-oriented flight training) programs, it should be taught long before a pilot reaches an airline interview.

LOFT TRAINING

Using computers and FTDs can go a long way in teaching LOFT. Once while giving ground trainer instruction with a student, I simulated radio failure. To isolate the student from the simulated environment and in an attempt to reproduce a real environment, I closed the door to the FTD so that the student was truly alone, as would be the case with a single pilot in the airplane.

After issuing a holding pattern instruction, complete with an expect further clearance time, I stopped responding to the student's radio calls. The student was not sure what to do because he was not completely playing the role of the simulation, but he did leave the hold at the proper EFC time and proceeded to an approach.

The student had to choose an approach based on his perception of the wind and traffic flow. He set up an approach to the destination airport and began inbound. The student's anxiety over the fact that nobody was talking to him began to mount up. Eventually, he could not stand it any longer. Before the airplane reached the decision height, he got up from the pilot's seat, opened the door, and came out! I asked him why he decided to jump from his airplane before landing. He said, "I thought you had gone to lunch and left me in there!"

The instructor should make it clear to the student that, even though in truth an FTD will not leave the ground, they must do everything as if they truly were in flight. This is obviously easier to say than to believe.

Many other methods have been used by creative flight instructors during LOFT. While in a Boeing 737 simulator, a first officer was told through her headset that the simulated flight was about to receive a bird strike through her front window. She was instructed to "play dead" after the bird hit the window. Then, sure enough, the out-the-cockpit view screen on the first officer's side pictured a shattered window and the pilot, playing the part well, slumped over. The captain, who did not know the first officer was in on the ruse, had to handle all the inflight duties himself, including handling the rapid decompression from the broken window.

On another day a flightcrew in a simulator cruising at a high altitude was told that a bomb threat had been called in against their airplane. In the scenario the bomber left the message that the bomb would go off whenever the airplane descended below 5,000 feet. What should the flightcrew do about this problem? Land somewhere that the airport elevation was above 5,000 feet, of course! The crew was expected to find several higher-than-5,000-feet airports and then calculate, accounting for winds, fuel, and runway length, which airport to approach.

The computer programmer had already designed into the situation only one airport that would meet all the situation requirements: above 5,000 feet, within fuel range, and with a long enough runway. The simulation observers waited to see if the crew would choose the correct airport and to do so fast enough to turn and get to that airport. The situation required the pilots to work as a team, to create a solution, to understand the fuel remaining and the fuel consumption rate, to calculate groundspeed with existing winds, and to take quick, accurate, decisive action.

As you can see, much more is gained in flight training with situation training than would have been the case if the pilot were simply asked to calculate a groundspeed, for example.

Some of us are still apprehensive around computers. No matter what your opinion of the growing computer technologies, they are a part of our aviation lives now. Our airplanes will fly more efficiently with computers, and our pilot training can be more efficient as well. If you are not comfortable with computer training yet, it might simply be a matter of exposure. Try out the new CBT programs and training devices, and you should see the advantages. As a prospective professional pilot, ready or not, you will be judged on how well you work with computer technology. If you are not computer-literate today, you should take steps now to get onboard. Your career might very well depend on it.

14
Multiengine rating practical test standards

PILOTS NEVER GET PAST "CHECKRIDITIS." THINK OF THE NERVOUSNESS AS part of the test. Applicants blame a checkride failure on the fact that they were nervous, which might not be a valid reason. Plenty of things happen in everyday flying that will make you nervous, in which case you must perform better than any other time.

What if the left engine caught on fire? An engine fire is enough to make anybody nervous. If I am so nervous that I cannot do my job, then I am not a pilot. The problem will get worse if I freeze at the controls and do nothing because I am nervous. Pilots must work through the nervousness and still take corrective action to meet any situation.

What is the worst thing that can happen on a checkride? You can fail. A checkride failure does not scare me as much as an engine failure on takeoff, or getting hit by lightning, or a midair collision. If I stop being a pilot at the first sign of stress and nervousness, then I shouldn't have become a pilot.

Dealing with the checkride nervousness is just as much a part of the test as preflight, stalls, and single-engine landings. We will always be nervous, but it can never be an excuse for our lack of preparation. The best remedy for checkriditis is confidence. Confidence comes from hard work, study, and proficiency.

The checkride will begin with the examiner asking the question, "Is this going to be an IFR or VFR multiengine rating test?" Remember that you are committed when you answer the question. The examiner will look over your logbook and certificate to be sure that you qualify for the test. The examiner will double-check to see that the application for airman certificate or rating form is correctly filled out and signed by the applicant and instructor.

The examiner is supposed to tell you where restrooms are, where the water fountain or soda machines can be found, and whether or not smoking will be permitted during the test. After all this, the real test begins.

You will notice that your flight instructor, who has been with you through thick and thin, is nowhere to be found. Applicants always get this great sense of aloneness when the test gets down to business. The first oral exam question is important for psychological reasons. After hours of study, you just want to see if it has all paid off. The effort will pay nice dividends if you have prepared properly.

Do not expect the oral exam questions to be single-information questions. An example of a single-information question: What color is the position light on the airplane's right wing? To answer this question, the applicant has to remember a single piece of knowledge. No reasoning was required, just rote memorization.

The examiner is more likely to ask: "You are flying at night and you see another airplane at your altitude and at your 2 o'clock position. All you can see is a green wingtip light. Who has the right-of-way?" This question requires the applicant to know many more bits of knowledge and to group them together to reason out a proper course of action. In the oral exam expect questions that will force you to produce some judgment.

If you only memorize a list of airplane speeds, capacities, and procedures, without truly understanding how to utilize the speeds, capacities, and procedures, then failure is probable. An examiner might ask single-information questions, but only to set up thought-provoking questions.

The study questions in the next subsection are single-information questions that are included here to help get you started. Many are questions for a chain that starts with a single-information question, then progresses to the real heart of the matter. Go through the questions with the airplane's manuals at your side. The questions concerning a particular airplane can be used as an open-book test of the operating handbook.

MULTIENGINE ORAL EXAMINATION QUESTIONS

Does the airplane have a critical engine?

If the airplane has counterrotating propellers, the answer is no. Only when both engines turn the same direction does one become critical. Refer to chapter 1.

What makes an engine critical?

If both engines turn the same way (clockwise, as seen from the cockpit), P factor will shift the thrust vector to the right. The shifted thrust vector lengthens the lever arm, and yaw becomes more effective. Refer to chapter 1.

What type engine does the airplane have?

Refer to the airplane's operating handbook or other aircraft documents.

What do the numbers and letters of the airplane's engine type mean?

Numbers, such as 360, represent piston displacement. The letter O represents opposed; L represents left-turning or counterrotating. Refer to the airplane's operating handbook or other aircraft documents for specific information.

What is piston displacement?

The piston displacement is the area that all cylinders sweep out during their top-dead-center to bottom-dead-center stroke.

What is the brake horsepower of the engines?

Refer to the airplane's operating handbook or other aircraft documents.

What is the difference between brake horsepower and thrust horsepower?

Brake horsepower (BHP) is the power produced by the engine that is delivered to the propeller. Thrust horsepower (THP) is the actual power from the propeller. Because no propeller is 100 percent efficient, BHP will always be greater than THP. The invention of the constant-speed propeller narrowed the gap between BHP and THP. Refer to chapter 4.

What engine-driven accessories are attached to the engines?

Oil pumps, fuel pumps, vacuum pumps, magnetos, prop governors, tachometers, alternators, and the like are attached to the engines. Accessories and the normal friction of parts inside the engine equal *friction horsepower* (FHP). Engine designers must allow for this loss of power from friction. The theoretical value of horsepower is called *indicated horsepower* (IHP): IHP – FHP = BHP.

How do engine-driven accessories affect brake horsepower?

Because any friction or drag on the engine reduces the power delivered to the propeller shaft, any accessories will reduce BHP. We are willing to accept this BHP reduction in return for the beneficial aspects of accessories: magnetos fire spark plugs; vacuum pumps help spin gyro instruments; and oil pumps move the engine lubricant.

What is the first indication of an engine failure (multiengine airplane)?

When an engine fails, the first indication will be a yaw and roll motion toward the failed engine. The pilot must react instinctively with rudder to keep the airplane straight. Never fly a multiengine airplane with your feet flat on the floor. You must have your feet on the rudder pedals, ready to react.

What items should be systematically checked if engine roughness occurs?

Verify this with the POH, but the primary items are:

- Mixtures—adjust as necessary.
- Fuel selectors—on proper tank.
- Crossfeed—operated properly.
- Electric fuel pumps—on.

- Carburetor heat—on.
- Magnetos—check separately.

How long do you wait for an oil pressure indication before shutting down an engine at engine start?

Verify with the POH, but the rule of thumb is 30 seconds in summer and 60 seconds in winter.

What is the procedure when the cylinder head temperature becomes too hot?

1. Reduce power.
2. Open cowl flaps.
3. Enrich the mixture.
4. Lower the nose if climbing (best climb cooling speed).

Why is it a poor procedure to idle an engine for long periods of time?

Idling uses the idle circuit of the carburetor, which does not meter fuel as accurately as the main metering system will at faster RPMs. The idle circuit might run the engine rich, which will not burn cleanly. This can cause carbon deposits to foul the spark plugs causing that engine to run rough. It is a good idea to operate the idle circuit (throttle pulled all the way back) for a short period to ensure that the idle circuit is working and that the engine will not quit at low idle.

What is the normal magneto drop during the runup and what are the limitations?

Refer to the airplane's POH. A 100–150 RPM drop is normal, and the difference between the two magnetos on one engine should be within 50 RPM of each other. Allow plenty of warm-up time prior to the engine run-up.

What type of oil should be used in the airplane's engines?

Refer to the airplane's operating handbook or other aircraft documents.

Would a different season of the year or different climate determine which oil to use?

Yes. Outside-air temperatures determine the oil viscosity used in an airplane. Oil must be thick enough to lubricate, but not break down under heat, plus thin enough to properly flow through the engine and lubricate. Check the engine manufacturer's recommendations for proper oil grade within a certain outside-air temperature range.

What is the purpose of carburetor heat?

Carburetor heat provides heated air to the carburetor in the event of icing. Carb heat is also the alternate source of engine air. You should know where the heated air comes from in the airplane. Often the air is heated by contact with a hot exhaust pipe. This always opens the possibility of an exhaust system crack developing and contaminating the carburetor air. You should see an RPM drop when carb heat is applied because the warm air is less dense, which provides less combustion. The RPM reduction proves to the pilot that the heat system is working.

What is the minimum safe amount of oil in each engine?

Refer to the airplane's operating handbook or other aircraft documents.

Can the airplane's oil dipsticks be interchanged?

No. Usually there is a left-engine dipstick and a right-engine dipstick. They do not have duplicate scales. Because the engines are mounted on the wings and because the wings have a dihedral, the oil sits in the pan at an angle. The proper dipstick is needed to get the proper reading of the oil level.

Why are the prop controls pushed forward before landing?

The throttles should be placed full-forward, or at a climb setting in some models, to prepare for a possible go-around. If power were suddenly needed, you would want the propellers to be in position to accept the power. If you inadvertently left the props back, and then added full power, the effect would be like shooting the power of a cannon through the barrel of a rifle. The result would be less than full power (less than full thrust) and possible damage to the engine/prop combination.

What drives the airplane's propeller into a feathered position?

Refer to chapter 4. The airplane's operating handbook and other aircraft documents will have specific information.

How long does it take for the propeller to feather?

Refer to the airplane's operating handbook or other aircraft documents. It should take 8–10 seconds from the time the prop control is placed in the feather position until the propeller actually stops.

What brings the airplane's propeller out of feather?

The airplane's operating handbook or other aircraft documents will have specific information; general information is in chapter 4. Various systems will unfeather propeller blades: a spring in the hub, oil pressure, an accumulator.

What would happen if the prop-governor shaft broke?

If the shaft stopped turning, the flyweights in the governor would no longer have centrifugal force. The flyweights would fold in under the speeder spring's tension. What happens next depends on the airplane's system. Refer to chapter 4.

What would happen if the prop governor's speeder spring broke?

If the speeder spring broke, the flyweights would swing out unchecked by the speeder spring tension. What happens next depends on the airplane's system. Refer to chapter 4.

What is a synchrophaser?

A synchrophaser is the electronic device (described in chapter 4) that automatically places both engines at the exact same RPM. Synchronizing the propellers reduces vibration and the annoying prop noise oscillations.

What holds the gear up in the retracted position?

Refer to the airplane's operating handbook or other aircraft documents. Most are held up by hydraulic pressure.

What happens if the hydraulic system malfunctions or leaks?

Refer to the airplane literature for specific information. Normally, the pressure holding the gear up will be slowly released if the system developed a leak. The landing gear would extend slowly. The pressure sensor of the landing gear system should feel this loss of pressure and bring the gear back up; however, the additional pressure could force the system to leak more. The danger is that if the gear comes out slowly, it will not have the full benefit of a gravity-assist to swing and lock in place. Put the landing gear down while there is still fluid in the system. Land as soon as practical.

How long does landing gear extension or retraction take?

Refer to the airplane's operating handbook or other aircraft documents. It is important to watch for when the landing gear completes its travel. The landing gear's hydraulic pump should automatically turn off when the system pressure reaches its upper pressure limit; however, if the system's pressure sensor malfunctions, the pump will continue to run. This can damage or disable the pump because it is not designed to operate for long periods of time. The attentive pilot should notice if the pump continues to operate past the proper length of time. If the pump does not stop automatically, the pilot should turn off the pump by pulling out the circuit breaker.

What causes the airplane's landing gear to retract?

Most light-twin airplanes use hydraulic fluid pushed by an electric pump. Refer to the airplane's operating handbook or other aircraft documents.

What causes the airplane's landing gear to move to the down-and-locked position?

Refer to the airplane's operating handbook or other aircraft documents.

What can be done if the landing gear does not extend?

The airplane's handbook will have an emergency gear extension checklist. Check the landing gear's electric pump circuit breaker to ensure that it is pushed in. Check the master switch. Verify that the landing gear selector switch is in the down position, then extend the gear manually.

What is the emergency gear-extension speed?

Refer to the airplane's operating handbook or other aircraft documents.

How does the emergency gear extension system work?

Most emergency landing gear extension systems release pressure in the lines, which allows the gear to free fall into place. Refer to the airplane's operating handbook or other aircraft documents for specific information.

What will happen to the landing gear during an electrical failure?

If the system uses an electric pump to move the hydraulic fluid, then the failure of the electrical system will fail the pump. You will need to use the emergency extension system. Refer to the airplane's operating handbook or other aircraft documents.

What is a squat switch and how does it work?

The squat switch is a device that prevents the landing gear from retracting while the airplane is on the ground. The electric landing gear pump will only operate if current is sent from the primary electrical bus, through the squat switch, and then on to the pump. When the weight of the airplane is on the landing gear's oleo strut, the strut is compressed. In this position, the squat switch is open, and the electrical connection to the pump is broken. No electricity gets through; therefore, the pump cannot turn, and the gear cannot fold up. When the airplane is in the air, no weight is on the strut, so the strut extends. The extension closes the squat switch, and the electrical connection is made to the pump. This allows the pump to operate and move the hydraulic fluid, which actuates the landing gear. Refer to the airplane's operating handbook or other aircraft documents for specific information.

Where are any squat switches located on the airplane?

Refer to the airplane's operating handbook or other aircraft documents.

What causes the green gear-down-and-locked light, or lights, to illuminate?

The individual landing gears have a set of contacts, similar to a squat switch, between the primary electrical bus and the green landing-gear-down light. When the landing gear reaches the down-and-locked position, the contacts connect, and the light comes on.

Where is the landing gear hydraulic fluid reservoir located in the airplane?

Refer to the airplane's operating handbook or other aircraft documents.

Why is the landing gear operation speed (V_{LO}) different than the landing gear extended speed (V_{LE})?

Landing gear that is already down and locked can withstand greater loads than during extension or retraction. This is why V_{LE} is faster than V_{LO}. Landing gear doors that are in transit might cup the wind and produce excessive drag, which might adversely affect airspeed at a crucial moment. Depending on the direction of gear travel, an excessive relative wind might thrust the landing gear up into the wells, where they can become jammed.

Where is the brake hydraulic fluid reservoir located in the airplane?

Refer to the airplane's operating handbook or other aircraft documents.

When the landing gear is fully retracted, what makes the landing gear hydraulic system pump stop pumping?

The hydraulic system has a pressure sensor that monitors the number of pounds per square inch that the system is producing in the lines. The pressure sensor has an upper and lower range. When the landing gear is fully retracted, the hydraulic lines will continue to pressurize for a short time after the gear is up. When the pressure builds to the upper pressure limit, the sensor automatically turns off the pump motor. If at any time the pressure falls below the lower limit (leak in a line), the sensor will turn the pump motor on and pump the pressure to the upper limit again. Refer to the airplane's POH to determine the upper and lower pressure limits.

How are the landing gear lights dimmed?

The normal brightness of the landing gear position lights on the panel is too bright for night vision; therefore, the lights need to be dimmable. The lights may be dimmed one of two ways. A shutter might be turned to squint out the light. A dimmer setting for all panel lights might include the landing gear position indicators. On some models, the gear lights automatically dim when the navigation lights are turned on. The manufacturer figured that if it is dark enough to turn on the position lights, then it is also dark enough to turn down the cabin lights, including the gear lights. (Students beware. It is a favorite flight-instructor trick to turn on the navigation lights and dim the gear lights when you are not looking. During the daytime, it will look as if the lights are not on at all. Woe be unto you if you land without double-checking the gear lights on short final.)

What is the normal final approach speed?

The safe final approach speed will vary from airplane to airplane. The speed also depends on the use of flaps. Read what the manufacturer has to say about the matter. I like to play it safe and hug the blue line into the flare.

When does the landing gear horn sound?

The landing gear warning horn should sound if the gear handle is ever placed in the UP position while on the ground. If the squat switch system is working properly, the gear should not retract, even with the handle up. The horn will also sound anytime either throttle is retarded below an engine setting sufficient to sustain flight and all three gears are not down and locked, or anytime flaps are extended past an intermediate position while all three gears are not down and locked. Refer to the POH for specific details.

When is the landing gear retracted on takeoff?

The landing gear should only be retracted when no more runway or runway overrun is available. If an engine fails after liftoff, and if there is still enough runway to land straight ahead, you can set the airplane right back down, but only if the landing gear is still down.

What is the recommended main gear and nose gear tire pressure for the airplane?

Refer to the airplane's operating handbook or other aircraft documents.

What does the stall warning horn and landing gear warning horn sound like?

It is very important that you know the difference in the sound of the stall horn and the landing gear unsafe horn. Most manufacturers make the horns sound different; others make one horn a constant sound and the other horn an intermittent sound. Refer to the airplane's operating handbook or other aircraft documents.

The battery is dead, so you call for an APU start. The lineman that brings over the power cart asks, "Do you want this set on 12 or 24 volts?" What will you tell the lineman?

Refer to the airplane's operating handbook or other aircraft documents.

What are the procedures for starting using external power?

The procedure depends on the individual system. Some systems require that the master switch be ON and others have it turned OFF. Refer to the airplane's operating handbook or other aircraft documents.

Where are the batteries located?

Refer to the airplane's operating handbook or other aircraft documents.

Does the battery have ventilation? If so, how is it ventilated? If so, why does it need ventilation?

Vents near a battery will circulate fresh air over the battery. The entrance vent is cut into the wind so that ram-air is forced inside. The exit vent is cut away from the wind so that the air is drawn outside. If the battery ever received an overcharge from the alternator and the battery acid boiled, it would be important to keep the acid's fumes out of the cabin.

Does the airplane have an alternator or a generator?

Refer to the airplane's operating handbook or other aircraft documents.

Which items draw the most electrical current?

The largest electrical draw is usually the landing gear pump motor, followed by the wing flaps' motor, the heater-air blower, the fresh-air blower, the landing lights, and the pitot-tube heater. This information would be important if you found yourself in flight with battery power only. You might need to prioritize the essential equipment based upon power needs.

What happens if the alternator voltage becomes too high?

The system is protected by an over-voltage relay that essentially takes the alternator off line whenever the voltage exceeds a preset limit. The limit is usually 17 volts on 12-volt systems and 31 volts on 24-volt systems.

What is the airplane's maximum alternator output?

Refer to the airplane's operating handbook or other aircraft documents.

What is the difference between an alternator and a generator?

A generator produces electrical power by turning a turbine. An alternator must first receive an electrical current before it can produce a stepped-up current. This distinction is important when it becomes necessary to take an alternator or generator off line due to a malfunction.

What should be done if the alternator overvoltage light illuminates?

When the electrical system warning light comes on, the battery is probably supplying all the electrical power because a spike or other charge in excess of the system tolerance has caused the alternator to be taken off line for its own protection. If the problem was caused by a one-time spike in the system, you can bring the alternator back on line and turn off the warning light by recycling the master switch. If this does not solve the problem, or if the system takes the alternator off line a second time, reduce the electrical load to conserve battery power, and land as soon as practical.

How much fuel does the airplane hold?

Refer to the airplane's operating handbook or other aircraft documents.

One engine has failed enroute and has been secured. You decided to extend the airplane's range by transferring fuel from the dead-engine side and burning it in the good engine. What is the procedure for doing this in the airplane?

Refer to chapter 5 for general information. Refer to the airplane's operating handbook or other aircraft documents for specific information.

When should electric fuel pumps be used?

Turn on electric fuel pumps during any crucial phase of flight where an engine failure would be particularly dangerous: takeoff, go-around, switching fuel tanks, and the like. Refer to chapter 5.

Why should electric fuel pumps be used?

Using the electric fuel pumps plus the engine-driven pumps improves the safety margin if an engine-driven fuel pump fails during a crucial phase of flight. Refer to chapter 5.

Where are the electric fuel pumps?

Check the operating handbook for the exact location. You should hear the pumps clicking during engine start.

Would tip tanks affect stall/spin recovery?

Yes. The best spin, if there is such, is nose low, tight, and fast. A nose-low, fast-rotation spin is closer to a recovery attitude than a nose-high, slow-rotation flat spin. Tip tanks that are full of fuel place weight a longer distance away from the center of gravity, and this would cause the spin to fly out and move to a flatter mode. (When figure skaters fly into a spin and tuck their arms in tight, the spin accelerates, but when their arms are extended outward, the spin slows down. Tip tanks are like extended arms.) Tip tanks could induce an unrecoverable flat spin. Remember that multiengine airplanes are not required to do spin testing for certification. If you spin a twin, you become the test pilot.

How are the engines primed?

Refer to the airplane's operating handbook or other aircraft documents.

What is the proper nose strut inflation? What is the proper main gear strut inflation?

Refer to the airplane's operating handbook or other aircraft documents.

What is the ground limitation for pitot heat?

Refer to the airplane's POH for specifics. The pitot heat should be turned on for short intervals while on the ground to prevent overheating. Airflow in flight will prevent overheating.

What is the cold-start procedure?

Refer to the airplane's operating handbook or other aircraft documents.

What is the origin of cabin heat?

Refer to the airplane's operating handbook or other aircraft documents.

Where are the static ports?

The number and location of the outside static ports is important. The static system normally has a port on each side of the airplane. The port lines join to make a Y-shape inside. This Y arrangement reduces static pressure errors due to airplane slip. Avoiding errors in a slip is especially important in multiengine airplanes that due tend to slip during engine out procedures. For the exact port locations, refer to the airplane's POH.

Where is the alternate static port?

Refer to the airplane's operating handbook or other aircraft documents. If the outside static ports ever get clogged by ice or other debris, the pilot must be able to vent the system by using the alternate static source. The pilot must be familiar with the operation and location of the alternate static vent switch.

What are the gyro suction limits?

Refer to the airplane's operating handbook or other aircraft documents.

How is a vacuum pump failure indicated in the airplane?

The suction or instrument air gauge will show a pressure that is below acceptable limits. Refer to the airplane's operating handbook or other aircraft documents.

If the vacuum pump failed in flight, what instruments would be affected?

The vacuum suction or instrument air system turns the gyroscopes in the attitude gyro and the directional gyro instruments. Early detection of a vacuum pump failure is essential so that the pilot can change her scan to include properly operating instruments.

How is the static system drained?

Refer to the airplane's operating handbook or other aircraft documents. Water from rain can easily get into the pitot static system. You have probably seen the three pitot/static system instruments jump while flying in the rain. This happens when water gets into the lines and momentarily causes a false reading. Many systems provide a way to drain the water.

What is the limit on cranking the starter?

Refer to the airplane's operating handbook or other aircraft documents. The starter should never be allowed to grind the propeller around for long periods of time. The maximum time a starter should be engaged is 30 seconds. If the engine does not start, wait at least 2 minutes for the starter to cool before cranking again.

What do cowl flaps do?

Cowl flaps are doors that open underneath the engine compartment. When the doors are open, the relative wind that moves over the opening produces a low-pressure area. The low pressure at the door draws air out of the engine compartment, which aids cooling. Because the cowl flaps do add drag to the airplane, they should be closed when the airplane is flying fast enough that ram air provides adequate cooling. Refer to the airplane's operating handbook or other aircraft documents.

What are the possible flap settings of the airplane?

Refer to the airplane's operating handbook or other aircraft documents.

How are the flaps operated?

Refer to the airplane's operating handbook or other aircraft documents. Some flaps are moved by an electric motor; others are manually operated by a handle.

Where is the external power plug located?

Refer to the airplane's operating handbook or other aircraft documents.

What should be done if a cabin door or luggage compartment door opens in flight?

Return to the field in a normal manner. Have a passenger hold the door during landing flare.

What is the airplane's basic empty weight?

Refer to the airplane's weight and balance form, the airplane's operating handbook, and other aircraft documents.

What is the airplane's maximum landing weight?

Refer to the POH to determine if the airplane has a specific maximum landing weight. The landing weight of many airplanes is less than the takeoff weight. When landing, the airplane is subjected to negative-G loading. The airplane might not absorb negative-G stresses as well as positive-G stresses. If the airplane is heavy, and a hard landing is made, the negative-G loading can be exceeded. For this reason, some airplanes must land at a much lighter weight compared to takeoff weight.

Why are maximum ramp weight and maximum takeoff weight different?

Ramp weight is heavier than maximum takeoff weight to allow for fuel burn, which reduces weight during taxi and runup.

Does the airplane have a zero fuel weight?

Refer to chapter 5 and the airplane's POH.

Can the airplane be flown with four average persons on board, full fuel, and full baggage?

Check the weight and balance information carefully. Multiengine training airplanes are not designed for travel comfort. A full load of fuel, passengers, and baggage probably cannot be carried.

What happens when the CG is too far forward?

Rotation and flare are difficult. A pilot risks touching down nosewheel first due to unexpected resistance to the elevator back pressure during takeoff and landing.

What happens when the CG is too far aft?

Rotation might be premature. The airplane's longitudinal stability is reduced, which might provoke a stall. If a stall or spin is encountered, the recovery might be difficult or impossible.

Where is the datum line on the airplane?

Recall that the datum is the reference position for measuring arm to stations. Check the airplane's weight and balance information for the datum position. Many single-engine airplane's use the firewall as the datum. Many multiengine airplanes use the plane of propeller rotation as the datum.

What does the basic empty weight include?

Basic empty weight is the airplane and all permanently attached equipment, including the weight of full engine oil, hydraulic fluids, and unusable fuel. The weight and balance information required to be carried on the airplane will have a list of all items that make up basic empty weight.

What happens to the CG as fuel is burned?

This depends entirely on the position of the various fuel tanks. If the tanks are in the wings, the CG location will not change drastically because the CG range is also within the wing's chord line, but the CG might move slightly. If the CG is already on the forward or aft limit, the range could be exceeded with even a small change in CG caused by fuel burn. Refer to the airplane's operating handbook or other aircraft documents.

What happens to the CG when the landing gear is retracted?

The landing gear folds up and the weight of the tires, struts, and extensions will come to rest in a new position. Depending on the landing gear design, the CG might shift as the gear is retracted or extended. Refer to the airplane's operating handbook or other aircraft documents.

What V speeds make up the fast limit and slow limit of the airplane's normal operating range (green arc)?

The slow end of the green arc is V_{S1} and the fast end is V_{NO}. Refer to the airplane's operating handbook and airspeed indicator.

What V speeds make up the fast limit and slow limit of the airplane's flap operating range (white arc)?

The slow end of the white arc is V_{SO} and the fast end is V_{FE}. Refer to the airplane's operating handbook and airspeed indicator.

What V speeds make up the fast limit and slow limit of the airplane's caution range (yellow arc)?

The slow end of the yellow arc is V_{NO} and the fast end is the red-line V_{NE}. Refer to the airplane's operating handbook and airspeed indicator.

Why did the manufacturer of the airspeed indicator leave off any indication of design maneuvering speed (V_A)?

The design maneuvering speed (V_A) changes with the weight of the airplane. V_A increases as the airplane weight increases. Because the airplane is constantly changing weight, V_A cannot be indicated on the airspeed indicator with a constant value.

What does the blue radial line of the airspeed indicator represent?

The blue radial line is only indicated on multiengine airplanes to represent V_{YSE}, which is the best single-engine rate of climb speed. (You will become quite accustomed to hanging on the blue line during multiengine training.)

Why does the multiengine airplane's airspeed indicator have two red lines?

Multiengine airplane airspeed indicators have two red lines, one at the slow end of the speed range and one at the fast end. (Refer to chapter 1.) The slow red line is V_{MC}, the minimum control speed. The fast red line is V_{NE}, the never-exceed speed. Refer to the airplane's operating handbook or airspeed indicator.

What is the maximum demonstrated crosswind component of the airplane?

Most manufacturers include a graph of crosswind components in the airplane's POH. Refer to the airplane's operating handbook or other aircraft documents.

What are the maneuvering limits (positive and negative Gs) of the airplane?

The G loading that an airplane is stressed to handle depends on its certification category. Normal category is stressed to +3.8 Gs and −1.52 Gs. Utility category is +4.4 Gs and −1.76 Gs. Aerobatic category is +6.0 Gs and −3.0 Gs. Refer to the POH or the airworthiness certificate for the category.

How does an increase in altitude affect the true airspeed (TAS) of a stall?

The true airspeed of a stall increases with an increase in altitude.

How does an increase in altitude affect the indicated airspeed (IAS) of a stall?

The indicated airspeed of a stall remains the same as altitude increases.

How does an increase in altitude affect the true airspeed of V_{MC}?

V_{MC}'s true airspeed decreases as altitude increases. Refer to chapters 1 and 12.

What steps must be taken if an engine failure occurs during flight below V_{MC}?

Never let this situation develop. The only recovery is to reduce power on both engines, lower the nose, and accelerate to a speed that is faster than V_{MC} in order to maintain aircraft control. Read more about this in chapters 1 and 2.

When is the gear extended before landing with one engine inoperative?

Lower the landing gear when you are ready to begin the descent from pattern altitude. The landing gear will produce drag, which will increase the sink rate. Use good judgment regarding the wind and other traffic. The gear can be lowered anytime that you need to descend anyway.

What is the final approach speed for the airplane on one engine?

Refer to the airplane's operating handbook or other aircraft documents. I try to hold the blue line until I am sure that a go-around is not needed, then I reduce speed to the manufacturer's recommended speed, followed by flare and touchdown.

When are the flaps extended on a single-engine approach?

Flaps are optional. After the landing gear is down, and the proper adjustments have been made, the flaps can be lowered only after a landing is assured. If the flaps are brought in too early, you might end up struggling to the runway. Adding flaps too early on the approach will cause the airplane to be too low. This will require you to advance power on the good engine. Stepping on the brake and the gas pedal at the same time doesn't make good sense.

How do you crossfeed in the airplane?

Refer to the airplane's operating handbook or other aircraft documents and follow any prescribed checklists. Refer to chapter 5.

What are the normal panel indications when an engine has failed?

The manifold pressure gauge and tachometer will have the same indication as when an engine is operating. The pilot cannot tell by looking outside if the engine has failed because the propeller is windmilling. Rely on the dead-foot/dead-engine method. Read chapter 3. If the airplane is equipped with a fuel-flow meter, a failed engine might be detected by watching a significant reduction in fuel consumption. When the dead engine has had time to cool off, the exhaust gas temperature gauge and the cylinder head temperature gauge will show falling temperatures.

What are the normal panel indications when an engine is shut down?

The engine that has been feathered and secured should have the following engine instrument indications: oil pressure is zero, amp meter is zero, alternator out, vacuum suction is zero, RPM is zero, and manifold pressure reads the ambient pressure.

What is the maximum allowable RPM drop during the runup's feathering check?

Refer to the airplane's operating handbook or other aircraft documents. The norm is a 500 RPM drop.

What are the airplane certification standards for computing V_{MC}?

Refer to chapter 1 for more discussion and details:
- The critical engine is inoperative and windmilling.
- Not more than a 5° bank toward the operative engine.
- Landing gear retracted.
- Flaps in the takeoff position.
- The most rearward CG.
- Cowl flaps in the takeoff position.
- Airplane at gross weight.
- Ground effect negligible.
- Maximum available power on the operating engine.
- Sea-level conditions.
- Trimmed for takeoff.

What is V_{MC}?

Simple definition: The minimum flight speed at which the airplane is directionally controllable with one engine inoperative.

What is the highest single drag item on the airplane?

A windmilling propeller. Have your flight instructor perform a drag demonstration so that you can see and feel the effects of drag on the engine while only one engine is operating. This demonstration is discussed in chapter 12.

What is the second highest drag component on the airplane?

Full flaps. This is why flaps come up early in any recovery procedure and stay up if there is any hope of climbing on one engine. Refer to chapter 3.

How would V_{MC} be affected with a larger engine?

V_{MC} would increase. More power means more yaw that must be overcome with rudder. When greater rudder force is required, the speed must also be faster. Refer to chapter 1.

How would V_{MC} be affected by turbocharging?

A turbocharger makes it possible for an engine to maintain sea-level power at higher altitudes. If power output remains constant, then V_{MC} will remain constant. At a certain altitude, the turbocharger's compressor will be turning at maximum speed, and power will consequently start to decrease as if the engine were normally aspirated. When the power starts to diminish, V_{MC} will get slower. Refer to chapters 1 and 12.

Choose the better takeoff procedure:

A. Rotate at V_{MC} +5 knots, then climb out with a shallow climb angle, and gain as much speed as possible.

B. Rotate at V_{MC} +5 knots, then climb out with a steep climb angle, and hold the blue line.

Answer B is the better selection. Certain pilots might argue that a shallow climbout is easier on passengers, and the extra speed would be helpful if an engine quit. The problem is that the extra speed will quickly evaporate during the first few seconds of the emergency. Altitude is more important. Altitude is extremely hard to come by on just one engine, but altitude gives you the room to adjust airspeed and remain above terrain. The passengers must accept the steeper climbout. Gain altitude as quickly as possible by using the blue-line speed of V_{YSE}.

What is accelerate-stop distance?

Refer to the airplane's operating handbook or other aircraft documents. The accelerate-stop distance is the length of runway used by an airplane from a standing start to liftoff speed, and then, after an engine has failed, braking from liftoff speed to a complete stop. If the distance is longer than the runway, the airplane will run off the far end of the runway while the pilot applies the brakes. The distance to stop is always longer than the distance to accelerate to liftoff speed; in certain conditions, the stop distance might be twice as far as the accelerate distance. You should be very familiar with the performance charts pertaining to accelerate-stop distance calculations. Refer to chapter 2.

What is the airplane's single-engine service ceiling and single-engine absolute ceiling?

Refer to the airplane's operating handbook or other aircraft documents. There is a limit to how high any airplane can climb. Airplanes that are not turbocharged are limited to the lower thick-air altitudes. Even with both engines operating, there is a density altitude that is as high as the airplane can go. Recall from chapter 1 that when an engine fails, there is a 50-percent loss of power, but an 80-percent loss of performance. This means that if you are flying at the maximum two-engine altitude when one engine fails, you will find yourself sinking, even though you have full power on the good engine. This is because the single-engine absolute ceiling is lower than the two-engine absolute ceiling. The definition of *absolute ceiling* is the maximum density altitude where the airplane is capable of maintaining level flight. The *single-engine service ceiling* is the density altitude where only a 50-foot per minute climb is possible. Become familiar with the airplane's single-engine service and absolute ceiling numbers. You will be surprised by how low the altitudes are.

If the single-engine absolute ceiling is 4,000 feet density altitude, and the actual density altitude at the airport where you plan to take off is 5,000 feet, should you take off?

The safe answer is no, do not take off until the density altitude has improved. If you do take off and one engine fails, you will not able to climb to safety under any circumstances. The altitude where level flight can be maintained would be 1,000 feet lower than the ground; therefore, any struggle to fly the airplane would be a dangerous waste of time.

You are taking off in a DC-7 (four engines) but the number one engine is inoperative. What will be the three-engine takeoff procedure?

This is the last question. Yes, it is a little unusual. I include it because it is the last question that I was asked on my ATP oral exam. I told the examiner that I had only seen the cutaway nose section of a DC-7 at the National Air and Space Museum. That did not get me off the hook. I went on to explain that flying a four-engine airplane with only three operable engines would take a special flight permit from the FAA. "Yes, of course," the examiner said, "but what about the takeoff procedure?" I said that I would start out with full power on engines 2 and 3, which are the two inboard engines. This would give me symmetrical thrust during the beginning of the takeoff roll. Then, after the speed becomes fast enough to make the rudder effective, I would come in with partial power on the number 4 engine, which is the outboard engine on the right wing. The number 2 and 3 engines would cancel out each other's yaw, and the rudder would cancel out the yaw of the number 4 engine. The examiner accepted the answer. I became an ATP later that day. Good luck to you on the DC-7 questions . . . .

MULTIENGINE LAND (AMEL) PRACTICAL TEST STANDARDS

Note: An applicant seeking initial certification as a commercial pilot with an airplane multiengine land class rating will be evaluated in all TASKS listed within this section.

Contents

C. Diversion

D. Lost Procedures

VII. SLOW FLIGHT AND STALLS

   A. Maneuvering during Slow Flight

   B. Power-off Stalls

   C. Power-on Stalls

   D. Spin Awareness

VIII. EMERGENCY OPERATIONS

   A. Emergency Descent

   B. Maneuvering with One Engine Inoperative

   C. Engine Inoperative Loss of Directional Control Demonstration

   D. Engine Failure during Takeoff before V_{MC} (Simulated)

   E. Engine Failure after Liftoff (Simulated)

   F. Approach and Landing with an Inoperative Engine

   G. Systems and Equipment Malfunctions

   H. Emergency Equipment and Survival Gear

IX. MULTIENGINE OPERATION

   A. Performance and Limitations

   B. Operation of Systems

   C. Flight Principles—Engine Inoperative

X. HIGH-ALTITUDE OPERATIONS

   A. Supplemental Oxygen

   B. Pressurization

XI. POST-FLIGHT PROCEDURES

   A. After Landing

   B. Parking and Securing

I. AREA OF OPERATION: PREFLIGHT PREPARATIONS

A. TASK: CERTIFICATES AND DOCUMENTS

References: FAR Parts 43, 61, and 91; AC 61-21, AC 61-23; Pilot's Operating Handbook and FAA Approved Airplane Flight Manual

Objective: To determine that the applicant:

1. Exhibits knowledge of the elements related to certificates and documents by explaining—

   a. pilot certificate privileges and limitations.

   b. medical certificate, class, and duration.

   c. pilot logbook or flight record.

2. Exhibits knowledge of the elements related to certificates and documents by locating and explaining the—

   a. airworthiness and registration certificates.

   b. operating limitations, placards, instrument markings, handbooks, and manuals.

c. weight and balance data, and equipment list.

d. airworthiness directives, maintenance requirements, tests, and appropriate records.

B. TASK: WEATHER INFORMATION

References: AC 00-6, AC 0045, AC 61-21, AC 61-23, AC 61-84; AIM

Objective: To determine that the applicant:

1. Exhibits knowledge of the elements related to weather information from various sources with emphasis on—

a. PIREPs.

b. SIGMETs and AIRMETs.

c. wind shear reports.

2. Makes a competent go/no-go decision based on the available weather information.

C. TASK: CROSS-COUNTRY FLIGHT PLANNING

References: AC 61-21, AC 61-23, AC 61-84; Navigational Charts, Airport/Facility Directory, AIM

Note: In-flight demonstrations of cross-country procedures by the applicant are tested under area of operation NAVIGATION.

Objective: To determine that the applicant:

1. Exhibits knowledge of the elements related to cross-country flight by presenting a preplanned VFR cross-country flight, as previously assigned by the examiner. It shall be planned using real-time weather to the first fuel stop necessary. Computations shall be based on maximum-passenger, baggage, and/or cargo loads.

2. Uses appropriate, current aeronautical charts.

3. Properly identifies airspace, obstructions, and terrain features.

4. Selects easily identifiable enroute checkpoints.

5. Selects most favorable altitudes or flight levels, considering weather conditions and equipment capabilities.

6. Computes headings, flight time, and fuel requirements.

7. Selects appropriate navigation facilities and communication frequencies.

8. Extracts and records pertinent information from NOTAM's Airport/Facility Directory and other flight publications.

9. Completes a navigation log and simulates filing a VFR flight plan.

D. TASK: NATIONAL AIRSPACE SYSTEM

References: FAR Part 91, AIM

Objective: To determine that the applicant exhibits knowledge of the elements related to the National Airspace System by explaining:

1. Basic VFR Weather Minimums for all class airspace.

2. Airspace classes including their boundaries, and pilot certification and airplane equipment requirements for the following:

a. Class A.

b. Class B.

    c. Class C.

    d. Class D.

    e. Class E.

    f. Class G.

  3. Special-Use Airspace and other airspace areas.

E. TASK: MINIMUM EQUIPMENT LIST

References: FAR Part 91

Objective: To determine that the applicant exhibits knowledge of the elements related to the FAA-approved minimum equipment list by explaining:

1. Which aircraft requires the use of a minimum equipment list.
2. Airworthiness limitations imposed on aircraft operations with inoperative instruments or equipment.
3. Requirements for a letter of authorization (LOA) from the FAA Flight Standards District Office.
4. Supplemental Type Certificates.
5. Instrument and equipment exceptions.
6. Special flight permits.
7. Procedures for deferring maintenance on aircraft without an approved minimum equipment list.

F. TASK: AEROMEDICAL FACTORS

References: AC 61-21, AC 67-2; AIM

Objective: To determine that the applicant exhibits knowledge of the elements related to the Aeromedical Factors by explaining:

1. The symptoms, causes, effects and corrective actions of at least four of the following:
   a. hypoxia.
   b. hyperventilation.
   c. middle ear and sinus problems.
   d. spatial disorientation.
   e. motion sickness.
   f. carbon monoxide poisoning.
   g. stress and fatigue.
2. The effects of alcohol and drugs, including over-the-counter drugs.
3. The effects of nitrogen excesses during scuba dives upon a pilot and passenger in flight.

G. TASK: PHYSIOLOGICAL ASPECTS OF NIGHT FLIGHT

References: AC 61-21, AC 67-2; AIM

Objective: To determine that the applicant exhibits knowledge of the elements related to the physiological aspects of night flight by explaining:

1. Function of various parts of the eye essential for night vision.
2. Adaptation of the eye to changing light.
3. Correct use of the eye to accommodate changing light.
4. Coping with illusions created by various light conditions.

5. Effects of pilot's physical condition on visual acuity.

6. Methods for increasing vision effectiveness.

H. TASK: LIGHTING AND EQUIPMENT FOR NIGHT FLYING

References: AC 61-21, Pilot's Operating Handbook, FAA-Approved Airplane Flight Manual

Objective: To determine that the applicant:

1. Exhibits knowledge of the elements related to lighting and equipment for night flying by explaining:

   a. types and use of various personal lighting devices.

   b. required equipment, additional equipment recommended, and location of external navigation lighting of the airplane.

   c. meaning of various airport and navigation lights, method of determining their status, and procedure for airborne activation of runway lights.

2. Locates and identifies switches, spare fuses, and circuit breakers pertinent to night operations.

II. AREA OF OPERATION: PREFLIGHT PROCEDURES

A. TASK: PREFLIGHT INSPECTION

References: AC 61-21; Pilot's Operating Handbook and FAA-Approved Airplane Flight Manual

Objective: To determine that the applicant:

1. Exhibits knowledge of the elements related to a preflight visual inspection, including which items must be inspected, for what reason, and how to detect possible defects.

2. Inspects the airplane by systematically following a prescribed checklist.

3. Verifies that the airplane is in condition for safe flight, notes any discrepancy, and accurately judges whether the airplane requires maintenance.

B. TASK: COCKPIT MANAGEMENT

Reference: AC 61-21, Pilot's Operating Handbook, FAA-Approved Airplane Flight Manual

Objective: To determine that the applicant:

1. Exhibits knowledge of the elements related to efficient cockpit management procedures and related safety factors.

2. Organizes and arranges material and equipment in a manner that makes the items readily available.

3. Briefs, or causes the briefing of, occupants on the use of safety belts and emergency procedures.

4. If applicable, briefs crew appropriately.

5. Completes the prescribed checklist.

C. TASK: ENGINE STARTING

References: AC 61-21, AC 61-23, AC 91-13, AC 91-55; Pilot's Operating Handbook and FAA-Approved Airplane Flight Manual

Objective: To determine that the applicant:

1. Exhibits knowledge of the elements related to correct engine-starting procedures, including the use of an external power source, starting under various atmospheric conditions, awareness of other persons and property during start, and the effects of using incorrect starting procedures.
2. Accomplishes correct starting procedure.
3. Completes the prescribed checklist.

D. TASK: TAXIING

References: AC 61-21, Pilot's Operating Handbook and FAA-Approved Airplane Flight Manual

Objective: To determine that the applicant:

1. Exhibits knowledge of the elements related to recommended taxi procedures, including the effect of wind on the airplane during taxiing and the appropriate control position for such conditions.
2. Positions flight controls, properly considering wind.
3. Performs a brake check immediately after the airplane begins movement.
4. Controls direction and speed without excessive use of brakes.
5. Complies with airport surface markings, signals, and ATC clearances.
6. Avoids other aircraft and hazards.
7. Completes the prescribed checklist.

E. TASK: BEFORE-TAKEOFF CHECK

References: AC 61-21; Pilot's Operating Handbook and FAA-Approved Airplane Flight Manual

Objective: To determine that the applicant:

1. Exhibits knowledge of the elements related to the before-takeoff check, including the reasons for checking each item and how to detect possible malfunctions.
2. Positions the airplane properly, considering other aircraft, the surface conditions, and, if applicable, the wind conditions.
3. Divides attention inside and outside of the cockpit.
4. Ensures that the engine temperatures and pressures are suitable for run-up and takeoff.
5. Accomplishes the before-takeoff check and ensures that the airplane is in a safe operating condition.
6. Reviews takeoff performance airspeeds and expected takeoff distances.
7. Describes takeoff emergency procedures and, if applicable, briefs crew on procedures.
8. Assures no conflict with traffic prior to taxiing into takeoff position.
9. Completes the prescribed checklist.

III. AREA OF OPERATION: AIRPORT OPERATIONS

A. TASK: RADIO COMMUNICATIONS AND ATC LIGHT SIGNALS

References: AC 61-21, AC 61-23; AIM

Objective: To determine that the applicant:

1. Exhibits knowledge of the elements related to radio communications, radio failure, and ATC light signals.
2. Selects the appropriate frequencies for the facilities to be used.
3. Transmits using recommended phraseology.
4. Acknowledges radio communications and complies with instructions.
5. Uses prescribed procedures following radio communications failure.
6. Interprets and complies with ATC light gun signals.

B. TASK: TRAFFIC PATTERNS
   References: AC 61-21, AC 61-23; AIM
   Objective: To determine that the applicant:
   1. Exhibits knowledge of the elements related to traffic pattern procedures at each class airspace airport, runway incursion avoidance, collision and wind-shear avoidance, and approach procedure when wind shear is reported.
   2. Follows the established traffic pattern procedures, instructions, and rules.
   3. Maintains adequate spacing from other traffic.
   4. Establishes an appropriate distance from the runway or landing.
   5. Avoids wake turbulence encounters.
   6. Corrects for wind drift to maintain proper ground track.
   7. Remains oriented to the runway and landing area in use.
   8. Maintains and holds the traffic pattern altitude, ±50 feet (20 meters) and appropriate airspeed, ±5 knots.
   9. Completes the prescribed checklist.

C. TASK: AIRPORT AND RUNWAY MARKING AND LIGHTING
   References: AC 61-21; AIM
   Objective: To determine that the applicant:
   1. Exhibits knowledge of the elements related to airport and runway markings and lighting.
   2. Identifies and interprets airport, runway, and taxiway markings and lighting.

IV. AREA OF OPERATION: TAKEOFFS, LANDINGS, AND GO-AROUNDS
A. TASK: NORMAL AND CROSSWIND TAKEOFFS AND CLIMB
   Reference: AC 61-21; Pilot's Operating Handbook and FAA-Approved Airplane Flight Manual

Note: If a calm weather condition exists, the applicant's knowledge of the crosswind elements shall be evaluated through oral testing; otherwise, a crosswind takeoff and climb shall be demonstrated.

   Objective: To determine that the applicant:
   1. Exhibits knowledge of the elements related to normal and crosswind take-offs and climb.
   2. Positions the flight controls and flaps for the existing conditions.
   3. Taxis into the takeoff position and aligns the airplane on the runway centerline.
   4. Advances the throttles to takeoff power.

5. Rotates at recommended airspeed and accelerates to the best single-engine climb speed or V_Y, whichever is greater, ±5 knots during the climb.
6. Retracts the landing gear and flaps after a positive rate of climb indication. Climbs at V_Y ±5 knots to a safe maneuvering altitude.
7. Maintains takeoff power to a safe maneuvering altitude, then sets climb power.
8. Maintains directional control and proper wind drift correction throughout takeoff and climb.
9. Uses noise abatement procedures as required.
10. Completes the prescribed checklist.

B. TASK: NORMAL AND CROSSWIND APPROACHES AND LANDINGS

References: AC 61-21; Pilot's Operating Handbook and FAA-Approved Airplane Flight Manual

Note: If a calm weather condition exists, the applicant's knowledge of the crosswind elements shall be evaluated through oral testing; otherwise, a crosswind takeoff and climb shall be demonstrated.

Objective: To determine that the applicant:

1. Exhibits knowledge of the elements related to normal and crosswind approach and landing.
2. Considers the wind condition, landing surface, and obstructions.
3. Selects a suitable touchdown point.
4. Establishes the approach and landing configuration and adjusts the power controls as required.
5. Maintains a stabilized approach and recommended approach airspeed, with gust factor applied, ±5 knots.
6. Makes smooth, timely, and correct control application during roundout and touchdown.
7. Remains aware of the possibility of wind shear and/or wake turbulence.
8. Touches down smoothly at approximate stalling speed at a specified point or within 200 feet (60 meters) beyond a specified point with no drift and the airplane's longitudinal axis aligned with the runway centerline.
9. Maintains crosswind correction and directional control throughout the approach and landing.
10. Completes the prescribed checklist.

C. TASK: SHORT-FIELD TAKEOFF AND CLIMB

Reference: AC 61-21; Pilot's Operating Handbook and FAA-Approved Airplane Flight Manual

Note: In airplanes with V_X values within 5 knots of V_{MC}, the use of V_Y or the manufacturer's recommendation might be more appropriate for this demonstration.

Objective: To determine that the applicant:

1. Exhibits knowledge of the elements related to short-field takeoff and climb.
2. Positions the flight controls and flaps for the existing conditions.
3. Positions the airplane for maximum utilization of available takeoff area.

4. Advances the throttles to takeoff power.

5. Rotates at recommended airspeed.

6. Climbs at manufacturer's recommended configuration and airspeed, or in their absence at V_X, +5 -0 knots until obstruction is cleared, or until the airplane is at least 50 feet (20 meters) above the surface.

7. After clearing the obstruction, accelerates to and maintains V_Y, ±5 knots.

8. Retracts the landing gear and flaps after a positive rate of climb indication.

9. Maintains takeoff power to a safe maneuvering altitude, then sets climb power.

10. Maintains directional control and proper wind drift correction throughout takeoff and climb.

11. Completes the prescribed checklist.

D. TASK: SHORT-FIELD APPROACH AND LANDING

References: AC 61-21; Pilot's Operating Handbook and FAA-Approved Airplane Flight Manual

Objective: To determine that the applicant:

1. Exhibits knowledge of the elements related to a short-field approach and landing.

2. Considers wind conditions, landing surface, and obstructions.

3. Selects a suitable touchdown point.

4. Establishes the recommended approach and landing configuration, and adjusts attitude and power as required.

5. Maintains a stabilized approach, controlled rate of descent, and recommended airspeed (or, in the absence of, not more than 1.3 V_{SO}) with gust correction factor applied ±5 knots.

6. Makes timely, and correct control application during roundout and touchdown.

7. Remains aware of the possibility of wind shear and/or wake turbulence.

8. Touches down smoothly at approximate stalling speed, at a specified point or within 100 feet (30 meters) beyond a specified point with little or no float, with no drift, and with the airplane's longitudinal axis aligned with the runway centerline.

9. Maintains crosswind correction and directional control throughout the approach and landing.

10. Applies brakes as necessary to stop in the shortest distance consistent with safety.

11. Completes the prescribed checklist.

E. TASK: GO-AROUND

References: AC 61-21; Pilot's Operating Handbook and FAA-Approved Airplane Flight Manual

Objective: To determine that the applicant:

1. Exhibits knowledge of the elements related to go-around.

2. Makes a timely decision to discontinue the approach to landing.

3. Applies takeoff power immediately and establishes the pitch attitude that will slow or stop the descent.

4. Retracts flaps to approach setting.

5. Retracts the landing gear after a positive rate of climb indication.

6. Trims the airplane to accelerate to best single-engine climb speed or V_Y, whichever is greater, before the final flap retraction, then climbs at the appropriate speed ±5 knots.

7. Maintains takeoff power to a safe maneuvering altitude, then sets climb power.

8. Maintains proper wind drift correction and obstruction clearance throughout the transition to climb.

9. Completes the prescribed checklist.

V. AREA OF OPERATION: PERFORMANCE MANEUVERS

A. TASK: STEEP TURNS

Reference: AC 61-21; Pilot's Operating Handbook and FAA-Approved Airplane Flight Manual

Objective: To determine that the applicant:

1. Exhibits knowledge of the elements related to steep turns.

2. Selects an altitude that allows the task to be completed no lower than 3,000 feet (920 meters) AGL or the manufacturer's recommended altitude, whichever is higher.

3. Establishes and maintains the manufacturer's recommended entry speed (or in its absence, the design maneuvering speed) ±5 knots.

4. Smoothly enters a coordinated steep turn with a 50° bank, ±5°, immediately followed by at least a 360° turn in the opposite direction.

5. Divides attention between airplane control and orientation.

6. Rolls out on the entry heading ±5°.

7. Maintains the entry altitude throughout the maneuver ±100 feet (30 meters).

B. TASK: ENGINE FAILURE DURING STRAIGHT-AND-LEVEL FLIGHT AND TURNS (by reference to instruments only)

References: FAR Part 61; AC 61-21, AC 61-27; FAA-S-8081-4

Objective: To determine that the applicant:

1. Exhibits knowledge of the elements related to engine failure during straight-and-level flight and turns.

2. Recognizes engine failure promptly during straight-and-level flight and standard rate turns.

3. Sets the engine controls, reduces drag, and identifies and verifies the inoperative engine.

4. Attains the best engine inoperative airspeed and appropriately trims the airplane and maintains control.

5. Follows the prescribed checklist to verify procedures for securing the inoperative engine.

6. Establishes a bank toward the operating engine(s) as necessary for best performance.
7. Attempts to determine the reason for the engine malfunction.
8. Monitors the operating engine(s) and updates decisions based on observational feedback.
9. Determines if it is feasible to restart the affected engine; if so, follows appropriate restart procedures.
10. Demonstrates coordinated flight while flying straight-and-level and while turning in both directions.
11. Maintains the specified altitude ±100 feet (30 meters) if within the airplane's capability, the specified airspeed ±10 knots, and the specified heading ±10° if straight-and-level, or the specified bank within ±10° of the standard rate bank angle if in a turn.

C. TASK: INSTRUMENT APPROACH—ALL ENGINES OPERATING (by reference to instruments only)
   References: FAR Part 61; AC 61-21, AC 61-27; FAA-S-8081-4
   Objective: To determine that the applicant:
   1. Exhibits knowledge of the elements related to a published instrument approach with all engines operating.
   2. Sets the navigation and communication equipment used during the approach and uses the proper communications technique.
   3. Requests and receives an actual or simulated ATC clearance for an instrument approach.
   4. Follows instructions and instrument approach procedures correctly.
   5. Maintains a specified airspeed within 10 knots and an altitude within 100 feet (30 meters) prior to the final approach fix.
   6. Establishes a rate of descent that will ensure arrival at the MDA or DH, whichever is appropriate, in a position from which a normal landing can be made either straight-in or circling.
   7. Allows, while on the final approach segment, no more than three-quarter-scale deflection of the localizer/glide slope indicators, CDI, or within 10° in the case of RMI or NDB indicators.
   8. Avoids descent below the published minimum altitude on straight-in approaches or exceeding the visibility criteria for the aircraft category on circling approaches.
   9. Executes a missed approach procedure at the designated MAP.
   10. Completes the prescribed checklist.

D. TASK: INSTRUMENT APPROACH—ONE ENGINE INOPERATIVE
   References: FAR Part 61; AC 61-21, AC 61-27; FAA-S-8081-4
   Objective: To determine that the applicant:
   1. Exhibits knowledge of the elements related to multiengine procedures used during a published instrument approach with one engine inoperative.

2. Sets the navigation and communication equipment used during the approach and uses the proper communications technique.
3. Requests and receives an actual or simulated ATC clearance for an instrument approach.
4. Recognizes engine failure promptly.
5. Sets the engine controls, reduces drag, and identifies and verifies the inoperative engine.
6. Attains the best engine inoperative airspeed and appropriately trims the airplane and maintains control.
7. Follows the prescribed checklist to verify procedures for securing the inoperative engine.
8. Establishes a bank toward the operating engine, as necessary, for best performance.
9. Attempts to determine the reason for the engine malfunction.
10. Monitors the operating engine(s) and updates decisions based on observational feedback.
11. Determines if it is feasible to restart the affected engine; if so, follows appropriate restart procedures.
12. Follows instructions and instrument approach procedures correctly.
13. Maintains a specified airspeed within 10 knots and an altitude within 100 feet (30 meters) prior to the final approach fix.
14. Establishes a rate of descent that will ensure arrival at the MDA or DH, whichever is appropriate, in a position from which a normal landing can be made either straight-in or circling.
15. Allows, while on final approach segment, no more than three-quarter-scale deflection of the localizer/glide slope indicators, CDI, or within 10° in the case of RMI or NDB indicators.
16. Avoids descent below the published minimum altitude on straight-in approaches or exceeding the visibility criteria for the aircraft category on circling approaches.
17. Executes a missed approach procedure at the designated MAP.
18. Completes the prescribed checklist.

VI. AREA OF OPERATION: NAVIGATION
A. TASK: PILOTAGE AND DEAD RECKONING
References: AC 61-21, AC 61-23, AC 61-84
Objective: To determine that the applicant:
1. Exhibits knowledge of the elements related to pilotage and dead reckoning.
2. Correctly flies to at least the first planned checkpoint to demonstrate accuracy in computations, considers available alternates, and takes suitable action for various situations, including possible route alteration by the examiner.
3. Follows the course solely by reference to landmarks.
4. Identifies landmarks by relating the surface features to chart symbols.

5. Navigates by means of precomputed headings, groundspeed, and elapsed time.
6. Verifies the airplane's position within 1 nautical mile (1.85 km) of flight planned route at all times.
7. Arrives at the enroute checkpoints and destination within 3 minutes of the ETA.
8. Corrects for, and records, the difference between preflight fuel, ground-speed, and heading calculations and those determined enroute.
9. Maintains appropriate altitude ±100 feet (30 meters) and established head-ing ±10°.
10. Completes all prescribed checklists.

B. TASK: RADIO NAVIGATION AND RADAR SERVICES

References: AC 61-21, AC 61-23

Objective: To determine that the applicant:
1. Exhibits knowledge of the elements related to radio navigation and ATC radar services.
2. Selects and identifies the appropriate facilities.
3. Locates the airplane's position relative to the navigation facility.
4. Intercepts and tracks a given radial or bearing.
5. Locates position using cross radials or bearings.
6. Recognizes and describes the indication of station passage.
7. Recognizes signal loss and takes appropriate action.
8. Utilizes proper communication procedures when using ATC radar services.
9. Maintains the appropriate altitude ±100 feet (30 meters).

C. TASK: DIVERSION

References: AC 61-21, AC 61-23

Objective: To determine that the applicant:
1. Exhibits knowledge of the elements related to procedures for diversion.
2. Selects an appropriate alternate airport and route.
3. Diverts toward the alternate airport promptly.
4. Makes an accurate estimate of heading, groundspeed, arrival time, and fuel consumption to the alternate airport.
5. Maintains the appropriate altitude ±100 feet (30 meters) and established heading ±10°.

D. TASK: LOST PROCEDURE

References: AC 61-21, AC 61-23

Objective: To determine that the applicant:
1. Exhibits knowledge of the elements related to lost procedures.
2. Selects the best course of action when given a lost situation.
3. Maintains the original or appropriate heading, and if necessary, climbs.
4. Attempts to identify nearest prominent landmark(s).
5. Uses available navigation aids, or contacts an appropriate facility for assistance.

6. Plans a precautionary landing if deteriorating visibility and/or fuel exhaustion is impending.

VII. AREA OF OPERATION: SLOW FLIGHT AND STALLS
A. TASK: MANEUVERING DURING SLOW FLIGHT

References: AC 61-21; Pilot's Operating Handbook and FAA-Approved Airplane Flight Manual

Objective: To determine that the applicant:

1. Exhibits knowledge of the elements related to flight characteristics and controllability associated with maneuvering during slow flight.
2. Selects an entry altitude that will allow the task to be completed no lower than 3,000 feet (920 meters) AGL or the manufacturer's recommended altitude, whichever is higher.
3. Stabilizes and maintains the airspeed at 1.2 V_{S1}, ±5 knots.
4. Establishes straight-and-level flight and level turns, with gear and flaps selected as specified by the examiner.
5. Maintains the specified altitude ±50 feet (20 meters).
6. Maintains the specified heading during straight flight ±5°.
7. Maintains specified bank angle ±10° during turning flight.
8. Rolls out on specified headings ±5°.
9. Divides attention between airplane control and orientation.

B. TASK: POWER-OFF STALLS

References: AC 61-21, AC 61-67; Pilot's Operating Handbook and FAA-Approved Airplane Flight Manual

Objective: To determine that the applicant:

1. Exhibits knowledge of the elements related to aerodynamic factors associated with power-off stalls and how this relates to actual approach and landing situations.
2. Selects an entry altitude that allows the task to be completed no lower than 3,000 feet (920 meters) AGL or the manufacturer's recommended altitude, whichever is higher.
3. Establishes the stall entry from both straight and turning flight.
4. Slows the airplane to normal approach speed and establishes the approach and landing configuration.
5. Sets power to approach power while establishing the approach attitude.
6. Maintains the specified heading ±10° in straight flight; a 20° angle of bank ±10° in turning flight.
7. Recognizes and announces the onset of the stall by identifying the first aerodynamic buffeting or decay of control effectiveness.
8. Promptly recovers as the stall occurs by reducing the pitch attitude and by simultaneously applying power, according to the manufacturer's recommendation. Reduces drag as necessary.

9. Recovers to the point where adequate control effectiveness is regained with the minimum loss in altitude.

10. Allows the airplane to accelerate to approach speed, and resumes the approach.

C. TASK: POWER-ON STALLS

Reference: AC 61-21, AC 61-67; Pilot's Operating Handbook and FAA-Approved Airplane Flight Manual

Note: In few very high-performance aircraft, the power setting may have to be reduced below the PTS guideline setting to prevent excessively high pitch attitudes (greater than 30° nose up). These low power settings would make the evaluation of this maneuver unrealistic and unfeasible. These maneuvers may be deemed inappropriate with regard to this TASK for INITIAL commercial pilot certification.

Objective: To determine that the applicant:

1. Exhibits knowledge of the elements related to aerodynamic factors associated with power-on stalls and how this relates to actual takeoff and departure situations.

2. Selects an entry altitude that allows the task to be completed no lower than 3,000 feet (920 meters) AGL or the manufacturer's recommended altitude, whichever is higher.

3. Establishes the takeoff or departure configuration, and slows the airplane to normal liftoff speed.

4. Sets power to the manufacturer's recommended power-on stall power setting while establishing the climb attitude (in the absence of a manufacturer's recommended power setting, use no less than approximately 55 to 60 percent of full power as a guideline).

5. Maintains the specific heading ±10° in straight flight; a 20° angle of bank ±10° in turning flight.

6. Recognizes and announces the onset of the stall by identifying the first aerodynamic buffeting or decay of control effectiveness.

7. Promptly recovers as the stall occurs by reducing the pitch attitude and by simultaneously applying power, according to the manufacturer's recommendation. Reduces drag as necessary.

8. Recovers to the point where adequate control effectiveness is regained with the minimum loss in altitude.

9. Allows the airplane to accelerate to the best angle of climb speed with simulated obstacles or the best rate of climb speed without simulated obstacles, and resumes the climb.

D. TASK: SPIN AWARENESS

References: AC 61-21, AC 61-67; Pilot's Operating Handbook and FAA-Approved Airplane Flight Manual

Objective: To determine that the applicant:

1. Exhibits knowledge of the elements related to spin dynamics by explaining:
   a. the aerodynamic factors, including instrument indications, that occur in a spin.
   b. the phases of a spin with regard to uncoordinated flight, the vertical and rotational velocities, and its rotation about the axis perpendicular to the Earth's surface.
2. Exhibits knowledge of the elements related to spins by explaining:
   a. flight situations where unintentional spins might occur.
   b. the technique used to recognize and recover from unintentional spins.

VIII. AREA OF OPERATION: EMERGENCY OPERATIONS
A. TASK: EMERGENCY DESCENT
References: AC 61-21; Pilot's Operating Handbook and FAA-Approved Airplane Flight Manual

Objective: To determine that the applicant:
1. Exhibits knowledge of the elements related to an emergency descent.
2. Recognizes situations, such as depressurization, cockpit smoke and/or fire, that require an emergency descent.
3. Establishes the prescribed airspeed and configuration for the emergency descent as recommended by the manufacturer without exceeding safety limitations.
4. Uses proper engine control settings.
5. Exhibits orientation, division of attention, and proper planning.
6. Recognizes the requirement to establish positive load factors during the descent.
7. Completes the prescribed checklist.

B. TASK: MANEUVERING WITH ONE ENGINE INOPERATIVE
References: AC 61-21; Pilot's Operating Handbook and FAA-Approved Airplane Flight Manual

Note: The feathering of one propeller must be demonstrated in multiengine airplanes equipped with propellers that can be safely feathered and unfeathered in flight. An appropriately equipped aircraft must be provided by the applicant. The maneuver shall be performed at altitudes and positions where safe landings at established airports can be readily accomplished in the event difficulty is encountered in restarting and/or unfeathering. In the event a propeller cannot be unfeathered during the practical test, it shall be treated as an emergency.

Objective: To determine that the applicant:
1. Exhibits knowledge of the elements related to maneuvering with one engine inoperative.
2. Selects an entry altitude that will allow the task to be completed no lower than 3,000 feet (920 meters) AGL or the manufacturer's recommended altitude, whichever is higher.

3. Sets the engine controls, identifies and verifies the simulated inoperative engine, reduces drag.

4. Attains the best engine inoperative airspeed and appropriately trims the airplane and maintains control.

5. Follows the prescribed checklist to verify procedures for securing the inoperative engine.

6. Establishes a bank toward the operating engine as necessary for best performance.

7. Monitors the operating engine(s) and updates decisions based on observational feedback.

8. Restarts the affected engine using appropriate restart procedures.

9. Maintains the specified altitude ±100 feet (30 meters), when straight-and-level, and levels off from climbs and descents, at specified altitudes, ±100 feet (30 meters).

10. Completes the prescribed checklist.

C. TASK: ENGINE INOPERATIVE—LOSS OF DIRECTIONAL CONTROL DEMONSTRATION

References: AC 61-21; FAA-Approved Airplane Flight Manual and Pilot Operating Handbook

Note: Airplanes with normally aspirated engines will lose power as altitude increases because of the reduced density of the air entering the induction system of the engine. This loss of power will result in a V_{MC} lower than the stall speed at higher altitudes. Also, some airplanes have such an effective rudder that even at sea level, V_{MC} is lower than stall speed. For these airplanes, a demonstration of loss of directional control may be safely conducted by limiting travel of the rudder pedal to simulate maximum available rudder. Limiting travel of the rudder pedal should be accomplished at a speed well above the power-off stall speed (approximately 20 knots). This will avoid the hazards of stalling one wing with maximum allowable power applied to the engine on the other wing. In the event of any indication of stall prior to loss of directional control, recover to the entry airspeed. The demonstration should then be accomplished with the rudder pedal blocked at a higher airspeed.

Do not perform this maneuver by increasing the pitch attitude to a high angle with both engines operating and then reducing power on the critical engine. This technique is hazardous and may result in loss of airplane control.

Objective: To determine that the applicant:

1. Exhibits knowledge of the elements related to engine inoperative-loss of directional control by explaining:

   a. the meaning of the term "critical engine."

   b. effects of density altitude on the V_{MC} demonstration.

   c. effects of airplane weight and center of gravity on control.

   d. reasons for variations in V_{MC}.

   e. relationship of V_{MC} to stall speed.

f. reasons for loss of directional control.

g. indications of loss of directional control.

h. importance of maintaining proper pitch and bank attitude, and proper coordination of controls.

i. loss of directional control recovery procedure.

j. engine failure during takeoff, including planning, decisions, and single-engine operations.

2. Exhibits skills in performing an engine inoperative-loss of directional control demonstration:

a. selects an entry altitude that will allow the task to be completed no lower than 3,000 feet (920 meters) AGL or the manufacturer's recommended altitude, whichever is higher.

b. configures the airplane at V_{SSE}/V_{YSE} as appropriate, as follows:

(1) landing gear retracted.

(2) flaps set for takeoff.

(3) cowl flaps set for takeoff.

(4) trim set for takeoff.

(5) propellers set for high RPM.

(6) power on critical engine reduced to idle.

(7) power on operating engine set to takeoff maximum available power.

c. establishes a single engine climb attitude with the airspeed at approximately 10 knots above V_{SSE}.

d. establishes a bank toward the operating engine as required for best performance and controllability.

e. increases the pitch attitude slowly to reduce the airspeed at approximately 1 knot per second while applying rudder pressure to maintain directional control until full rudder is applied.

f. recognizes and announces the first indications of loss of directional control, stall warning, or buffet.

g. recovers promptly by simultaneously reducing power sufficiently on the operating engine while decreasing the angle of attack as necessary to regain airspeed and directional control with a minimum loss of altitude. Recovery SHOULD NOT be attempted by increasing the power on the simulated failed engine.

h. recovers within 20° of the entry heading.

i. accelerates to V_{XSE}/V_{YSE} as appropriate, ±5 knots, during the recovery.

D. TASK: ENGINE FAILURE DURING TAKEOFF BEFORE V_{MC}

References: AC 61-21; Pilot's Operating Handbook and FAA-Approved Airplane Flight Manual

Note: Engine failure shall not be simulated at a speed greater than 50 percent of the calculated V_{MC}.

Objective: To determine that the applicant:

1. Exhibits knowledge of the elements related to the procedure used for engine failure during takeoff prior to reaching V_{MC}.
2. Utilizes the prescribed emergency procedure.
3. Promptly and smoothly closes the throttle(s) when simulated engine failure occurs.
4. Maintains directional control within 15 feet (10 meters) of the runway centerline while applying the brakes as necessary.

E. TASK: ENGINE FAILURE AFTER LIFTOFF (SIMULATED)

References: AC 61-21; Pilot's Operating Handbook and FAA-Approved Airplane Flight Manual

Objective: To determine that the applicant:

1. Exhibits knowledge of the elements related to the procedure used for engine failure after liftoff.
2. Promptly recognizes engine failure, maintains directional control, and utilizes the prescribed emergency procedure.
3. Identifies and simulates feathering the propeller of the failed engine while continuing to climb. The examiner shall than establish zero-thrust on the inoperative engine.
4. Reduces drag by raising the gear and flaps, if utilized, when a positive rate of climb is established.
5. Promptly and smoothly accelerates to V_{YSE} if obstructions are present, establishes V_{XSE} or V_{MC} +5, whichever is greater, until obstruction is cleared, then V_{YSE}.
6. Follows the prescribed engine failure takeoff checklist after reaching 400 feet (130 meters) or safe obstruction clearance altitude.
7. Establishes a bank toward the operating engine as necessary for best performance.
8. Attempts to determine the reason for the engine malfunction.
9. Monitors the operating engine(s) and updates decisions based on observational feedback.
10. Determines if it is feasible to restart the affected engine; if so, follows appropriate restart procedures.
11. Returns for landing at the airport or suitable landing area.

F. TASK: APPROACH AND LANDING WITH AN INOPERATIVE ENGINE (SIMULATED)

References: AC 61-21; Pilot's Operating Handbook and FAA-Approved Airplane Flight Manual

Objective: To determine that the applicant:

1. Exhibits knowledge of the elements related to approach and landing procedures to be used in various emergency situations.

2. Recognizes engine failure promptly.
3. Sets the engine controls, reduces drag, and identifies and verifies the inoperative engine.
4. Attains the best engine inoperative airspeed and appropriately trims the airplane and maintains control.
5. Follows the prescribed checklist to verify procedures for securing the inoperative engine.
6. Establishes a bank toward the operating engine as necessary for best performance.
7. Attempts to determine the reason for the engine malfunction.
8. Monitors the operating engine(s) and updates decisions based on observational feedback.
9. Determines if it is feasible to restart the affected engine; if so, follows appropriate restart procedures.
10. Plans and follows a flight pattern to the selected landing area, considering altitude, wind, terrain, obstructions, and other factors.
11. Completes the prescribed checklist.

G. TASK: SYSTEMS AND EQUIPMENT MALFUNCTIONS

References: AC 61-21; Pilot's Operating Handbook and FAA-Approved Airplane Flight Manual

Objective: To determine that the applicant:

1. Exhibits knowledge of the elements related to causes, indications, and pilot actions for various systems and equipment malfunctions.
2. Analyzes the situation and takes appropriate action for simulated emergencies, pertaining to:
   a. importance of availability and use of an emergency checklist.
   b. partial power loss.
   c. engine roughness or overheat.
   d. loss of oil pressure.
   e. fuel starvation.
   f. smoke and fire.
   g. icing.
   h. pressurization.
   i. pitot-static system, vacuum/pressure system, and associated flight instruments.
   j. electrical.
   k. landing gear.
   l. flaps.
   m. inadvertent door opening.
   n. emergency exits.
   o. any other emergency unique to the airplane flown.

H. TASK: EMERGENCY EQUIPMENT AND SURVIVAL GEAR

References: AC 61-21; Pilot's Operating Handbook and FAA-Approved Airplane Flight Manual

Objective: To determine that the applicant:

1. Exhibits knowledge of the elements related to emergency equipment appropriate to the airplane used for the practical test by describing:
   a. location in the airplane.
   b. method of operation.
   c. servicing requirements.
   d. method of safe storage.
2. Exhibits knowledge of the elements related to survival gear by describing:
   a. survival gear appropriate for operation in various climatological and topographical environments.
   b. location in the airplane.
   c. method of operation.
   d. servicing requirements.
   e. method of safe storage.

IX. AREA OF OPERATION: MULTIENGINE OPERATIONS

A. TASK: PERFORMANCE AND LIMITATIONS

References: AC 61-21, AC 61-23, AC 61-84, AC 91-23; Pilot's Operating Handbook and FAA-Approved Airplane Flight Manual

Objective: To determine that the applicant:

1. Exhibits knowledge of the elements related to performance and limitations by explaining the use of charts, tables, and data to determine performance and the adverse effects of exceeding limitations.
2. Computes weight and balance, including adding, removing, and shifting weight. Determines if the weight and center of gravity will remain within limits during all phases of flight.
3. Describes the effects of various atmospheric conditions on the airplane's performance.
4. Determines whether the computed performance is within the airplane's capabilities and operating limitations.

B. TASK: OPERATION OF SYSTEMS

References: AC 61-21; Pilot's Operating Handbook and FAA-Approved Airplane Flight Manual

Objective: To determine that the applicant exhibits knowledge of the elements related to the appropriate normal operating procedures and limitations of the following systems by explaining:

1. Primary flight controls and trim.
2. Flaps, leading edge devices, and spoilers.
3. Powerplants.

4. Propellers.
5. Landing gear.
6. Fuel, oil, and hydraulic systems.
7. Electrical system.
8. Pitot-static system, vacuum/pressure system, and associated flight instruments.
9. Environmental system.
10. Deicing and anti-icing systems.
11. Avionics systems.

C. TASK: FLIGHT PRINCIPLES—ENGINE INOPERATIVE

References: AC 61-21, AC 61-23

Objective: To determine that the applicant:

1. Exhibits knowledge of the elements related to engine inoperative flight principles by explaining:
   a. effects of density altitude.
   b. importance of reducing drag and banking properly into the good engine(s).
   c. importance of establishing and maintaining proper airspeed.
   d. importance of maintaining proper pitch and bank attitudes, and proper coordination of controls.
   e. takeoff emergencies, including planning, decisions, and single-engine operation when failure occurs prior to V_{MC} and after liftoff.

2. Demonstrates knowledge of the effects of various airspeeds and configurations on performance during inoperative engine operation by:
   a. selecting an entry altitude that will allow the task to be completed no lower than 3,000 feet (920 meters) AGL or the manufacturer's recommended altitude, whichever is higher.
   b. establishing V_{YSE} with critical engine, if applicable, at zero thrust.
   c. varying the airspeed from V_{YSE} and demonstrating the effect of the airspeed changes on performance.
   d. maintaining V_{YSE} and demonstrating each of the following on performance:
      (1) extension of landing gear.
      (2) extension of flaps.
      (3) extension of both landing gear and flaps.
      (4) windmilling of propeller on the inoperative engine.

X. AREA OF OPERATION: HIGH-ALTITUDE OPERATIONS

Note: This area of operation applies only to that applicant whose airplane is equipped for high-altitude operations; otherwise, this shall be orally tested.

A. TASK: SUPPLEMENTAL OXYGEN

References: FAR Part 91; AC 61-107; Pilot's Operating Handbook, FAA-Approved Airplane Flight Manual, AIM

Objective: To determine that the applicant:

1. Exhibits knowledge of the elements related to supplemental oxygen by explaining:

   a. regulatory requirements for use of supplemental oxygen.

   b. distinction between "aviators' breathing oxygen" and other types.

   c. method of determining oxygen service availability.

   d. operational characteristics of continuous flow, demand, and pressure-demand oxygen systems.

   e. care and storage of high-pressure oxygen bottles.

2. Uses supplemental oxygen promptly and properly when physiological or regulatory requirements prescribe its use.

B. TASK: PRESSURIZATION

References: FAR Part 91, AC 61-21, AC 61-107, Pilot's Operating Handbook, FAA-Approved Airplane Flight Manual, AIM

Objective: To determine that the applicant:

1. Exhibits knowledge of the elements related to pressurization by explaining:

   a. regulatory requirements for use of pressurized airplane systems.

   b. operational characteristics of the cabin-pressure control system.

   c. physiological hazards associated with high-altitude flight and decompression.

   d. operational and physiological reasons for completing emergency descents.

   e. need for wearing safety belts and for rapid access to supplemental oxygen.

2. Operates the pressurization system properly, and reacts promptly and properly to pressurization malfunctions.

XI. POST-FLIGHT PROCEDURES

A. TASK: AFTER LANDING

References: AC 61-21; Pilot's Operating Handbook and FAA-Approved Airplane Flight Manual

Objective: To determine that the applicant:

1. Exhibits knowledge of the elements related to after-landing procedures, including local and ATC procedures.

2. Selects a suitable parking area while considering proper wind correction technique and obstacle clearance.

3. Completes all prescribed checklists.

B. TASK: PARKING AND SECURING

References: AC 61-21; Pilot's Operating Handbook and FAA-Approved Airplane Flight Manual

Objective: To determine that the applicant:

1. Exhibits knowledge of the elements related to ramp safety, parking hand signals, shutdown, securing, and post-flight inspection.

2. Parks the airplane properly, considering the safety of nearby persons and property.

3. Follows the recommended procedure for engine shutdown, securing the cockpit, and deplaning passengers.
4. Secures the airplane properly.
5. Performs a satisfactory post-flight inspection.
6. Completes the prescribed checklist.

Most applicants who attempt the multiengine practical test are already commercial pilots or are becoming a commercial pilot as a part of the multiengine checkride; however, it is possible to take the private pilot checkride in a multiengine airplane. Upon successful completion of the multiengine private pilot test, the new pilot can only fly multiengine airplanes, because their certificate will read "Private Pilot, Multiengine Land."

The private pilot multiengine examination combines all multiengine tasks such as "Engine failure on takeoff before V_{MC}," and all private pilot tasks such as "S-turns across a road." There is also a requirement to fly the multiengine airplane by reference to flight instruments only, but no instrument approaches are required.

While training in the multiengine airplane toward the private pilot certificate, you can solo the multiengine airplane before passing a checkride with the proper flight instructor endorsement. Rarely does a person's very first solo flight take place in a multiengine airplane. It can happen, however, particularly if you own the multiengine airplane and choose to fly it during your training.

15
The multiengine
flight instructor

IF YOUR CAREER GOALS INVOLVE THE AIRLINES OR CORPORATIONS, YOU will need all the multiengine flight time possible as outlined in chapter 10. Time spent in the multiengine airplane giving instruction to others is usually the first opportunity for young pilots to build multiengine experience.

The bad news is that multiengine flight instruction can be very hazardous. The multiengine instructor must really know the airplane and its capabilities. There are more opportunities to get into trouble while sitting in the right seat of a light multiengine airplane than in any other type of instruction.

PRIMARY INSTRUCTION FIRST

You must graduate to multiengine instruction. I would not want a rookie instructor teaching from the start in a multiengine airplane. So many things learned by giving primary instruction prove to be priceless in a multiengine airplane. Instructors learn to divide their attention with primary students. Experienced instructors do a better job of looking out for traffic. Experienced instructors can keep one eye on the student and one eye on the airplane.

After giving a few hundred hours of instruction, your time in the air (and the student's time) is used more efficiently. You become a better teacher because you have explained many ideas to all types of students. Experienced instructors know what does and does not work. All these lessons learned by teaching in a single-engine airplane are necessary for good, safe, multiengine instruction.

You never stop learning and growing. I fully understood instrument flying only when I became an instrument instructor. Likewise, I fully understood multiengine flying only when I became a multiengine instructor.

Giving multiengine flight instruction is a real challenge. You must teach new concepts to students every day. The students who come to get their multiengine ratings probably have never talked about zero sideslip, V_{MC}, accelerate-stop distance, crossfeeding an engine, or feathering a propeller. This will all be new to them. It will be up to you to truly understand these topics and relate the art and science of multiengine flight to them.

INSTRUCTOR CHECKRIDE

A multiengine flight instructor certificate requires another checkride that will be similar to the original multiengine rating test, but now you fly from the right seat and you must be able to teach all the multiengine concepts. Start instructing in a single-engine airplane because training for a flight instructor certificate with a multiengine rating would be very expensive without the single-engine experience. Additionally, you could only instruct in multiengine airplanes.

There is no multiengine instructor written test, so expect a vigorous oral exam to begin the practical test. Regulation 91.191 says that to qualify for the multiengine instructor test, you must have logged a minimum of 15 hours in multiengine airplanes. The 6–10 hours or more that you spent working toward your original multiengine rating do not count toward the 15 because you were not yet rated in a multiengine airplane during your training. This means that the 15 hours must all come after passing your first multiengine checkride.

Later, when you are giving multiengine instruction, the FAA requires under regulation 91.195 that you have 5 hours of pilot-in-command time in any multiengine airplane in which you teach.

The flight test will be easier and shorter if you already have a flight instructor certificate with an airplane single-engine rating. The multiengine instructor practical test standard says that if you have been previously tested on a specified area of operation, then you need not be tested again.

The areas eliminated from your multiengine instructor test if you already have a single-engine instructor certificate are:

- Area of operation I—Fundamentals of instructing.
- Area of operation II—Technical subject areas.
- Area of operation III—Preflight preparation.

- Area of operation IV—Preflight lesson on a maneuver to be performed in flight.
- Area of operation VI—Ground and water operations.
- Area of operation VII—Airport operations.
- Area of operation IX—Fundamentals of flight.
- Area of operation XI—Basic instrument maneuvers.
- Area of operation XII—Performance maneuvers.
- Area of operation XIII—Ground reference maneuvers.
- Area of operation XVI—After-landing procedures (seaplane).

Quite a bit is cut out, but realize that according to the standards: "At the discretion of the examiner, the applicant's competence in all areas of operation may be evaluated." This means that the examiner might require an applicant to prepare a lesson plan, discuss the laws of learning, or fly an S turn on the multiengine instructor test.

These areas of operation would become the basis for the multiengine instructor test (edited) if you already have a single-engine instructor certificate:

- Area of operation V—Multiengine operations: operation of systems; performance and limitations; flight principles with an engine inoperative; emergency procedures.
- Area of operation VIII—Takeoffs and climbs: normal and crosswind takeoff and climb; short-field takeoff and climb.
- Area of operation X—Stalls and maneuvering during slow flight: power-on stalls; power-off stalls; maneuvering during slow flight.
- Area of operation XIV—Emergency operations: system and equipment malfunctions; maneuvering with one engine inoperative; engine inoperative loss of directional control demonstration (V_{MC} demo); demonstrating the effects of various airspeeds and configurations during engine inoperative performance; engine failure during takeoff before V_{MC}; engine failure after liftoff; approach and landing with an inoperative engine; emergency equipment and survival gear.
- Area of operation XV—Approaches and landings (airplane): normal and crosswind approach and landing; go-around; short-field approach and landing.

METHOD OF OPERATION

After becoming a multiengine instructor, you will need to have a talk with yourself to determine exactly what your limitations will be. I struck a compromise in the previous chapter on multiengine airwork.

One school of thought says that you should teach total realism in multiengine training. You should actually feather an engine on takeoff, and you should make real engine-failed approaches and landings. The other school of thought never actually shut down an engine in flight. Always simulate the engine failure with the throttle, never the mixture control or the fuel selector valve.

The first school is too dangerous and the second school does not offer real multi-engine training. I split the difference at 3,000 feet AGL, or higher if recommended by the manufacturer. Above 3,000 feet AGL, I use the mixture control or selector valve to shut down, feather, and then secure engines. Below 3,000 feet AGL, I use the throttle only to simulate an engine failure.

You must develop some personal minimums as a multiengine instructor. There are certain things that you will not do. Remember when you first got your instrument rating? The new rating in your wallet said that you could legally fly in any instrument weather, but you didn't. If you were smart, your first solo IFR experience was an approach with a relatively high ceiling so that you broke out of the clouds well above the decision height. Your confidence grew, and you became comfortable with lower and lower ceilings.

The same is true with multiengine instruction. At first, you will not even simulate an engine failure upon takeoff below 500 feet AGL. You might lower that to 300 feet after learning more about the airplane and yourself. Only you can know your comfort level. Do not get pushed into a situation that you cannot get out of.

Takeoff engine-failure simulations should be accomplished by bringing one throttle back to idle. The student should go through the procedure in response to a failure. If and when the student calls for prop feathering, I will advance the idle throttle to a position that gives zero thrust, which simulates the drag of a feathered prop. I do not place the throttle to zero thrust until the student calls "prop to feather." If he forgets that part of the procedure, he is going to have sore leg muscles.

Always be ready for your student to do something unexpected. Never hesitate to pull back both mixture controls to save a situation. For instance, you are on a takeoff roll with a multiengine student. As a test for the student, prior to obtaining V_{MC} you call out, "Fire in the left engine!" The student, rather than pulling back both throttles, retards only the left one.

If you are not ready, you will soon be off the side of the runway and into the grass. Pull back both mixture controls, and keep the nose straight with rudder. Anticipate. Be 110 percent attentive while providing multiengine instruction.

Would you ever pull both mixtures in flight? Yes, if the alternative is a low-altitude V_{MC} roll. You have lifted off the runway with a multiengine student on his third lesson, and you simulate right-engine failure by pulling the right throttle back to idle. Your eager student, his mind a blur, quickly pulls the right engine into feather, and locks his elbow holding full power on the left engine.

It happens so fast that verbal instructions cannot prevent it. The airplane is losing speed and altitude. The airplane starts to yaw to the right. "Pull the rip cord" this instant: both mixture controls. Remember that it's always better to pancake in with the wheels down than to crash upside down and out of control. If this hypothetical situation scares you, you are not alone.

Protect yourself

Do not simulate takeoff engine failures until you have some confidence in your student's airspeed control. Do not simulate takeoff engine failures near V_{MC}. Do not simulate takeoff engine failures immediately as the wheels leave the ground.

Perform engine shutdowns at a safe altitude. You must know the specific airplane well to confidently shut down an engine. You need to know the manufacturer's V_{SSE} speed by heart. V_{SSE} is the *minimum safe single-engine* speed used to intentionally render an engine inoperative for training purposes.

Whenever you intend to shut down and feather an engine, have a plan of action already in mind if the engine does not restart. The airplane's mechanical well-being often determines which engine to shut down. You need to know which engine is easier to start. You need to know which starter does not always engage the first time. You need to know any other factor that would affect an engine restart.

At high altitude, you can keep the identity of the failed engine a secret. Down low, when the throttle is used to simulate engine failure, the student can clearly see which engine is pulled back. Up high, where you do complete engine shutdowns, hide the engine failure from the student. If you fail an engine by using the fuel selector valve, move the valve after distracting the student, or cover up both valves with a chart or checklist.

Cover the valves when you are not going to fail an engine; the student will not know for sure when the engine might fail or which engine it will be. If you fail the engine with the mixture control, you can place a chart or checklist into the control pedestal between the right-engine prop control and the left-engine mixture control. The student will know an engine is about to fail, but he won't know which one.

Think ahead

Think about the wind at the home airport before you shut down an engine. Provided that both engines start equally well, which engine should be shut down in the following situation? Runway 18 is being used at home. The wind is from 220° at 15 knots. You are 5 miles from the airport at 5,000 feet AGL, and you have reached the point in the lesson where you want to teach the student to recognize engine failure, feather the prop, and secure the engine.

The left engine is better. Let's assume that a restart fails and several additional attempts also fail. Now you are faced with actually landing with a single engine. Wind at the airport will require a right crosswind technique. This means the centerline-aligned approach will carry the right wing low. If the left engine is dead, you should fly with the right wing low anyway.

To reduce sideslip drag, you will make the approach with the airplane banked into the good engine. Everything will work out if the good engine is on the same side that the wind is coming from. Imagine how awkward and dangerous the approach would be with the left wing down in a right crosswind. Plan ahead so that this never happens.

It is also a good idea to have some engine-out boundaries. Never let yourself get too far from a suitable airport while practicing engine-out procedures. The distance depends on altitude and wind. If you were just at the minimum 3,000 feet AGL and stuck with an engine that would not restart, you could be in trouble if you must fly to the airport against a strong breeze.

Never attempt to fly slowly or execute a stall with one engine inoperative. Never simulate an engine failure when flying slower than V_{SSE}.

NO RIDERS

Think twice about allowing riders on multiengine flight lessons. Another student might benefit from observation, but other factors are involved. I will not do V_{MC} demonstrations with a backseat passenger. Any extra weight in the rear moves the center of gravity, which increases V_{MC}. The bookspeed for V_{MC} is calculated with an aft CG, but a minimal surprise factor is preferred during V_{MC} work; the calculated speed of V_{MC} and the actual speed of V_{MC} can be quite different.

Instructing might be just what you need to gain that expensive and irreplaceable multiengine time. It can be great fun, but approach it very seriously. Do your homework. Know your airplane inside and out. Be ready to react to student mistakes regardless of the student's experience. Always leave yourself an out.

The following is an abbreviated copy of the Multiengine Flight Instructor Practical Test Standards. All individual seaplane tasks have been removed and all tasks that would be included in an initial flight instructor test have also been removed. What remains is the actual multiengine flight instructor practical test if you start the test as a single-engine flight instructor.

MULTIENGINE FLIGHT INSTRUCTOR PRACTICAL TEST STANDARDS

V. AREA OF OPERATION: MULTIENGINE OPERATIONS
Note: The examiner **will select TASKS A, B, C, and D.**

A. TASK: OPERATION OF SYSTEMS (AMEL and AMES)
   References: AC 61-21; FAA S-8081-1, FAA-S-8081-2; Pilot's Operating Handbook, FAA-Approved Airplane Flight Manual
   Objective: To determine that the applicant exhibits instructional knowledge of the elements related to the operation of systems, as applicable to the airplane used for the practical test, by describing:
   1. Primary flight controls and trim.
   2. Pitot static/vacuum system and associated instruments.
   3. Landing gear.
   4. Wing flaps, leading edge devices, and spoilers.
   5. Powerplant, including controls, indicators, cooling, and fire detection.
   6. Propellers, including controls and indicators.
   7. Fuel, oil, and hydraulic systems.
   8. Electrical system.
   9. Environmental system.
   10. Deicing and anti-icing systems.
   11. Avionics system.
   12. Any system unique to the airplane flown.

B. TASK: PERFORMANCE AND LIMITATIONS (AMEL and AMES)

References: AC 61-21, AC 61-23, AC 61-84, AC-91-23; FAA-S-8081-1, FAA-S-8081-2; Pilot's Operating Handbook, FAA-Approved Airplane Flight Manual

Objective: To determine that the applicant exhibits instructional knowledge of the elements related to performance and limitations by describing:

1. Determination of weight and balance condition.
2. Use of performance charts, tables, and other data in determining performance in various phases of flight.
3. Effects of exceeding limitations.
4. Effects of atmospheric conditions on performance.
5. Factors to be considered in determining that the required performance is within the airplane's capabilities.

C. TASK: FLIGHT PRINCIPLES—ENGINE INOPERATIVE (AMEL and AMES)

References: AC 61-21; FAA-S-8081-1, FAA-S-8081-2; Pilot's Operating Handbook, FAA-Approved Airplane Flight Manual

Objective: To determine that the applicant exhibits instructional knowledge of the elements related to flight principles-engine inoperative by describing:

1. Effects of density altitude.
2. Importance of reducing drag.
3. Importance of establishing and maintaining proper airspeed.
4. Importance of maintaining proper pitch and bank attitudes, and proper coordination of controls.
5. Effects of weight and center of gravity.
6. Critical engine.
7. Reasons for loss of directional control.
8. Indications of approaching loss of directional control.
9. Reasons for variations in V_{MC}.
10. Relationship of V_{MC} to stall speed, including determination of whether a loss of directional control demonstration can be safely accomplished.
11. Takeoff emergencies, including planning, decisions, and single-engine operations.

D. TASK: EMERGENCY PROCEDURES (AMEL and AMES)

References: AC 61-21; FAA-S-8081-1, FAA-S-8081-2; Pilot's Operating Handbook, FAA-Approved Airplane Flight Manual

Objective: To determine that the applicant exhibits instructional knowledge of the elements of emergency procedures appropriate to the airplane used for the practical test by describing:

1. Importance of availability and use of an emergency checklist.
2. Possible causes of partial or complete power loss in various flight situations.
3. Procedures to be followed if partial or complete power loss occurs during any phase of flight.
4. Procedures to be followed in icing conditions.
5. Procedures to be followed in the event of instrument malfunction.
6. Recommended recovery procedure from an unintentional spin.
7. Any other emergency appropriate to the airplane flown.

VIII. AREA OF OPERATION: TAKEOFF AND CLIMBS

Note: The examiner **will select at least one TASK.**

A. TASK: NORMAL AND CROSSWIND TAKEOFF AND CLIMB (AMEL and AMES)

References: AC 60-14, AC 61-21; FAA-S-8081-1, FAA-S-8081-2; Pilot's Operating Handbook, FAA-Approved Airplane Flight Manual, Seaplane Manual.

Objective: To determine that the applicant:

1. Exhibits instructional knowledge of the elements of a normal and crosswind takeoff and climb by describing—
   a. review of wind conditions.
   b. takeoff hazards.
   c. use of wing flaps.
   d. alignment with takeoff path.
   e. initial positioning of flight controls.
   f. power application.
   g. directional control during acceleration on the surface.
   h. crosswind control technique during acceleration on the surface.
   i. rotation at airspeed appropriate for the airplane flown.
   j. how to establish the single-engine best rate of climb pitch attitude.
   k. how to establish and maintain V_Y.
   l. how to establish and maintain cruise climb airspeed and the appropriate power setting.
   m. crosswind correction and track during climb.
   n. use of checklist.
   o. difference between a normal and a glassy-water takeoff (seaplane).
2. Exhibits instructional knowledge of common errors related to a normal and crosswind takeoff and climb by describing—
   a. improper initial positioning of flight controls or wing flaps.
   b. improper power application.
   c. inappropriate removal of hand from throttles.
   d. poor directional control.
   e. improper use of ailerons.

    f. rotation at improper airspeed.

    g. failure to establish and maintain proper climb configuration.

    h. drift during climb.

  3. Demonstrates and simultaneously explains a normal or a crosswind takeoff and climb from an instructional standpoint.

  4. Analyzes and corrects simulated common errors related to a normal or a crosswind takeoff and climb.

B. TASK: SHORT-FIELD TAKEOFF AND CLIMB (AMEL)

References: AC 60-14, AC 61-21; FAA-S-8081-1, FAA-S-8081-2; Pilot's Operating Handbook, FAA-Approved Airplane Flight Manual

Objective: To determine that the applicant:

  1. Exhibits instructional knowledge of the elements of a short-field takeoff and climb by describing—

    a. review of wind conditions

    b. takeoff and climb hazards, particularly those related to obstacles.

    c. use of wing flaps.

    d. how to position and align the airplane for maximum utilization of available takeoff area.

    e. initial positioning of flight controls.

    f. power application.

    g. directional control during acceleration on the surface.

    h. rotation at the airspeed appropriate for airplane used in the practical test.

    i. initial climb attitude and airspeed (V_X) until obstacle is cleared (50 feet/16 meters AGL).

    j. acceleration to V_Y and establishment and maintenance of V_Y.

    k. how to establish and maintain cruise climb airspeed and the appropriate power setting.

    l. track during climb.

    m. use of checklist.

  2. Exhibits instructional knowledge of common errors related to a short-field takeoff and climb by describing—

    a. failure to position the airplane for maximum utilization of available takeoff area.

    b. improper initial positioning of flight controls and wing flaps.

    c. improper power application.

    d. inappropriate removal of hand from throttles.

    e. poor directional control.

    f. improper use of ailerons.

    g. improper use of brakes.

    h. rotation at improper airspeed.

    i. failure to establish and maintain proper climb configuration and airspeeds.

    j. drift during climb.

3. Demonstrates and simultaneously explains a short-field takeoff and climb from an instructional standpoint.

4. Analyzes and corrects simulated common errors related to a short-field takeoff and climb.

X. AREA OF OPERATION: STALLS AND MANEUVERING DURING SLOW FLIGHT

Note: The examiner **will select at least one TASK**. Stalls will not be performed with one engine at reduced power or inoperative and the other engine(s) developing effective power.

Stalls using high power settings should not be performed. The high pitch angles necessary to induce these stalls could possibly result in uncontrollable flight.

Examiners and instructors should be alert to the possible development of high sink rates when performing stalls in multiengine airplanes with high wing loadings; therefore, the altitude loss during stall entries should be no more than 50 feet.

A. TASK: POWER-ON STALLS (AMEL and AMES)

References: AC 60-14, AC 61-21; FAA-S-8081-1, FAA-S-8081-2; Pilot's Operating Handbook, FAA-Approved Airplane Flight Manual

Objective: To determine that the applicant:

1. Exhibits instructional knowledge of the elements of power-on stalls, in climbing flight (straight or turning), with selected landing gear and flap configurations, by describing—

   a. aerodynamics of power-on stalls.

   b. relationship of various factors such as landing gear and flap configuration, weight, center of gravity, load factor, and bank angle to stall speed.

   c. flight situations where unintentional power on stalls may occur.

   d. recognition of the first indications of power-on stalls.

   e. performance of power-on stalls in climbing flight (straight or turning).

   f. entry technique and minimum entry altitude.

   g. coordination of flight controls.

   h. recovery technique and minimum recovery altitude.

2. Exhibits instructional knowledge of common errors related to power-on stalls, in climbing flight (straight or turning), with selected landing gear and flap configurations, by describing—

   a. failure to establish the specified landing gear and flap configuration prior to entry.

   b. improper pitch, heading, and bank control during straight-ahead stalls.

   c. improper pitch and bank control during turning stalls.

   d. rough or uncoordinated control technique.

   e. failure to recognize the first indications of a stall.

   f. failure to achieve a stall.

   g. improper torque correction.

    h. poor stall recognition and delayed recovery.

    i. excessive altitude loss or excessive airspeed during recovery.

    j. secondary stall during recovery.

3. Demonstrates and simultaneously explains power-on stalls, in climbing flight (straight or turning), with selected landing gear and flap configurations, from an instructional standpoint.

4. Analyzes and corrects simulated common errors related to power-on stalls, in climbing flight (straight and turning), with selected landing gear and flap configurations.

B. TASK: POWER-OFF STALLS (AMEL and AMES)

    References: AC 60-14, AC 61-21; FAA-S-8081-1, FAA-S-8081-2; Pilot's Operating Handbook, FAA-Approved Airplane Flight Manual

    Objective: To determine that the applicant:

1. Exhibits instructional knowledge of the elements of power-off stalls, in descending flight (straight or turning), with selected landing gear and flap configurations, by describing—

    a. aerodynamics of power-off stalls.

    b. relationship of various factors such as landing gear and flap configuration, weight, center of gravity, load factor, and bank angle to stall speed.

    c. flight situations where unintentional power-off stalls may occur.

    d. recognition of the first indications of power-off stalls.

    e. performance of power-off stalls in descending flight (straight or turning).

    f. entry technique and minimum entry altitude.

    g. coordination of flight controls.

    h. recovery technique and minimum recovery altitude.

2. Exhibits instructional knowledge of common errors related to power off stalls, in descending flight (straight or turning), with selected landing gear and flap configurations, by describing—

    a. failure to establish the specified landing gear and flap configuration prior to entry.

    b. improper pitch, heading, and bank control during straight-ahead stalls.

    c. improper pitch and bank control during turning stalls.

    d. rough or uncoordinated control technique.

    e. failure to recognize the first indications of a stall.

    f. failure to achieve a stall.

    g. improper torque correction.

    h. poor stall recognition and delayed recovery.

    i. excessive altitude loss or excessive airspeed during recovery.

    j. secondary stall during recovery.

3. Demonstrates and simultaneously explains power-off stalls, in descending flight (straight or turning), with selected landing gear and flap configurations, from an instructional standpoint.

4. Analyzes and corrects simulated common errors related to power-off stalls, in descending flight (straight or turning), with selected landing gear and flap configurations.

C. TASK: MANEUVERING DURING SLOW FLIGHT (AMEL and AMES)

References: AC 60-14, AC 61-21; FAA-S-8081-1, FAA-S-8081-2; Pilot's Operating Handbook, FAA-Approved Airplane Flight Manual

Objective: To determine that the applicant:

1. Exhibits instructional knowledge of the elements of maneuvering during slow flight by describing—
   a. relationship of configuration, weight, center of gravity, maneuvering loads, angle of bank, and power to flight characteristics and controllability.
   b. relationship of the maneuver to critical flight situations, such as go-arounds.
   c. performance of the maneuver with selected landing gear and flap configurations in straight-and-level flight and level turns.
   d. specified airspeed for the maneuver.
   e. coordination of flight controls.
   f. trim technique.
   g. re-establishment of cruise flight

2. Exhibits instructional knowledge of common errors related to maneuvering during slow flight by describing—
   a. failure to establish specified gear and flap configuration.
   b. improper entry technique.
   c. failure to establish and maintain the specified airspeed.
   d. excessive variations of altitude and heading when a constant altitude and heading are specified.
   e. rough or uncoordinated control technique.
   f. improper correction for torque effect.
   g. improper trim technique.
   h. unintentional stalls.
   i. inappropriate removal of hand from throttles.

3. Demonstrates and simultaneously explains maneuvering during slow flight from an instructional standpoint.

4. Analyzes and corrects simulated common errors related to maneuvering during slow flight.

XIV. AREA OF OPERATION: EMERGENCY OPERATIONS

Note: The examiner **will select TASKS A, B, C, D, E, F, and G.**

A. TASK: SYSTEMS AND EQUIPMENT MALFUNCTIONS

References: AC 61-21; FAA-S-8081-1, FAA-S-8081-2; Pilot's Operating Handbook, FAA-Approved Airplane Flight Manual

Note: The examiner will not simulate a system or equipment malfunction in a manner that may jeopardize safe flight or result in possible damage to the airplane.

> *Objective:* To determine that the applicant exhibits instructional knowledge of the elements related to systems and equipment malfunctions, appropriate to the airplane used for the practical test, by describing recommended pilot action for:

1. Smoke, fire, or both, during ground or flight operations.
2. Rough running engine, partial power loss, or sudden engine stoppage.
3. Propeller malfunction.
4. Loss of engine oil pressure.
5. Fuel starvation.
6. Engine overheat.
7. Hydraulic system malfunction.
8. Electrical system malfunction.
9. Carburetor or induction icing.
10. Door or window opening in flight.
11. Inoperative or "runaway" trim.
12. Landing gear or flap malfunction.
13. Pressurization malfunction.
14. Any other system or equipment malfunction.

B. TASK: MANEUVERING WITH ONE ENGINE INOPERATIVE

> *References:* AC 60-14, AC 61-21; FAA-S-8081-1, FAA-S-8081-2; Pilot's Operating Handbook, FAA-Approved Airplane Flight Manual

Note: The feathering of one propeller shall be demonstrated in any multiengine airplane equipped with propellers which can be safely feathered and unfeathered in flight. Feathering for pilot flight test purposes should be performed only under such conditions and at such altitudes (no lower than 3,000 feet/1,000 meters above the surface) and positions where safe landings on established airports can be readily accomplished, in the event difficulty is encountered in unfeathering. At altitudes lower than 3,000 feet above the surface, simulated engine failure will be performed by throttling the engine and then establishing zero thrust. In the event a propeller cannot be unfeathered during the practical test, it should be treated as an emergency.

> *Objective:* To determine that the applicant:

1. Exhibits instructional knowledge of the elements related to maneuvering with one engine inoperative by describing—
    a. flight characteristics and controllability associated with maneuvering with one engine inoperative.
    b. use of prescribed emergency checklist to verify accomplishment of procedures for securing inoperative engine.
    c. proper adjustment of engine controls, reduction of drag, and identification and verification of the inoperative engine.

       d. how to establish and maintain the best engine inoperative airspeed.

       e. proper trim technique.

       f. how to establish and maintain a bank, as required, for best performance.

       g. appropriate methods to be used for determining the reason for the malfunction.

       h. importance of establishing a heading toward the nearest suitable airport or seaplane base.

       i. importance of monitoring and adjusting the operating engine.

       j. performance of straight-and-level flight, turns, descents, and climbs, if the airplane is capable of those maneuvers under existing conditions.

2. Exhibits instructional knowledge of common errors related to maneuvering with one engine inoperative by describing—

       a. failure to follow prescribed emergency checklist.

       b. failure to recognize an inoperative engine.

       c. hazards of improperly identifying and verifying the inoperative engine.

       d. failure to properly adjust engine controls and reduce drag.

       e. failure to establish and maintain the best engine inoperative airspeed.

       f. improper trim technique.

       g. failure to establish and maintain proper bank for best performance.

       h. failure to maintain positive control while maneuvering.

       i. hazards of attempting flight contrary to the airplane's operating limitations.

3. Demonstrates and simultaneously explains maneuvering with one engine inoperative from an instructional standpoint.

4. Analyzes and corrects simulated common errors related to maneuvering with one engine inoperative.

C. TASK: ENGINE INOPERATIVE LOSS OF DIRECTIONAL CONTROL DEMONSTRATION (AMEL and AMES)

    References: AC 60-14, AC 61-21; FAA-S-8081-1, FAA-S-8081-2; Pilot's Operating Handbook, FAA-Approved Airplane Flight Manual

Note: FAR Part 1 defines V_{MC} as minimum control speed with the critical engine inoperative. There is a density altitude above which the stalling speed is higher than the engine inoperative minimum control speed. When this density altitude exists close to the ground because of high elevations, high temperatures, or both, an effective flight demonstration of loss of directional control may be hazardous and should not be attempted. If it is determined prior to flight that the stall speed is above or equal to V_{MC}, this flight demonstration is impracticable. In this case, the significance of the engine inoperative minimum control speed should be emphasized through oral questioning, including the results of attempting engine inoperative flight below that speed, the recognition of loss of directional control, and proper recovery techniques.

    Recovery should be made by simultaneously reducing the power on the operating engine and reducing the angle of attack as necessary to regain directional control and airspeed. Recoveries should not be attempted by increasing power on the simulated failed engine.

Performing this maneuver by increasing pitch attitude to a high angle with both engines operating and then reducing power on the critical engine should be avoided. This technique is hazardous and may result in loss of aircraft control.

Objective: To determine that the applicant:

1. Exhibits instructional knowledge of the elements related to engine inoperative loss of directional control by describing—
   a. causes of loss of directional control at airspeeds less than V_{MC}, the factors affecting V_{MC}, and the safe recovery procedures.
   b. establishment of airplane configuration, adjustment of power controls, and trim prior to the demonstration.
   c. establishment of engine inoperative pitch attitude and airspeed.
   d. establishment of a bank attitude as required for best performance.
   e. entry technique to demonstrate loss of directional control.
   f. indications that enable a pilot to recognize loss of directional control.
   g. proper recovery technique.
2. Exhibits instructional knowledge of common errors related to engine inoperative loss of directional control by describing—
   a. inadequate knowledge of the causes of loss of directional control at airspeeds less than V_{MC}, factors affecting V_{MC}, and safe recovery procedures.
   b. improper entry procedures, including pitch attitude, bank attitude, and airspeed.
   c. failure to recognize imminent loss of directional control.
   d. failure to use proper recovery technique.
   e. rough and/or uncoordinated control technique.
3. Demonstrates and simultaneously explains engine inoperative loss of directional control from an instructional standpoint.
4. Analyzes and corrects simulated common errors related to engine inoperative loss of directional control.

D. TASK: DEMONSTRATING THE EFFECTS OF VARIOUS AIRSPEEDS AND CONFIGURATIONS DURING ENGINE INOPERATIVE PERFORMANCE

References: AC 60-14, AC 61-21; FAA-S-8081-1, FAA-S-8081-2; Pilot's Operating Handbook, FAA-Approved Airplane Flight Manual

Objective: To determine that the applicant:

1. Exhibits instructional knowledge of the elements related to the effects of various airspeeds and configurations during engine inoperative performance by describing—
   a. selection of proper altitude for the demonstration.
   b. proper entry procedure to include pitch attitude, bank attitude, and airspeed.

   c. effects on performance of airspeed changes at, above, and below V_{YSE}.
   d. effects on performance of various configurations—
      (1) extension of landing gear.
      (2) extension of wing flaps.
      (3) extension of both landing gear and wing flaps.
      (4) windmilling of propeller on inoperative engine.
   e. airspeed control throughout the demonstration.
   f. proper control technique and procedures throughout the demonstration.
2. Exhibits instructional knowledge of common errors related to the effects of various airspeeds and configurations during engine inoperative performance by describing—
   a. inadequate knowledge of the effects of airspeeds above or below V_{YSE} and of various configurations on performance.
   b. improper entry procedures, including pitch attitude, bank attitude, and airspeed.
   c. improper airspeed control throughout the demonstration.
   d. rough and/or uncoordinated control technique.
   e. improper procedures during resumption of cruise flight.
3. Demonstrates and simultaneously explains the effects of various airspeeds and configurations during engine inoperative performance from an instructional standpoint.
4. Analyzes and corrects simulated common errors related to the effects of various airspeeds and configurations during engine inoperative performance.

E. TASK: ENGINE FAILURE DURING TAKEOFF BEFORE V_{MC}
Note: Engine failure will not be simulated at a speed greater than 50 percent V_{MC}.
   References: AC 60-14, AC 61-21; FAA-S-8081-1, FAA-S-8081-2; Pilot's Operating Handbook, FAA-Approved Airplane Flight Manual
   Objective: To determine that the applicant:
   1. Exhibits instructional knowledge of the elements related to engine failure during takeoff before V_{MC} by describing—
   a. use of prescribed emergency procedure.
   b. prompt closing of throttles.
   c. how to maintain directional control.
   d. proper use of brakes (landplane).
   2. Exhibits instructional knowledge of common errors related to engine failure during takeoff before V_{MC} by describing—
   a. failure to follow prescribed emergency procedure.
   b. failure to promptly recognize engine failure.
   c. failure to promptly close throttles following engine failure.
   d. faulty directional control and use of brakes.
   3. Demonstrates and simultaneously explains a simulated engine failure during takeoff before V_{MC} from an instructional standpoint.

4. Analyzes and corrects simulated common errors related to engine failure during takeoff before V_{MC}.

F. TASK: ENGINE FAILURE AFTER LIFTOFF (AMEL and AMES)

References: AC 60-14, AC 61-21; FAA-S-8081-1, FAA-S-8081-2; Pilot's Operating Handbook, FAA-Approved Airplane Flight Manual

Objective: To determine that the applicant:

1. Exhibits instructional knowledge of the elements related to engine failure after liftoff by describing—

   a. use of prescribed emergency checklist to verify accomplishment of procedures for securing the inoperative engine.

   b. proper adjustment of engine controls, reduction of drag, and identification and verification of the inoperative engine.

   c. how to establish and maintain a pitch attitude that will result in the best engine inoperative airspeed, considering the height of obstructions.

   d. how to establish and maintain a bank as required for best performance.

   e. how to maintain directional control.

   f. methods to be used for determining reason for malfunction.

   g. monitoring and proper use of the operating engine.

   h. an emergency approach and landing, if a climb or level flight is not within the airplane's performance capability.

   i. positive airplane control.

   j. how to obtain assistance from the appropriate facility.

2. Exhibits instructional knowledge of common errors related to engine failure after liftoff by describing—

   a. failure to follow prescribed emergency checklist.

   b. failure to properly identify and verify the inoperative engine.

   c. failure to properly adjust engine controls and reduce drag.

   d. failure to maintain directional control.

   e. failure to establish and maintain a pitch attitude that will result in best engine inoperative airspeed, considering the height of obstructions.

   f. failure to establish and maintain proper bank for best performance.

3. Demonstrates and simultaneously explains a simulated engine failure after liftoff from an instructional standpoint.

4. Analyzes and corrects simulated common errors related to engine failure after liftoff.

G. TASK: APPROACH AND LANDING WITH AN INOPERATIVE ENGINE (AMEL and AMES)

References: AC 60-14, AC 61-21; FAA-S-8081-1, FAA-S-8081-2; Pilot's Operating Handbook, FAA-Approved Airplane Flight Manual

Objective: To determine that the applicant:

1. Exhibits instructional knowledge of the elements related to an approach and landing with an inoperative engine by describing—

a. use of the prescribed emergency checklist to verify accomplishment of procedures for securing the inoperative engine.
b. proper adjustment of engine controls, reduction of drag, and identification and verification of the inoperative engine.
c. how to establish and maintain best engine-inoperative airspeed.
d. trim technique.
e. how to establish and maintain a bank as required for best performance.
f. the monitoring and adjusting of the operating engine.
g. proper approach to selected touchdown area, at the recommended airspeed.
h. proper application of flight controls.
i. how to maintain a precise ground track.
j. wind shear and turbulence.
k. proper timing, judgment, and control technique during roundout and touchdown.
l. directional control after touchdown.
m. use of brakes (landplane).

2. Exhibits instructional knowledge of common errors related to an approach and landing with an inoperative engine by describing—
a. failure to follow prescribed emergency checklist.
b. failure to properly identify and verify the inoperative engine.
c. failure to properly adjust engine controls and reduce drag.
d. failure to establish and maintain best engine inoperative airspeed.
e. improper trim technique.
f. failure to establish proper approach and landing configuration at appropriate time and in proper sequence.
g. failure to use proper technique for wind shear or turbulence.
h. inappropriate removal of hand from throttles.
i. faulty technique during roundout and touchdown.
j. improper directional control after touchdown.
k. improper use of brakes (landplane).

3. Demonstrates and simultaneously explains an approach and landing with a simulated inoperative engine from an instructional standpoint.

4. Analyzes and corrects simulated common errors related to an approach and landing with an inoperative engine.

H. TASK: EMERGENCY EQUIPMENT AND SURVIVAL GEAR

References: AC 61-21; FAA-S-8081-1, FAA-S-8081-2; Pilot's Operating Handbook, FAA-Approved Airplane Flight Manual

Objective: To determine that the applicant exhibits instructional knowledge of the elements related to emergency equipment and survival gear appropriate to the airplane flown by describing—

1. Locations in the airplane.
2. Purpose.
3. Method of operation or use.
4. Servicing.
5. Storage.
6. Equipment and gear appropriate for operation in various climates, over various types of terrain, and over water.

XV. AREA OF OPERATION: APPROACHES AND LANDINGS

Note: The examiner **will select at least one TASK.**

A. TASK: NORMAL AND CROSSWIND APPROACH AND LANDING

References: AC 60-14, AC 61-21; FAA-S-8081-1, FAA-S-8081-2; Pilot's Operating Handbook, FAA-Approved Airplane Flight Manual, Seaplane Manual

Objective: To determine that the applicant.

1. Exhibits instructional knowledge of the elements of a normal and a crosswind approach and landing by describing—

   a. how to determine landing performance and limitations.

   b. configuration, power, and trim.

   c. obstructions and other hazards which should be considered.

   d. a stabilized approach at the recommended airspeed to the selected touchdown area.

   e. coordination of flight controls.

   f. a precise ground track.

   g. wind shear and wake turbulence.

   h. most suitable crosswind technique.

   i. timing, judgment, and control technique during roundout and touchdown.

   j. directional control after touchdown.

   k. use of brakes (landplane).

   l. use of checklist.

2. Exhibits instructional knowledge of common errors related to a normal and a crosswind approach and landing by describing—

   a. improper use of landing performance data and limitations.

   b. failure to establish approach and landing configuration at appropriate time or in proper sequence.

   c. failure to establish and maintain a stabilized approach.

   d. inappropriate removal of hand from throttles.

   e. improper technique during roundout and touchdown.

   f. poor directional control after touchdown.

   g. improper use of brakes (landplane).

3. Demonstrates and simultaneously explains a normal or a crosswind approach and landing from an instructional standpoint.

4. Analyzes and corrects simulated common errors related to a normal or crosswind approach and landing.

B. TASK: GO-AROUND (AMEL and AMES)

References: AC 60-14, AC 61-21; FAA-S-8081-1, FAA-S-8081-2; Pilot's Operating Handbook, FAA-Approved Airplane Flight Manual

Objective: To determine that the applicant:

1. Exhibits instructional knowledge of the elements of a go-around by describing—
   a. situations where a go-around is necessary.
   b. importance of making a prompt decision.
   c. importance of applying takeoff power immediately after the go-around decision is made.
   d. importance of establishing proper pitch altitude.
   e. wing flaps retraction.
   f. use of trim.
   g. landing gear retraction.
   h. proper climb speed.
   i. proper track and obstruction clearance.
   j. use of checklist.

2. Exhibits instructional knowledge of common errors related to a go-around by describing—
   a. failure to recognize a situation where a go-around is necessary.
   b. hazards of delaying a decision to go around.
   c. improper power application.
   d. failure to control pitch altitude.
   e. failure to compensate for torque effect.
   f. improper trim technique.
   g. failure to maintain recommended airspeeds.
   h. improper wing flaps or landing gear retraction procedure.
   i. failure to maintain proper track during climb-out.
   j. failure to remain well clear of obstructions and other traffic.

3. Demonstrates and simultaneously explains a go-around from an instructional standpoint.

4. Analyzes and corrects simulated common errors related to a go-around.

C. TASK: SHORT-FIELD APPROACH AND LANDING (AMEL)

References: AC 60-14, AC 61-21; FAA-S-8081-1, FAA-S-8081-2; Pilot's Operating Handbook, FAA-Approved Airplane Flight Manual

Objective: To determine that the applicant:

1. Exhibits instructional knowledge of the elements of a short-field approach and landing by describing—
   a. how to determine landing performance and limitations.
   b. configuration and trim.

    c. proper use of pitch and power to maintain desired approach angle.

    d. barriers and other hazards which should be considered.

    e. effect of wind.

    f. selection of touchdown and go-around points.

    g. a stabilized approach at the recommended airspeed to the selected touchdown point.

    h. coordination of flight controls.

    i. a precise ground track.

    j. timing, judgment, and control technique during roundout and touchdown.

    k. directional control after touchdown.

    l. use of brakes.

    m. use of checklist.

2. Exhibits instructional knowledge of common errors related to a short-field approach and landing by describing—

    a. improper use of landing performance data and limitations.

    b. failure to establish approach and landing configuration at appropriate time or in proper sequence.

    c. failure to establish and maintain a stabilized approach.

    d. improper technique in use of power, wing flaps, and trim.

    e. inappropriate removal of hand from throttles.

    f. improper technique during roundout and touchdown.

    g. poor directional control after touchdown.

    h. improper use of brakes.

3. Demonstrates and simultaneously explains a short-field approach and landing from an instructional standpoint.

4. Analyzes and corrects simulated common errors related to a short-field approach and landing.

16
Instrument multiengine flying and the ATP

INSTRUMENT FLYING AND MULTIENGINE FLYING ARE TWO DIFFERENT skills, but in every pilot's career, there comes a time when they merge. It was once assumed that a pilot with an instrument rating who took and passed a noninstrument multiengine practical test could put it all together and fly safely as a instrument/multiengine pilot. The previous instrument training was supposed to "overlap" the new multiengine training that a pilot received.

A series of accidents in the early 1980s, however, changed all that. The accidents involved pilots flying in a multiengine airplane through instrument conditions. In each case the probable cause of the accident was related to a conflict rather than a coordination of instrument and multiengine skills. The FAA began to realize that a person with instrument skills or a person with multiengine skills does not automatically have the combination of instrument/multiengine skills. So the multiengine testing procedures were changed.

Today, you must announce at the beginning of the multiengine checkride whether you are seeking an IFR or a VFR multiengine rating (see chapter 12). If you indicate IFR, there is no turning back. If while on the IFR multiengine checkride you fail on an instrument-related task, you cannot change your mind and say, "I really only wanted the VFR multiengine ride." The Practical Test Standards (PTS) are clear on the difference between the IFR and VFR multiengine tests. Following is the note pertaining to IFR and VFR examinations from the PTS:

Note: If an applicant holds a private or commercial pilot certificate with airplane single-engine land and instrument ratings and seeks to add an airplane multiengine land rating, the applicant is required to demonstrate competency in all TASKS of Area of Operation VI.

If the applicant elects not to demonstrate competency in instrument flight, the applicant's multiengine privileges will be limited to VFR only. To remove this restriction, the pilot must demonstrate competency in all TASKS of Area of Operation VI. If the applicant elects to demonstrate competency in the TASKS of Area of Operation VI, then fails one or more of those TASKS, the applicant will have failed the practical test. After the test is initiated, the applicant will not be permitted to revert to the "VFR only" option.

So if a person seeks an IFR multiengine rating, he or she must take and pass all the tasks of Area of Operation VI. What are these tasks? Area of Operation VI has three sections:

VI. INSTRUMENT FLIGHT
    A. Engine Failure During Straight-And-Level Flight and Turns
    B. Instrument Approach—All Engines Operating
    C. Instrument Approach—One Engine Inoperative

If a person is only interested in a VFR multiengine rating, he or she takes the entire multiengine test, except Area of Operation VI. Area of Operation VI is the attempt by the FAA to ensure that a pilot can blend instrument and multiengine skills safely. This blend is no longer assumed, but must be tested.

ONE ENGINE INOPERATIVE INSTRUMENT APPROACH

The biggest challenge of the IFR portion of the multiengine flight test is the "one engine inoperative" instrument approach. The examiner will ask the applicant to perform an instrument approach, and at some point, the examiner will also simulate a failed engine. This simulated engine failure usually occurs at the busiest point in the approach. The examiner will wait until you are in the middle of reading back an approach clearance, selecting a frequency, or making an intercept to pull a throttle back.

Because this is an actual instrument approach that will terminate low to the ground, the examiner should not pull back a mixture control, but rather simulate with the throttle control. The PTS outlines what the applicant is expected to do:

Area of Operation VI
Task C: INSTRUMENT APPROACH—ONE ENGINE INOPERATIVE (AMEL)
1. *Objective.* To determine that the applicant:
   a. Exhibits commercial pilot knowledge by explaining the multiengine procedures used during a published instrument approach with one engine inoperative.
   b. Requests and receives an actual or simulated clearance for a published instrument approach.
   c. Recognizes engine failure promptly.
   d. Sets the engine controls, reduces drag, and identifies and verifies the inoperative engine.
   e. Establishes the best engine-inoperative airspeed and trims the airplane.
   f. Verifies the accomplishment of the prescribed checklist procedures for securing the inoperative engine.
   g. Establishes and maintains a bank toward the operating engine, as necessary, for best performance.
   h. Attempts to determine the reason for the engine malfunction.
   i. Requests and receives an actual or simulated clearance for a published instrument approach with one engine inoperative.
   j. Follows instructions and instrument approach procedures.
   k. Recites the missed approach procedure and decides on the point at which the approach will continue or discontinue, considering the performance capability of the airplane.
   l. Descends on course so as to arrive at the DH or MDA, whichever is appropriate, in a position from which a normal landing can be made straight-in or circling.
   m. Maintains the specified airspeed, +/- 10 knots.
   n. Avoids full-scale deflection on the CDI or glideslope indicators, descent below minimums, or exceeding the radius of turn as dictated by the visibility minimums for the aircraft approach category, while circling.
   o. Communicates properly with ATC.
   p. Completes a safe landing.

As you can see, you would have your hands full. An instrument approach alone is a challenge, and an engine failure is a challenge. When they happen on top of one another, it will be more than an unprepared pilot can handle. Look at letter *h*, above: "Attempts to determine the reason for the engine malfunction." This calls for the pilot in mid-approach to troubleshoot the problem. Imagine holding a localizer against a strong crosswind and a failed engine, reporting the outer marker inbound, memorizing the missed approach procedure, and still finding time to determine what has gone wrong with the bad engine. All the time spent learning the airplane's systems and practicing the emergency procedures will pay off here.

Speaking of the missed approach procedure, look at letter *k*: "Recites the missed approach procedure and decides on the point at which the approach will continue or discontinue, considering the performance capability of the airplane." You cannot assume that with one engine failed, it is even possible to execute a missed approach procedure. The procedure might call for a climb that one engine cannot provide.

In light of this situation, the pilot might need to alter the instrument approach and stay higher than MDA or DH. Of course, by doing this, the pilot runs the risk of not getting under the clouds and ever seeing the airport. It could be a tough call: Do I continue a descent down to an altitude that is in fact below a "point of no single-engine return?" Doing this will increase my chances of seeing the runway, but I better eventually get below the clouds because the low altitude and poor single-engine climb performance makes a missed approach impossible. Or do I stay high at or above a safe go-around altitude and hope the clouds are not down at minimums? The answer to these questions require the pilot to determine where a "point of no single-engine return" is located based on many factors.

How steeply must I climb during the missed approach procedure to miss the terrain? How will the wind and temperature affect the situation? Is the engine failure under control or is there a greater danger from fire? All this and more must be considered within only a few seconds.

For pilots on checkrides, this task is somewhat easier because we know the situation is coming. A single-engine instrument approach will not be an unexpected event to a person on the IFR multiengine test. The applicant could think this through even before takeoff and have a plan of action ready. In reality, we should always be that prepared. Pilots should think about these actions on every multiengine approach in anticipation of the time when they encounter an actual emergency during, or prior to, an instrument approach.

If the pilot does descend below the clouds and spots the airport while on an instrument approach with one engine failed, he or she will need to face yet another decision. Should I land straight in or circle to land? This should also have been anticipated. If a straight-in landing is possible, the pilot should just continue to descend with landing gear down. If a circle to land is required, this will probably mean that the landing gear must be temporally raised to reduce drag in the level flight portion of the circle maneuver.

All this and more was discussed in chapter 12 and certainly will be explained further by your own flight instructor. However, the idea of instrument/multiengine involves more than checkride procedures. For most pilots, the instrument/multiengine plateau is the highest elevation reached prior to becoming a professional pilot. The instrument/multiengine level is required to move on to charter flying, corporations, or the airlines, so this level is the master's degree of flying. The master's level requires a higher level of thinking and problem-solving.

REAL-WORLD TRAINING

An important but often unspoken part of the master's level is the fact that you no longer are a student and therefore should not think like a student. This is not to say that you ever stop learning—in that sense, we are all students. However, this idea is different. Instrument/multiengine pilots must function in the real world, not the flight training world, and unfortunately, there is a difference. Are there things that we do in the training environment for the sake of training that we would not do in the real-world environment?

I believe the answer is yes. Hence, real problems can develop. When brought up in the training environment, some students can only function in that environment and do not understand the difference between the training and real-world environments. Here are some examples to illustrate this concept. See if you recognize yourself in any of these circumstances.

After a student and an instructor fly for approximately one hour, conducting instrument approaches and multiengine emergency procedures, they fly back toward the home airport. The home airport has an instrument approach that is incorporated into the flight lesson. The instructor simulates a radar vector to this approach. What is this student thinking about this approach? The student is probably thinking that this approach is simply being used to conclude the lesson. The student might know that the instructor is due back to begin another flight lesson. The student personally might also need to be on the ground so that he or she can make it to work on time.

The student also realizes that the weather is actually VFR and wearing the "hood" is just a game instructors play. The student and instructor are both now solidly in the "last approach syndrome." It would be a real surprise to both of them if they were not able to land at the end of this approach. Has either one of them even looked at the missed approach procedure?

Contrast that training situation with another flight to the same airport using the same instrument approach. This time the pilot has flown several hours to get here. The clouds are low and the outcome of the approach is seriously in doubt. The AWOS or ATIS report of the cloud bases are making the pilot think a missed approach is inevitable. It will be a surprise if the airport is spotted and a landing made.

Do you see how differently the pilots in the two situations are thinking? The pilot in the training environment figures that a landing is assured, and a missed approach would be a surprise. The pilot in the real environment assumes a missed approach is assured, and a landing would be a pleasant surprise. What will the pilot who has only been exposed to the training environment do when he or she is faced with a real-world situation? The "train-brain" pilot will be tempted to fly below the MDA or delay a missed approach past the missed approach point because it has not entered his or her mind yet that a missed approach is inevitable. People get killed when they use a training environment thought process in the real world.

This "train-brain" tendency comes up again and again. One time, I was conducting an IFR check with a student. As a part of the test, we flew an NDB approach about 35 miles away from his home airport. The approach turned out to be a disaster; everything went wrong. When the flight was over, the student said, "You know it really was not fair to make me fly that NDB down there because I have never practiced that one."

How would you have responded? This comment told me more about this student's lack of preparedness for the real world than any blown approach ever could have. In his mind, the only "fair" approaches were the ones that his instructor and he had drilled on over and over again. I guess this guy expected to have an instrument rating someday that was restricted to only the three or four instrument approaches that he had worked on.

Have you ever pulled out a few most often flown instrument approach charts from the chart book? Students do this on checks many times. By the time I get to the airplane, the student has selected about four approaches out of the big book and attached them to a knee board. I can only assume that these are the student's most practiced approaches. I guess these students expect me to have them fly only one of these that they have chosen.

There is a fine line here. Is pulling approach charts out of the book just good planning, or is it a crutch? It might be good planning, but in a real-world environment, how can any pilot know before takeoff which approaches he or she might need to fly on that particular flight? The wind, traffic conflicts, or a missed approach could cause a pilot to end up flying an approach that could not have been planned for. When charts get pulled out the question remains: Could this student find an approach other than what was preselected and fly an unplanned approach with equal accuracy?

Flying the airplane and simultaneously thumbing through the chart book to find a specific approach is not that easy. Students who pull charts beforehand, but who must later find another chart from the book, almost always will loose their heading and altitude while fumbling around in the book. When something does not go according to plan, the student begins to panic and his or her flying skills suffer. This is classic "train-brain."

In the training environment, the situation is controlled and the outcome is known; pulling charts might be good lesson planning. But in the real-world environment, the outcome is unknown and the student's skills should not be limited. Flight instructors start out with students in the training environment, but eventually good instructors must introduce the real environment.

One time on an IFR check, I had a student who pulled off his IFR hood when we reached an approach's MDA. Of course, I had not wanted the student to see the airport yet, hoping to watch him track to the missed approach point. "Why did you take the hood off?" I asked. "Because I'm at MDA. We're done!" the student said, a little agitated that I had even asked such a question. What is wrong with this situation? The student had been exposed only to the training environment where instructors have the power to make clouds go away at convenient times. Was that student ready for the real world of IFR?

Decision training must be a part of real-world training. On many occasions I have kept students in simulated IFR conditions to the missed approach point during an approach that they thought was the last of the day. Early in the approach I will say, "I will let you know if we ever get out of these (simulated) clouds." However, I say that without any intention of saying anything else throughout the remainder of the approach. When the student nears the decision height, the student might fail to make a decision. On several occasions students have descended to DH on the glideslope and arrived at the point where a go-around must begin if the runway is not in sight.

All along, the students expected me to say, "OK, take your hood off" before arrival at DH, but I said nothing. They panic. They actually turn their head and look through the long IFR hood at me with a question on their face. They want to know why I did not make the clouds go away, and at this point, they have not contemplated the possibility of a missed approach. This indecision will cause us to get off the localizer and below DH before a confused student, totally saturated in "train-brain," does anything. Why did the student pause? Why wasn't the student applying full power at the DH? Because the student was not thinking in the real-world environment.

A good instrument/multiengine instructor will foster thinking from the real world. Usually we imagine instrument/multiengine training to be filled with physical skills, such as holding a rudder against a good engine when the other engine has failed or making a localizer and glideslope intercept. But good instruction to the master's degree level should also include thinking skills.

THE INNER GAME OF FLYING

In *The Inner Game of Tennis*, Timothy Gallway maintains that tennis players reach a high level of skill where the winner relies more on thinking skills than on physical skills. When I play tennis, I usually beat myself. I hit the ball out of bounds or into the net, or I never hit it at all. But when two really good tennis players get together neither can rely on the other to mess up. If you are playing Andre Agassi, Pete Sampras, or Steffi Graf, you cannot expect your opponent to miss any shots. At the level, they can hit the backhand, forehand, lob, or any other shot you hit at them.

So how is it possible to beat a player at that level? The only way is to outsmart them. You must think better than the opponent. You must have a plan, a strategy. You need to think two and three shots ahead. If you and I were to watch two players on that level, we would be seeing two physical athletes in action. However, to the athletes themselves, they see two minds in action. At that level the action is beyond the physical and is controlled by the mental.

Is there an inner game of instrument/multiengine flight? In early instrument training, pilots are shown how to fly the approaches (make the shots). We have NDBs, VORs, and ILS. Tennis players have the backhand, net charge, and forehand volley. At some point, the pilot becomes proficient at performing the approaches. However, just like a tennis player who learns all the shots but still gets beaten badly by a player on the mental level, the "approach pilot" is not yet an "instrument pilot." The true, real-world instrument/multiengine pilot flies the airplane physically but operates on a higher mental level. On this higher level, controllers and pilots communicate with more than just words. The pilot is aware of other traffic and his or her own place in the "big picture." Any airplane problems that might come up can be dealt with because there is mental capability to spare. The pilot is viewing the "mental radar screen" and can see the situation clearly.

Once when I was working with an instrument/multiengine student, we were being radar vectored for an NDB approach to runway 18. The vectors led us east of the airport and final approach course on a heading of north. We were essentially on a wide left downwind to the approach. The NDB pointer crept from about a 300 relative bearing, past our left wing, and then behind.

Based on our position to the approach, I was expecting a left turn to a heading that would aim us at an approach course intercept. At about this time, the controller addressed us and said, "Turn left heading 040." Turn left to 040° was wrong. The controller had made a minor slip of the tongue. I reasoned that he had probably meant 240°, since that would have been a good intercept vector. Even if he had actually wanted us to fly 040, he would not have turned us to the left from 360 to 040.

But the student I was with was not playing the inner game. The student made a left turn all the way back around to the heading of 040 and sat contentedly as we flew off in the wrong direction. Within a minute the controller saw us striking off into uncharted territory and turned us around. Later on the ground, I asked the student why we made that turn. "Because the controller told us to!" I tried to remind him that there is no such thing as "controller in command" and that every ATC assignment given to a pilot must be evaluated.

Yes, the controller made a slight error, but the pilot had made the larger mistake. The student should have been seeing our position in his imagination and our relative position to the anticipated approach intercept. Had he done so, it would have made no sense to make a 320° heading change to a direction that took us away from the approach. He would have questioned the assignment and made arrangements to fix the problem.

Instead, he was blindly aiming the airplane around the sky, unaware of the world around him. He could have responded to the controller's request to "turn left to 040" by saying, "OK, you want us to turn left to zero forty," with emphasis on the words *left* and *zero* and in a questioning tone of voice. The controller would have certainly realized that what was really being said was, "Hey, didn't you mean 240?" The controller would have made the correction, the intercept would have gone smoothly, and traffic would not get backed up.

Another time I was flying into Washington National Airport in a Beechcraft Duchess. Airline pilots call National Airport "the DC-3 airport that time forgot," because today's airliners require a larger comfort zone than the airport has to offer. Nevertheless, a Duchess is much slower than the rest of the air traffic inbound to National. I was still way back in the sequence to the airport and planning to maintain my cruise speed all the way to the threshold. The radio work was rapid, and I sensed urgency in the controller's voice when I heard the following conversation between the approach controller and a Bonanza pilot who was also inbound.

Controller: Bonanza 1234A, what will be your approach speed on final?

Bonanza pilot: Ninety knots.

I did not have time to think about it right then, but what was the controller really asking? You would guess that a controller at Washington National Airport is not a rookie. He had probably controlled thousands of airplanes like a Bonanza. Do you really think he did not already have a pretty good idea what the normal Bonanza approach speed was?

The controller was speaking in code. He really was telling the Bonanza pilot to keep his speed fast if he had any hope of keeping up with the traffic flow. But, the pilot did not see the big picture. He was not playing the inner game. He said, "90 knots," which told the controller with whom he was dealing: someone without the master's degree.

Once, I overheard two pilots complaining about the poor ATC service that they had received the last time that they had flown to a Class C airport. "Those controllers made us fly 30 miles out of the way!" That was all I heard of the story, so I imagined how the entire story could have gone:

Pilot: Nashville Approach, this is 22B.

Controller: Aircraft calling Nashville, standby.

Then, with no delay:

Pilot: Nashville 22B, roger that, standing by.

Then, after a delay and conversations with other aircraft:

Controller: 22B, what is your full call sign?

Pilot: N5122B

Controller: Remain clear of Class C airspace. What is your type aircraft?

Pilot: 22B is a Cessna 152.

Controller: 22B, what are your intentions?

Pilot: I am landing at Nashville.

Controller: 22B, squawk 4152.

Pilot: 4151, roger.

Controller: 22B, squawk four-*one*-five-*two*, and do you have information Golf?

Pilot: I'll go get Golf, roger.

Controller: 22B, remain this frequency, traffic one o'clock four miles a King Air descending out of four-thousand. (Spell out?)

No response from 22B.

Controller: 22B, did you copy traffic?

Pilot: Nashville approach 22B is back with you with information Golf.

Let's stop this conversation right here and ask this question. What does this controller think of this pilot? The controller has absolutely no way of knowing whether or not this pilot is a great stick-and-rudder guy, but from the poor radio technique alone, the controller probably will have no confidence in this pilot. If later during this flight, a tight situation occurs that requires a high level of awareness and pilot-system technique, will the controller believe the pilot can do the job?

Let's say that 22B, a Cessna 152, is directed to set up on a 5-mile left base to runway 20L at Nashville. Meanwhile, a United 737 is on a 15-mile final also for runway 20L. If the Cessna pilot keeps a fast speed, holds the base leg tight, and cuts into final early, there should be no problem. But if the Cessna pilot slows down to 65 knots and flies an uncontrolled airport traffic pattern, there will be a conflict.

If you were the controller seeing the Cessna and 737 on the radar screen, and after having the previous conversation with the Cessna pilot, what would you do? Now you know why some pilots get vectored "30 miles out of the way."

Controllers make judgments as to whether or not the pilots they are working with can play the mental game and control accordingly. An inner game controller can quickly determine whether or not you are in the same league with him and with other pilots on the frequency. When controllers know that you are not playing the game, they can and will take advantage of this fact.

Have you ever been given a heading to fly that was not really where you wanted to go, and it seemed the controller had forgotten about you? He did not forget. You were given what I call a "limbo heading." The controller saw a potential conflict between two airplanes. Not necessarily a collision conflict, but probably a sequencing conflict. The controller decides that he or she needs more time between airplanes, and therefore, somebody up there is going to have to be delayed.

Now controllers know that pilots hate to do holding patterns. And controllers hate to give out holding patterns because deep-down, they know that making a pilot hold is an admission that their "flow control" techniques did not work out. If the controller assigns a hold to a pilot, the pilot might even believe that the hold was the "fault" of the controller. Human nature says that controllers do not want to be shown up by pilots, and vice versa. So the controller wants to avoid assigning a hold to anybody.

Yet someone must be delayed, but who? The controller will pick out the pilot that up to this point has not been playing the inner game: "Cessna 46Q, fly heading 270." The heading of 270 takes that airplane out of the mix and buys the time necessary to work out the problem. The controller is betting that the pilot of 46Q will not know any better and will quietly fly out of the situation. Eventually, 46Q will be dealt with, but in the meantime, the problem gets solved and nobody holds. Everyone on the frequency can see what is going on except the poor unaware pilot of 46Q.

Of course, there are times when an airplane needs to be flown in a direction that normally would not make sense. At those times, as a situationally aware pilot, I want to know what the reason for that heading is. I will say, "Tulsa Approach, give us an idea how long we will be on this heading." Now I am speaking in code. I am really saying, "You will have to tell me what is going on or put someone else on this limbo heading!"

One day, I took off into the clouds on a multiengine instrument flight with a student. We were going to fly about 35 miles away to practice an SDF approach, and then return for an ILS approach. After takeoff, climb, radar identification, and level off, the student asked, "Should we get a Mode C readout from the controller?" We both were aware that the Mode C transponder had been reported as intermittent by pilots of that airplane on a previous flight. But I figured since we had been flying straight and level indicating 3,000 feet, if the controller had seen anything drastically different than 3,000 feet, he would have said something already. "Let's save that question for later," I told the student.

We flew on through the clouds, executed the SDF approach, and started our trip home. The ILS approach at the home airport had a localizer that pointed out in the general direction of the airport with the SDF. Normally when flying between these two airports, the controllers would have you intercept the localizer and track inbound. But this time, the controller gave us a heading that would only parallel the localizer.

By listening on the frequency only a short time, I became aware that another airplane coming from the opposite direction was also headed for that same ILS. The controller had not yet decided which airplane would fly the approach first, so he placed both airplanes in limbo headings. We were not going the wrong direction, but we were not intercepting the approach course either.

As the next few minutes passed, I could tell that we were closer, but that the other airplane was faster. The controller had not made up his mind. We were watching the ADF needle, tuned to the ILS approach's compass locator, and I knew that the moment of truth would soon be at hand. A decision needed to be made by the controller in the next few seconds or things would get messed up. That is when I keyed the mike and said, "Seymour Approach, this is 79N, can you give us a Mode C readout?" The controller replied, "79N, I have you at 3,000 feet. . .ah. . .turn right heading 080, intercept the localizer, you are cleared for the ILS runway 5 approach."

I knew that the controller had been wrestling with the decision and had not made a choice. I waited until the moment when some decision had to be made, and at that moment, I made sure he was thinking about me. I did not care about the Mode C readout, but using that question, I provoked a decision in my favor. We flew the approach as fast as was practical, so we would not hold up the airplane in trail, and it all worked out great.

Be careful, however; this information is powerful. This is not about a "me-first" attitude. There will be times when the inner game will dictate that you go last and hold in the meantime. But seeing the big picture will make you more efficient and safer. When pilots and controllers work together above the physical and into the mental level, there is an unspoken confidence in each other that produces a unique synergy. This level is where instrument/multiengine pilots belong. If your flight instructor is simply putting you under the hood, making you fly an approach, and pulling back an engine, you truly are not receiving the best instruction. Look for the inner game, and begin to play.

AIRLINE TRANSPORT PILOT CERTIFICATE

If the instrument/multiengine level is the master's degree, the ATP should be seen as the PhD. When you think of the ATP, you think of a person completely in control of any flying situation. That might not be completely true; however, ATP certification carries with it substantial clout.

On the ATP checkride and theoretically at any other time, the ATP must "show mastery of the aircraft with the successful outcome of any task never in doubt." The ATP certificate can be obtained in either a multiengine or single-engine airplane. Pilot career climbers most often will want the multiengine ATP certificate because multi-engine flying pays the most and carries the prestige. You know that you have really "arrived" when your pilot seat is forward of the airplane's nose wheel!

That being said, you can take the ATP checkride in the same airplane that you took your original multiengine checkride in. The airplane does not have to be "big" to be an ATP airplane. To become eligible for the ATP certificate a person must:

1. Have a first-class medical certificate.
2. Pass the ATP written test.
3. Read, write, and understand the English language.
4. Speak English without an accent or impediment of speech.
5. Be a high-school graduate (or equivalent per the FAA Administrator's opinion).
6. At least 1,500 flight hours as a pilot, including:
   a. 250 flight hours in airplanes for an airplane ATP certificate.
   b. 500 flight hours of cross country time, 100 of which are in airplanes for the airplane ATP certificate.
   c. 100 flight hours of night time, 25 of which are in airplanes for the airplane ATP certificate.
   d. 75 hours of actual or simulated instrument time, at least 50 hours of which were in actual flight.
7. Be 23 years of age.
8. Be of good moral character.

Everything but the "good moral character" part is easily determined. I had an inspector tell me that in his view a criminal record should prevent a person from becoming an ATP because you cannot have good moral character and a criminal record. But that opinion was his personal belief and not the official interpretation of the FAA. If you have a criminal record and want to be an ATP, you should choose your inspectors carefully.

It is also possible to take and pass the ATP practical test before you turn 23 years old. The test is given as normal, but if you pass, you will not get a temporary pilot certificate. Instead, you will get a letter from the examiner stating that you passed the test but do not meet the age requirement. The letter can be exchanged for the ATP certificate when you turn 23. I have had a few former students/flight instructors who had such a letter. Guess where they were at 7:30 A.M. on the morning of their 23rd birthday? You got it. They were standing at their local FAA office door, waiting for it to open.

Before 1996 you had to get a permit to take the ATP written exam. The permit, which was FAA Form 8060-7, could only be obtained from an FAA inspector. The inspector verified that the pilot held a first-class medical certificate and had 1,500 hours in his or her logbook. When I received my permit, the inspector went through every page of the three logbooks I had at the time. He asked many questions about flights I had taken, instruction I had received, and the flight hours I had accumulated. When he got to 1,500 hours of time, he stopped. Then he gave me the permit that allowed me to take the ATP written *one time.* You made sure not to fail that test, because a failure would mean another trip to the FAA office for another permit and the inevitable questions about why you failed the first time.

Today the use of FAA Form 8060-7 has been suspended, and you do not need a permit. However, the minimum requirements have not changed. Any person can take the ATP written exam, but on the date that the test is taken, that person must have a first- class medical certificate and 1,500 hours of legitimate flight time (ground trainer time doesn't count). Later when the ATP practical test is administered, the examiner will check the dates and verify the flight time in the logbook. If the examiner discovers that a person did not meet all the requirements on the day he or she took the written test, that person will no longer be eligible for the ATP practical test.

The ATP checkride is essentially a detailed equipment test and a super instrument/multiengine flight test. The ATP Practical Test Standards spell out the equipment knowledge in detail. Review "Part 1, Equipment Knowledge" in the test that appears later in this chapter.

The airplane that must be provided on the flight portion of the ATP practical test does not have to have all the equipment listed in Part 1, Task A, so don't panic. The test standards state: "The applicant is required to provide an appropriate and airworthy aircraft for the practical test. Its operating limitations must not prohibit the tasks required on the practical test. Flight instruments required are those necessary for controlling the aircraft without outside reference. The aircraft must have radio equipment for communications with air traffic control and the performance of instrument approach procedures." The airplane does not have to have a flight management system, ice protection devices, pressurization systems, or Doppler radar. However, you should have complete knowledge of anything the airplane does have. The PTS goes on to say that the level of ATP equipment knowledge should be equal to that contained in the airplane's operating handbook or FAA-approved airplane flight manual and the minimum equipment list. (To refresh your memory, review chapter 7 on the MEL and AFMs.)

INSTRUMENT MULTIENGINE FLYING AND THE ATP

The flight portion of the ATP is a combination of instrument skills, multiengine skills, combined instrument/multiengine skills, and a ton of common sense. The instrument skills required include everything from an under-the-hood instrument takeoff to holding patterns, in-flight emergencies, and various instrument approaches. The multiengine skills are basically the same as from the Multiengine Practical Test Standards (chapter 14).

For the instrument/multiengine combination skills, the ATP test requires an instrument takeoff. The takeoff is usually performed while wearing an IFR hood. This means that you take off looking inside only at the DG, or if you're lucky, at a localizer needle if that runway has one.

Once in the air, the examiner may elect to simulate the failure of one engine while you are still under the hood. The ATP test standard says that this failed engine simulation cannot occur closer to the ground than 500 feet, but this still means that you must deal with a takeoff engine failure with reference to inside instruments alone. Now you are flying simulated IFR and simulated engine failure in combination.

There are several other examples of this combination throughout the test. Look at the following ATP test outline and note where these combinations can exist:

Area of Operation: Preflight Preparation
I. Equipment Knowledge
  A. Equipment Examination
  B. Performance and Limitations

Area of Operation 2
 I. Preflight Procedures
  A. Preflight Inspection
 II. Ground Operations
  A. Powerplant Start
  B. Taxiing
  C. Pretakeoff Checks
III. Takeoff and Departure Maneuvers
  A. Normal and Crosswind Takeoff
  B. Instrument Takeoff
  C. Powerplant Failure during Takeoff
  D. Rejected Takeoff
  E. Instrument Departure
IV. Inflight Maneuvers
  A. Steep Turns
  B. Approaches to Stalls
  C. Powerplant Failure—Multiengine airplanes
  D. Powerplant Failure—Single-engine airplanes
  E. Specific Flight Characteristics

V. Instrument Procedures
   A. Instrument arrival
   B. Holding
   C. Precision Instrument Approaches
   D. Nonprecision Instrument Approaches
   E. Circling Approach
   F. Missed Approach
VI. Landings and Approaches to Landings
   A. Normal and Crosswind Approaches and Landings
   B. Landing from a Precision Approach
   C. Approach and Landing with a (Simulated) Powerplant Failure—Multiengine Airplanes
   D. Landing from a Circling Approach
   E. Rejected Landing
   F. Landing from a Zero or Nonstandard Flap Approach
VII. Normal and Abnormal Procedures
VIII. Emergency Procedures
IX. Post-flight Procedures
   A. After-Landing
   B. Parking and Securing

In the late 1980s, I used to tell up-and-coming pilots: "Don't worry about the cost of your ATP. Whomever you are working for when you get 1,500 hours will pay for it!" And that advice was good most of the time. During the late-1980's pilot-hiring boom (chapter 17), I could not keep a flight instructor when they accumulated between 800 to 1,200 hours. By the time they got 1,500 hours, they were already on the flight line for somebody and their ATP was being incorporated into a routine Part 135 or 121 check. In other words, the company they worked for would pay the pilot to get the ATP. One of those former students who passed the ATP practical test but got a letter instead of a certificate because he was not 23 yet, actually became an ATP and a captain on his birthday. The airline was counting off the days until he turned 23 so that they could promote him to four strips.

Unfortunately, today this is not happening. Pilot hiring goes through cycles, so perhaps by the time you read this, pilots with 800 hours will again be hired by the airlines. As of this writing, however, you should expect to pay for your own ATP. If you are applying for a job, you'll need to have the airline transport pilot certificate listed on your résumé, as well as the 1,500 hours required for the ATP.

The "magic number" for total flight hours that makes a pilot marketable moves up and down like the tide. Whenever this number is below 1,500 hours, employers pay for ATPs. When the magic number is higher than 1,500 hours, pilots pay for ATPs. In the mid 1990s, the magic number is higher than 1,500 hours and is hovering around

2,000 hours (500 of which must be multiengine time). That means you need to save your money, then seek out quality instruction.

PRACTICAL TEST STANDARDS FOR ATP CERTIFICATE

The following is the Practical Test Standards for the airline transport pilot certificate:

Part 1, Airplanes

Section One: Area of Operation

PREFLIGHT PREPARATION
I. EQUIPMENT KNOWLEDGE

   A. TASK: EQUIPMENT EXAMINATION
      References: FAR Part 61; Pilot's Operating Handbook, FAA-Approved Airplane Flight Manual (AFM)
   Objective: To determine that the applicant:

   1. Exhibits adequate knowledge appropriate to the airplane; its systems and components; its normal, abnormal, and emergency procedures; and uses the correct terminology with regard to the following items–
      a. landing gear—indicators, brakes, antiskid, tires, nose-wheel steering, and shock absorbers.
      b. powerplant—controls and indications, induction system, carburetor and fuel injection, turbocharging, cooling, fire detection/protection, mounting points, turbine wheels, compressors, deicing, anti-icing, and other related components.
      c. propellers—type, controls, feathering/unfeathering, autofeather, negative torque sensing, synchronizing, and synchrophasing
      d. fuel system—capacity; drains; pumps; controls; indicators; crossfeeding; transferring; jettison; fuel grade, color, and additives; fueling and defueling procedures; and substitutions, if applicable.
      e. oil system—capacity, grade, quantities, and indicators.
      f. hydraulic system—capacity, pumps, pressure, reservoirs, grade, and regulators.
      g. electrical system—alternators, generators, battery, circuit breakers and protection devices, controls, indicators, and external and auxiliary power sources and ratings.
      h. environmental systems—heating, cooling, ventilation, oxygen and pressurization, controls, indicators, and regulating devices.
      i. avionics and communications—autopilot; flight director; Electronic Flight Indicating Systems (EFIS); Flight Management System(s) (FMS); Long Range Navigation (LORAN) systems; Doppler Radar; Inertial Navigation Systems (INS); Global Positioning System (GPS/DGPS-NVGPS); VOR, NDB, ILS/MLS, RNAV systems and components; indicating devices; transponder; and emergency locator transmitter.

       j. ice protection—anti-ice, deice, pitot-static system protection, propeller, windshield, wing and tail surfaces.

       k. crewmember and passenger equipment—oxygen system, survival gear, emergency exits, evacuation procedures and crew duties, and quick donning oxygen mask for crewmembers and passengers.

       l. flight controls—ailerons, elevator(s), rudder(s), control tabs, balance tabs, stabilizer, flaps, spoilers, leading edge flaps/slats and trim systems.

  2. Exhibits adequate knowledge of the contents of the Operating Handbook or AFM with regard to the systems and components listed in paragraph 1 (above); the Minimum Equipment List (MEL), if appropriate; and the Operations Specifications, if applicable.

B. TASK: PERFORMANCE AND LIMITATIONS

References: FAR Parts 1, 61, 91; Pilot's Operating Handbook, AFM

Objective: To determine that the applicant:

  1. Exhibits adequate knowledge of performance and limitations, including a thorough knowledge of the adverse effects of exceeding any limitation.

  2. Demonstrates proficient use of (as appropriate to the airplane) performance charts, tables, graphs, or other data relating to items such as—

       a. accelerate-stop distance.

       b. accelerate-go distance.

       c. takeoff performance, all engines, engine(s) inoperative.

       d. climb performance including segmented climb performance; with all engines operating; with one or more engine(s) inoperative; and with other engine malfunctions as may be appropriate.

       e. service ceiling, all engines, engines(s) inoperative, including drift down, if appropriate.

       f. cruise performance.

       g. fuel consumption, range, and endurance.

       h. descent performance.

       i. go-around from rejected landings.

       j. other performance data (appropriate to the airplane).

  3. Describes (as appropriate to the airplane) the airspeeds used during specific phases of flight.

  4. Describes the effects of meteorological conditions upon performance characteristics and correctly applies these factors to a specific chart, table, graph, or other performance data.

  5. Computes the center-of-gravity location for a specific load condition (as specified by the examiner), including adding, removing, or shifting weight.

  6. Determines if the computed center of gravity is within the forward and aft center-of-gravity limits, and that lateral fuel balance is within limits for takeoff and landing.

  7. Demonstrates good planning and knowledge of procedures in applying operational factors affecting airplane performance.

Part 1, Airplanes

Section Two: Areas of Operation

I. PREFLIGHT PROCEDURES

A. TASK: PREFLIGHT INSPECTION

References: FAR Parts 61, 91; Pilot's Operating Handbook, AFM

Note: If a flight engineer (FE) is a required crewmember for a particular type airplane, the actual visual inspection may be waived. The actual visual inspection may be replaced by using an approved pictorial means that realistically portrays the location and detail of inspection items. On airplanes requiring an FE, an applicant must demonstrate adequate knowledge of the FE functions for the safe completion of the flight if the FE becomes ill or incapacitated during flight.

Objective: To determine that the applicant:

1. Exhibits adequate knowledge of the preflight inspection procedures, while explaining briefly—
   a. the purpose of inspecting the items which must be checked.
   b. how to detect possible defects.
   c. the corrective action to take.
2. Exhibits adequate knowledge of the operational status of the airplane by locating and explaining the significance and importance of related documents such as—
   a. airworthiness and registration certificates.
   b. operating limitations, handbooks, and manuals.
   c. minimum equipment list (MEL) (if appropriate).
   d. weight and balance data.
   e. maintenance requirements, tests, and appropriate records applicable to the proposed flight or operation; and maintenance that may be performed by the pilot or other designated crewmember.
3. Uses the approved checklist to inspect the airplane externally and internally.
4. Uses the challenge-and-response (or other approved) method with the other crewmember(s), where applicable, to accomplish the checklist procedures.
5. Verifies the airplane is safe for flight by emphasizing (as appropriate) the need to look at and explain the purpose of inspecting items such as—
   a. powerplant, including controls and indicators.
   b. fuel quantity, grade, type, contamination safeguards, and servicing procedures.
   c. oil quantity, grade, and type.
   d. hydraulic fluid quantity, grade, type, and servicing procedures.
   e. oxygen quantity, pressures, servicing procedures, and associated systems and equipment for crew and passengers.
   f. landing gear, brakes, and steering system.
   g. tires for condition, inflation, and correct mounting, where applicable.

    h. fire protection/detection systems for proper operation, servicing, pressures, and discharge indications.

    i. pneumatic system pressures and servicing.

    j. ground environmental systems for proper servicing and operation.

    k. auxiliary power unit (APU) for servicing and operation.

    l. flight control systems including trim, spoilers, and leading/trailing edge.

    m. anti-ice, deice systems, servicing, and operation.

6. Coordinates with ground crew and ensures adequate clearance prior to moving any devices such as door, hatches, and flight control surfaces.

7. Complies with the provisions of the appropriate Operations Specifications, if applicable, as they pertain to the particular airplane and operation.

8. Demonstrates proper operation of all applicable airplane systems.

9. Notes any discrepancies, determines if the airplane is airworthy and safe for flight, or takes the proper corrective action.

10. Checks the general area around the airplane for hazards to the safety of the airplane and personnel.

II. GROUND OPERATIONS

A. TASK: POWERPLANT START

References: FAR Part 61; Pilot's Operating Handbook, AFM

Objective: To determine that the applicant:

1. Exhibits adequate knowledge of the correct powerplant start procedures, including the use of an auxiliary power unit (APU) or external power source, starting under various atmospheric conditions, normal and abnormal starting limitations, and the proper action required in the event of a malfunction.

2. Ensures the ground safety procedures are followed during the before-start, start, and after-start phases.

3. Ensures the use of appropriate ground crew personnel during the start procedures.

4. Performs all items of the start procedures by systematically following the approved checklist items for the before-start, start, and after-start phases.

5. Demonstrates sound judgment and operating practices in those instances where specific instructions or checklist items are not published.

B. TASK: TAXIING

References: FAR Part 61; Pilot's Operating Handbook, AFM

Objective: To determine that the applicant:

1. Exhibits adequate knowledge of safe taxi procedures (as appropriate to the airplane including push-back or powerback, as may be applicable).

2. Demonstrates proficiency by maintaining correct and positive airplane control. In airplanes equipped with float devices, this includes water taxiing, approaching a buoy, and docking.

3. Maintains proper spacing on other aircraft, obstructions, and persons.

4. Accomplishes the applicable checklist items and performs recommended procedures.

5. Maintains desired track and speed.

6. Complies with instructions issued by ATC (or the examiner simulating ATC).

7. Observes runway hold lines, localizer and glideslope critical areas, and other surface control markings and lighting.

8. Maintains constant vigilance and airplane control during taxi operations.

C. TASK: PRETAKEOFF CHECKS

References: FAR Part 61, Pilot's Operating Handbook, AFM

Objective: To determine that the applicant:

1. Exhibits adequate knowledge of the pretakeoff checks by stating the reason for checking the items outlined on the approved checklist and explaining how to detect possible malfunctions.

2. Divides attention properly inside and outside the cockpit.

3. Ensures that all systems are within their normal operating range prior to beginning, during the performance of, and at the completion of those checks required by the approved checklist.

4. Explains, as may be requested by the examiner, any normal or abnormal system operating characteristic or limitation; and the corrective action for a specific malfunction.

5. Determines if the airplane is safe for the proposed flight or requires maintenance.

6. Determines the airplane's takeoff performance, considering such factors as wind, density altitude, weight, temperature, pressure altitude, and runway condition and length.

7. Determines speeds/V-speeds and properly sets all instrument references, flight director and auto pilot controls, and navigation and communications equipment.

8. Reviews procedures for emergency and abnormal situations which may be encountered during takeoff, and states the corrective action required of the pilot in command and other concerned crewmembers.

9. Obtains and correctly interprets the takeoff and departure clearances as issued by ATC.

III. TAKEOFF AND DEPARTURE MANEUVERS

A. TASK: NORMAL AND CROSSWIND TAKEOFF

References: FAR Part 61; Pilot's Operating Handbook, AFM

Objective: To determine that the applicant:

1. Exhibits adequate knowledge of normal and crosswind takeoffs and climbs including (as appropriate to the airplane) airspeeds, configurations, and emergency/ abnormal procedures.

2. Notes any obstructions or other hazards that might hinder a safe takeoff.

3. Verifies and correctly applies correction for the existing wind component to the takeoff performance.

4. Completes required checks prior to starting takeoff to verify the expected powerplant performance. Performs all required pretakeoff checks as required by the appropriate checklist items.

5. Aligns the airplane on the runway centerline.

6. Applies the controls correctly to maintain longitudinal alignment on the centerline of the runway prior to initiating and during the takeoff.

7. Adjusts the powerplant controls as recommended by the FM-approved guidance for the existing conditions.

8. Monitors powerplant controls, settings, and instruments during takeoff to ensure all predetermined parameters are maintained.

9. Adjusts the controls to attain the desired pitch attitude at the predetermined airspeed/V-speed to attain the desired performance for the particular takeoff segment.

10. Performs the required pitch changes and, as appropriate, performs or calls for and verifies the accomplishment of gear and flap retractions, power adjustments, and other required pilot-related activities at the required airspeed/V-speeds within the tolerances established in the Pilot's Operating Handbook or AFM.

11. Uses the applicable noise abatement, wake turbulence avoidance procedures, as required.

12. Accomplishes or calls for and verifies the accomplishment of the appropriate checklist items.

13. Maintains the appropriate climb segment airspeed/V-speeds.

14. Maintains the desired heading within ±5° and the desired airspeed/V-speed within ±5 knots or the appropriate V-speed range.

B. TASK: INSTRUMENT TAKEOFF

References: FAR Part 61; AC 61-27; Pilot's Operating Handbook, AFM, AIM

Objective: To determine that the applicant:

1. Exhibits adequate knowledge of an instrument takeoff with instrument meteorological conditions simulated at or before reaching an altitude of 100 feet (30 meters) AGL. If accomplished in a flight simulator, visibility should be no greater than one-quarter (¼) mile, or as specified by operator specifications.

2. Takes into account, prior to beginning the takeoff, operational factors which could affect the maneuver, such as Takeoff Warning Inhibit Systems or other airplane characteristics, runway length, surface conditions, wind, wake turbulence, obstructions, and other related factors that could adversely affect safety.

3. Accomplishes the appropriate checklist items to ensure that the airplane systems applicable to the instrument takeoff are operating properly.

4. Sets the applicable radios/flight instruments to the desired setting prior to initiating the takeoff.
5. Applies the controls correctly to maintain longitudinal alignment on the centerline of the runway prior to initiating and during the takeoff.
6. Transitions smoothly and accurately from visual meteorological conditions to actual or simulated instrument meteorological conditions.
7. Maintains the appropriate climb attitude.
8. Complies with the appropriate airspeeds/V-speeds and climb segment airspeeds.
9. Maintains desired heading within ±5° and desired airspeeds within ±5 knots.
10. Complies with ATC clearances and instructions issued by ATC (or the examiner simulating ATC).

C. TASK: POWERPLANT FAILURE DURING TAKEOFF

References: FAR Part 61; AC 61-21; Pilot's Operating Handbook, AFM; DOT/FAA Takeoff Safety Training Aid

Objective: To determine that the applicant:

1. Exhibits adequate knowledge of the procedures used during powerplant failure on takeoff, the appropriate reference airspeeds, and the specific pilot actions required.
2. Takes into account, prior to beginning the takeoff, operational factors that could affect the maneuver, such as Takeoff Warning Inhibit Systems or other airplane characteristics, runway length, surface condition, wind, wake turbulence, obstructions, and other related factors that could affect safety.
3. Completes required checks prior to starting takeoff to verify the expected powerplant performance. Performs all required takeoff checks as required by the appropriate checklist items.
4. Aligns the airplane on the runway.
5. Applies the controls correctly to maintain longitudinal alignment on the centerline of the runway prior to initiating and during the takeoff.
6. Adjusts the powerplant controls as recommended by the FAA-approved guidance for existing conditions.
7. Single-engine airplanes: Established a power-off descent approximately straight-ahead, if the powerplant failure occurs after becoming airborne.
8. Continues the takeoff (in multiengine airplane) if the powerplant failure occurs at a point where the airplane can continue to a specified airspeed and altitude at the end of the runway commensurate with the airplane's performance capabilities and operating limitations.
9. Maintains (in multiengine airplane), after a simulated powerplant failure and after a climb has been established, the desired heading within ±5°, desired airspeed within ±5 knots, and, if appropriate for the airplane, established a bank of approximately 5°, or as recommended by the manufacturer, toward the operating powerplant.

10. In a multiengine airplane the published V_1, V_R, and/or V_2 speeds, the failure of the most critical powerplant should be simulated at a point:
    a. after V_1 and prior to V_2, if in the opinion of the examiner, it is appropriate under prevailing conditions; or
    b. as close as possible after V_1, when V_1 and V_2 or V_1 and V_R are identical.
11. In a multiengine airplane for which no V_1, V_R, or V_2 speeds are published, the failure of the most critical powerplant should be simulated at a point after reaching a minimum of V_{MCA} and, if accomplished in the aircraft, at an altitude not lower than 500 feet AGL.
12. Maintains the airplane alignment with the heading appropriate for climb performance and terrain clearance when powerplant failure occurs.

D. TASK: REJECTED TAKEOFF

References: FAR Part 61; AC 61-21; Pilot's Operating Handbook, AFM; DOT/FM Takeoff Safety Training Aid

Objective: To determine that the applicant understands when to reject or continue the takeoff:

1. Exhibits adequate knowledge of the technique and procedure for accomplishing a rejected takeoff after powerplant/system(s) failure/warnings, including related safety factors.
2. Takes into account, prior to beginning the takeoff, operational factors which could affect the maneuver, such as Takeoff Warning Inhibit Systems or other airplane characteristics, runway length, surface conditions, wind, obstructions, and other related factors that could affect takeoff performance and could adversely affect safety.
3. Aligns the airplane on the runway centerline.
4. Performs all required pretakeoff checks as required by the appropriate checklist items.
5. Adjusts the powerplant controls as recommended by the AFM-approved guidance for the existing conditions.
6. Applies the controls correctly to maintain longitudinal alignment on the centerline of the runway.
7. Aborts the takeoff if, in a single-engine airplane, the powerplant failure occurs prior to becoming airborne, or in a multiengine airplane, the powerplant failure occurs at a point during the takeoff where the abort procedure can be initiated and the airplane can be safely stopped on the remaining runway/stopway. If a flight simulator is not used, the powerplant failure should be simulated before reaching 50 percent of V_{MC}
8. Reduces the power smoothly and promptly, if appropriate to the airplane, when powerplant failure is recognized.
9. Uses spoilers, prop reverse, thrust reverse, wheel brakes, and other drag/braking devices, as appropriate, maintaining positive control in such a manner as to bring the airplane to a safe stop. Accomplishes the appropriate

powerplant failure or other procedures and/or checklists as set forth in the Pilot Operating Handbook or AFM.

E. TASK: INSTRUMENT DEPARTURE

References: FAR Part 61; AC 61-27; Pilot's Operating Handbook, AFM, AIM

Objective: To determine that the applicant:

1. Exhibits adequate knowledge of SIDs, Enroute Low/High Altitude Charts, STARs and related pilot/controller responsibilities.
2. Uses the current and appropriate navigation publications for the proposed flight.
3. Selects and uses the appropriate communications frequencies, and selects and identifies the navigation aids associated with the proposed flight.
4. Performs the appropriate checklist items.
5. Establishes communications with ATC, using proper phraseology.
6. Complies, in a timely manner, with all instructions and airspace restrictions.
7. Exhibits adequate knowledge of two-way radio communications failure procedures.
8. Intercepts, in a timely manner, all courses, radials, and bearings appropriate to the procedure, route, clearance, or as directed by the examiner.
9. Maintains the appropriate airspeed within ±10 knots, headings within ±10°, altitude within ±100 feet (30 meters); and accurately tracks a course, radial, or bearing.
10. Conducts the departure phase to a point where, in the opinion of the examiner, the transition to the enroute environment is complete.

IV. INFLIGHT MANEUVERS

A. TASK: STEEP TURNS

References: FAR Part 61; AC 61-27; FSB Report; Pilot's Operating Handbook, AFM

Objective: To determine that the applicant:

1. Exhibits adequate knowledge of steep turns (if applicable to the airplane) and the factors associated with performance; and, if applicable, wing loading, angle of bank, stall speed, pitch, power requirements, and over-banking tendencies.
2. Selects an altitude recommended by the manufacturer, training syllabus, or other training directive, but in no case lower than 3,000 feet (900 meters) AGL.
3. Establishes the recommended entry airspeed.
4. Rolls into a coordinated turn of 180° or 360° with a bank of at least 45°. Maintains the bank angle within ±5° while in smooth, stabilized flight.
5. Applies smooth coordinated pitch, bank, and power to maintain the specified altitude within ±100 feet (30 meters) and the desired airspeed within ±10 knots.

6. Rolls out of the turn (at approximately the same rate as used to roll into the turn) within ±10° of the entry or specified heading, stabilizes the airplane in a straight-and-level attitude or, at the discretion of the examiner, reverses the direction of turn and repeats the maneuver in the opposite direction.

7. Avoids any indication of an approaching stall, abnormal flight attitude, or exceeding any structural or operating limitation during any part of the maneuver.

B. TASK: APPROACHES TO STALLS

References: FAR Part 61; AC 61-21; FSB Report; Pilot's Operating Handbook, AFM

Note: THREE approaches to stall are required, as follows (unless otherwise specified by the FSB Report):

1. One in the takeoff configuration (except where the airplane uses only zero-flap takeoff configuration) or approach configuration.
2. One in a clean configuration
3. One in a landing configuration.

One of these approaches to a stall must be accomplished while in a turn using a bank angle of 15 to 30°.

Objective: To determine that the applicant:

1. Exhibits adequate knowledge of the factors which influence stall characteristics, including the use of various drag configurations, power settings, pitch attitudes, weights, and bank angles. Also, exhibits adequate knowledge of the proper procedure for resuming normal flight.

2. Selects an entry altitude, when accomplished in an airplane, that is in accordance with the AFM or Operating Handbook, but in no case lower than an altitude that will allow recovery to be safely completed at a minimum of 3,000 feet (900 meters) AGL. Stalls accomplished in an FTD or flight simulator, the entry altitude may be at low, intermediate, or high altitude as appropriate for the airplane and the configuration, at the discretion of the examiner.

3. Observes the area is clear of other aircraft prior to accomplishing an approach to a stall.

4. While maintaining altitude, slowly establishes the pitch attitude (using trim or elevator/stabilizer), bank angle, and power setting that will induce stall at the desired target airspeed.

5. Announces the first indication of an impending stall (such as buffeting, stick shaker, decay of control effectiveness, and any other cues related to the specific airplane design characteristics) and initiates recovery or as directed by the examiner (using maximum power or as directed by the examiner).

6. Recovers to a reference airspeed, altitude and heading, allowing only the acceptable altitude or airspeed loss, and heading deviation.

7. Demonstrates smooth, positive airplane control during entry, approach to a stall, and recovery.

C. TASK: POWERPLANT FAILURE—MULTIENGINE AIRPLANE

References: FAR Part 61; Pilot's Operating Handbook, AFM

Note: When not in an FTD or a flight simulator, the feathering of one propeller must be demonstrated in any multiengine airplane equipped with propellers which can be safely feathered and unfeathered while airborne. In a multiengine jet airplane, one engine must be shut down and a restart must be demonstrated while airborne. Feathering or shutdown should be performed only under conditions, and at such altitudes (no lower than 3,000 feet [900 meters] AGL) and in a position where a safe landing can be made at an established airport in the event difficulty is encountered in unfeathering the propeller or restarting the engine. At an altitude lower than 3,000 feet (900 meters) AGL, simulated engine failure will be performed by setting the powerplant controls to simulate zero-thrust. In the event propeller cannot be unfeathered or engine air started during the test, it should be treated as an emergency.

When authorized and conducted in a flight simulator, feathering or shutdown may be performed in conjunction with any procedure or maneuver and at locations and altitudes at the discretion of the examiner. However, when conducted in an FTD, authorizations shall be limited to shutdown, feathering, restart, and/or unfeathering procedures only. See Appendix 1.

Objective: To determine that the applicant:

1. Exhibits adequate knowledge of the flight characteristics and controllability associated with maneuvering with powerplant(s) inoperative (as appropriate to the airplane).
2. Maintains positive airplane control. Establishes a bank of approximately 5°, if required, or as recommended by the manufacturer, to maintain coordinated flight, and properly trims for that condition.
3. Sets powerplant controls, reduces drag as necessary, correctly identifies and verifies the inoperative powerplant(s) after the failure (or simulated failure).
4. Maintains the operating powerplant(s) within acceptable operating limits.
5. Follows the prescribed airplane checklist, and verifies the procedures for securing the inoperative powerplant(s).
6. Determines the cause for the powerplant(s) failure and if a restart is a viable option.
7. Maintains desired attitude within ±100 feet (30 meters), when a constant altitude is specified and is within the capability of the airplane.
8. Maintains the desired airspeed within ±10 knots.
9. Maintains the desired heading within ±10° of the specified heading.
10. Demonstrates proper powerplant restart procedures (if appropriate) in accordance with FM-approved procedure/checklist or the manufacturer's recommended procedures and pertinent checklist items.

D. TASK: POWERPLANT FAILURE—SINGLE-ENGINE AIRPLANE

References: FAR Part 61; AC 61-21; Pilot's Operating Handbook, AFM

Note: No simulated powerplant failure shall be given by the examiner in an airplane when an actual touchdown could not be safely completed should it become necessary.

Objective: To determine that the applicant:

1. Exhibits adequate knowledge of the flight characteristics, approach and forced (emergency) landing procedures, and related procedures to use in the event of a powerplant failure (as appropriate to the airplane).
2. Maintains positive airplane control throughout the maneuver.
3. Establishes and maintains the recommended best glide airspeed, +5 knots, and configuration during a simulated powerplant failure.
4. Selects a suitable airport or landing area which is within the performance capability of the airplane.
5. Establishes a proper flight pattern to the selected airport or landing area, taking into account altitude, wind, terrain, obstructions, and other pertinent operational factors.
6. Follows the emergency checklist items appropriate to the airplane.
7. Determines the cause for the simulated powerplant failure (if altitude permits) and if a restart is a viable option.
8. Uses airplane configuration devices such as landing gear and flaps in a manner recommended by the manufacturer and/or approved by the FAA.

E. TASK: SPECIFIC FLIGHT CHARACTERISTICS

References: FAR Part 61; FSB Report; Pilot's Operating Handbook, AFM
Objective: To determine that the applicant:

1. Exhibits adequate knowledge of specific flight characteristics appropriate to the specific airplane, as identified by the FSB Report, such as Dutch Rolls in a Boeing 727 or Lear Jet.
2. Uses proper technique to enter into, operate within, and recover from specific flight situations.

V. INSTRUMENT PROCEDURES

Note: TASKS B through F are not required if the applicant holds a private pilot or commercial pilot certificate and is seeking a type rating limited to VFR. If TASK D, Nonprecision Instrument Approach Procedures, is performed in a training device (other than an FTD or flight simulator) and the applicant has completed an approved training course for the airplane type involved, not more than one (1) of the required instrument procedures may be observed by a person qualified to act as an instructor or check airman under that approved training program. The instrument approaches are considered to begin when the airplane is over the initial approach fix for the procedure being used and end when the airplane touches down on the runway or when transition to a missed approach configuration is completed. Instrument conditions need NOT be simulated below the minimum altitude for the approach being accomplished.

A. TASK: INSTRUMENT ARRIVAL

References: FAR Part 61; Pilot's Operating Handbook, AFM, AIM; Enroute Low/High Altitude Charts, Profile Descent Charts, STARs, Instrument Approach Procedure Charts
Objective: To determine that the applicant:

1. Exhibits adequate knowledge of Enroute Low/High Altitude Charts, STARs, Instrument Approach Charts, and related pilot and controller responsibilities.
2. Uses the current and appropriate navigation publications for the proposed flight.
3. Selects, and correctly identifies all instrument references, flight director and autopilot controls, and navigation and communications equipment associated with the arrival.
4. Performs the airplane checklist items appropriate to the arrival.
5. Establishes communications with ATC, using proper phraseology.
6. Complies, in a timely manner, with all ATC clearances, instructions, and restrictions.
7. Exhibits adequate knowledge of two-way communications failure procedures.
8. Intercepts, in a timely manner, all courses, radials, and bearings appropriate to the procedure, route, ATC clearance, or as directed by the examiner.
9. Adheres to airspeed restrictions and adjustments required by regulations, ATC, the Pilot Operating Handbook, the AFM, or the examiner.
10. Establishes, where appropriate, a rate of descent consistent with the airplane operating characteristics and safety.
11. Maintains the appropriate airspeed/V-speed within ±10 knots, but not less than V_{REF}, if applicable; heading ±10°; altitude within ±100 feet (30 meters); and accurately tracks radials, courses, and bearings.
12. Complies with the provisions of the Profile Descent, STAR, and other arrival procedures, as appropriate.

B. TASK: HOLDING

   References: FAR Part 61; Pilot's Operating Handbook, AFM, AIM; Enroute Low/High Altitude Charts, STARs, Instrument Approach Procedure Charts

   Objective: To determine that the applicant:

1. Exhibits adequate knowledge of holding procedures for standard and nonstandard, published and nonpublished holding patterns. If appropriate, demonstrates adequate knowledge of holding endurance, including, but not necessarily limited to, fuel on board, fuel flow while holding, fuel required to alternate, etc.
2. Changes to the recommended holding airspeed appropriate for the airplane and holding altitude, so as to cross the holding fix at or below maximum holding airspeed.
3. Recognizes arrival at the clearance limit or holding fix.
4. Follows appropriate entry procedures for a standard, nonstandard, published, or nonpublished holding pattern.
5. Complies with ATC reporting requirements.

6. Uses the proper timing criteria required by the holding altitude and ATC or examiner's instructions.

7. Complies with the holding pattern leg length when a DME distance is specified.

8. Uses the proper wind-drift correction techniques to maintain the desired radial, track, or bearing.

9. Arrives over the holding fix as close as possible to the "expect further clearance" time.

10. Maintains the appropriate airspeed/V-speed within ±10 knots, altitude within ±100 feet (30 meters), headings within ±10°; and accurately tracks radials, courses, and bearings.

C. TASK: PRECISION INSTRUMENT APPROACHES

References: FAR Part 61; AC 61-27; Pilot's Operating Handbook, AFM, AIM; Instrument Approach Procedure Charts

Note: Two precision approaches, utilizing airplane NAVAID equipment for centerline and glideslope guidance, must be accomplished in simulated instrument conditions to 200 feet above the runway/touchdown zone elevation. At least one approach must be flown manually. The second approach may be flown via the autopilot, if appropriate, and if the 200-foot altitude does not violate the authorized minimum altitude for autopilot operation. Manually flown precision approaches may use raw data displays or may be flight director assisted, at the discretion of the examiner.

For multiengine airplanes at least one manually controlled precision approach must be accomplished with a simulated failure of one powerplant. The simulated powerplant failure should occur before initiating the final approach segment and must continue to touchdown or throughout the missed approach procedure.

As the markings on localizer/glideslope indicators vary, a one-quarter scale deflection of either the localized or glideslope indicator is when it is displaced one-fourth of the distance that it may be deflected from the on glideslope or on localizer position.

Objective: To determine that the applicant:

1. Exhibits adequate knowledge of the precision instrument approach procedures with all engines operating, and with one engine inoperative.

2. Accomplishes the appropriate precision instrument approaches as selected by the examiner.

3. Establishes two-way communications with ATC using the proper communications phraseology and techniques, either personally, or, if appropriate, directs co-pilot/safety pilot to do so, as required for the phase of flight or approach segment.

4. Complies, in a timely manner, with all clearances, instructions, and procedures.

5. Advises ATC anytime the applicant is unable to comply with a clearance.

6. Establishes the appropriate airplane configuration and airspeed/V-speed, considering turbulence, wind shear, micro burst conditions, or other meteorological and operating conditions.

7. Completes the airplane checklist items appropriate to the phase of flight or approach segment, including engine-out approach and landing checklists, if appropriate.

8. Prior to beginning the final approach segment, maintains the desired altitude +100 feet (30 meters), the desired airspeed within ±10 knots, the desired heading within ±5°; and accurately tracks radials, courses, and bearings.

9. Selects, tunes, identifies, and monitors the operational status of ground and airplane navigation equipment used for the approach.

10. Applies the necessary adjustments to the published Decision Height and visibility criteria for the airplane approach category as required, such as—
    a. Notices to Airmen, including Flight Data Center Procedural NOTAMs.
    b. inoperative airplane and ground navigation equipment.
    c. inoperative visual aids associated with the landing environment.
    d. National Weather Service (NWS) reporting factors and criteria.

11. Establishes a predetermined rate of descent at the point where the electronic glideslope begins which approximates that required for the airplane to follow the glideslope.

12. Maintains a stabilized final approach, arriving at Decision Height with no more than one-quarter scale deflection of the localizer, or the glideslope indicators and the airspeed/V-speed within ±5 knots of that desired.

13. Avoids descent below the Decision Height before initiating a missed approach procedure or transitioning to a landing.

14. Initiates immediately the missed approach when at the Decision Height, and the required visual references for the runway are not distinctly visible and identifiable.

15. Transitions to a normal landing approach only when the airplane is in a position from which a descent to a landing on the runway can be made at a normal rate of descent using normal maneuvering.

16. Maintains localizer and glideslope within one-quarter scale deflection of the indicators during the visual descent from Decision Height to a point over the runway where glideslope must be abandoned to accomplish a normal landing.

D. TASK: NONPRECISION INSTRUMENT APPROACHES

References: FAR Part 61; AC 61-27; Pilot's Operating Handbook, AFM, AIM; Instrument Approach Procedure Charts

Note: The applicant must accomplish at least two nonprecision approaches. The examiner will select nonprecision approaches that are representative of that which the applicant is likely to use. The second nonprecision approach will utilize a navigational aid other than the one used for the first approach.

Objective: To determine that the applicant:

1. Exhibits adequate knowledge of nonprecision approach procedures representative of those the applicant is likely to use.

2. Accomplishes the nonprecision instrument approaches selected by the examiner.

3. Establishes two-way communications with ATC as appropriate to the phase of flight or approach segment and uses proper communications phraseology and techniques.
4. Complies with all clearances issued by ATC.
5. Advises ATC or the examiner anytime the applicant is unable to comply with a clearance.
6. Establishes the appropriate airplane configuration and airspeed, and completes all applicable checklist items.
7. Maintains, prior to beginning the final approach segment, the desired altitude ±100 feet (30 meters), the desired airspeed ±10 knots, the desired heading ±5°; and accurately tracks radials, courses, and bearings.
8. Selects, tunes, identifies, and monitors the operational status of ground and airplane navigation equipment used for the approach.
9. Applies the necessary adjustments to the published Minimum Descent Altitude and visibility criteria for the airplane approach category when required, such as—
   a. Notices to Airmen, including Flight Data Center Procedural NOTAMs.
   b. inoperative airplane and ground navigation equipment.
   c. inoperative visual aids associated with the landing environment.
   d. National Weather Service (NWS) reporting factors and criteria.
10. Establishes a rate of descent that will ensure arrival at the Minimum Descent Altitude (at, or prior to reaching, the visual descent point [VDP] if published) with the airplane in a position from which a descent from MDA to a landing on the intended runway can be made at a normal rate using normal maneuvering.
11. Allows, while on the final approach segment, not more than quarter-scale deflection of the Course Deviation Indicator (CDI) or ±5° in the case of the RMI or bearing pointer, and maintains airspeed within ±5 knots of that desired.
12. Maintains the Minimum Descent Altitude, when reached, within -0, +50 feet (-0, +15 meters) to the missed approach point.
13. Executes the missed approach if the required visual references for the intended runway are not distinctly visible and identifiable at the missed approach point.
14. Executes a normal landing from a straight-in or circling approach when instructed by the examiner.

E. TASK: CIRCLING APPROACH
   References: FAR Part 61; AC 61-27; Pilot's Operating Handbook, AFM, AIM; Instrument Approach Procedure Charts
   Objective: To determine that the applicant:
   1. Exhibits adequate knowledge of circling approach categories, speeds, and procedures to a specified runway.
   2. Accomplishes the circling approach selected by the examiner.

3. Demonstrates sound judgment and knowledge of the airplane maneuvering capabilities throughout the circling approach.

4. Confirms the direction of traffic and adheres to all restrictions and instructions issued by ATC.

5. Descends at a rate that ensures arrival at the MDA at, or prior to, a point from which a normal circle-to-land maneuver can be accomplished.

6. Avoids descent below the appropriate circling Minimum Descent Altitude or exceeding the visibility criteria until in a position from which a descent to a normal landing can be made.

7. Maneuvers the airplane, after reaching the authorized circling approach altitude, by visual references to maintain a flight path that permits a normal landing on a runway at least 90° from the final approach course.

8. Performs the procedure without excessive maneuvering and without exceeding the normal operating limits of the airplane (the angle of bank should not exceed 30°).

9. Maintains the desired altitude within -0, +100 feet (-0, +30 meters), heading/track within ±5°, the airspeed/V-speed within ±5 knots, but not less than the airspeed as specified in the pilot operating handbook or the AFM.

10. Uses the appropriate airplane configuration for normal and abnormal situations and procedures.

11. Turns in the appropriate direction, when a missed approach is dictated during the circling approach, and uses the correct procedure and airplane configuration.

12. Performs all procedures required for the circling approach and airplane control in a smooth, positive, and timely manner.

F. TASK: MISSED APPROACH

References: FAR Part 61; AC 61-27; Pilot's Operating Handbook, AFM, AIM; Instrument Approach Procedure Charts

Note: The applicant must be required to perform at least two missed approaches with at least one missed approach from a precision approach (ILS, MLS, or GPS). A complete approved missed approach must be accomplished at least once. Additionally, in multiengine airplanes, a missed approach must be accomplished with one engine inoperative (or simulated inoperative). The engine failure may be experienced anytime prior to the initiation of the approach, during the approach, or during the transition to the missed approach attitude and configuration.

Going below the MDA or DH, as appropriate, prior to the initiation of the missed approach shall be considered unsatisfactory performance. However, satisfactory performance may be concluded if the missed approach is properly initiated at DH and the airplane descends below DH only because of the momentum of the airplane transitioning from a stabilized approach to a missed approach.

Objective: To determine that the applicant:

1. Exhibits adequate knowledge of missed approach procedures associated with standard instrument approaches.

2. Initiates the missed approach procedure promptly by the timely application of power, establishes the proper climb attitude, and reduces drag in accordance with the approved procedures.

3. Reports to ATC, beginning the missed approach procedure.

4. Complies with the appropriate missed approach procedure or ATC clearance.

5. Advises ATC anytime the applicant is unable to maneuver the airplane to comply with a clearance.

6. Follows the recommended airplane checklist items appropriate to the go-around procedure for the airplane used.

7. Requests clearance, if appropriate, to the alternate airport, another approach, a holding fix, or as directed by the examiner.

8. Maintains the desired altitudes ±100 feet (30 meters), airspeed ±5 knots, heading ±5°; and accurately tracks courses, radials, and bearings.

VI. LANDINGS AND APPROACHES TO LANDINGS

Note: Notwithstanding the authorizations for the combining of maneuvers and for the waiver of maneuvers, the applicant must make at least three (3) actual landings (one to a full stop). These landings must include the types listed in this AREA OF OPERATION, however, more than one type may be combined where appropriate (i.e., crosswind and landing from a precision approach or landing with simulated powerplant failure, etc.).

For all landings in airplanes, touchdown should be 500 to 3,000 feet (150 to 900 meters) past the runway threshold, not to exceed one-third of the runway length, with the runway centerline between the main gear.

A. TASK: NORMAL AND CROSSWIND APPROACHES AND LANDINGS

References: FAR Part 61; AC 61-21; Pilot's Operating Handbook, AFM

Note: In an airplane with a single powerplant, unless the applicant holds a commercial pilot certificate, he/she must accomplish accuracy approaches and spot landings from an altitude of 1,000 feet (300 meters) or less, with the engine power lever in idle and 180° of change in direction. The airplane must touch the ground in a normal landing attitude beyond and within 200 feet (60 meters) of a designated line or point on the runway. At least one landing must be from a forward slip. Although circular approaches are acceptable, 180° approaches using two 90° turns with a straight base leg are preferred.

Objective: To determine that the applicant:

1. Exhibits adequate knowledge of normal and crosswind approaches and landings including recommended approach angles, airspeeds, V-speeds, configurations, performance limitations, wake turbulence, and safety factors (as appropriate to the airplane).

2. Establishes the approach and landing configuration appropriate for the runway and meteorological conditions, and adjusts the powerplant controls as required.

3. Maintains a ground track that ensures the desired traffic pattern will be flown, taking into account any obstructions and ATC or examiner instructions.

4. Verifies existing wind conditions, makes proper correction for drift, and maintains a precise ground track.

5. Maintains a stabilized approach and the desired airspeed/V-speed within ±5 knots.

6. Accomplishes a smooth, positively controlled transition from final approach to touchdown.

7. Maintains positive directional control and crosswind correction during the after-landing roll.

8. Uses spoilers, prop reverse, thrust reverse, wheel brakes, and other drag/braking devices, as appropriate, in such a manner to bring the airplane to a safe stop.

9. Completes the applicable after-landing checklist items in a timely manner and as recommended by the manufacturer.

B. TASK: LANDING FROM A PRECISION APPROACH

References: FAR Part 61; AC 61-27; Pilot's Operating Handbook, AFM, AIM
Note: If circumstances beyond the control of the applicant prevent an actual landing, the examiner may accept an approach to a point where, in his/her judgment, a safe landing and a full stop could have been made. Where a simulator, approved for landing from a precision approach, is used, the approach may be continued through the landing and credit given for one of the landings required by this AREA OF OPERATION.

Objective: To determine that the applicant:

1. Exhibits awareness of landing in sequence from a precision approach.

2. Considers factors to be applied to the approach and landing such as displaced thresholds, meteorological conditions, NOTAMs, and ATC or examiner instructions.

3. Uses the airplane configuration and airspeed/V-speeds, as appropriate.

4. Maintains, during the final approach segment, glideslope and localizer indications within applicable standards of deviation, and the recommended airspeed/V-speed ±5 knots.

5. Applies gust/wind factors as recommended by the manufacturer, and takes into account meteorological phenomena such as wind shear, microburst, and other related safety of flight factors.

6. Accomplishes the appropriate checklist items.

7. Transitions smoothly from simulated instrument meteorological conditions at a point designated by the examiner, maintaining positive airplane control.

8. Accomplishes a smooth, positively controlled transition from final approach to touchdown.

9. Maintains positive directional control and crosswind correction during the after-landing roll.

10. Uses spoilers, prop reverse, thrust reverse, wheel brakes, and other drag/braking devices, as appropriate, in such a manner to bring the airplane to a safe stop after landing.

11. Completes the after-landing checklist items in a timely manner and as recommended by the manufacturer.

C. TASK: APPROACH AND LANDING WITH (SIMULATED) POWERPLANT FAILURE–MULTIENGINE AIRPLANE

References: FAR Part 61; AC 61-21; Pilot's Operating Handbook, AFM

Note: In airplanes with three powerplants, the applicant shall follow a procedure (if approved) that approximates the loss of two powerplants, the center and one outboard powerplant. In other multiengine airplanes, the applicant shall follow a procedure which simulates the loss of 50 percent of available powerplants, the loss being simulated on one side of the airplane.

Objective: To determine that the applicant:

1. Exhibits adequate knowledge of the flight characteristics and controllability associated with maneuvering to a landing with (a) powerplant(s) inoperative (or simulated inoperative) including the controllability factors associated with maneuvering, and the applicable emergency procedures.
2. Maintains positive airplane control. Establishes a bank of approximately 5°, if required, or as recommended by the manufacturer, to maintain coordinated flight, and properly trims for that condition.
3. Sets powerplant controls, reduces drag as necessary, correctly identifies and verifies the inoperative powerplant(s) after the failure (or simulated failure).
4. Maintains the operating powerplant(s) within acceptable operating limits.
5. Follows the prescribed airplane checklist, and verifies the procedures for securing the inoperative powerplant(s).
6. Proceeds toward the nearest suitable airport.
7. Maintains, prior to beginning the final approach segment, the desired altitude ±100 feet (30 meters), the desired airspeed ±10 knots, the desired heading ±5°; and accurately tracks courses, radials, and bearings.
8. Establishes the approach and landing configuration appropriate for the runway or landing area, and meteorological conditions; and adjusts the powerplant controls as required.
9. Maintains a stabilized approach and the desired airspeed/V-speed within ±5 knots.
10. Accomplishes a smooth, positively controlled transition from final approach to touchdown.
11. Maintains positive directional control and crosswind corrections during the after-landing roll.
12. Uses spoilers, prop reverse, thrust reversers, wheel brakes and other drag/braking devices, as appropriate, in such a manner to bring the airplane to a safe stop after landing
13. Completes the after-landing checklist items in a timely manner, after clearing the runway, and as recommended by the manufacturer.

D. TASK: LANDING FROM A CIRCLING APPROACH

References: FAR Part 61; AC 61-27; Pilot's Operating Handbook, AFM, AIM

Objective: To determine that the applicant:

1. Exhibits adequate knowledge of a landing from a circling approach.
2. Selects, and complies with, a circling approach procedure to a specified runway.
3. Considers the environmental, operational, and meteorological factors which affect a landing from a circling approach.
4. Confirms the direction of tram and adheres to all restrictions and instructions issued by ATC.
5. Descends at a rate that ensures arrival at the MDA at, or prior to, a point from which a normal circle-to-land maneuver can be accomplished.
6. Avoids descent below the appropriate circling MDA or exceeding the visibility criteria until in a position from which a descent to a normal landing can be made.
7. Accomplishes the appropriate checklist items.
8. Maneuvers the airplane, after reaching the authorized circling approach altitude, by visual references, to maintain a flight path that permits a normal landing on a runway at least 90° from the final approach course.
9. Performs the maneuver without excessive maneuvering and without exceeding the normal operating limits of the airplane. The angle of bank should not exceed 30°.
10. Maintains the desired altitude within +100, -0 feet (+30, -0 meters), heading within ±5°, and approach airspeed/V-speed within ±5.
11. Uses the appropriate airplane configuration for normal and abnormal situations and procedures.
12. Performs all procedures required for the circling approach and airplane control in a timely, smooth, and positive manner.
13. Accomplishes a smooth, positively controlled transition to final approach and touchdown.
14. Maintains positive directional control and crosswind correction during the after-landing roll.
15. Uses spoilers, prop reverse, thrust reverse, wheel brakes, and other drag/braking devices, as appropriate, in such a manner to bring the airplane to a safe stop.
16. Completes the after-landing checklist items, after clearing the runway, in a timely manner and as recommended by the manufacturer.

E. TASK: REJECTED LANDING

References: FAR Part 61; AC 61-21; Pilot's Operating Handbook, AFM; FSB Report

Note: The maneuver may be combined with instrument, circling, or missed approach procedures, but instrument conditions need not be simulated below 100 feet (30 meters)

above the runway. This maneuver should be initiated approximately 50 feet (15 meters) above the runway and approximately over the runway threshold or as recommended by the FSB Report.

For those applicants seeking a VFR-only type rating in an airplane not capable of instrument flight, for those cases where this maneuver is accomplished with a simulated engine failure, it should not be initiated at speeds or altitudes below that recommended in the pilot's operating manual.

Objective: To determine that the applicant:

1. Exhibits adequate knowledge of a rejected landing procedure, including the conditions that dictate a rejected landing, the importance of a timely decision, the recommended airspeed/V-speeds, and also the applicable "clean-up" procedure.
2. Makes a timely decision to reject the landing for actual or simulated circumstances and makes appropriate notification when safety-of-flight is not an issue.
3. Applies the appropriate power setting for the flight condition and establishes a pitch attitude necessary to obtain the desired performance.
4. Retracts the wing flaps/drag devices and landing gear, if appropriate, in the correct sequence and at a safe altitude, establishes a positive rate of climb and the appropriate airspeed/V-speed within ±5 knots.
5. Trims the airplane as necessary, and maintains the proper ground track during the rejected landing procedure.
6. Accomplishes the appropriate checklist items in a timely manner in accordance with approved procedures.

F. TASK: LANDING FROM A ZERO OR NONSTANDARD FLAP APPROACH

References: FAR Part 61; AC 61-21; FSB Report; Pilot's Operating Handbook, AFM

Note: This maneuver need not be accomplished for a particular airplane type if the administrator has determined that the probability of flap extension failure on that type airplane is extremely remote due to system design. The examiner must determine whether checking on slats only and partial-flap approaches are necessary for the practical test.

Objective: To determine that the applicant:

1. Exhibits adequate knowledge of the factors which affect the flight characteristics of an airplane when full or partial flaps, leading edge flaps, and other similar devices become inoperative.
2. Uses the correct airspeeds/V-speeds for the approach and landing.
3. Maintains the proper airplane pitch attitude and flight path for the configuration, gross weight, surface winds, and other applicable operational considerations.
4. Uses runway of sufficient length for the zero or nonstandard flap condition.

5. Maneuvers the airplane to a point where, in the opinion of the examiner, touchdown at an acceptable point on the runway and a safe landing to a full stop could be made.

6. If a landing is made, uses spoilers, prop reverse, thrust reverse, wheel brakes, and other drag/braking devices, as appropriate, in such a manner to bring the airplane to a safe stop.

VII. NORMAL AND ABNORMAL PROCEDURES

References: FAR Part 61; Pilot's Operating Handbook, AFM
Objective: To determine that the applicant:

1. Possesses adequate knowledge of the normal and abnormal procedures of the systems, subsystems, and devices relative to the airplane type (as may be determined by the examiner); knows immediate action items to accomplish, if appropriate, and proper checklist to accomplish or to call for, if appropriate.

2. Demonstrates the proper use of the airplane systems, subsystems, and devices (as may be determined by the examiner) appropriate to the airplane such as—
   a. powerplant.
   b. fuel system.
   c. electrical system.
   d. hydraulic system.
   e. environmental and pressurization systems.
   f. fire detection and extinguishing systems.
   g. navigation and avionics systems.
   h. automatic flight control system, electronic flight instrument system, and related subsystems.
   i. flight control systems.
   j. anti-ice and deice systems.
   k. airplane and personal emergency equipment.
   l. other systems, subsystems, and devices specific to the type airplane, including make, model, and series.

VIII. EMERGENCY PROCEDURES

References: FAR Part 61; Pilot's Operating Handbook, AFM
Objective: To determine that the applicant:

1. Possesses adequate knowledge of the emergency procedures (as may be determined by the examiner) relating to the particular airplane type.

2. Demonstrates the proper emergency procedures (as must be determined by the examiner) relating to the particular airplane type, including—
   a. emergency descent (maximum rate).
   b. inflight fire and smoke removal.
   c. rapid decompression.
   d. emergency evacuation.
   e. others (as may be required by the AFM).

3. Demonstrates the proper procedure for any other emergency outlined (as must be determined by the examiner) in the appropriate approved AFM.

IX. POST-FLIGHT PROCEDURES

A. TASK: AFTER LANDING
References: Pilot's Operating Handbook, AFM
Objective: To determine that the applicant:

1. Exhibits adequate knowledge of safe after-landing/taxi procedures as appropriate.
2. Demonstrates proficiency by maintaining correct and positive control. In airplanes equipped with float devices, this includes water taxiing, approaching a buoy, and docking.
3. Maintains proper spacing on other aircraft, obstructions, and persons.
4. Accomplishes the applicable checklist items and performs the recommended procedures.
5. Maintains the desired track and speed.
6. Complies with instructions issued by ATC (or the examiner simulating ATC).
7. Observes runway hold lines, localizer and glideslope critical areas, and other surface control markings and lighting.
8. Maintains constant vigilance and airplane control during the taxi operation.

B. TASK: PARKING AND SECURING
References: Pilot's Operating Handbook, AFM
Objective: To determine that the applicant:

1. Exhibits adequate knowledge of the parking and the securing airplane procedures.
2. Has adequate knowledge of the airplane forms/logs to record the flight time/discrepancies.

17
Why multiengine?

WHY IS IT IMPORTANT TO GET A MULTIENGINE RATING? YOU MIGHT have access to a multiengine airplane and learning to flying it would represent a new challenge. Even a private pilot checkride can be taken in a multiengine airplane. Yet for most pilots the step from single- to multiengine is not taken "because it is there." Rather, it is taken as a necessary step on a career path.

Climbing the aviation career ladder to corporations or airlines cannot be accomplished without a multiengine rating and multiengine flight time. If a piloting career is your goal, you must cultivate what will make you attractive to companies in the future. Your pilot logbook must become an unshakable legal document that clearly explains the course you have taken to reach the goal.

Not long after I passed the commercial pilot checkride, and with barely 300 hours of flight time, I was introduced at a gathering as a "commercial pilot." A man asked me, "So what airline do you fly for?" It was a little embarrassing trying to explain that just because I had a commercial certificate did not mean that I could fly for a commercial airline. There is a large gap between certification and marketability.

When a corporation or airline hires an individual, they look at many factors: personality, references from previous employers, drug tests, knowledge of airplane systems, regulations and instrument procedures, ease with relationships, previous FAA violations, and many others. But the factor that gets you in the door to the interview in the first place is flight time. Building the flight time that will attract an interview and, hopefully, professional pilot employment is a skill all its own.

QUANTITY AND QUALITY FLIGHT TIME

Your flight time must take into account two factors: quantity and quality. When a pilot first gets the commercial certificate and has as little as 200 hours of flight time in his or her logbook, quantity is more important than quality. This pilot must increase flight time or wither on the vine. At this point, the amount of time is more important than what kind of time. The pilot must build flight time from 200 to approximately 1,000 hours. During this stretch, an hour of Cessna 150 time is just as valuable as anything else.

Although quantity is most important during this period, quality should not be ignored. For instance, flights to Atlanta, Georgia, are more valuable than flights to Edenton, North Carolina. The actual time in the logbook might be the same for both flights, but the level of pilot skill required and experience gained from the flight is greater in Atlanta.

A flight in actual instrument conditions is more valuable than a flight in VFR. A flight that deals with northern winter weather is more valuable than a flight into southern summer weather. Flight instruction given is more valuable than a sightseeing flight. A night Part 135 cargo flight is more valuable than a dual cross-country with a student pilot. Anything "scheduled" is more valuable than anything unscheduled.

After the pilot puts together around 1,000 hours, the quantity versus quality equation begins to turn around. Now it becomes more important to have meaningful hours rather than plentiful hours, and this is where multiengine time makes all the difference. A pilot with 2,500 single-engine hours is not as valuable as a pilot with 2,000 hours, if 500 of those 2,000 are in a multiengine airplane. Here the quantity (2,500) is just not as good as the quality (2,000/500). Employers expect the quantity but look for quality.

FLIGHT TIME MINIMUMS

Airline companies publicly issue minimum flight times for pilots who they would consider for employment. There is some variation between companies, but most lump all multiengine time together. A check airman with American Eagle told me, "All multiengine time is counted the same." This means that flight time in a Piper Seminole is as good as in a Beech Baron. Once in the interview, the larger equipment might make a difference to the individual conducting the interview, but as far as the "foot in the door" requirement, all reciprocating multiengine time is equal. Turbine flight time does carry extra clout, but first-job employers rarely include turbine time minimums in their published numbers.

I teach a college course in air transportation that details how to get a job in the aviation industry. Each year I assign every student an airline company. The airlines chosen are usually the kind considered to be entry-level: commuters and regional carriers. The student then is required to do extensive research on that airline so he or she can make an educated employment decision about that company.

This is not an ordinary college paper. Students must dig past the company's "propaganda" to get the real story of the company. They must interview company officials, talk to the pilots, study the company's financial position, discover if airplanes are on order, and familiarize themselves with the hiring process, including minimum flight, education, and health requirements. They must also understand the management and union relationship, predict the company's expansion or bankruptcy, and understand the motivation of the airline to make interline agreements with other carriers.

I tell students that by the end of the class, if they are not dating the company president's son or daughter, they have not done the job completely. Armed with all this information, the student can make a better employment decision.

Every airline studied in the class requires multiengine time in their published minimums. Here is a sample of airline requirements from research taken from the early 1990s. Some of these airlines went out of business; others have been swallowed up by other airlines. The figures reveal a multiengine pattern. The first number is the airline's minimum total flight time. The second number is the airline's minimum multiengine flight time.

- Air LA 1500/250
- Air Midwest 1500/300
- Air Nevada 1500/100
- Air Wisconsin 1500/500
- Allegheny/USAir 1500/500
- Aloha Island Air 800/300
- Alpha Air 1200/200
- Aspen Airways 2500/500
- Business Exp 1500/500
- Cavair 1600/100
- CC Air/USAir 1500/200
- Comair 2500/750
- Commutair/USAir 1500/300
- Crown Airways 1500/500
- Eastern/B Harbour 1200/200
- Express/NW Airlink 1500/500
- GP Express 1500/500
- Great Lakes 1500/200
- Henson/USAir 2000/500
- Horizon Air 1200/300
- Jetstream Int'l 1500/500

- Kitty Hawk Cargo 1500/150
- Long Island Air 1000/150
- Mesaba 1000/100
- MidAtlantic Freight 1200/25
- Midwest Express 2000/1000
- Mohawk 1500/500
- MountainAir Cargo1000/100
- Nashville/Flagship 1500/300
- New England Air 2000/500
- Pan Am Express 2000/500
- Precision 1500/500
- Scenic 3000/1000
- Simmons 1500/300
- Skyfreighters 1500/150
- SkyWest Airlines 1000/100
- StatesWest Airlines 2000/500
- Sunshine Air 3000/1000
- TransStates 1500/500
- TransWorld Exp 1500/500
- US Check 1200/25
- Virgin Air 1500/200

The times shown were given from the companies themselves at the time of the research. These times can and do change from day to day depending on the company needs. The real reason these numbers are published by the companies is to discourage pilots with less time from flooding their personnel office with résumés and phone calls. There are plenty of cases where pilots were hired with less than the stated minimum times, but normally you will need much more than the stated minimum to compete for the job.

Total time minimum requirements run from 1,000 to 3,000 hours, with 1,500 being about average. The list of stated multiengine minimum time ranges from 25 hours to 1,000 hours, with the average somewhere around 500. Is 1,500 total and 500 multiengine the magic mix of quantity and quality? Maybe not. Remember, these are numbers the company uses to "qualify" candidates for employment. Hiring decisions are also made on such "unlogable" factors such as personality, work ethic, and luck.

PILOT EMPLOYMENT ECONOMICS

In the late 1980s pilots were being hired at an alarming rate by airline companies. Two factors came together to fuel the hiring frenzy. The 1978 deregulation act took the federal government out of the airline business. Prior to deregulation, airline companies were paid to fly to certain airports. The government decided that many communities needed airline service so that their populations, job markets, and tax bases would grow.

If an airline company lost money while servicing such a community, the federal government would simply write them a check to cover their loss. This guaranteed the airlines a profit. It also eliminated the need for one airline to compete with another on the basis of ticket price. The airlines were wealthy, stable, and stationary. Unfortunately, this system kept ticket prices artificially high, and consumer groups wanted competition in the market to drive prices lower.

After deregulation, if an airline company lost money flying to a particular city, it no longer could turn to the government for dollars. Smart business sense says that a company should always maximize profits, or if that is not possible, at least minimize loses. With this strategy in mind, many cities lost their major air carrier service because the airline lost money.

Small airlines with smaller airplanes came to the rescue. The smaller turboprop commuter airplanes were best suited to make a profit on short hops to a larger airport to connect with larger airlines. Hence, the hub-and-spoke system was born. More than 500 small airlines sprang up to fill the gaps left by the major carriers. These airlines needed pilots, and when companies need pilots, the market is right for pilot hiring.

At the same time that deregulation was being felt, the military changed its strategy in regard to pilots. Traditionally, pilots got their training in the military and then went to work for airlines. The airlines relied on a steady stream of pilots with previous big airplane experience from the military.

Once the military saw many of their training dollars lost to the civilian airlines, they started paying military pilots more as an incentive to stay in the service. It worked. In 1985, for the first time, more civilian-trained pilots were hired by major airlines than military-trained pilots.

I spoke to a Navy pilot flying a P-3 Orion from Pax River and asked him if he was considering the airlines when his Navy obligation was completed. He replied, "I would like to leave the Navy so my family would not get transferred so often, but if I leave the Navy now and go to the airlines, it will take me at least five years to make what I already make now. I cannot afford the pay cut, so I'm staying in the Navy."

In the late 1980s, airlines needed pilots and the traditional source of pilots, the military, was drying up. The only other source was civilian pilots, but civilian pilots just did not have the military pilot's flight time and experience. Something had to give. The minimum requirements for the airlines took a dive to meet the reality of what civilian pilots had to offer. The requirement for a four-year college degree was dropped. The requirement that pilots have 20/20 uncorrected vision was eliminated. Minimum flight requirements plummeted.

The demand for pilots went up because more airlines went into operation. At the same time, the supply of pilots to meet the demand dropped due to fewer military pilots coming out. These market forces produced the "pilot boom." Airlines needed pilots more than pilots needed airlines; therefore, pilots could be selective.

Then the early 1990s arrived. Tough economic times caused airlines to lose millions of dollars and forced many of them into bankruptcy. The reduced profitability of flights reduced the demand for pilots. The hiring requirements began to increase. Market forces shifted. Pilots needed airlines more than airlines needed pilots. Now airlines could be selective.

Many airlines now require pilots to pay for their own training once hired or as a prerequisite for hiring. This training is usually a type rating or toward a type rating for a specific airplane flown by the airline. The cost of this training is approximately $10,000, and this is added to the previous cost of the private, instrument, commercial, and multiengine ratings. Several commuter airline officials who I have talked to have made it clear: as long as there are pilots who will pay the $10,000, they will continue to require it.

By the mid 1990s, there have been some signs of recovery. Some airlines have dropped the employee-paid training requirement and moved toward employee repayment plans for longevity, and internship programs.

I have had a unique view on all of this because I have trained many of the pilots who were the beneficiaries of the pilot hiring boom and who have struggled through the pilot glut—the shift in pilot requirements clearly. In 1987, I could not keep pilot graduates after they had 800 hours because they were hired almost automatically by commuter airlines. In 1988, former students needed only 1,000 hours. In 1989, it took about 1,200 hours, and the competition was tougher.

By 1990, the target for marketability was 1,500 to 1,800 hours. In 1991, 1992, and 1993, more than 2,000 hours were required just to be considered. By 1994, it took 2,500 hours and/or $10,000 for the prerequisite training.

The ratio of total time to multiengine time has shifted as well. In 1987 not much more than a fresh multiengine rating was needed. The ratio was about 8:1, or only one hour of multiengine time for every 8 hours total. In 1990 the ratio was 5:1. In 1993 and 1994, the average was approximately 3:1. In 1996, the ratio went back to 5:1.

Prospective pilots must be keenly aware of the market fluctuations. The minimum flight times required for employment are constantly in transition and are driven by the economy, politics, and consumer demand.

BUILDING FLIGHT TIME

We have established that a large amount of total time and valuable multiengine time will be required to get an airline or corporate career off the ground. Now the most pressing question is "How do I get this flight time?" Flying time is expensive; pilots cannot simply buy 2,000 hours in both single- and multiengine airplanes. It must be accumulated in other ways. Unfortunately, some of the "other ways" are illegal and getting caught could render your logbook and your aviation career dreams moot.

The need to build flight time actually starts after a pilot receives the private pilot certificate. As a student pilot the flight time is dictated by the flight instructor and the Federal Aviation Regulations. Private pilots know that they must gain flight time in order to get an instrument rating and a commercial certificate. Pilots need maximum flight hours on minimum dollars, and here some problems can arise. Let these next few pages be a guide to staying out of trouble, and to building acceptable flight time.

THE EXPENSE-SHARING MISUNDERSTANDING

The Federal Aviation Regulations (FARs) outline the privileges and limitations of a private pilot in FAR 61.118. Most private pilots have memorized 61.118(b), which states: "A private pilot may share the operating expenses of a flight with his passengers." We are quick to realize that this regulation does not say that expenses must be shared equally; however, there are some major misunderstandings about this rule.

The general paragraph at the beginning of 61.118 says: "A private pilot may NOT act as pilot in command of an aircraft that is carrying passengers or property for compensation or hire." The intent of Part 61 is to prevent private pilots from becoming professional pilots until they get further training and certificates. But the "shared expenses" rule seems to be an exception to the "no compensation or hire" rule. When is it legal to share expenses with passengers and when is it not legal? The answer seems to lie within the original intent or reason for the flight. Look at these two similar examples.

Situation 1 A private pilot is walking out the door of the FBO to preflight a single-engine rented airplane. He is planning to fly to another airport 100 miles away in order to practice VFR navigation and to build his total and cross-country flight time. A friend of his sees him walking to the plane and calls to him, "Do you mind if I ride along with you?" The private pilot remembers the expense-sharing rule and says, "Sure you can ride along, but this flight is going to cost me about a hundred bucks. Do you mind chipping in a little of the cost?" The passenger agrees to help pay, and they take off.

Situation 2 A relative of a private pilot calls and says that she must attend a meeting in a city 100 miles away. The relative asks if the private pilot could fly her to the city for the meeting. The private pilot says, "Sure, I'll fly you over there, but that trip will cost about a hundred bucks. Do you mind chipping in a little of the cost?" The relative agrees, and the private pilot takes the relative to the meeting.

Are these flights legal? They could both be to the same airport, they could both cost the same, and they could involve a passenger sharing expenses of the exact same dollar amount. Both situations sound the same. Both situations look the same to anyone watching the takeoff. But the FAA currently does not think they are the same. The FAA feels that Situation 2 is a direct violation of FAR 61.118.

How can pilots know how the FAA feels about a particular regulation? You might think that this question would have a simple answer: just read the regulation. It is not that simple, however, because different readers of the regulation might have different interpretations. Even FAA officials will give opposing interpretations on any given regulation. The ultimate way to learn what the FAA really means by their regulations is to look at what will trigger the FAA to prosecute a pilot.

In one recent case, the private pilot in question got a telephone call in the middle of the night from a neighbor. The neighbor had discovered that his father had fallen ill and wanted the private pilot to immediately fly him to see the sick father. The private pilot took off with the neighbor at 4 A.M. on a mission of mercy. The private pilot asked the neighbor to share expenses of the flight, which the neighbor gladly did at the time. Later, the neighbor thought the shared cost of the flight was excessive and called the FAA to ask what he thought was a harmless question about how much airplanes cost to fly. The FAA issued an emergency revocation of the private pilot's certificate.

During the investigation of this private pilot, the FAA turned up two other flights that they felt were violations. One took place when the private pilot flew in a guest speaker to his child's school science fair. The private pilot took a tax deduction for the flight on the basis that the cost of the flight was his donation to a charity. The other flight in question involved the same private pilot transporting an elderly lady across the state to consult with a physician about her medical treatment.

In the case of each flight, the FAA charged that the private pilot accepted compensation in the form of money or tax advantage that was outside the law. The FAA believed that the original intent of each flight was to transport another person. The only reason the flights were taken in the first place was to carry a passenger. If the passenger had not needed transportation, the flight would not have been made. The private pilot had not originally planned on making these flights, so shared expenses in these cases were illegal compensation.

The FAA issued a violation. A judge agreed with the FAA and suspended the private pilot's certificate for 180 days. The case was under appeal at the time of this writing, but even if the case is overturned on appeal, the pilot will always have this violation on his record. With airlines being very selective today, any violation of a pilot's FAA record means a professional pilot career can be forgotten.

You might be saying, "How can the FAA possibly know my true intent on any flight?" They can't. The FAA knows that people violate the shared-expense rule every day. That is why when they do catch somebody, they might "throw the book at him" to make the pilot an example to other violators who have not been caught yet. Each pilot must use good judgment with FAR 61.118 because your flight time investment and your hopes for a flying career rest on every flight.

Commercial considerations

Many believe that when they become a commercial pilot, their troubles of this nature are over. Nothing could be further from the truth. Commercial pilots have even more issues to resolve. FAR 61.139 says: "The holder of a commercial pilot certificate may act as pilot in command of an aircraft carrying passengers or property for compensation or hire." This regulation seems to leave the door open for just about anything. It also seems to say that commercial pilots can accept payments for their services as a pilot anytime a customer agrees to pay. What this regulation does *not* say is more important, and this can be a real pilot trap.

Part 135 regulations govern air-taxi operators, more commonly called charter pilots. To complete a flight that falls under FAR Part 135 rules, a pilot must have much more flight time and testing than it takes to get a commercial pilot certificate. If a commercial pilot ever makes a flight that could be considered a Part 135 operation without proper certification beyond the commercial certificate, the pilot is taking a tremendous risk.

So what can a commercial pilot legally do? On January 19, 1996, an amendment to the FARs went into force that was intended to clarify the issue. Prior to this date, Part 135.1(b) listed activities that require a commercial pilot certificate but at the same time are *not* considered a Part 135 operation. Regulation 135.1 now outlines what *is* considered a Part 135 operation.

The new regulation refers us to FAR Part 119 for more restrictions. Unfortunately, Part 119 is not very familiar to most pilots. Federal Aviation Regulations books customarily include Parts 1, 61, 91, 121, 135, and 830; they usually do not contain Part 119.

Part 119, which was amended on February 26, 1996, contains regulations pertaining to air carriers and commercial operators. In short, this regulation says that even with a commercial pilot certificate, there are only a few operations you can legally conduct. FAR Part 119.1(e) is the new list of operations that are legal with a commercial certificate alone. It states:

This part does not apply to—

1. Student instruction;
2. Nonstop sightseeing flights in aircraft with 30 or fewer passenger seats and payload capacity of less than 7,500 pounds, that begin and end at the same airport, and are conducted within a 25 statue mile radius of the airport;
3. Ferry or training flights;
4. Aerial work operations, including—
   i. Crop dusting, seeding, spraying and bird chasing;
   ii. Banner towing;
   iii. Aerial photography or survey;
   iv. Fire fighting;
   v. Helicopter construction operations or repair work;
   vi. Powerline or pipeline patrol;
5. Sightseeing flights in Hot Air Balloons;
6. Nonstop flights conducted with a 25 statute mile radius of the airport of takeoff for the purpose of intentional parachute jumps.

There are some other possibilities for helicopters, but this is the entire list for airplanes. Ideally, FAR 61.139 would have Part 119(e) listed under privileges and limitations of commercial pilots because this list better represents the legal privileges. The 1996 amendment has made this regulation harder, not easier, to find and therefore will probably trap more pilots.

Situation 1 A commercial pilot flies an airplane carrying a passenger to a basketball game. The operating expense of the flight is $100. The commercial pilot charges the passenger $150. The commercial pilot pays the expense of the airplane and keeps $50 for his services. Is this a legal situation?

No. Anytime a person or property departs from one airport and lands at another airport on a flight that was solicited, a charter flight has occurred. This falls under Part 135 and a commercial pilot certificate alone does not qualify the pilot to make the flight.

Situation 2 A commercial pilot flies an airplane carrying a passenger to a basketball game. The operating expense of the flight is $100. The commercial pilot charges the passenger $100. The commercial pilot pays the expense of the airplane, keeps no money for himself, and records the flight in his logbook. Is this a legal situation?

No. According to the FAA, and backed up in the courts, this also is a violation because the pilot did receive compensation. The compensation was not money, but rather flight time in the logbook. Any compensation on a flight of this nature is illegal.

Situation 3 A commercial pilot flies an airplane carrying a passenger to a basketball game. The operating expense of the flight is $100. The commercial pilot and passenger equally share the expense of the flight. Is this situation legal?

Part 61.139 on Commercial Pilot privileges does not make any mention of a commercial pilot sharing expenses. In practice, the FAA allows commercial pilots to share expenses as long as the "intent of the flight" issue is resolved properly. If the sole reason for this trip is to carry the passenger, then this situation, too, is illegal.

Situation 4 A commercial pilot who also holds a flight instructor certificate flies an airplane carrying a passenger to a basketball game. The operating expense of the flight is $100. The commercial pilot/flight instructor charges the passenger $100 for the airplane plus an hourly instruction fee of $20 per hour for two hours and $5 for a new pilot logbook. The passenger pays a total of $145, and the instructor records the flight in the passenger's newly acquired logbook as dual instruction received. The instructor then records the time in his own logbook under dual-instruction given. Is this a legal situation?

This one is tough. Clearly the instructor is using his instructor certificate to get around the Part 119 restriction. The passenger was not truly a flight student. Why did the instructor believe that this new student's first lesson needed to be a cross-country flight? This will be the FAA's first question. The FAA would surely contend that this is also a violation of Part 135, Part 119, and an abuse of the flight instructor certificate. This pilot would be in deep trouble.

Situation 5 The commercial pilot/flight instructor is also a big basketball fan. Never mind. . .

You can see that an endless number of gray-area situations can develop. The bottom line is not what the pilot thinks, but what the FAA will violate a pilot for. Consider the FAA a sleeping giant. If you operate in these gray areas as a matter of practice and one day accidentally awaken the angry giant, he will not be in a good mood, and your certificates and career will hang by a thread.

Reality

So what are the chances of getting caught? The FAA is understaffed and overworked. How can they possibly place every flight and every airport under surveillance? They can't. Chances are that if you are violating Part 135 regulations, it won't be the FAA who catches you, anyway. The Part 135 and 119 operators themselves serve as rent-a-cops.

Place yourself in the position of a Part 135 operator who has spent thousands of dollars on airplanes, advertising, office supplies, telephone systems, and pilot training. You have spent thousands of hours preparing manuals and pilot folders that are acceptable to the FAA for certification. You have coped with surprise FAA inspections and petty details. You are honestly trying to play by the rules.

One day you look out your office window and see a small single-engine airplane pull up to the FBO and unload passengers carrying briefcases. At the very least you will be suspicious. You might even call the FAA to report the small airplane's tail number because this lowly commercial pilot is stealing your business. If you are the pilot of the small airplane, beware. The chances of getting turned in are greater than the chances of the FAA outright catching you.

After reading this, you might feel a little boxed in. There don't seem to be many legal ways to build the vital flight time. Flight instruction is first on the commercial pilot privileges list (operations excluded from Part 119) and is probably the most readily available legal operation. There are geographic pockets where banner towing, aerial photography, or sightseeing flights are plentiful, but these pockets are sparse. Many of these operations are also seasonal and cannot be counted on for long-term time building. The question remains: where are pilots supposed to get valuable flight time?

I was interviewing a pilot once and the subject of flight time naturally came up in the conversation. He said he had been working on building his time various ways. His previous instructor had told him, "If you do not have much flight time, you must create some." This very curious statement opens up new gray areas of flight time. Without knowing anything was wrong, you might have fallen into some of the following traps.

FLIGHT SIMULATORS

Many questions come up about flight simulators and how this time should be used. First, it is important to get terminology correct. According to FAA Advisory Circular 120-45A, an "*airplane simulator* is a full-size replica of a specific type or make, model, and series airplane cockpit, including assemblages of equipment and programs necessary. The device must simulate the airplane in ground and flight operations, a force cueing system which provides cues at least equivalent to that of three degrees" of free motion.
Most flight schools do not have anything that fits this description. Full-motion flight simulators are usually found in major airline training facilities. These simulators are boxed-in cockpits that stand high above the floor on legs. Hydraulics in the legs allow the entire box to pitch, roll, and yaw in response to the pilots control inputs and simulated weather conditions.

The advisory circular offers one more definition: "An *airplane training device* is a full-scale replica of an airplane's instruments, equipment, panels, and controls in an open flight deck or an enclosed airplane cockpit, including assemblage of equipment and programs necessary to represent the airplane in ground and flight conditions to the extent of the systems installed in the device; does not require a force (motion) cueing or visual system." This means that training devices do not move and are generic; they do not need to be an exact replica of a particular airplane.

Based on these definitions most flight students use training devices not flight simulators.

Can any simulator (training device) time be used as flight time? The answer is definitely no. FAR Part 1.1 defines flight time as "the time from the moment the aircraft first moves under its own power for the purpose of flight until the moment it comes to rest at the next point of landing." Actual flight time can only be recorded if it takes place in an aircraft that moves. Part 1.1 further defines an aircraft as "a device that is used or intended to be used for flight in the air." A flight simulator/training device cannot move under its own power with the intention of flight, nor can it be used for flight in the air.

Yet there are still some instructors and even examiners who count simulator time as flight time. Where does the confusion come from? FAR 61.65(e) details the flight experience needed to qualify for an instrument rating. The regulation says that a pilot must have at least 125 hours of "pilot flight time." The applicant must also have had 40 hours of instrument instruction. Of these 40 hours, 20 hours can be in an approved instrument ground trainer (device). Also, 15 hours of the 40 must be "flight" instruction with an instrument flight instructor (CFII).

The applicant therefore must have 20 hours in an aircraft, and may have up to 20 hours in the ground trainer. The 20 flight hours must all be with an instructor, 15 of which with a CFII. None of these requirements reduces the applicants total flight time requirement of 125 hours. A pilot is *not* eligible for an instrument rating with 105 flight hours and 20 hours of ground trainer time.

Several pilots have been stripped of the instrument rating because they got through an FAA checkride without the examiner seeing the problem. But the FAA office in Oklahoma City never misses this mistake. Many more Instrument applicants have been disappointed when a sharp examiner refused to give the checkride under these conditions.

More confusion comes from FAR 61.129, dealing with the requirements for a commercial pilot certificate. Section (b), titled "Flight Time as Pilot," requires "a total of at least 250 hours of flight time as pilot, which may include not more than 50 hours of instruction from an authorized instructor in a ground trainer." This all but suggests that, in this case, 50 hours of simulator time can be used as flight time. This leads to misinterpretation and mistakes in logbooks.

In practice this regulation allows for 50 hours of simulator time in lieu of 50 hours flight time. The applicant can go to the commercial checkride with 200 hours of flight time and 50 hours ground trainer time. The instrument ground trainer requirements and the commercial ground trainer allowance are apparently contradictory. The only possible exception that would allow ground trainer time to count toward flight time is when it is specifically authorized by an official of the FAA, and only then under a strictly controlled and inspected environment.

How should flight simulator time be logged? Flight simulator/ground trainer time is logged under the column in most logbooks listing "training device" or "simulator." It also can be counted under "instruction" or "dual received" for the purpose of proving an applicant has had the allowed 20 hours toward an instrument rating or to prove the applicant is current for flight under IFR.

Simulator and ground trainer time can never be logged under "total duration of flight" or "flight time." In addition, all simulator and training device time must be signed off by a ground or flight instructor. FAR 61.189 requires the instructor to certify the time spent in a ground trainer by signing his or her name and giving his or her certificate number.

There is no such thing as "solo simulator." If you operate a simulator or ground trainer alone, the time spent cannot be used toward an instrument rating or to maintain instrument currency. If you have been logging simulator/ground trainer time as flight time, and that time is now included in what you are calling your "total time," you should go back and subtract it out.

There is nothing outright illegal about including simulator time; however, no employer will allow it. If you land an interview with a company and they find out you have logged flight time inappropriately, the interview will conclude very quickly. If you have used simulator/ground trainer time to qualify for an FAA certificate that specifically requires flight time, your certificate is in jeopardy, even if you have the proper flight time now. Double-check your logbooks. Do not let the airline interviewer spot this problem before you do.

SAFETY PILOTS

Some pilots have built flight time by creating "safety pilot" time. (If you want to start a fight, just walk into any hangar in America and take either side of this controversy.) In order for instrument-rated pilots to fly in IFR conditions, according to FAR 61.57, they must have logged 6 hours of actual or simulated instrument time. Of the 6 hours, 3 hours can be in a ground trainer. Also, at least 6 instrument approaches are required, and they can all be in the simulator. This must be accomplished within any 6-month time block.

If a pilot fails to get this experience within the 6-month period, he or she can no longer act as pilot in command under IFR. The FAA then gives the pilot an additional 6-month grace period to get current. During the grace period, if the pilot lacks the portion of the currency requirement that must be accomplished in an airplane, the pilot must simulate instrument conditions while actually flying in VFR conditions.

However, it is simply not safe to fly with an IFR hood on with nobody looking out for traffic. This is where the "safety pilot" comes in. FAR 61.51(c)(4) says, "A pilot may log as instrument flight time only that time during which he operates the aircraft solely by reference to instruments, under actual or simulated instrument flight conditions. Each entry must include the place and type of each instrument approach completed, and the name of the safety pilot for each simulated instrument flight." A safety pilot is someone who will look for traffic while the instrument pilot flies under the hood. The safety pilot must be rated and current in the airplane used.

The pilot flying under the hood may log pilot in command time for this flight, but can the safety pilot log any flight time? FAR 61.51(c)(3) says, "A pilot may log as second-in-command time all flight time during which he acts as second-in-command of an aircraft on which more than one pilot is required under the type certification of the aircraft, or the regulations under which the flight is conducted." Under FAR 61.51(c)(4), a safety pilot is required.

So, in this situation, two pilots are required, and 61.51(c)(3) says that anytime two pilots are required, one pilot can log second-in-command. Second-in-command time does increase total flight time. This means that two private pilots flying a Cessna 150 could both log flight time as long as one of the pilots flies under the hood.

Now apply this idea to the concept of quality flight time. I do not feel the Cessna 150 second-in-command time is very valuable. If a potential employer calls you in for an interview, they will be looking for the quality of your time, not necessarily the quantity. If you have just barely met the airline's or Part 135 operator's minimum time requirements on the strength of single-engine second-in-command time, your application will be disregarded. My advice is that you keep this flight time out of your logbook.

Can a safety pilot log the time as pilot in command? This is up for interpretation. It is possible for two pilots in the same airplane to both log pilot in command for simultaneous flight time. But FAR 61.51(c)(2)(iii) allows it only under the condition where "a certificated flight instructor may log as pilot in command time all flight time during which he acts as a flight instructor."

When an instructor is instructing in flight, he or she logs the time PIC. If the pilot receiving instruction is at least a private pilot in an aircraft the pilot is rated to fly, that pilot can also log PIC. By this regulation, it appears that the only time two pilots can simultaneously log PIC is when one is an instructor. If the safety pilot is not an instructor, then it seems pilot-in-command time would not be allowed.

However, a ruling has been made that would allow both pilot and the safety pilot to log pilot-in-command time if they agree before takeoff to allow the safety pilot to manipulate the controls at some point during the flight. There is a distinction made here between logging PIC and acting as PIC.

When planning a flight career, it is best to stay away from any questionable flight time situations. You might in your heart believe that a particular way to log flight time is valid, but your heart has nothing to do with it. What counts is what an airline interviewer believes and what will persuade him or her to hire you.

Controversial flight time is anathema to the airlines and air-taxi operators. They have enough problems without dealing with the FAA in some future investigation about your flight time. They will always take a pilot with a spotlessly clean logbook over one who has built time in the gray areas. Do not be short-sighted and pursue quick time over the quality time.

HITCHHIKING ON 135

Many pilots have built time while riding along on Part 135 air-taxi airplanes. This also creates problems. First, if you do not meet the Part 135 air-taxi flight time minimums, you cannot log anything as PIC that is truly a Part 135 operation. FAR Part 135.243 requires a pilot to have 500 hours of pilot time to qualify as a VFR-only Part 135 pilot in command. The same regulation requires 1,200 hours for IFR pilot-in-command operations. Even if you meet these minimums, you still cannot log the flight time unless you actually work for and have been tested by the Part 135 operator.

Take a situation where a charter airplane leaves airport A and flies to airport B. At airport B paying passengers are picked up and flown to airport C. Flying the airplane is a legal and certified Part 135 IFR pilot. The 135 pilot's best friend, who is also a pilot but not employed by the 135 company, is riding along. Can the friend who rides along log any of this trip? Yes, but only that part of the flight that could be considered under Part 91 flight rules and not Part 135 flight rules.

The leg from airport A to airport B was essentially a deadhead leg. No passengers were on board, so there was no requirement for Part 135. The pilots could agree before takeoff that the ride-along pilot is PIC for the first leg. The leg from airport B to airport C does require a qualified Part 135 pilot because passengers are on board, but the ride-along pilot does not qualify and therefore cannot log the flight time.

Then deadhead legs on Part 135 airplanes are not technically Part 135 operations and are then outside the FAA's Part 135 jurisdiction. Deadhead ride-along pilots might be prohibited by the Part 135 operator's procedures manual or by their insurance carrier. If you already are a Part 135 pilot, you might be placing your job and career on the line by allowing your pilot friends to ride along.

Ride-along pilots need to know that the Part 135 operator will not pay higher insurance premiums to protect an unneeded pilot. If anything should happen on the flight, a ride-along pilot will not be covered under any insurance. If an accident were to occur, the Part 135 operator could even take a ride-along pilot to court and claim that the pilot's inexperience caused the accident. The Part 135 operator could claim that the ride-along pilot was an illegal stowaway. The case might be in court for years and legal fees might financially drain the ride-along pilot.

It's not all bad. Some Part 135 operators will approve and even encourage ride-along pilots. They use riding along as a cheap way to train future pilots. Stay above board. Ask the Part 135 operator about the company policy on rider pilots. If logging deadhead legs is approved by the operator, and you are satisfied that the air-taxi is legal, safe, and properly insured, the exposure might even help you gain employment with the company in the future.

MILITARY CROSSOVER TIME

If you are a military pilot and seek a job in the civilian flight world, you will need to transfer your military flight experience to a civilian pilot certificate. The process involves taking your military flight records to your local FAA flight standards district office and having the records qualified. The FAA inspector will give a commercial-pilot written exam, and after passing the exam, the military pilot is awarded the Commercial Pilot Certificate. The procedure is straightforward, but the FAA is very stingy with anything they do not consider flight time.

A controversy has come up over military flight officers who fly in the backseat of a military airplane as a weapons systems officer (WSO). These people are trained to navigate all over the world, monitor airplane systems, and operate the armaments. But the FAA does not consider WSOs pilots because they do not actually fly the airplane. Some fighter backseats do have sticks so that WSOs can fly the airplane, but it is simply not recognized by the FAA.

Several years ago a WSO, upset that his time was not considered flight time by the local FAA, started calling around to other FSDO offices. He finally found an FAA inspector who could be convinced that WSO time was pilot time. The WSO cited FAR 61.155 pertaining to flight hours used to qualify as an airline transport pilot. FAR 61.155(d)(2) states that "a commercial pilot may credit the following flight time toward the 1,500 hours total flight time requirement . . . with flight engineer time acquired in airplanes required to have a flight engineer by their approved aircraft flight manuals, while participating at the same time in an approved pilot training program."

The regulation goes on to say that "the applicant (for the ATP) may not credit more than one hour for each three hours of flight engineer flight time so acquired, nor more than a total of 500 hours." The WSO argued that backseat fighter time was even more valuable than flight engineer time because backseaters do have a control stick. Therefore, backseaters should have at least the same 1-to-3 flight hour ratio as flight engineers. The FAA inspector accepted the argument.

The next day, the WSO drove 400 miles to that inspector's office and used WSO-backseat time to get a flight time credit toward the airline transport pilot certificate. When the WSO returned home, the word spread of his success. Soon, a steady stream of WSOs were quietly driving the 400 miles to see this one inspector.

It did not last long. The inspector finally stopped issuing the logbook certifications. The first WSO is now a captain for a regional air carrier. All other WSOs must start as student pilots with zero flight time when they become civilians.

FALSE RECORDS

Of course there are pilots who have more flight time in their logbooks than they have actually flown. FAR 61.59(a)(2) specifically speaks to logbook liars by saying, "No person may make or cause to be made any fraudulent or intentionally false entry in any logbook, record, or report that is required to be kept, made, or used to show compliance with any requirement for the issuance, or exercise of the privileges, or any certificate or rating under this part."

If a pilot is caught, according to FAR 61.59(b), "The commission by any person of an act prohibited under [the paragraph regarding logbook falsification] of this section is a basis for suspending or revoking any airman or ground instructor certificate or rating held by that person." Many pilots believe that the chances of getting caught are so small that there is no risk involved by padding the logbook. The FAA knows that pilots cheat in their logbooks every day. The agency also knows they cannot catch everyone. Those they do catch, however, get the maximum enforcement.

In the late 1980s, several flight instructors working together at an FBO in Nashville, Tennessee, lost their certificates due to falsifying records. The instructors were accused of adding flight time to individual flights. If a lesson took 1.2 hours, they might put 1.5 hours in their own logbook. They were also accused of logging the wrong airplanes. A lesson might have been accomplished in a Cessna 172, but they listed the flight in a Cessna 172RG.

The FAA proved that the flight instructors had falsified their logbooks by obtaining a subpoena not only for the pilot logbooks but for the airplane logbooks and FBO invoices. Then it was a simple matter of mathematics. The total time claimed by the instructors during one period of time was greater than the total hours on the school's airplanes during the same time period.

The FAA stripped the instructors of all their pilot certificates and ratings and banned them from flying for one year. This meant that they would have to wait a year, then start out again as student pilots. In addition, no company will hire any pilot who has previously had his or her certificates revoked.

LOGBOOK CERTIFICATION

Every would-be professional pilot will turn over their logbooks to the FAA at least once: for ATP certification. After accumulating 1,500 hours, pilots schedule an appointment with an FAA inspector. The pilot must bring his or her logbook and a first-class medical certificate to the meeting.

The inspector will go through each page of the logbook and ask questions about many entries. If it is approved, the inspector will certify the logbook and issue the pilot a permit to take the airline transport pilot written test one time. You do not want to fail this test. If you do, you must go back to the FAA and get another test permit and answer the inevitable questions about why you failed.

Getting your logbook FAA certified is a good idea. If a potential employer has a question about any of your flight time, having the flight time certified means that FAA has already given its approval.

Logbooks are also submitted for Part 135 review. In one case, a pilot who had been riding along on previous Part 135 flights had made 22 entries as pilot in command. The FAA believed this to be suspicious because of the amount of time recorded and took action against the pilot. The pilot testified at a hearing that she had only flown the airplane during deadhead legs.

The problem was that she logged the entire flight as PIC, including the portions that were Part 135 operations. A judge ruled that the logbook was intentionally false and ordered that her commercial pilot certificate be revoked. The case was appealed to the National Transportation Safety Board, but the board upheld the judge's order by saying that the pilot had "misrepresented her flight experience."

Pilots are always weighing risk in their piloting decisions. The risk of getting caught falsifying records might be small, but for future professional pilots, the risk is greater than most pilots think. The possible advantage a pilot gets by falsifying the logbook is just not worth gambling an entire career over.

The safest path to unquestionable flight time is by strict adherence to Part 119.1. This usually means a couple of years working as a flight instructor and then for a Part 119 or 135 operator. Multiengine time will mount with a Part 119 or 135 operator.

CAREER CLIMBING

The most likely career ladder starts with the commercial-pilot level, on to flight instructor to accumulate flight time quantity, then on to air-taxi work as a Part 135 pilot to get the quality multiengine time. So, the key to the best marketability often involves charter flying.

Unfortunately, charter and air-taxi is very sensitive to the business cycle. When business and corporations experience hard times, one of the first things cut out is travel. This means fewer charter flights and fewer multiengine hours for up- and-coming pilots. Part 135 flying is an unavoidable rung on the pilot career ladder, but it can be a roadblock as well.

Another way to build flight time is to work for someone who owns an airplane. When a business jet taxis into the ramp and unloads corporate executives, the pilot employed by the company that owns the airplane is operating under Part 91. As a Part 91 operator, the pilot does not need to worry about all those Part 135 restrictions. The problem is that many of these jobs require a good deal of flight time in order to meet the company's insurance requirements and are not considered time builders. Even so, many pilots have been at the right place at the right time and landed a corporate job (even single-engine) that provided accelerated flight time.

The best way to accumulate a large quantity of single-engine time and enough quality multiengine time to become job marketable is to work hard, and stay out of the gray areas.

Index

Illustrations are indicated in **boldface**.

INDEX

About the author

Paul A. Craig is the chief flight instructor at the Middle Tennessee State University Aerospace Department in Murfreesboro, Tennessee. He holds the Gold Seal Multiengine and Instrument Flight Instructor Certificate, as well as an Airline Transport Pilot Certificate. He is a recipient of the North Carolina Flight Instructor of the Year award and is an FAA safety program counselor. Craig speaks year-round to pilot proficiency award programs, flight instructor refresher clinics, and safety seminars. He has a Masters of Aerospace Education degree and a Specialist in Education degree. Currently he is working toward a Doctor of Education degree. He has contributed many articles to various aviation periodicals and is the author of two books in the Practical Flying Series: *Be a Better Pilot: Making the Right Decisions* and *Stalls and Spins*. He is also the author of *Light Airplane Navigation Essentials*. This being said, Craig is happiest in an airplane, instructing a student, shooting an ILS, or pulling an engine and feathering the prop.